BREAD

IS

GOLD

MASSIMO BOTTURA
& FRIENDS

BREAD

IS

GOLD

EXTRAORDINARY MEALS
WITH ORDINARY INGREDIENTS

Bread Is Gold

Bread Is Gold
by Massimo Bottura

Every morning over breakfast my brothers and I fought for the leftover pieces of bread from the previous night to dip in warm milk with a splash of coffee. We called this mess *zuppa di latte*, milk soup. I preferred the bread grated directly into the bowl and always asked my mother to help me. Then, to my delight, I poured in the sugar, lots of it, until my mother started yelling, "Massimooooo—that's too much sugar! Look at your spoon. It is standing up straight!" She loved to tell this story to strangers with the additional comment, "And look at him now—a famous cook!"

The endless bowls of milk soup that I devoured for breakfast and before heading off to bed were a memory like any other until my mother passed away. Only then did that flavor become an obsession. How could I transform a memory into something tangible, edible, and most important, emotional?

In the kitchen of my restaurant Osteria Francescana in Modena, we began experimenting with variations on toasted breadcrumbs, milk, and sugar. The mixture went through numerous stages of blending, filtering, and whipping until it turned into a cream of sorts. We added another layer to the recipe, a caramelized bread crunch, and then another again, salted bread ice cream. It tasted better than I remembered—the toasted, caramel, and salty flavors were comforting, even childish—but the layers of tonal beige were not inviting. More than that, the meaning was not clear. No one cared about a bowl of bread, milk, and sugar . . . except me. What the recipe needed was value.

Flipping through an art magazine at home, a gold-plated wastepaper basket by Swiss artist Sylvie Fleury caught my attention. She casts objects from popular culture in silver and gold. The ordinary suddenly became extraordinary. That was it! The message was to make visible the invisible.

Back in the kitchen, we molded melted sugars into a translucent gold-tinted sugar shell that looked like a piece of crumpled paper from the wastepaper basket. The dome was so fragile it fractured when touched. In this way, when you ate it, the golden mirage gave way to the formless soup of childhood memories. We put it on the menu and called it *Il pane è oro* or Bread Is Gold.

How could I have known at the time that the name "bread is gold" would take on a much deeper meaning than the recipe itself. That a recipe would become the anthem under which we chanted the unsung values of recovering recipes and all those discarded, undervalued, and neglected ingredients that have always played a central role in the Italian kitchen. I am an Italian chef. The most valuable lessons are to make the most of everything and to never throw anything edible away. No crumbs or bones or cheese rinds. A ragù is nothing more than a sauce made with scraps of meat or fish or vegetable trimmings.

By the end of 2013, Italy had begun a national discussion about the upcoming Expo 2015 in Milan. The food-focused theme had just been announced: "Feeding the Planet, Energy for Life." There was a mad rush by the press, and countries were announcing the chefs that would be cooking and representing them. We started receiving requests: Can you cook here? Can you set up a pop-up? At first I was flattered and then unsettled. I realized that no one was asking us chefs for our opinions or our ideas. No one was asking us *how* to feed the planet.

Around that time I had the privilege of meeting Davide Rampello. Davide is a notable Italian in the world of design and aesthetics. He had just been nominated the director of the Pavilion Zero, which aimed to illustrate Expo's theme through visuals and storytelling. I confided in him that I was dreaming about an Expo pavilion in which some of the world's best chefs could cook with the waste from Expo for people in need. Without hesitation, he remarked: "It would be a miracle, a twenty-first-century version of *Miracle in Milan*." He was referring to the 1951 neorealist film *Miracolo a Milano* directed by Vittorio De Sica, which tells the story of an orphan who is found in a cabbage patch, then swept up from poverty by a shining angel. The fairy tale is every man's dream of a better life. Davide clarified that what I was imagining was not a pavilion but a *refettorio*, the place where monks and nuns have shared meals for centuries. He explained that the word *refettorio* comes from the Latin *reficere,* which means to rebuild and restore. At the end of the week, Davide called me and said, "Caritas Ambrosiana, the biggest Catholic charity organization in Milan, is interested in your *refettorio*."

One week later, we had an appointment with Don Giuliano, the parish priest of two churches in the Greco neighborhood of Milan, just north of the central train station. In this forgotten quarter of Milan, the daily struggle is set to the soundtrack of passing trains. As I drove under train tracks and passed graffitied walls, I began to understand that the culture of food waste is much like the culture of peripheral neighborhoods of any city; what is unwanted gets pushed further away. Nestled among the warehouses, nondescript apartment buildings, and a fifteenth-century church, we found ourselves in front of Teatro Greco, a theater from the 1930s, long since abandoned.

Don Giuliano unlocked the doors to the theater and said, "What could be more appropriate than a theater for a *refettorio*? What does a theater put on stage if not the drama of life? Drama includes everything: life, death, joy, and moments of darkness."

His enthusiasm was contagious. The empty theater with its dusty upholstered chairs was waiting for a miracle. Could it be transformed into the communal dining hall I imagined, like in Santa Maria delle Grazie where Leonardo da Vinci painted the *Last Supper*? I envisioned the most spectacular *refettorio* ever seen, filled with art, light, beauty, cooking, and life named after the patron saint of Milan, Sant'Ambrogio.

Ludwig Wittgenstein, the Austrian linguistics philosopher, wrote in the early twentieth century, "Ethics and aesthetics are one and the same." I have always considered ethics and aesthetics as two sides of the same coin. Beauty without good isn't beautiful at all. And good needs beauty to convey its message. Davide, in his role as the former director of the Triennnale of Design in Milan, knew exactly whom to call for help. The architects and students from the Politecnico of Milan took on the renovation from theater to dining hall, complete with professional kitchen and walk-in refrigeration. Italian companies donated furniture and lighting. Thirteen designers each made a unique prototype monastic oak table following the principles of a convent table: solid, stable, and suitable for at least eight guests. Five Italian artists were commissioned to bring beauty: Mimmo Palladino created the external doorway to mark the entrance; Gaetano Pesce

made a fountain of life; Enzo Cucchi painted a thirty-nine-foot (twelve-meter) long fresco; Carlo Benvenuto made an existential photograph of a loaf of bread; and Maurizio Nannucci produced a neon sign mounted outside the building for everyone to see that read, NO MORE EXCUSES.

I invited friends and colleagues to cook during the six months of Expo. I called forty chefs in one day asking for their support. Most of them said, "Yes, we will come," even before I posed the question. Far too often at our restaurants and the food festivals we attend, we are only speaking to the converted. I asked them all, "Wouldn't it be refreshing to cook for people who had no idea who we were?"

Each chef would have the opportunity to meet the neighborhood children and cook lunch for them as well as create a meal for one hundred guests from local homeless shelters. The knowledge, creativity, and know-how of professional chefs was essential to prove that salvaged food, overripe or bruised and beyond expiration dates, as well as scraps and trimmings that otherwise would be thrown away, were not only edible, but even delicious.

The Refettorio Ambrosiano opened its doors on May 28, 2015, and thanks to the sustained work of Caritas Ambrosiana, continues to serve guests five days a week. We put words aside and took action. We learned that limitations inspire creativity. When putting food on the table is a challenge, miracles happen in the kitchen. We were enlightened by the genius of necessity. We brought dignity back to the table by changing the dynamics of the dining room and serving unexpected food to the most vulnerable. I wanted our guests to feel welcomed. I remember the very first nights at the Refettorio, when the guests barely spoke to each other. In a matter of weeks, guests and volunteers and chefs were joking around. The meal became a celebration. Most important, we gave food a voice, gave waste a place, and nourished a community. We confirmed what we had only imagined: that a meal can unite, revive, and renew. And during it all, we were reminded that cooking is an act of love.

In looking for solutions to fight food waste, we found incredible potential for a wider impact. We became aware that a good meal in a beautiful and welcoming environment can change a community. After our experience at the Refettorio Ambrosiano, my wife, Lara, and I founded a nonprofit association called Food for Soul to make places like these accessible to more people around the world.

Will the role of chefs define the future of food? Today chefs have a greater social responsibility than ever before. They are not only responsible for their customers at the table but also for the community at large—the artisans, the farmers, and the cheesemakers—as well as the next generation of chefs that will follow in their footsteps. Chefs are becoming ambassadors of culture, influential thinkers, and activists. There is more we chefs can do to make the world a better and more delicious place. As we cooked together at the Refettorio week after week, I imagined a cookbook that assembled recipes and stories about the beautiful and the ugly ingredients we cooked with, the food we served, the people we met, the many spontaneous acts of generosity. Cooking is about transformation. Real beauty is seeing the value in something that might not seem to have any value at all. Something recovered is something gained.

What surprised me is just how fabulous the recipes turned out to be. Working outside of our restaurant kitchens, with ingredients we did not choose, pushed our limits and our skills and forced us to rethink the life cycle of food. Every week chefs created meals out of thin air. Not only did they cook, but they took the time to write down the recipes and share them with us. I cannot thank them enough for giving their time and their ideas to this book.

The good thing is that you don't have to be a professional cook to make these recipes. These are recipes that can be cooked by anyone, anywhere, on the tightest budget. They do not require fancy equipment. They just require time and energy and creativity. Cooking with ingredients that otherwise would have been thrown away draws out the resourcefulness of a cook, any cook. These recipes were cooked for real people and written for home cooks. The quantities can be doubled and tripled and quadrupled for cafeterias, cooking schools, and large crowds.

The recipes in this book are odes to imperfection. On one hand they can be considered ordinary; on the other hand, they just might be the most extraordinary proof that cooking is a call to act. Recipes can change the way we look at the world. A crate of brown and bruised bananas that nobody wants can be a magical beginning of the next great recipe. We received many brown bananas and made banana ice cream every day for children in the neighborhood. But the day I learned how to make chutney out of the banana peels, I never looked at a banana in the same way.

You can learn to make pesto with popcorn or breadcrumbs instead of costly pine nuts. You can learn to make a ragù out of almost anything and everything. Eggs are often used in unexpected ways. Meat is often turned into hamburgers, meatballs, and meatloaves. Many recipes come with condiments, sauces, and side dishes. Ice cream is one of the joys in life and this book is full of ice-cream recipes, because it is one of the best ways to reclaim ingredients that are no longer perfect, such as fruit, vegetables, and dairy. But more important than the actual recipes is the resounding message: Improvise, experiment, and cook with urgency. Use this book as a guide and a starting point for cooking out of your pantry and refrigerator.

Food waste is one of the biggest problems of our century and our generation's cross to bear. Numbers are numbers. Almost one billion people are undernourished. One-third of the food we produce globally is wasted every year, including nearly *four trillion* apples. Just imagine how many apple pies we could make? If we don't do something about it now, the numbers will only get worse. I am an optimist and I believe that we are already making positive change. This is just one of many projects aimed at reducing food waste around the world. The good thing is that everyone can participate. A recipe after all is a solution to a problem. Choose to be part of the solution by cooking and sharing a meal around a table. It might be the most revolutionary thing you do all day.

Daniel Humm

There was a layer of dust on everything. We had been under renovation for three months and although we were basically ready to open when Daniel Humm, the Swiss chef behind Eleven Madison Park in New York City, and his team arrived, what they saw probably shocked them. I was sweeping the floor. My wife, Lara, and the project manager, Cristina, were outside removing the plastic from all the chairs that had just been delivered. Seen Lippert, a chef visiting from New York, was diligently cleaning the kitchen counters, stovetops, and surfaces that had never been used. We were still waiting for a few tables to arrive, but the refrigerator was full. The first delivery of ingredients had come in that morning: lots of strawberries in various stages of maturity; lots of zucchini (courgettes) with spotty signs of aging; turkey and beef hamburger patties still in their packages; and a bag of stale bread from the bakery across the street.

Daniel was the first chef to cook at the Refettorio. It wasn't my intention to put that kind of pressure on him because he is one of the nicest people I know. When I saw him in London only a month earlier, he mentioned he would be cooking in Milan in May for the James Beard Foundation and I jumped on the opportunity. Actually, we asked a lot of chefs to help us out that summer in the same way: If they were coming to town to visit or cook at Expo (the six-month universal exposition in Milan), we invited them to stay an extra day and cook with us. Surprisingly, many did, and even more surprisingly, we found that many chefs who had just prepared a high-end meal for paying guests, now brought a heightened sense of urgency and appreciation to the project of cooking with us in less than perfect circumstances.

I was thrilled that Daniel was here, but I was nervous. I had invited one of the best chefs in the world to cook in a soup kitchen with humble, even ugly, ingredients, for a group of people who had little or no idea who he was and probably did not even care. I wasn't sure he knew what he had gotten himself into. When Daniel arrived, I walked him around, describing every table and object.

I think he was touched to inaugurate the kitchen. He seemed to genuinely appreciate the craftsmanship that went into the oak tables, each one designed by a different artist, the artwork on the walls, the original cement tile floors, and the vaulted tin ceiling in the kitchen. Later he confessed to Lara, "You know when Massimo first told me about it, there were questions if this ever could happen, but Massimo is so passionate and when he starts talking you think that it is just talk, but it's all here, it's all real, and it's unbelievable."

We had opened a week early to receive Daniel and his team. Our guests were scheduled to begin coming for dinner the following week. That night, as a substitute, we hosted one hundred hot and tired high school students from Modena who were returning from a day at the Expo fairgrounds. Little did they know a three-Michelin-star chef would be cooking dinner. The group brought the energy and enthusiasm that we all needed to relieve the stress of the opening—and they were honored to be the first guests.

The meal was seasonal, tasty, and unfussy. Both strawberries and cherries were in season and, like so much seasonal fruit, were very perishable. In fact, there were large quantities of questionable strawberries to clean and separate for a gazpacho (a perfect substitution as tomatoes weren't in season yet, and the soup's pink color was a fun surprise). A gratin was a brilliant solution for the less than perfect condition of the zucchini and meat. An herbed tomato/meat was layered with the zucchini like a lasagna, topped with béchamel and grated Parmigiano, and baked. They made bread pudding for dessert, which is not an Italian recipe. I had never actually tasted bread pudding until that night, but over the months to come I would try many versions of it. In Italy, we use stale bread in many savory dishes, but very few sweet ones.

Being resourceful in the kitchen by working with what you have on hand is a skill and it takes practice. Daniel explained, "We went through a lot of ideas, very quickly, but one thing my mom always used to make was gazpacho, which is the perfect recipe for overripe tomatoes and day-old bread. But we were cooking in May and there were not any overripe tomatoes, so when we saw the crates of strawberries, the decision was made on the spot!" The recipes they made are perfect for large gatherings because they can be made ahead of time and then brought to temperature at the last minute. Gazpacho, gratin, and bread pudding all make great leftovers, too, because they taste even better the next day.

Daniel is not a big talker. He has an ability to listen and synthesize his thoughts with great economy. At the end, he told me, "When you look at a lot of famous traditional dishes, they have been created out of necessity, right? And mostly waste, stuff that was left over." Daniel, with his Swiss precision, had just summed up the project that we had only just begun.

Daniel Humm

STRAWBERRY GAZPACHO

Serves 8

- 11 oz (310 g) stale bread, cut into ⅓-inch (1 cm) cubes
- 2 red bell peppers, diced
- 1 green bell pepper, diced
- 4 English cucumbers, peeled, seeded, and diced
- 2 garlic cloves, sliced
- 1¾ lb (800 g) strawberries, halved
- ⅔ cup (165 ml) canned tomato juice
- ¾ cup (175 ml) extra-virgin olive oil, plus more for drizzling
- generous ⅓ cup (85 ml) red wine vinegar
- Salt
- Handful of small basil leaves
- Freshly ground black pepper

Preheat the oven to 350°F (180°C/Gas Mark 4). Line a baking sheet with parchment paper.

Arrange 7 oz (200 g) of the bread on the baking sheet and toast until golden brown, about 12 minutes. Set the croutons aside.

In a large bowl, toss together the remaining bread, bell peppers, cucumbers, garlic, strawberries, tomato juice, olive oil, and vinegar. Cover and marinate overnight in the fridge.

Transfer the ingredients to a blender and blend until smooth. Strain through a fine-mesh sieve. Season to taste with salt.

To serve, ladle the soup into bowls. Drizzle with olive oil and garnish with the basil, black pepper, and croutons.

📷 P. 15

RECIPE NOTES: _____
_____
_____
_____
_____
_____
_____
_____
_____
_____
_____
_____
_____
_____
_____
_____
_____
_____

ZUCCHINI AND BEEF GRATIN

Serves 8

- 2¼ cups (120 ml) extra-virgin olive oil
- 2 onions, diced
- 3 garlic cloves, minced
- 2¼ lb (1 kg) ground (minced) beef, lamb, turkey, or pork
- Salt
- 1 can (28 oz/795 g) whole peeled tomatoes
- Leaves from 2 sprigs oregano, chopped
- 2 teaspoons dried thyme
- 7 zucchini (courgettes), cut into slices ¼ inch (6 mm) thick
- 7 tablespoons (100 g) butter
- ¾ cup (100 g) all-purpose (plain) flour
- 4¼ cups (1 liter) milk, warmed
- 3 large eggs

In a large pot, heat 4 tablespoons of the olive oil over medium heat. Add the onions and garlic and cook until tender, about 7 minutes. Add the meat, season with salt, and cook, stirring occasionally, until cooked through, about 15 minutes. Remove the meat from the pot and set aside. Drain off any rendered fat. Add the tomatoes, oregano, and thyme to the pot and season with salt. Cook over low heat until thick, about 10 minutes. Return the meat to the pan and stir to combine. Set the sauce aside.

In another large pot, heat 4 tablespoons of the olive oil over high heat. Season the zucchini (courgette) slices with salt. Working in small batches, add to the pot and sear, caramelizing the slices on both sides, about 4 minutes. Add more oil as necessary. Transfer to paper towels to drain any excess oil. Set aside.

In a medium pot, melt the butter over medium heat until foamy but not browned. Slowly add the flour and cook, whisking constantly, for about 7 minutes. Slowly add the milk, continuing to whisk until the milk comes to a simmer and thickens, about 10 minutes. Season to taste with salt. Strain the béchamel through a fine-mesh sieve.

Preheat the oven to 375°F (190°C/Gas Mark 5).

In a large bowl, whisk the eggs with a wire whisk. Slowly whisk 1 cup (200 ml) of the warm béchamel into the eggs, whisking constantly so as not to cook the eggs. Stir into the remaining béchamel.

Spread one-sixth of the meat mixture in the bottom of each of two 9 x 13-inch (23 x 33 cm) baking pans. Make a single layer of zucchini over the beef. Continue making alternate layers of beef and zucchini in both pans, finishing with the zucchini. Cover both pans completely with the béchamel mixture. Transfer to the oven and bake until bubbling on the sides and the center of the béchamel is completely set, about 6 minutes. Let stand at room temperature for at least 10 minutes before serving.

📷 P. 16

RECIPE NOTES: _____
_____
_____

BREAD PUDDING WITH RED WINE CHERRY SAUCE AND VANILLA ICE CREAM

Serves 8

BREAD PUDDING
2 tablespoons (30 g) butter
scant 2 cups (450 ml) milk
scant 2 cups (450 ml) heavy (whipping) cream
2 vanilla beans, split lengthwise
4 eggs
4 egg yolks (see Note)
¾ cup plus 2 tablespoons (175 g) granulated sugar
¼ teaspoon salt
2¼ lb (1 kg) stale brioche, diced

VANILLA ICE CREAM
6⅓ cups (1.5 liters) heavy (whipping) cream
1 vanilla bean, split lengthwise
4 egg yolks (see Note)
scant 1 ½ cups (285 g) granulated sugar
½ teaspoon salt

RED WINE CHERRY SAUCE
1½ cups (375 ml) red wine
4½ oz (125 g) dried cherries
4 tablespoons granulated sugar
2 teaspoons cornstarch (cornflour)

MAKE THE BREAD PUDDING

In a medium pot, combine the milk and cream and bring to a simmer over medium heat. Remove the milk from the heat and scrape in the vanilla seeds and add the pods. Cover and let steep at room temperature for 20 minutes.

Preheat the oven to 350°F (180°C/Gas Mark 4). Butter two 9-inch (22 cm) round cake pans.

In a large bowl, whisk together the whole eggs, egg yolks, and sugar, whisking well to combine. Strain the steamed milk mixture through a fine-mesh sieve and slowly add it to the egg mixture, whisking constantly so as not to cook the eggs. Whisk in the salt. Divide the diced bread among the prepared pans and pour the custard over the bread to completely cover. Top each pan with several nubs of butter. Wrap each pan tightly with foil.

Transfer the pans to one or more roasting pans and add water to come halfway up the sides of the pans. Transfer to the oven and bake the puddings until the custard is set, 45 minutes to 1 hour. Remove the foil and bake until the tops are golden brown, about 15 minutes more. Let stand at room temperature for 15 minutes before serving.

>>

MAKE THE VANILLA ICE CREAM

In a medium pot, bring the cream to a simmer over medium heat. Remove the cream from the heat and scrape in the vanilla seeds, adding the pods as well. Cover and let steep at room temperature for 30 minutes. Strain the mixture through a fine-mesh sieve.

In a large bowl, whisk together the egg yolks and sugar until creamy. Slowly whisk the cream mixture into the egg mixture, whisking constantly so as not to cook the eggs. Transfer to a medium pot and cook over medium heat, whisking constantly until the mixture reaches 181°F (83°C). Whisk in the salt. Strain the mixture again through a fine-mesh sieve into a clean bowl and chill over a bowl filled with ice and water.

Transfer to an ice-cream machine and process according to the manufacturer's instructions. (If you don't have an ice-cream machine, freeze the mixture until hard enough to scoop.)

MAKE THE RED WINE CHERRY SAUCE

Set up a large bowl of ice and water. In a medium pot, combine the wine and half of the dried cherries. Bring to a simmer over medium heat and cook to reduce the wine by one-fourth, about 12 minutes. Transfer to a blender, add the sugar and cornstarch, and blend. Strain the mixture through a fine-mesh sieve into a clean pot. Bring to a simmer over medium heat and cook, whisking constantly, for 10 minutes. Add the remaining cherries and cook for 5 minutes more. Remove from the heat and let cool.

TO SERVE

Serve the warm bread pudding topped with the ice cream and the red wine cherry sauce.

Note: Save the egg whites to make Meringues (pages 32 or 387).

RECIPE NOTES: _____
_____
_____
_____
_____
_____
_____
_____
_____
_____
_____
_____
_____
_____
_____
_____
_____
_____

Massimo Bottura

I was up all night thinking about the day to come. As soon as I entered the Refettorio, I went straight into the walk-in refrigerator to see what was there. Knowing that the flow of surplus could vary from day to day, we built a large walk-in refrigerator so there would be enough food to prepare meals for one hundred guests at dinner and the one hundred children who often joined us for lunch. Since this was one of the very first meals, the refrigerator was still quite empty. Over the months, it would become a reliable pantry for chefs. Today it looked cavernous. Nevertheless, the more I looked, the more I found. To my surprise, the room was fragrant. I found a box of small bunches of basil stacked one on top of the other. They looked about a week old, with only a few green leaves poking out of the browning bouquet. And the first thing that came to mind was pesto.

Then the truck pulled up. Every morning, a refrigerated truck arrived from Expo with surplus food that was no longer deemed good enough to sell. Over the next months we would become familiar enough with the driver to know, by the expression on his face, if the truck was bountiful or bare. No matter what arrived, we were thankful. The circumstances dictated the cooking and we all became obsessed with cleaning out the refrigerator and using every ingredient. It was challenging and rewarding to be a chef in that kitchen. It brought out the best in everyone.

On that day Cristina was more nervous than me. She was the project manager of the Refettorio and constantly running between the kitchen and the truck, assisting the visiting chefs, and solving any and every problem. Although she is quite petite, her endearing Venezuelan accent and energetic voice holds everyone's attention: chefs and volunteers alike. Only one year earlier, when mutual friend and fellow Venezuelan, Sasha Correa, introduced Cristina to us, she was studying gastronomic history in the nearby university town of Bologna. She told us that when she had left Venezuela it was hard to find sugar and milk, and today even bread was scarce.

For this reason, she was writing her thesis on Italian recipes that use day-old bread. I knew then she would be perfect for the job.

Davide di Fabio, Jessica Rosval, and Laura Cattani from Osteria Francescana were working in the Refettorio kitchen that day. Davide rummaged through the pantry and took out a case of canned beans, then grabbed some vegetables, and several Parmigiano rinds. He had an idea for a summer version of *pasta e fagioli* (a classic Italian pasta and bean soup) that he would transform into a savory bean salad served with a crudité of chopped vegetables and diced Parmigiano rinds for texture and flavor.

Jessica and Laura had spent the morning picking out the green basil leaves from the browned bunches. Davide looked at the little pile of leaves and shook his head: not enough for a classic Ligurian pesto—a mixture of basil, pine nuts, Parmigiano cheese, and olive oil. So he suggested adding other aromatic greens, like mint. Then when it turned out there were no pine nuts, I said, "What about breadcrumbs?"

Fresh bread is perfect to serve with a meal. The next day it is still good for toast or bruschetta. After a couple of days, when it is too hard to even cut, making breadcrumbs is the best way to recover this precious ingredient. Italian cuisine offers an almost infinite number of recipes using breadcrumbs, from savory to sweet. Davide grated hard bread and sautéed the crumbs in olive oil. He placed the ingredients in a blender, added ice to keep the fragile but vibrant greens from overheating and tasting bitter, and whipped it into the texture and color of the classic recipe. I wondered if our guests would notice the difference.

Who would our guests be that night? When Daniel Humm had cooked the week before, we had invited high school students visiting Expo to fill the dining hall. This night would be the first time that a chef would cook for guests invited by Caritas Ambrosiana from nearby homeless shelters. I would come to know many by name as the

summer progressed, but at the time I didn't know what to expect. They were all passing through a fragile moment in their lives. In addition to our guests, we often served elementary and middle school kids from day camps in Greco and surrounding neighborhoods in Milan. This program was part of our mission to engage the local community about Expo's theme: Feeding the planet.

I will admit that we cheated a little bit when it came to the dessert. I had asked Cristina several days before to be sure the ingredients needed for the dessert Bread Is Gold were in the pantry. I was sure we would have plenty of day-old bread, but I also wanted to make sure that enough milk and sugar were there. We all felt that it was important to serve Bread Is Gold, or at least a version of it, because it represented so much more than a dessert: To me it was the way to celebrate the spirit of the entire project. We adapted the recipe for the circumstances using thinly sliced bread dusted with gold powder to cover the salty bread ice cream, crunchy caramelized croutons, and sweet cream. All the flavors were present and all of the emotions. We went out into the dining room to serve the half-empty room. The guests were reserved, ate quickly, and left quietly.

It had been a long day. I sat down with my head in my hands wondering if this project was really going to work. The priest Don Giuliano, who had dined with the guests that evening, put his hand on my shoulder and assured me that it had gone well. He said, "Massimo, the message you shared tonight with the guests is that their life is precious. They will eventually see that there are no other intentions than to sit together at a table and share a meal in a safe and beautiful place. And really, what more can any of us ask for in life?"

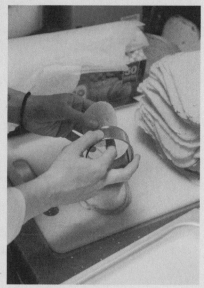

SUMMER VEGETABLES AND BEANS

Serves 8

5 oz (150 g) Parmigiano-Reggiano cheese rinds
3¾ cups (21 oz/600 g) canned kidney beans or other
    canned beans, drained
3½ oz (100 g) stale bread, cut into ⅓-inch (1 cm) cubes
¼ lb (120 g) radicchio, finely chopped
¼ lb (100 g) red, yellow, and green bell peppers, diced
2 oz (60 g) carrots, cut into ¼-inch (5 mm) dice
2 oz (60 g) celery, cut into ¼-inch (5 mm) dice
1 tablespoon diced onion (¼ inch/5 mm)
scant ½ cup (10 g) basil leaves, finely chopped
½ cup (130 ml) extra-virgin olive oil
⅓ cup (80 ml) white wine vinegar
Salt and freshly ground black pepper

In a large pot, combine the Parmigiano rinds with 3 quarts
(3 liters) cold water and cook over medium heat for 1 hour.
Remove the rinds and set aside. Add the beans and cook
over medium heat until soft and creamy, about 30 minutes.
Set aside.

Preheat the oven to 350°F (180°C/Gas Mark 4). Line a
baking sheet with parchment paper.

Arrange the bread on the baking sheet and toast until
golden brown, about 12 minutes. Set the croutons aside.

In a large bowl, combine the radicchio, bell peppers,
carrots, celery, onion, and basil. Add the olive oil, vinegar,
and salt and pepper to taste, and toss. Let rest for 2 hours.

To serve, ladle the beans and broth into bowls and top
with the vegetable mixture. Garnish with the croutons and
thin shavings of the Parmigiano rinds.

Note: Save any extra broth to make risottos or soups.

📷   P. 23

RECIPE NOTES: _____
_____
_____
_____
_____
_____
_____
_____
_____
_____
_____
_____
_____
_____
_____
_____
_____
_____

PASTA WITH MINT AND BREADCRUMB PESTO

Serves 6

MINT AND BREADCRUMB PESTO

7 oz (200 g) basil leaves
2 oz (50 g) parsley leaves
4 oz (120 g) mint leaves
1 oz (25 g) stale bread, finely crumbled (scant ½ cup)
2 garlic cloves, chopped
2 tablespoons plus 2 teaspoons extra-virgin olive oil
generous ½ cup (50 g) freshly grated Parmigiano-
    Reggiano cheese
1 tablespoon sea salt

PASTA

1 tablespoon coarse salt
1 lb (600 g) fusilli pasta or other short pasta
Freshly grated Parmigiano-Reggiano cheese, for serving

MAKE THE MINT AND BREADCRUMB PESTO

In a blender or food processor, combine the basil, parsley,
mint, breadcrumbs, garlic, and 5 ice cubes and pulse until
finely chopped. Add the olive oil, Parmigiano, and salt and
pulse to incorporate.

PREPARE THE PASTA

Bring a large pot of lightly salted water to a boil over medium
heat. Add the fusilli and cook until al dente. Toss the pasta
with the pesto. Sprinkle with the grated Parmigiano and serve.

RECIPE NOTES: _____
_____
_____
_____
_____
_____
_____
_____
_____
_____
_____
_____
_____
_____
_____
_____
_____
_____
_____

Serves 6

BREAD CRISPS
3½ oz (100 g) stale bread, sliced ⅛ inch (3 mm) thick
    and cut into six 4 inch (10 cm) rounds (see Note)
0.35 oz (10 g) edible gold powder

BREAD AND SUGAR CREAM
3½ oz (100 g) stale bread (see Note)
½ cup (100 g) packed light brown sugar
3⅓ cups (800 ml) milk
3 tablespoons heavy (whipping) cream

SALTED CARAMEL ICE CREAM
⅔ cup (150 ml) heavy (whipping) cream
¾ cup (150 g) packed light brown sugar
1½ teaspoons salt
⅔ cup (150 ml) milk

CARAMEL CROUTONS
3½ oz (100 g) bread, cut into small pieces (see Note)
4 tablespoons packed light brown sugar

MAKE THE BREAD CRISPS

Preheat the oven to 350°F (180°C/Gas Mark 4). Line a baking sheet with parchment paper.

Arrange the bread on the baking sheet ¾ inch (2 cm) apart. Bake until crispy and golden brown, about 4 minutes. Let cool. Sprinkle with the gold powder.

MAKE THE BREAD AND SUGAR CREAM

In a medium pan, heat the bread and brown sugar over medium heat and cook until caramelized, about 3 minutes. Add half the milk and simmer until almost all the liquid has evaporated. Add the remaining milk and the cream, bring to a boil, and cook for 3 minutes. Remove from the heat and let cool. Transfer to a blender and blend on high speed until smooth, about 3 minutes. Strain through a fine-mesh sieve two times. Cover and refrigerate. Once cold, whisk until stiff peaks form and transfer to a pastry (piping) bag.

>>

MAKE THE SALTED CARAMEL ICE CREAM

In a small pot, bring the cream to a boil over medium heat.

In a medium pan, melt the brown sugar over medium heat until completely melted, about 3 minutes. Add the warmed cream and salt, remove from the heat, and whisk. Strain through a fine-mesh sieve into a clean pan. Add the milk and generous ¾ cup (200 ml) water. Return to the heat and bring to 104°F (40°C) over medium heat, then simmer for 2 minutes until it reaches 176°F (80°C). Remove from the heat and let cool. Cover and refrigerate until well chilled. Transfer to an ice-cream machine and process according to the manufacturer's instructions. (If you don't have an ice-cream machine, freeze the mixture until hard enough to scoop.)

MAKE THE CARAMEL CROUTONS

In a medium pan, heat the bread and brown sugar over medium heat and cook, stirring, until the sugar caramelizes and coats the bread, about 5 minutes. Transfer to a baking sheet lined with parchment paper and let cool. Store in an airtight container.

TO SERVE

Place a scoop of the salted caramel ice cream on each plate and top with 5 caramel croutons, 1 tablespoon bread and sugar cream, 5 more caramel croutons, and 1 more tablespoon bread and sugar cream. Garnish with 1 bread crisp.

Note: Save the leftover bread for the bread and sugar cream and caramel croutons.

P. 25

RECIPE NOTES: _____
_____
_____
_____
_____
_____
_____
_____
_____
_____
_____
_____
_____
_____
_____
_____
_____
_____
_____
_____
_____

Mauro Colagreco

Mauro Colagreco was the third chef to cook at the Refettorio and the first chef to cook both lunch and dinner. In addition to the guests, a group of children from a neighboring school were invited to lunch that day. His menu had touches of both French and Italian cuisine with a playfulness that is Mauro's signature. He was born in Argentina in 1976 and moved to France in 2001 to work with some of the great chefs—Bernard Loiseau, Alain Passard, Alain Ducasse, and Guy Martin—before opening his own restaurant, Mirazur, in Menton on the southern border between France and Italy. Mirazur is on a cliff looking over the sea. It is technically in France, but Italian influences, ingredients, and language are everywhere, especially in the markets of nearby Ventimiglia, Italy.

Mauro describes his unique blend of cultures and kitchens: "I'm from Argentina. My grandparents left Italy. There was war, famine, and Mussolini. They escaped to Argentina with what little they had. At my grandmother's there were always beautiful things to eat. That is Italy. Italian cuisine has always been about being able to cook with everyday products. Make do with what you have."

That day Mauro did not have to make do. He got lucky. He unloaded lots of great ingredients from the truck: red peppers, eggs, potatoes, goat cheese, and many cartons of heavy (whipping) cream. But the real surprise was an entire wheel of Castelmagno cheese, a cow's milk cheese from the Piedmont region of Italy that dates back to the thirteenth century and is primarily used for making fondue or added to risotto. It is a prestigious product, and not something I ever expected to see in the Refettorio. Mauro had already decided that he wanted to make homemade pasta for the occasion but the kitchen was not equipped with a pasta machine. Cristina got on the phone and began calling around to see if there was anyone in the neighborhood who could lend us one. Finally, Vittoria, one of the evening volunteers, arrived with a manual, hand-cranked one. It would have to do.

Making ravioli is a challenge for most people, even good chefs, but making six hundred ravioli for 150 people is a serious undertaking. Fortunately, Mauro brought two chefs from Mirazur with him that day, Antonio from Naples and Davide from Milan. They ended up making ravioli all day. Mauro decided to make the ravioli as kid friendly and colorful as he could, with a bright red pepper sauce. Filled with braised radicchio, Tropea red onions, and Castelmagno cheese, the ravioli touched on the bitter notes that Italians are accustomed to and love. But the real surprise was yet to come!

The main course was prepared in the form of a nest, a shredded potato nest with a poached egg placed inside. It was so picturesque, the kids were initially afraid to ruin it and then they discovered the joy of poking the runny poached egg and watching the plate become engulfed in a creamy yellow mess. They squealed and laughed and the room was filled with energy. Mauro was smiling too.

That evening the volunteers arrived earlier than expected. They diligently cleaned the silverware and set the tables. An older gentleman named Carlo took the lead cutting the bread and sending out the baskets to be placed on the table. This was only the third night of service since opening the Refettorio and everyone was taking the job very seriously. Looking back at these early days, the awkward silences and empty chairs, we would marvel at how only a few weeks later we would be calling each other by name.

Spirits were higher than the night before. A few smiles were exchanged and several guests thanked the chef when they left. As the room emptied, I looked over at Mauro leaning against the wall. He was exhausted. He had been in the kitchen since early that morning working really hard. The team had made more than six hundred ravioli, 150 potato nests with poached eggs, and hundreds of meringues. There was more than just cooking happening here; there was dedication. He had faced this challenge like everything else in his life and career: with absolute conviction—and a smile.

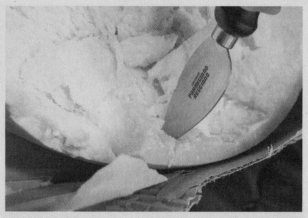

June 9

POTATO SALAD WITH MOZZARELLA AND SCALLIONS

Serves 6

> 2¼ lb (1 kg) potatoes
> 2 quarts (2 liters) beef broth
> 3 scallions (spring onions), chopped
> 10 basil leaves
> 3 tablespoons extra-virgin olive oil
> Salt and freshly ground black pepper
> 7 oz (200 g) mozzarella cheese, cut into ¾ -inch (2 cm) cubes
> 6 eggs

In a medium pot, combine the potatoes and broth and bring to a boil over medium heat. Cook until the potatoes are soft, about 15 minutes. Reserving the broth, drain the potatoes. When cool enough to handle, cut them into ¾ - to 1-inch (3 cm) cubes and transfer to a bowl. Add the scallions (spring onions), basil, and olive oil and toss to combine. Season to taste with salt and pepper. Add the mozzarella and toss to combine.

Bring a medium pot of lightly salted water to a boil over medium heat. Crack the eggs one by one into the water and cook for 6 minutes. Carefully remove with a slotted spoon.

To serve, divide the potato salad among 6 plates and top each with an egg.

RECIPE NOTES: _____
_____
_____
_____
_____
_____
_____
_____
_____
_____
_____
_____
_____
_____
_____
_____
_____
_____
_____
_____
_____
_____
_____
_____
_____
_____
_____

POTATO NEST
WITH POACHED EGG AND GOAT CHEESE SAUCE

Serves 6

> 2 cups (475 ml) sunflower oil, for deep-frying
> 3 potatoes, peeled
> 6 eggs
> 1¼ cups (300 ml) goat milk
> 7 oz (200 g) soft goat cheese
> Salt and freshly ground black pepper
> Small basil leaves, for garnish

In a medium pot, heat the sunflower oil to 265°F (130°C).

Using a grater, finely grate the potatoes to obtain fine strings. Form 6 nests. One by one, carefully place the nests in the oil and fry until golden brown, about 4 minutes. Transfer to paper towels to drain.

Bring a medium pot of lightly salted water to a boil over medium heat. Crack the eggs into the boiling water one by one and cook for 6 minutes. Carefully remove with a slotted spoon.

In a medium pot, bring the goat milk to a simmer over medium heat and reduce until creamy, about 10 minutes. Remove from the heat, stir in the goat cheese, and mix well to obtain a smooth sauce.

To serve, place a nest on each plate and top with an egg. Drizzle the egg with the goat cheese sauce. Garnish with salt, pepper, and basil.

📷   P. 31

RECIPE NOTES: _____
_____
_____
_____
_____
_____
_____
_____
_____
_____
_____
_____
_____
_____
_____
_____

Mauro Colagreco

CASTELMAGNO AND RADICCHIO RAVIOLI

Serves 6

CHARRED PEPPER SAUCE
10 red bell peppers
1 tablespoon extra-virgin olive oil
2 white onions finely chopped
scant ½ cup (100 ml) balsamic vinegar
4¼ cups (1 liter) vegetable stock

CASTELMAGNO AND RADICCHIO RAVIOLI
3¾ cups plus 1½ tablespoons (500 g) all-purpose (plain) flour
4 egg yolks
3 eggs
1 tablespoon extra-virgin olive oil
2 Tropea onions or other red onion, minced
4 heads Treviso radicchio, thinly sliced
20 basil leaves, chopped
Salt and freshly ground black pepper
¾ lb (350 g) Castelmagno cheese or other mild blue
    cheese, grated
2 tablespoons (30 g) butter
3½ oz (100 g) Parmigiano-Reggiano cheese, grated

MAKE THE CHARRED RED PEPPER SAUCE

Heat a cast-iron pan over high heat. Add the peppers and grill until lightly burned, 10 minutes. Peel, seed, and finely slice.

In a medium pot, heat the olive oil over medium heat. Add the onions and peppers and sauté until soft, 10 minutes. Add the vinegar to deglaze. Add the broth and cook for 1 hour. Transfer to a blender and blend until smooth.

MAKE THE CASTELMAGNO AND RADICCHIO RAVIOLI

In a large bowl, combine the flour, egg yolks, and eggs and work to form a smooth dough. Cover the surface directly with plastic wrap (clingfilm) and let rest for 1 hour.

In a medium pot, heat the oil over medium heat. Add the onions and brown, 4 minutes. Add the radicchio and cook until wilted, 5 minutes. Remove and stir in the basil. Season to taste with salt and pepper, and let cool. Add the Castelmagno and mix to combine. Transfer to a pastry (piping) bag.

Divide the pasta dough in half. Roll each half into a rectangle on a floured surface until 1/16 inch (1 mm) thick. Place 1 tablespoon of the filling about 1½ inches (4 cm) apart over one piece of dough and top with the other piece. Press to seal and cut into 2-inch (5 cm) square ravioli.

Bring a large pot of lightly salted water to a boil over medium heat. Add the ravioli and cook for 1 minute. Drain and gently toss with the butter and Parmigiano.

TO SERVE

Place a spoonful of the red pepper sauce on the bottom of each plate and top with the ravioli.

 P. 33

VANILLA CUSTARD
WITH BREAD ICE CREAM AND MERINGUES

Serves 6 to 8

BREAD ICE CREAM
7 oz (200 g) stale bread, torn into pieces
4¼ cups (1 liter) heavy (whipping) cream
3 egg yolks
1 cup (200 g) granulated sugar

MERINGUES
1¼ cups (250 g) granulated sugar
5 egg whites

VANILLA CUSTARD
generous 2 cups (500 ml) milk
1 vanilla bean, split lengthwise
6 egg yolks
generous ¾ cup (170 g) granulated sugar

MAKE THE BREAD ICE CREAM

In a large bowl, soak the bread in the cream until soft, about 30 minutes. Transfer to a blender and blend until smooth. Transfer to a medium pot and bring to a boil over medium heat.

In a medium bowl, whisk the egg yolks and sugar until creamy. Slowly add one-fourth of the bread mixture, stirring constantly. Return to the pot and heat to 185°F (85°C). Pass through a fine-mesh sieve and let cool for 1 hour. Transfer to an ice-cream machine and process according to the manufacturer's instructions. (If you don't have an ice-cream machine, freeze the mixture until hard enough to scoop.)

MAKE THE MERINGUES

Preheat the oven to 250°F (120°C/Gas Mark ½). Line a baking sheet with parchment paper.

In a small pot, combine the sugar and 5 tablespoons water and heat to 248°F (120°C), stirring until dissolved. Set aside.

In a stand mixer, beat the egg whites at medium speed until stiff peaks form. Add the sugar syrup, increase the speed to high, and mix until fluffy. Transfer to a pastry (piping) bag and pipe spheres on the baking sheet. Bake until firm, 15 minutes.

MAKE THE VANILLA CUSTARD

Place the milk in a medium pot and scrape in the vanilla seeds. Bring to a boil over medium heat.

In a medium bowl, whisk the egg yolks and sugar until fluffy. Slowly add one-fourth of the milk mixture, stirring constantly. Return to the pot and heat to 181°F (83°C). Pass through a fine-mesh sieve into a bowl and set the bowl in a larger bowl filled with ice and water to cool.

TO SERVE

Place a spoonful of the vanilla custard in each bowl and top with a scoop of the bread ice cream. Garnish with a meringue.

Mauro Colagreco

René Redzepi

I met René Redzepi during the summer of 2000 at Ferran Adrià's restaurant elBulli. We were in very different stages of our careers. I was five years into my second restaurant and my wife was eight months pregnant with our second child. René was a kid ready to take on the world. His mission of putting Nordic cuisine on the map was still a pipe dream. I liked René because he wasn't there stealing secret recipes or hunting for techniques like most of the chefs around us. He was there to soak up Ferran's folly and magic. We all worked like dogs and were so tired that we took catnaps between lunch and dinner leaning against the maritime pines in the shade.

After elBulli, René returned to Denmark and eventually opened Noma, a restaurant that changed the face of Nordic gastronomy forever. We reunited in 2009 in Copenhagen for the first gathering of Cook It Raw, a chef-driven event focused on sustainability. Success had driven him into the limelight and yet he remained the earnest young man I knew back then; determined, focused, and always looking ahead. We became close again and on occasion we conspired about organizing something really off the hook and unexpected, like cooking for people who didn't know or care who we were, but I don't think either one of us ever imagined that someday we would end up cooking in a soup kitchen.

René had been addressing the issue of food waste by installing a policy of "Trash Cooking" at Noma, which meant that virtually nothing edible would be wasted: skins, seeds, guts, etc. were used to make something rather than being thrown away. René explained that Trash Cooking was used not only to address food waste, but also for innovation: "When we'd run out of ingredients, we started looking at what we threw in the trash. And it was a huge creative catalyst for us. An eye-opener."

At the Refettorio we were not using food from the trash can but products that were at high risk of being thrown into the trash. Every morning we received wilted vegetables; bruised or overripe fruit; and meat, fish, chicken, and dairy close to their expiration dates. We wanted to show the public that with some imagination chefs could turn these ingredients into tasty and healthy meals.

When I arrived, the kitchen was going at full speed. René and Beau Clugston, the Australian-born sous-chef of Noma at the time, had already unloaded the truck and were prepping for dinner. Across the kitchen I spotted our mutual friend, food journalist Joanna Savill, who had chosen to spend her two-week Italian holiday volunteering in the Refettorio kitchen. She was elbow deep in strawberry mush. Her fingers were red, cut, and chafed from going through fifteen blue plastic crates of strawberries. René was burning limes over an open flame on the stovetop while a large pot of broth was simmering. Beau was slicing eggplants (aubergines) into disks. Alessandra, a pastry chef from Modena, was shaping the hamburger buns. René gave me a quick rundown of the situation while he worked: "This morning we found a lot of fruit, almost no vegetables, some hamburger patties, some herbs, and two cases of limes. It was pointless to come with an idea, because you don't know what's going to come in. What if you'd decided on a ragù and fish came in?"

Letting nothing get in the way of flavor, René sautéed wilted zucchini (courgettes), pureed them, and served them with the pasta. He transformed random vegetables into a rich and flavorful burnt lime soup, and a tray of strawberries into heavenly ice cream. Working in the Refettorio kitchen meant being very resourceful and looking in every nook and cranny for ingredients that could make a difference. For example, René found two bags of popcorn kernels in the pantry and put them on the counter. Over at the basil counter, there were fifty or more bunches of browned basil to weed through for pesto but we were low on pine nuts. Pesto for two hundred people requires a lot of pine nuts and there was only a small package. So René started making popcorn. He blended it with the basil, oil, garlic, and cheese in the mixer. And it worked. The rest of the popcorn was served in place of bread.

René is at his most articulate when he is moving around the kitchen and talking at the same time. Our guests were about to arrive and he was checking on the hamburger buns in the oven, adding greens to each bowl of soup, and putting everything in place for the rush of service while he talked about why he was here cooking: "I think everybody has a responsibility. You know. So why shouldn't a chef also? If you're a chef, if you're a lawyer, or if you're the CEO of a company, it's the same gesture. But I believe it comes naturally for a lot of cooks to want to take care of somebody, because that's what we do every day. You feed them. You feed people."

All of us—the kitchen staff and the volunteers serving the meal—took this dinner very seriously. René and Beau had cooked the night before at the Bulgari Hotel for elite guests and we could all see he was dedicating the same amount of attention to this meal. The food had to be served at the right temperature and plated properly. Most of all, it had to be good. There were no excuses.

After service we were all exhausted, some of us were eating, others were cleaning the kitchen, and René and Beau were packing up their things. Just before René rolled his suitcases out the door, he said to me: "Do you know the first memory I have of you, Massimo, is overcooked pasta at elBulli? Somebody overcooked the pasta and you freaked out, really freaked out and you threw it into the ocean . . . the pasta! Do you remember that? So I guess the pasta needs to be cooked right . . . otherwise it gets wasted!"

René Redzepi

BURNT LIME SOUP

Serves 8

LIME OIL
Grated zest of 1 lime
scant ½ cup (100 ml) grapeseed oil

VEGETABLE BROTH
6 limes
3 tablespoons grapeseed oil
3½ oz (100 g) white onions, slivered
7 oz (200 g) Jerusalem artichokes, sliced ⅓ inch
    (1 cm) thick
3½ oz (100 g) carrots, sliced ⅓ inch (1 cm) thick
3½ oz (100 g) turnips, sliced 13 inch (1 cm) thick
3½ oz (100 g) celeriac, peeled and sliced ⅓ inch
    (1 cm) thick
3½ oz (100 g) potatoes, peeled and sliced ⅓ inch
    (1 cm) thick
3½ oz (100 g) apples, sliced ⅓ inch (1 cm) thick
1 bunch lemon thyme
¼ oz (10 g) dried mushrooms
16 chicory leaves
16 mustard leaves
Salt and freshly ground black pepper
scant ½ cup (10 g) basil, chopped
scant ½ cup (10 g) cilantro (coriander), chopped

MAKE THE LIME OIL

In a small bowl, whisk together the lime zest and grapeseed oil. Set aside.

MAKE THE VEGETABLE BROTH

Char the limes until completely blackened over the open flame of a stove burner (or under a hot broiler [grill] if you don't have a gas stove). Let cool, then quarter. Set aside.

In a large pot, heat the grapeseed oil over medium heat. Add the onions and sauté until translucent, about 6 minutes. Add the Jerusalem artichokes, carrots, turnips, celeriac, potatoes, and apples and cook until aromatic, about 10 minutes. Add the lemon thyme, dried mushrooms, and 2 quarts (2 liters) water and bring to a boil over medium heat. Reduce to a simmer, add the limes, and cook to reduce by half, about 40 minutes. Add the chicory and mustard leaves and let rest for 10 minutes. Season to taste with salt and pepper.

TO SERVE

Ladle the soup into 8 bowls. Sprinkle with the basil and cilantro (coriander) and drizzle with the lime oil.

Note: You can use any root vegetables you have on hand.

 P. 39

PASTA WITH POPCORN PESTO

Serves 8

POPCORN PESTO
3 tablespoons corn oil
generous 2 tablespoons popcorn kernels
1 garlic clove, minced
Leaves from 4 bunches basil, washed and chopped
Leaves from 1 bunch cilantro (coriander), washed
    and chopped
1¼ cups (275 ml) extra-virgin olive oil
3½ oz (100 g) pine nuts (see Note)
Grated zest of 1 lemon, plus more to taste
Salt and freshly ground black pepper

PASTA
2¼ lb (1 kg) short pasta (such as penne, tortiglioni, or fusili)
Extra-virgin olive oil, for drizzling
Freshly grated Parmigiano-Reggiano cheese, for serving

MAKE THE POPCORN PESTO

In a medium pot, heat the corn oil over high heat. Just as the oil begins to smoke, add the popcorn and quickly cover with a lid. Vigorously shake the pan while the popcorn begins to pop. Once the popping begins to subside, remove from the heat and continue shaking for about 1 minute. Once cool, remove the popcorn and discard any unpopped kernels. Transfer to a food processor and blend into medium-size bits. Set aside.

In a blender, combine the garlic, basil, cilantro (coriander), and olive oil and process until smooth. Add the pine nuts and pulse until lightly crush. Transfer to a large bowl. Add the lemon zest and season to taste with salt and pepper. Add the popcorn and gently mix to combine. Set aside.

PREPARE THE PASTA

Bring a large pot of lightly salted water to a boil over medium heat. Add the pasta and cook until al dente. Drain and transfer to the bowl with the popcorn pesto. Gently stir to coat the pasta evenly. Adjust the seasoning with salt, pepper, and lemon zest.

To serve, divide the pasta among 8 bowls and garnish with a drizzle of olive oil and some Parmigiano.

Note: If you don't have pine nuts, add more popcorn.

RECIPE NOTES: _____
_____
_____
_____
_____
_____
_____
_____
_____

René Redzepi

HAMBURGERS
WITH EGGPLANT AND HOMEMADE KETCHUP

Serves 8

CRUMBLED HAMBURGERS

1½ lb (700 g) ground (minced) beef
½ cup (30 g) chopped parsley
½ cup (30 g) chopped lovage or celery leaves
1½ teaspoons sea salt
1 teaspoon freshly ground black pepper
1¼ teaspoons freshly ground mustard seeds
    or mustard powder
2 teaspoons grapeseed oil
1½ cups (200 g) all-purpose (plain) flour
8 eggs, lightly beaten
7 oz (200 g) stale bread, finely crumbled (3½ cups)

HOMEMADE KETCHUP

1 tablespoon grapeseed oil
2 shallots, finely minced
2 garlic cloves, finely minced
3 tablespoons sherry vinegar
1 cup (9 oz/250 g) tomato paste (puree)
5 sprigs thyme
2 fresh bay leaves
Salt

FRIED EGGPLANT

2 lb (800 kg) eggplants (aubergines), cut crosswise
    in slices ⅓ inch (1 cm) thick
Salt
2 cups (440 ml) grapeseed oil
4 tablespoons balsamic vinegar

FOR ASSEMBLY AND SERVING

3 tablespoons grapeseed oil, for the burgers
Salt
8 brioche hamburger buns, homemade (recipe follows)
    or store-bought
7 tablespoons (100 g) butter, melted
3½ oz (100 g) Parmigiano-Reggiano cheese, thickly shaved,
    for serving

MAKE THE CRUMBLED HAMBURGER

In a large bowl, mix together the beef, parsley, lovage, salt, pepper, mustard, and oil. Vigorously fold and beat the meat with the palm of your hand until the mixture becomes more opaque and white, about 5 minutes (the mixture should not be crumbly). Divide evenly into 8 portions and shape into patties.

Set up 3 shallow bowls: one for the flour, a second for the eggs, and a third for the breadcrumbs. Coat the patties in the flour, dusting off any excess, then quickly dip into the eggs, and finally into the breadcrumbs. Transfer to a container, cover, and refrigerate until ready to cook.

>>

MAKE THE HOMEMADE KETCHUP

In a pan, heat the grapeseed oil over medium heat. Add the shallots and garlic and sauté until lightly golden, 5 minutes. Add the vinegar, stirring to release any caramelized bits on the bottom of the pan. Reduce the heat to medium-low and add the tomato paste (puree), thyme, bay leaves, and 1 cup (250 ml) water, stirring to mix thoroughly. Simmer until the consistency of ketchup, 5 minutes. Remove the thyme stems and bay leaves and season to taste with salt. Set aside.

MAKE THE FRIED EGGPLANT

Line baking sheets with parchment paper. Arrange the eggplants (aubergines) on the lined sheets, sprinkle with salt on both sides, and let stand for 30 minutes. Transfer to paper towels and press to absorb the excess liquid.

In a large frying pan, heat the grapeseed oil over medium-high heat. Working in batches, add the eggplant without overcrowding the pan and cook until lightly browned, about 3 minutes. Turn and brown the other side. Transfer to a tray lined with paper towels to absorb any excess oil. Transfer to another tray and drizzle with the balsamic vinegar. Set aside.

TO ASSEMBLE

Preheat the oven to 325°F (160°C/Gas Mark 3).

In a large frying pan, heat the grapeseed oil over medium-high heat. Working in batches, add the hamburger patties, reduce the heat to medium, and cook until browned, 5 minutes. Flip and brown on the other side, 5 minutes more. Transfer to a tray lined with paper towels and season with salt.

Meanwhile, place the fried eggplant on a baking sheet and transfer to the oven to reheat.

Split the buns horizontally, place on a baking sheet cut side up, and toast in the oven for 2 minutes. Spread the toasted buns with the melted butter.

TO SERVE

Place the patties in the buns and top with 3 or 4 pieces of fried eggplant, slathering a small spoonful of the tomato ketchup over each piece. Garnish with thick shavings of Parmigiano.

BRIOCHE BUNS

Makes 30 buns

1 tablespoon plus 2 teaspoons active dried yeast
7 tablespoons granulated sugar
scant ½ cup (100 ml) milk
5¾ cups (750 g) all-purpose (plain) flour
8 eggs
4 teaspoons salt
2 sticks plus 5 tablespoons (300 g) butter, cubed,
    at room temperature
1 tablespoon sesame seeds

>>

René Redzepi

In a bowl, combine the yeast and 1½ tablespoons of the sugar. In a medium pot, warm the milk over medium heat to 77°F (25°C). Pour over the yeast and sugar and whisk until small bubbles form. Cover with plastic wrap (clingfilm) and let sit for 10 minutes. Remove the plastic wrap and transfer to a stand mixer fitted with the dough hook attachment. Add the flour and 7 of the eggs and mix on low speed for 1 minute. Add the remaining 5½ tablespoons sugar and salt and mix on medium speed for 10 minutes. Add the butter, one piece at a time, and beat until fully incorporated. Transfer to a large container coated with cooking spray. Cover with plastic wrap and let rise for 8 hours.

Line a baking sheet with parchment paper or coat with cooking spray. Divide the dough into 2-ounce (60 g) portions, shape into balls, and place on the baking sheet. Cover with plastic wrap and let rise until the buns have doubled in size, 30 to 45 minutes.

Preheat the oven to 350°F (180°C/Gas Mark 4).

In a small bowl, whisk the remaining egg. Apply a thin layer of the whisked egg to the buns, and lightly sprinkle with the sesame seeds.

Bake until golden brown and 203°F (95°C) in the center, 10 to 15 minutes. Let cool on wire racks.

STRAWBERRIES WITH BANANA BREAD

Serves 8

MACERATED STRAWBERRIES
1 lb 2 oz (500 g) strawberries, quartered
⅓ cup (75 ml) red verjus or raspberry vinegar
¾ cups (90 g) powdered (icing) sugar
Salt (optional)

STRAWBERRY SORBET
1½ gelatin sheets
1¾ lb (750 g) strawberries, chopped
2 tablespoons birch syrup (or substitute with maple syrup)
¼ cup (50 g) granulated sugar
1½ tablespoons condensed milk

BANANA BREAD
1 stick plus 2 tablespoons (150 g) butter
2¾ cups (380 g) all-purpose (plain) flour
2½ teaspoons baking soda (bicarbonate of soda)
½ teaspoons salt
5 overripe bananas (see Note)
1⅛ cups (215 g) packed dark brown sugar
6 eggs

GARNISH
Lemon verbena leaves, pineapple mint leaves, or edible flower petals

>>

MAKE THE MACERATED STRAWBERRIES

In a large bowl, combine the strawberries and verjus. Using a small sieve, dust the powdered (icing) sugar over the fruit. Gently mix, cover, and refrigerate for 30 minutes. Adjust the sweetness with more sugar and season with salt, if needed. Cover and set aside.

MAKE THE STRAWBERRY SORBET

In a small bowl, soak the gelatin in cold water until soft, about 10 minutes. Drain and set aside.

In a medium pot, combine the strawberries, birch syrup, sugar, and condensed milk and cook until the strawberries have softened and released most of their liquid, about 20 minutes. Remove a small amount of the strawberry liquid and transfer to a small bowl. Add the gelatin and stir to dissolve. Return to the strawberry mixture. Using a hand blender or food processer, blend until smooth. Pass through a fine-mesh sieve into a bowl and place in larger bowl filled with ice and water to cool.

Transfer the cooled mixture to an ice-cream machine and process according to the manufacturer's instructions. (If you don't have an ice-cream machine, freeze the mixture until hard enough to scoop.)

MAKE THE BANANA BREAD

Preheat the oven to 350°F (180°C/Gas Mark 4). Coat a 5 x 9-inch (13 x 23 cm) baking pan with cooking spray, line with parchment paper, and coat the paper with cooking spray.

In a small pot, heat the butter over low heat and stir until light brown. Set aside.

In a medium bowl, sift together the flour, baking soda (bicarbonate of soda), and salt. Set aside.

In a stand mixer fitted with the paddle attachment or using a hand mixer, mix the bananas and brown sugar on medium-low speed until smooth. Add the eggs, one at a time, on medium speed, beating well after each addition. Turn the speed down to low and carefully add the dry ingredients in three additions. Add the butter and mix to combine.

Pour the batter into the prepared baking pan and bake until a wooden skewer inserted in the center comes out clean, 15 to 20 minutes, rotating the pan front to back halfway through. Let cool in the pans on a wire rack.

TO SERVE

Divide the macerated strawberries among 8 bowls and garnish with the lemon verbena, pineapple mint, or flower petals. Top with a scoop of the strawberry sorbet and a slice of the banana bread.

Note: Save the peels to make Banana Peel Chutney (page 158).

RECIPE NOTES: _____
_____
_____
_____

Yoshihiro Narisawa

Yoshihiro Narisawa has become a friend over the past decade. Nari, as I have always called him, speaks fluent Italian. He trained in Europe for nine years working in Switzerland, France, and Italy before returning to Japan and opening Les Créations de Narisawa. His knowledge of Italian culinary traditions often leads us into heated discussions about the parallels in flavor and practice between Italian and Japanese cuisine. Nari and I both embrace the idea that the kitchen is a place for continual evolution.

Over the past years I have witnessed a shift in his practice toward a more pronounced Japanese identity with advocacy for sustainable, organic, and natural ingredients. In 2013 the restaurant, renamed Narisawa, was recognized internationally with the first Sustainable Restaurant Award from *Restaurant Magazine*. He explained, "In my restaurant, we don't waste food. The better parts we serve to our guests. The rest we cook for the staff. More than 90 percent of ingredients are delivered directly from the producers. I never ask for specific items. The producers send the products that are the freshest. The producers are very small, so this is one way of reducing waste for them, too."

On this day, something special was happening in the kitchen. Three professional chefs from Japan, France, and Italy had left their kitchens to turn tired ingredients into a delicious meal. Japanese chef Takahiko Kondo, a chef at Osteria Francescana for the past twelve years, was elbow deep in what looked like chocolate soup. Across the room was an unfamiliar face. It was Christian Julliard, Alain Ducasse's executive chef worldwide, who had stopped by early that morning to take a look at the kitchen in advance of Alain's own dinner. Christian didn't look around and walk out the door; he saw that there was far too much work for three people in the kitchen, so he rolled up his sleeves to brunoise twenty-two pounds (ten kilos) of onions for Nari's milk soup, a treasured childhood recipe.

And there was the familiar face of food journalist Joanna Savill. She had worked through crates of strawberries for René Redzepi the day before. Despite that, she returned for more torture. Nari had her peeling kilos and kilos of potatoes. She recalled, "Each peeled potato had to be cut carefully into neat triangles. All the same size. It took almost an entire morning. It was a little surprising to see them then boiled for a soup! But the soup was fabulous, so all that precision probably helped."

At the time I could not have imagined that this scene would repeat itself over and over again during the course of Expo: chefs, friends, and volunteers from around the world stopping by for a day or a week to lend a hand. Maybe this was the magical formula that made these meals so special. The people who dined at the Refettorio felt this energy. Nari recalled the guests saying, "Here, we're welcomed as guests and asked if the meal was nice or not. We feel very happy to be treated like that." Not only did our guests appreciate the meal but also the volunteers who set the tables, served, washed dishes, and cleaned up were eager to know all the details of the recipes. After service, we held a staff meal and there was always someone asking the chef about a favorite dish.

Nari was happy to see that people wanted to repeat the recipes, and that evening everyone was asking about the teriyaki sauce. That is when I began to think about writing this cookbook. We should at the very least document the recipes that were proof of what had happened. Recipes are often the best storytellers. Reading a recipe, I imagine the physical motions around the space, the sound of the cutting board, and the smells coming from the kitchen.

When everyone had gone, Nari and I walked back to the apartment. He told me that the essence of Japanese food culture is expressed in the words *itadakimasu* and *gochisosama deshita*. The first expresses gratitude to the ingredients and to nature, while the second expresses gratitude to the person who prepared the food. Japanese parents teach their children not to waste by repeating these words before every meal. I remembered this ritual from my travels to Japan and it sounded like the Japanese version of the Italian expression *buon appetito*, a common benediction that Pope Francis uses to bless the meal and spread the message: Treasure the moment, treasure each other, and treasure the food that you will be served. But then Nari told me about a word that I had never heard before, *mottainai*. Nari said, "It represents the soul of Japanese food culture because it expresses the idea of quality over quantity and implies *not* wasting." Later, I looked it up and found that it can be translated to "what a waste" or "don't be wasteful."

The Japanese have great respect for food and yet there are serious food waste problems in Japan, too. The pace of modern life and the race to make ends meet contribute to throwing away more than what we eat: here, there, and everywhere. We had only just begun to scratch the surface of the food-waste dilemma. A few well-cooked meals would not solve the problem, but I felt that doing something, however small, would have greater impact than sitting around and scratching my head. I said the word *mottainai* over and over again trying to remember it. What a waste. What a waste. What a waste.

Yoshihiro Narisawa

44

June 17 and 18

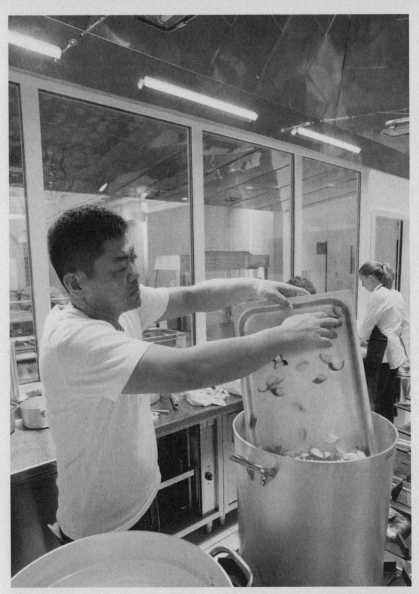

Serves 6

2 bay leaves
10 oz (280 g) root vegetables (such as potatoes, onions,
    carrots, and turnips), diced
4 oz (120 g) green vegetables (such as zucchini
    [courgettes], broccoli, and celery), diced
4 tablespoons (55 g) butter
½ cup (55 g) all-purpose (plain) flour
1⅓ cups plus 2 tablespoons (335 ml) milk
1 cup (160 g) canned beans
Salt and ground white pepper

In a large pot, bring 4 cups (960 ml) water and the bay leaves
to a simmer over medium heat. Cook the vegetables one at a
time until al dente, removing each with a slotted spoon and
setting aside before adding the next vegetable. Continue
this process until all the vegetables are cooked. Reserve the
cooking liquid.

In a medium pot, melt the butter over low heat. Add
the flour and cook, stirring constantly, until golden brown,
about 7 minutes. Add the milk and stir constantly until
velvety, about 15 minutes. Stir in a generous ¾ cup (200 ml)
of the reserved cooking liquid. Add the vegetables and the
beans and season to taste with salt and white pepper.
Ladle the soup into bowls.

RECIPE NOTES:

Yoshihiro Narisawa

TERIYAKI HAMBURGERS

Serves 6

HAMBURGERS
generous 1 cup (150 g) dried breadcrumbs
10 oz (300 g) ground (minced) beef
3½ oz (100 g) lard
½ cup (120 ml) milk
1 small onion, chopped
3 eggs
1 teaspoon salt
½ teaspoon freshly grated nutmeg
¼ teaspoon freshly ground black pepper
2 tablespoons extra-virgin olive oil

TERIYAKI SAUCE
2 tablespoons extra-virgin olive oil
2 red bell peppers, sliced
7 oz (200 g) mushrooms, quartered
1⅓ cups (320 ml) white wine
generous ⅔ cup (160 ml) soy sauce
½ cup plus 2 tablespoons (130 g) granulated sugar
2 tablespoons cornstarch (cornflour), sifted

MAKE THE HAMBURGERS

In a large bowl, combine the breadcrumbs, beef, lard, milk, onions, eggs, salt, nutmeg, and pepper and mix by hand until well incorporated. Form 6 patties.

In a medium frying pan, heat the olive oil over medium heat. Add the patties and cook until lightly browned on both sides, about 8 minutes.

MAKE THE TERIYAKI SAUCE

In a medium saucepan, heat the olive oil over medium heat. Add the red peppers and sauté until soft, about 6 minutes. Transfer to a plate. Add the mushrooms to the pan and sauté until soft, about 4 minutes. Add to the red peppers.

In a medium pot, bring the white wine to a simmer over medium heat and cook for 5 minutes. Add the soy sauce and sugar and mix well. Remove a small amount of the liquid and transfer to a small bowl. Add the cornstarch and stir to dissolve. Return to the pot, stirring constantly until the sauce is slightly thickened, about 10 minutes. Return the peppers and mushrooms to the pan.

TO SERVE

Place a hamburger patty on each plate and cover with the teriyaki sauce.

📷 P. 48

RECIPE NOTES:

CHOCOLATE BREAD WITH TOFFEE ICE CREAM

Serves 6

TOFFEE ICE CREAM
    2 eggs
    scant ½ cup (90 g) granulated sugar
    2 tablespoon condensed milk
    ¾ cup plus 2 tablespoons (215 ml) milk
    ¾ cup plus 2 tablespoons (215 ml) heavy (whipping) cream

CHOCOLATE BREAD
    2 eggs
    5½ tablespoons granulated sugar
    5 tablespoons unsweetened cocoa powder
    1¼ cups (288 ml) milk
    Twelve 1⅜-inch (3.5 cm) thick slices of stale bread

FRUIT SALAD
    7½ oz (210 g) assorted fruits (such as strawberries, melon,
        passion fruit, mango, pomegranate, and dragon fruit),
        peeled and diced

MAKE THE TOFFEE ICE CREAM

In a medium bowl, whisk together the eggs, sugar, and
condensed milk.
    In a medium pot, bring the milk to 176°F (80°C) over
low heat. Slowly stir one-fourth of the hot milk into the egg
mixture, stirring constantly. Transfer the warmed eggs to
the pot and cook at 180°F (82°C) for 15 minutes, stirring
constantly. Transfer to a large bowl of ice and water to
chill, then stir in the cream and return to the ice bath
until cold. Transfer to an ice-cream machine and process
according to the manufacturer's instructions. (If you don't
have an ice-cream machine, freeze the mixture until hard
enough to scoop.)

MAKE THE CHOCOLATE BREAD

Preheat the oven to 400°F (200°C/Gas Mark 6). Line a baking
sheet with parchment paper.
    In a medium bowl, whisk the eggs and sugar. Add the
cocoa powder and mix. Stir in the milk. Add the bread and
let soak until absorbed. Transfer the bread to the prepared
baking sheet and bake until browned, about 20 minutes.
Set aside at room temperature.

MAKE THE FRUIT SALAD

In a medium bowl, combine the fruit. Cover and refrigerate
for 10 minutes.

TO SERVE

Place 1 or 2 slices of the warm chocolate bread on each plate
and top with a scoop of the toffee ice cream. Serve with the
fruit salad.

Enrico & Roberto Cerea

Enrico and Roberto Cerea, otherwise known as Chicco and Bobo, are two of five brothers. They were all born in the kitchen of their family's restaurant Da Vittorio (named after their father) in the province of Bergamo in the northern region of Lombardy. At a young age both brothers packed their bags and left to work in the kitchens of some of the most renowned restaurants at that time. After living in France, Germany, Spain, and the United States, they came back home with big dreams for Da Vittorio, which in 2009 was awarded its third Michelin star. They are the perfect examples of old-school chefs with their crisp white jackets and polite manner.

When Chicco and Bobo arrived at the Refettorio they brought with them a troop of young chefs, each with a poly-styrene foam box in his hands. I immediately imagined tons of different cheeses, for which the Bergamo Valley is famous. However, when I took off a lid, I couldn't believe my eyes: It was lobster! Chicco and Bobo had brought the surplus of food from their last catering service. The night before they had served a large wedding party on the verdant lawns of Da Vittorio. The lobsters, beautiful vegetables, and edible flowers became a celebration that our guests would never forget.

Actually, our guests were not accustomed to finding luxury surprises, and when ingredients like tropical fruits and Castelmagno cheese were featured in a meal, they were suspicious of what was on their plate because it was the first time for many of them to taste or even see these ingredients. On that day, I was afraid that they would not react well to the lobsters that Chicco and Bobo had so generously shared with us. Fortunately, we had the aid of Marzia Molteni, a psychologist from Caritas who had ample experience working with people in vulnerable conditions. She was in charge of helping us communicate with our guests. It was not always easy to know how to approach them, or even how to introduce and serve the dishes. Some people asked for plain pasta and didn't even want to try the dishes prepared by the chefs because they were unfamiliar; others fought over who had a bigger portion of pasta that night. After more than twenty years running a restaurant, I knew well that customers can often be difficult. Marzia advised us on how to encourage them to try new foods without being intimidated. She was there every night keeping watch and making sure nothing got out of hand.

Chicco and Bobo intuitively understood that they had to find a way to cook the lobster so that it wouldn't seem threatening or foreign. After a lot of debate, they decided to batter and fry it, like a tempura. Who knew it was even lobster?

That night, they served a soup called *panada* made with stale bread and Parmigiano rinds; lobster tempura with fennel sauce and decorated with delicate edible flower petals; and a lemon cake served with a tropical fruit salad. The colorful dishes brightened the room and no one turned down the lobster. Actually, the guests said that they hoped we would have lobster again.

When the last bowl of fruit salad left the kitchen, Chicco and Bobo had the same gentle and relaxed smile they had at the beginning of the service. And of course, the same clean, crisp jackets. In fact, I couldn't resist splashing my fingers in the vanilla sauce to stain their sleeves. They looked at me in shock and then followed my lead. Just in the knick of time, Don Giuliano entered the kitchen as he did nightly. He looked at us in the same way he looks at the neighborhood boys when their soccer games start to get rough. Then he reached over and took a piece of cake from the counter, turned around to leave, and said, "How lucky we are tonight to have mischievous boys in the kitchen!"

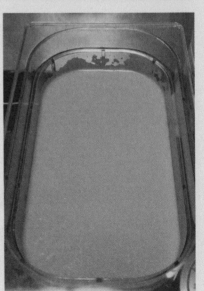

Serves 6

3 sage leaves
1 bay leaf
10½ oz (300 g) stale bread, chopped
Salt
6 tablespoons Parmigiano Cream (recipe follows)
2 tablespoons extra-virgin olive oil
1¾ oz (50 g) Parmigiano-Reggiano cheese, grated
Freshly ground black pepper

In a medium pot, combine 4¼ cups (1 liter) water, the sage and bay leaves and bring to a boil over medium heat. Add the bread, reduce the heat to low, and simmer for 30 minutes. Transfer to a blender and blend until smooth. Season to taste with salt.

To serve, ladle the soup into bowls. Add 1 tablespoon of the Parmigiano cream in the center, and drizzle with the olive oil. Garnish with the grated Parmigiano and freshly ground pepper.

PARMIGIANO CREAM

Makes 2¾ cups (650 ml)

generous 2 cups (500 ml) heavy (whipping) cream
5 oz (150 g) Parmigiano-Reggiano cheese, grated

In a medium pot, boil the cream over medium heat for 2 minutes. Remove from the heat and stir in the Parmigiano. Pass through a fine-mesh sieve, cover, and set aside at room temperature until ready to serve.

RECIPE NOTES: _____
_____
_____
_____
_____
_____
_____
_____
_____
_____
_____
_____
_____
_____
_____
_____
_____
_____
_____
_____

Serves 6

2 tablespoons plus 1¼ cups (300 ml) extra-virgin olive oil
1 white onion, slivered
3 fennel bulbs, trimmed and chopped
2 zucchini (courgettes), cut into 2-inch (5 cm) pieces
2 carrots, cut into 2-inch (5 cm) pieces
1 cauliflower, cut into 2-inch (5 cm) pieces
2½ cups (600 ml) milk
Salt and freshly ground black pepper
generous 1 cup (150 g) all-purpose (plain) flour
Meat from 6 lobster claws or other other firm fish
    or shellfish
Flower petals (such as carnations, calendula, dandelions,
    or other edible flower)

In a saucepan, heat 2 tablespoons of the olive oil over medium heat. Add the onion and cook until soft, about 5 minutes. Set aside.

Set up a bowl of ice and water. Bring a medium pot of salted water to a boil. Add the fennel and blanch for 3 seconds. Transfer to the ice bath to cool. Scoop out of the ice bath and set aside. Repeat for the zucchini (courgettes), carrots, and cauliflower.

In a medium saucepan, heat the milk over low heat. Add the blanched fennel and cook for 10 minutes. Transfer to a blender and blend until smooth. Season with salt and pepper. Set the fennel cream aside.

In a medium pot, heat 1¼ cups (300 ml) olive oil to 356°F (180°C).

In a medium bowl, mix the flour with a generous ¾ cup (200 ml) water and 4 ice cubes. Dip the lobster into the batter, add to the hot oil, and deep-fry until golden, about 1 minute. Drain on paper towels.

To serve, place a spoonful of the fennel cream on each dish. Top with the fried lobster and vegetables, and garnish with the flower petals.

📷   P. 55

RECIPE NOTES: _____
_____
_____
_____
_____
_____
_____
_____
_____
_____
_____
_____
_____
_____
_____
_____
_____

LEMON CAKE
WITH VANILLA CREAM AND TROPICAL FRUITS

Serves 6

TROPICAL FRUIT SALAD
2 mangoes, cut into ¾ -inch (2 cm) cubes
1 papaya, peeled, seeded, and cut into ¾ -inch (2 cm) cubes
1 pineapple, cut into ¾ -inch (2 cm) cubes
1 starfruit, sliced
5 passion fruits, halved

LEMON CAKE
7 cups (225 g) all-purpose (plain) flour
1 packet (7 g) active dry yeast
¼ teaspoon salt
7 tablespoons (100 g) butter, at room temperature
½ cup (110 g) granulated sugar
3 eggs
Juice and grated zest of 1 lemon
3 tablespoons plus 1 teaspoon milk

VANILLA CREAM
generous 2 cups (500 ml) milk
1 vanilla bean, split lengthwise
2 egg yolks (see Note)
5½ tablespoons granulated sugar

FOR SERVING
12 cape gooseberries

MAKE THE TROPICAL FRUIT SALAD

In a large bowl, combine the mangoes, papaya, pineapple, and starfruit. Scoop out the passion fruit pulp and strain, discarding the seeds. Add to the bowl and mix to combine.

MAKE THE LEMON CAKE

Preheat the oven to 350°F (180°C/Gas Mark 4). Line an 8-inch (20 cm) round baking ban and dust with flour.
    In a medium bowl, sift together the flour, yeast, and salt. Set aside.
    In a medium bowl, mix together the butter, sugar, eggs, and lemon juice and zest with a whisk until combined. Add the flour mixture and mix. Add the milk and mix until combined. Transfer to the prepared pan and bake until a wooden pick or tip of a knife comes out dry, about 45 minutes. Let cool in the pan on a wire rack.

>>

MAKE THE VANILLA CREAM

Place the milk in a medium saucepan and scrape in the vanilla seeds, adding the vanilla pod, too. Bring to a boil over medium heat and cook for 6 minutes. Remove from the heat.
    In a medium bowl, whisk together the egg yolks and sugar. Slowly add one-fourth of the hot milk. Transfer to the saucepan and heat to 181°F (83°C). Strain through a fine-mesh sieve into a bowl and set in a larger bowl of ice and water to cool down quickly. Cover and refrigerate.

TO SERVE

Place a slice of the lemon cake on each plate. Top with the fruit salad and the vanilla cream, and garnish with 2 cape gooseberries.

Note: Save the egg whites to make Meringues (pages 32 or 387). You can use any fruits you have on hand for the fruit salad.

📷   P. 57

RECIPE NOTES: _____
_____
_____
_____
_____
_____
_____
_____
_____
_____
_____
_____
_____
_____
_____
_____
_____
_____
_____
_____
_____
_____
_____
_____
_____
_____
_____
_____
_____
_____
_____

Enrico & Roberto Cerea

Yannick Alléno

I arrived at the Refettorio early, but Yannick Alléno was not there, so I walked across the street to the barbershop to get a haircut. A congregation of balding men blocked the doorway. I weaved through them and as soon as the barber sat me down, the questions began: "Are you that chef from the Refettorio? Are there really homeless people eating in there? What are you cooking?" I answered, "Actually, I'm waiting for the chef Yannick Alléno to arrive. He's from Paris, younger than me, and with more Michelin stars. He is a maverick in the kitchen and he's got really nice hair, too." They laughed. Most of these men have lived in or around this area their entire lives.

The barber said he was originally against the project because he was afraid that a soup kitchen would mean trouble for the quiet neighborhood. I reassured them that the Refettorio was one of the quietest places I've ever been, that the food was good, and that tonight it would be exceptional. When I stood up to go, they asked: "When can we come for dinner?" I invited them that night.

Yannick arrived with his partner Florence Cane, the general director of the Groupe Yannick Alléno, as well as editor of *Yam*, Yannick's gastronomy magazine. I first met Yannick and Florence in October of 2013. I was in Paris for an exhibition at l'École des Beaux-Arts called "Cookbook" curated by Andrea Petrini and Nicolas Bourriaud, then the school's director. Andrea and I crashed a *GQ* book party at the restaurant La Gazzetta and Yannick was standing at the bar. It was the perfect introduction to the emblematic French chef. He immediately started talking with passion about his fight to grow vegetables in Paris. He was dynamic and engaging. He had recently left Le Meurice (where he had been awarded three Michelin stars) to open his restaurant Le Cheval Blanc. His choice to leave marked a desire to explore, and move beyond the confines of classic French cuisine. It was a bold move and one that raised a lot of gossip and controversy at the time. Yannick

and Florence came to Modena to visit us soon after and we became fast friends.

It was 3 p.m. when Yannick arrived. In no time he put us all to work deboning chickens and preparing vegetables. There was a lot to do for a one hundred-person dinner that was only in a few hours. Yannick was very calm and very cool, because as much as the dinner was improvised, his technique and his palate were not. He knew exactly how to turn some zucchini (courgettes), peppers, cauliflower, chicken, tropical fruit, and day-old bread into a delicious and hearty meal.

I asked him what he was preparing. Yannick said, "I came with an evident spirit of French cuisine. I wanted to propose a classic, cold potage with cauliflower, nutmeg, and some vegetables. I'm going to make a poultry fricassee. You know, France is into sauce, so I will make a poultry sauce. We'll finish with something fresh like a fruit salad—I saw an overripe papaya and it could become a papaya salad with acidity from passion fruit—and bread pudding. Voilà."

What I learned that day is that Yannick is obsessed with sauce. Nothing was going to get in his way of making a sauce worthy of a Michelin three-star meal. "I made a jus with the chicken carcass; I added some carrots, some onion," he told me. "The sauce has to be reduced a lot. It has to be tasted and understood, then reduced more. It will have an intense taste, and be even tastier than it is now. That's what makes the dish. The sauce is the identity of French cuisine."

This lesson was valuable for everyone that day. The obsessive dedication to everything you do is what makes the difference between a good chef and a great one. At the end of the day it doesn't matter what ingredients you have available or where you are cooking; the intention, the obsession, and the work is all that matters.

As the juices on the stovetop were becoming a sauce, Yannick was opening the papaya. I was watching him from a corner of the room and I saw the expression on his face when he tasted it;

it wasn't that good. But he didn't throw it away. He cooked it. He transformed it into something edible, even good. He caught me watching him and said, "You see, suddenly, it is no longer waste because we recovered it. This exercise is pretty interesting. The idea behind it is fantastic: Transformation takes intelligence."

That is the value of technique and experience and why I had invited so many chefs to cook here in the first place. Yes, I knew they could make a delicious meal out of almost anything, but more important they could teach us all how to work with food that is on its way to the dumpster—food that is not so good or tasty. That is the value of having a chef like Yannick here in the Refettorio. That is the reason we are telling these stories.

The old men in the neighborhood were very happy that they had come. Later that summer they began to organize lunches every Thursday at the Refettorio for a crowd of over seventy people from the neighborhood.

The meal was perfect, and perfectly French, too. Francesco Vincezi, known as Vince, a young chef from Modena in charge of the pasta courses at Osteria Francescana, was helping that day. When he saw that Yannick had added pesto spaghetti to the main course, as the French often do, he looked astonished—Italians consider pasta worthy of its own course. Yannick laughed when I told him that Vince was not very happy about this and he responded: "Let me tell you a story. I was fifteen years old when I started working with Manuel Martinez at Le Relais Louis XIII. It was so hot that August I opened the window of the kitchen. I saw a man stealing the pastries I had just made. I ran out and tried to catch him but he got away. Months passed and when winter came I saw my chef giving that same man a bowl of soup. I said to Chef, 'He was the one who stole my pastries!' Chef replied, 'He was hungry.' Et voilà! I think cooks need to have a big heart." Now I understood why he added the spaghetti to the chicken fricassee. Yannick wanted to show our guests the meaning of French abundance as well as French perfection.

June 24

CHILLED CAULIFLOWER SOUP

Serves 6

CHILLED CAULIFLOWER SOUP
    1 large head of cauliflower, cut into 2-inch (5 cm) pieces
    4 cups (1 liter) milk
    2 teaspoons salt
    scant ½ cup (100 ml) heavy (whipping) cream

SAUTÉED ZUCCHINI AND POTATOES
    3 tablespoons extra-virgin olive oil
    1 onion, cut into ⅓-inch (1 cm) cubes
    3 zucchini (courgettes), cut into ⅓-inch (1 cm) cubes
    2 potatoes, cut into ⅓-inch (1 cm) cubes
    Leaves from 2 sprigs thyme, chopped
    Leaves from 2 sprigs oregano, chopped
    Salt and freshly ground black pepper

CROUTONS
    6 slices stale bread, cut into ⅓-inch (1 cm) cubes
    2 tablespoons extra-virgin olive oil
    Salt and freshly ground black pepper

FOR SERVING
    Freshly grated nutmeg
    Extra-virgin olive oil, for drizzling
    2 tablespoons chopped parsley

MAKE THE CHILLED CAULIFLOWER SOUP

In a medium pot, combine the cauliflower, milk, and salt, adding water if necessary to completely cover the cauliflower. Bring to a simmer over medium heat and cook until soft, about 10 minutes. Transfer to a blender and blend until smooth. Add the cream and adjust the seasoning if necessary. Cover and refrigerate.

SAUTÉ THE ZUCCHINI AND POTATOES

In a medium frying pan, heat 2 tablespoons of the olive oil over medium heat. Add the onions and sauté until soft but not browned, about 5 minutes. Add the zucchini (courgettes) and sauté until cooked.

In a separate medium frying pan, heat the remaining 1 tablespoon olive oil over high heat. Add the potatoes and sauté until cooked and slightly crispy, about 15 minutes.

In a medium bowl, combine the zucchini, potato, thyme, and oregano and season to taste with salt and pepper. Set aside.

>>

MAKE THE CROUTONS

Preheat the oven to 350°F (180°C/Gas Mark 4). Line a baking sheet with parchment paper.

In a medium bowl, toss the bread with the olive oil, and season with salt and pepper. Transfer to the prepared baking sheet and toast until golden brown, about 10 minutes.

TO SERVE

Ladle the chilled soup into bowls and top with a spoonful of the sautéed vegetables. Sprinkle with nutmeg, drizzle with olive oil, and garnish with parsley.

RECIPE NOTES: _____
_____
_____
_____
_____
_____
_____
_____
_____
_____
_____
_____
_____
_____
_____
_____
_____
_____
_____
_____
_____
_____
_____
_____
_____
_____
_____
_____
_____
_____
_____
_____
_____
_____

Yannick Alléno

CHICKEN FRICASSEE
WITH PEPPERS, SPINACH, AND PESTO PASTA

Serves 6

CHICKEN FRICASSEE
- 2 tablespoons (30 g) butter
- 1 chicken carcass, halved
- 1 onion, coarsely chopped
- 2 carrots sliced $\frac{1}{16}$ inch (2 mm) thick
- 3 celery stalks, sliced $\frac{1}{16}$ inch (2 mm) thick
- 2 shallots, sliced $\frac{1}{3}$ inch (1 cm) thick
- 1 garlic clove, chopped
- 1 tablespoon of tomato paste (puree)
- 6 boneless, skinless chicken thighs
- Salt and freshly ground black pepper
- 1 tablespoon extra-virgin olive oil

PEPPERS AND SPINACH
- 4 red or yellow bell peppers
- 2 tablespoons extra-virgin olive oil
- Salt and freshly ground black pepper
- 1 lb (500 g) spinach

PESTO PASTA
- 4 cups (100 g) fresh basil
- 3½ oz (100 g) Parmigiano-Reggiano cheese, grated, plus shaved Parmigiano for serving
- 3½ oz (100 g) stale bread, finely crumbled (1¾ cups)
- 4 tablespoons extra-virgin olive oil
- Salt and freshly ground black pepper
- 10 oz (300 g) spaghetti

MAKE THE CHICKEN FRICASSEE

In a large Dutch oven (casserole), heat the butter over medium heat. Add the chicken carcass and cook until browned, about 8 minutes. Add the onion, carrots, celery, shallots, and garlic and cook until soft, about 5 minutes. Add a generous 4 cups (1 liter) water and cook until reduced by half. Add the tomato paste (puree) and simmer until caramelized. Add a generous ¾ cup (200 ml) water and simmer over low heat for 30 minutes. Transfer to the oven and bake for 1 hour, skimming regularly and adding water if necessary. Strain and discard the solids. Transfer to a medium pot and simmer over low heat until reduced to about ¾ cup (200 ml), about 15 minutes. Set aside.

Preheat the oven to 350°F (180°C/Gas Mark 4).

Season the chicken thighs with salt and pepper. In a medium frying pan, heat the olive oil over high heat. Add the chicken and cook until browned on both sides, about 5 minutes. Transfer to a baking dish and add the chicken sauce. Bake until cooked through, about 20 minutes.

>>

PREPARE THE PEPPERS

Char the peppers over the open flame of a stove burner all over until the skin is completely blackened. (If you don't have a gas stove, char under a hot broiler [grill].) Transfer to a bowl, cover, and let sit for 20 minutes. Peel, seed, and slice the peppers. Toss with 1 tablespoon olive oil and season to taste with salt and pepper.

PREPARE THE SPINACH

In a medium frying pan, heat the remaining 1 tablespoon olive oil over medium heat. Add the spinach and sauté for 1 minute. Season to taste with salt and pepper.

MAKE THE PESTO PASTA

In a food processor, combine the basil, Parmigiano, and breadcrumbs and blend. With the machine running, slowly add the olive oil. Season to taste with salt and pepper.

Bring a large pot of lightly salted water to a boil over medium heat. Add the spaghetti and cook until al dente. Drain, reserving some of the pasta water. Toss with the pesto and loosen with the reserved pasta water, if necessary.

TO SERVE

Place a spoonful of chicken sauce on each plate and top with the chicken, peppers, and spinach. Serve the pasta alongside, sprinkled with Parmigiano shavings.

RECIPE NOTES: _____
_____
_____
_____
_____
_____
_____
_____
_____
_____
_____
_____
_____
_____
_____
_____
_____
_____
_____
_____
_____

BREAD PUDDING
WITH CANTALOUPE SORBET AND TROPICAL FRUITS

Serves 6 to 8

BREAD PUDDING
    1 lb 2 oz (500 g) stale bread, torn into 1¼ -inch
        (3 cm) pieces
    6 egg yolks (see Note)
    1 cup (200 g) granulated sugar
    4¼ cups (1 liter) heavy (whipping) cream
    1 vanilla bean, split lengthwise
    2 tablespoons (30 g) butter

CANTALOUPE SORBET
    1¼ cups (250 g) granulated sugar
    2¼ lb (1 kg) cantaloupe, cut into 1 inch (3 cm) chunks
    Juice of 3 lemons

TROPICAL FRUIT SALAD
    1 papaya, peeled, seeded, and diced
    1 mango, diced
    1 passion fruit, halved
    ½ teaspoon fresh ginger, minced
    2 teaspoons fresh lemon juice

MAKE THE BREAD PUDDING

Preheat the oven to 325°F (160°C/Gas Mark 3).
    Butter a 9-inch (23 cm) square baking dish and arrange the bread in one layer.
    In a medium bowl, whisk together the egg yolks and sugar.
    In a medium pot, bring the cream to a simmer over medium heat. Scrape in the vanilla seeds. Slowly incorporate the eggs into the hot cream, whisking constantly until the cream comes back to a simmer. Pour the mixture over the bread and let sit for 20 minutes.
    Transfer the baking dish to a roasting pan and add water to come halfway up the sides of the dish. Transfer to the oven and bake until firm, about 40 minutes. Let cool before cutting into slices ¾ inch (2 cm) thick.
    In a medium pan, melt the butter over medium heat. Add the pieces of bread pudding and cook until browned, about 1 minute per side.

MAKE THE CANTALOUPE SORBET

In a medium pot, bring the sugar and 1 cup (250 ml) water to a boil over medium heat until dissolved. Transfer to a blender, add the cantaloupe, and process until smooth. Add lemon juice to taste. Cover and refrigerate until well chilled. Transfer to an ice-cream machine and process according to the manufacturer's instructions. (If you don't have an ice-cream machine, freeze the mixture until hard enough to scoop.)

>>

MAKE THE TROPICAL FRUIT SALAD

In a medium bowl, combine the papaya and mango. Scoop in the passion fruit pulp, add the ginger and lemon juice, and mix.

TO SERVE

Place a slice of the bread pudding on each plate and top with the tropical fruit salad. Serve with a scoop of the cantaloupe sorbet.

Note: Save the egg whites to make Meringues (pages 32 or 387). You can use any fruits you have on hand for the fruit salad.

RECIPE NOTES: _____
_____
_____
_____
_____
_____
_____
_____
_____
_____
_____
_____
_____
_____
_____
_____
_____
_____
_____
_____
_____
_____
_____
_____
_____
_____
_____
_____
_____
_____
_____
_____
_____
_____
_____
_____

Gastón Acurio

Gastón Acurio is the father of contemporary Peruvian cuisine. He not only put the international spotlight on Peruvian food but also changed the way Peruvians think about their culinary heritage. He was the first Peruvian chef to bring forth the artisan, talk about indigenous ingredients, and give value to the riches and resources of Peru's remarkable biodiversity. His message traveled around the world through the restaurants he opened in Peru, Latin America, North America, and Europe. Gastón was also the driving force behind the culinary festival Mistura, which brought many chefs and journalists to meet artisans and discover new flavors. We are all at risk of losing our artisans and our heroic farmers, and he believes that chefs can make a difference when we stand united. "We've been trying to build a strong community between chefs all over the world that share principles and values around food and cooking," he told me.

Gastón and I hugged each other when he arrived at the Refettorio. I am always happy to see him. The kitchen was busy preparing lunch for a big group of kids. He thought that the best way to understand Italy was through its children. Milan is an immigrant destination and it is the most multicultural city in Italy. That day at lunch, there was a room full of elementary school children of every race, color, and continent. Gastón prepared a Peruvian lunch based on one of his favorite dishes. He began the meal with chicken and potatoes served with a *huancaína* sauce. "I'm making a dish that is one of the most humble, most popular, and democratic recipes in Peru," he said. "It's called *papa a la huancaína* and the sauce is made with chilies, day-old bread, and cheese." While the plates were being served, a young, eight-year-old boy asked to speak to Gastón. He said, "I was born in Italy but this is who I am!" He pointed to the sauce and we understood that his family was from Huancayo. Those flavors were so deeply rooted in him that he felt he belonged to them and they belonged to him.

Peruvian food is a confluence of diverse immigrant heritages. One of the best descriptions I have read is by Canadian food writer Alexandra Gill, who described it in an article in Canada's *The Globe and Mail*: "What do you get when you stir Chinese soy sauce, Japanese wasabi, Spanish chicken and beef, African pumpkin, Andean corn, and Incan potatoes in a melting pot bursting with citrusy chili peppers and black-mint pesto? This multicultural mash up is called Peruvian cuisine."

The second course was a Peruvian rice dish with vegetables served with a Nikkei-style sauce made with ginger and soy and individual omelets placed on top of the rice. Ninety kids at the table meant a lot of omelets. I'm not sure anyone imagined how many ninety omelets could be. The clock ticked and as it approached noon there was a mad rush to get the omelets made. Fortunately, Roberto Grau, Gaston's sous-chef, decided to call Diego Oka, Gastón's chef de cuisine at la Mar in Miami, who happened to be in Milan. Diego rushed over from another event to lend a hand. I watched this guy with amazement. He was a machine. He came to Modena that night and he ended up staying for three months, becoming part of our Osteria Francescana family.

That day Gastón served those kids so much more than lunch. He had opened his heart and shared himself, his country, and his heritage through food. He shared stories about the pre-Hispanic Inca culture in Peru and how Peruvian cuisine was born from a mix of that culture and immigrant cultures, such as Spanish, Japanese, Chinese and African. He was mentoring those kids as he had fostered Peruvian chefs and the public at large to look at their culinary heritage with pride and dignity. His cooking confirmed my belief that "food is culture." This moment convinced me that what we were doing here was not an act of charity, but spreading culture. Part of the fight against food waste is about understanding how other cultures make the most of ingredients. By looking at many culinary traditions we can form new culinary traditions that address not only the issue of food waste but also the power of food to unite people.

Gastón Acurio

June 25

Serves 6

1¼ lb (600 g) baby potatoes
Salt
6 oz (180 g) green beans
6 oz (180 g) carrots, quartered lengthwise
2 tablespoons canola (rapeseed) oil
1 lb (500 g) red bell peppers, chopped
5 oz (150 g) red onion, chopped
2 tablespoons chopped garlic
½ oz (15 g) ají amarillo or other fresh yellow chilies
1¼ cups (300 ml) milk
3 oz (80 g) queso fresco or other firm, fresh cheese
scant ½ cup (40 g) freshly grated Parmigiano-
    Reggiano cheese
1¾ oz (50 g) stale bread, cut into small pieces
6 black olives, pitted and chopped

In a large pot, combine the potatoes and 1 teaspoon salt and cover with water. Bring to a boil over medium heat and cook until soft and easily pierced with a wooden pick, about 8 minutes. Drain and let cool on a tray. Cut in half and set aside.

Set up a large bowl of ice and water. Bring a medium pot of salted water to a boil. Add the green beans and blanch for 10 seconds. Remove with a slotted spoon and immediately transfer to the ice bath to cool. Cut in half and set aside. Repeat the process for the carrots.

In a medium frying pan, heat the canola (rapeseed) oil over low heat. Add the bell peppers, onion, garlic, and chili and sauté for 1 minute. Transfer to a food processor. Add the milk, queso fresco, Parmigiano, and bread, and blend until smooth. Season to taste with salt.
Set aside the *huancaína* sauce.

To serve, divide the potatoes, green beans, and carrots among the plates and dress with the *huancaína* sauce. Garnish with the black olives.

Note: You can use any leftover *huancaína* sauce as a dip for vegetables or chips or as a sauce for chicken.

RECIPE NOTES:

ARROZ CHAUFA
AND SPANISH TORTILLA WITH NIKKEI SAUCE

Serves 6

ARROZ CHAUFA

4 tablespoons canola (rapeseed) oil, plus 1¼ cups
    (300 ml) for deep-frying
5 oz (150 g) capellini pasta, broken into smaller pieces
9 oz (250 g) boneless, skinless chicken thighs, cut into
    small pieces
9 oz (250 g) pork loin, cut into small pieces
¼ teaspoon salt, plus more for seasoning
1 oz (25 g) fresh ginger, finely chopped
2 garlic cloves, thinly chopped
½ medium head broccoli, roughly chopped
3 small zucchini (courgettes), diced
1 red bell pepper, diced
2½ cups (600 g) cooked long-grain rice
2 tablespoons plus 2 teaspoons oyster sauce
4 teaspoons soy sauce
1 teaspoon sesame oil
1 tablepoon granulated sugar

NIKKEI SAUCE

1½ tablespoons canola (rapeseed) oil
½ tablespoon garlic chopped
1 tablespoon chopped fresh ginger
½ tablespoon chopped scallions (spring onions),
    greens reserved for serving
1½ teaspoons oyster sauce
2 tablespoons plus 2 teaspoons chili-garlic sauce
2½ tablespoons Thai sweet chili sauce
2 cups (500 ml) chicken stock
1 tablespoon granulated sugar
1 teaspoon soy sauce
1 teaspoon sesame oil
1 tablespoon potato starch

OMELET

8 eggs
Pinch of salt
½ teaspoon sesame oil
½ teaspoon granulated sugar
3 tablespoons canola (rapeseed) oil

GARNISH

Chopped scallion (spring onion) greens
Chopped cilantro (coriander)

>>

MAKE THE ARROZ CHAUFA

In a medium heavy-bottomed pot, heat 1¼ cups (300 ml) of
the canola (rapeseed) oil over medium heat. Add the cappel-
lini and fry until golden brown, 1 minute. Set aside.

Season the chicken and pork with salt. In a large pan or
wok, heat 2½ tablespoons of the canola (rapeseed) oil over
medium heat. Add the chicken and pork and sauté until
golden brown, about 5 minutes. Transfer the chicken and
pork to a plate and set aside.

Clean the wok and heat the remaining 1½ tablespoons
canola oil over high heat. Add the ginger and garlic and sauté
until lightly browned, about 2 minutes. Add the broccoli,
zucchini (courgettes), and bell pepper and sauté for
2 minutes. Add the rice and brown for 2 minutes more,
stirring constantly. Add the oyster sauce, soy sauce, sesame
oil, the ¼ teaspoon salt, sugar, and fried pasta and sauté
until combined, about 3 minutes.

MAKE THE NIKKEI SAUCE

In a medium frying pan, heat the canola oil over medium heat.
Add the garlic, ginger, and scallions, and sauté. Add the oyster
sauce and cook over medium heat for 6 minutes. Add the
chili-garlic sauce and Thai sweet chili sauce and simmer for
5 minutes. Add the chicken stock, sugar, soy sauce, and
sesame oil and simmer for 8 minutes.

In a small bowl, dissolve the potato starch in 1½ tablespoons water. Add the mixture to the sauce and cook for
5 minutes to thicken. Remove from the heat but keep warm
for serving.

MAKE THE OMELET

In a medium bowl, whisk together the eggs, salt, sesame oil,
and sugar. In a small frying pan, heat 1½ teaspoons canola
oil over medium heat. Pour one-sixth of the egg mixture and
cook until lightly browned, about 5 minutes. Flip and cook
until lightly browned on the other side, about 3 minutes.
The tortilla should be moist inside. Repeat this process to
make 6 tortillas.

TO SERVE

Serve the *arroz chaufa* in a serving dish. Top with the tortilla
and drizzle with the Nikkei sauce. Sprinkle with the scallion
greens and chopped cilantro.

📷   P. 72

RECIPE NOTES: _____

_____

_____

_____

_____

_____

_____

_____

_____

TRES LECHES SPONGE CAKE
WITH DULCE DE LECHE ICE CREAM

Serves 8

TRES LECHES SPONGE CAKE
  4¼ cups (1 liter) milk
  2 cinnamon sticks
  1 vanilla bean, split lengthwise
  2⅓ cups (550 ml) heavy (whipping) cream
  1¾ cups (430 ml) condensed milk
  1 lb 5 oz (600 g) stale bread (preferably brioche),
    crusts trimmed

MANJAR BLANCO ICE CREAM
  generous 2 cups (500 ml) milk
  scant ½ cup (100 ml) heavy (whipping) cream
  ¼ cup (30 g) whole-milk powder
  1¾ oz (50 g) dextrose or glucose
  1½ tablespoons granulated sugar
  2 egg yolks (see Note)
  7 oz (200 g) manjar blanco or dulce de leche
  Pinch of salt

BERRY SAUCE
  ½ cup (100 g) granulated sugar
  3½ oz (100 g) strawberries
  3½ oz (100 g) raspberries and blueberries

MAKE THE TRES LECHES SPONGE CAKE

In a medium saucepan, combine the milk and cinnamon
sticks. Scrape in the vanilla seeds, add the pod as well.
Cook over medium heat until reduced by half, about 15
minutes. Strain into a medium bowl and let cool. Stir in the
cream and condensed milk. Cover and transfer the tres leches
sauce to the fridge to chill.

Place the bread snugly in a deep 8 x 12-inch (20 x 30 cm)
baking dish. Add the tres leches sauce, cover with plastic wrap
(clingfilm), and freeze for at least 6 hours or overnight. When
ready to serve, unmold and cut into 8 rectangles.

>>

MAKE THE MANJAR BLANCO ICE CREAM

In a medium pot, combine the milk, cream, milk powder, and
dextrose and cook over low heat for 7 minutes. In a medium
bowl, whisk together the sugar and egg yolks until creamy.
Whisk 2 cups (500 ml) of the hot milk mixture into the yolk
mixture. Transfer the warmed yolks to the pot and whisk
to combine. Cook until the mixture reaches 185°F (85°C).
Meanwhile, set up a large bowl of ice and water.

Stir the *manjar blanco* into the hot mixture, remove from
the heat, and set in the ice bath to quick-chill to 39°F (4°C).
Strain through a fine-mesh sieve, cover, and let rest in the
fridge for 10 hours.

Add the salt. Transfer to an ice-cream machine and process
according to the manufacturer's instructions. (If you don't have
an ice-cream machine, freeze the mixture until hard enough
to scoop.)

MAKE THE BERRY SAUCE

In a medium pot, heat the sugar over low heat until melted,
about 2 minutes. Add the berries and cook until soft, about
2 minutes more. Let cool, then cover and refrigerate to chill.

TO SERVE

Place 1 piece of the tres leches cake on each plate. Top with
a scoop of manjar blanco ice cream and drizzle with the
berry sauce.

Note: Save the egg whites to make Meringues (pages 32 or 387).

RECIPE NOTES: _____
_____
_____
_____
_____
_____
_____
_____
_____
_____
_____
_____
_____
_____
_____
_____
_____
_____
_____
_____
_____
_____
_____
_____

Andrea Berton & Davide Oldani

Andrea Berton and Davide Oldani are old friends from their days cooking at Gualtiero Marchesi in the 1980s. Although their paths diverged, they have always remained close, both working in Milan, each finding his own personal culinary expression.

Andrea is Friuliano. He has a staggering presence, very tall and at times intimidating. I've known him since 1994. We met the minute I walked into the kitchen at Hôtel de Paris in Monte Carlo. He had been working there nearly a year and took me under his wing. We have been friends ever since. In only a few years, he opened a series of successful restaurants in Milan: Pisacco, is an Italian bistro; Ristorante Berton, a Michelin contemporary fine dining restaurant; and Dry, the most recent, a combination pizzeria and cocktail bar.

Davide, on the other hand, is Milanese through and through. He is tan, fit, and stylish. He opened his restaurant D'O in the late 1990s with an inexpensive menu in a modern setting serving contemporary food. The restaurant received a Michelin star and Davide immediately became a pop icon in Italy.

Even though both of them were extremely busy with events around Expo, they were determined to find the time to cook a lunch and dinner at the Refettorio. The two of them had demonstrated their support over the months leading up to Refettorio's opening, including speaking at press conferences and showing up at fundraising events.

Neither of them could have imagined what a day it would be. Andrea was already at the Refettorio when Davide pulled up on his bicycle not looking like a chef at all. Don Giuliano—not looking anything like a priest in his blue pants, Polo shirt, and Birkenstock clogs—was also there, and about to head off on his mountain bike to make his routine stops at the local parishes. It was funny to see these two city boys on their bikes.

I came out and warned Davide that there was a problem: The gas wasn't working. This could complicate pre- paring lunch. Davide looked worried all of a sudden. He had planned to make a risotto called Panriso—a signature dish featuring sautéed breadcrumbs on top. The dish fit perfectly into the spirit of the Refettorio, using the breadcrumbs to add flavor and texture, and offered yet another clever idea for using day-old bread. However, without a stovetop, it would be impossible, so Davide turned his attention to making dessert. He found mascarpone and decided to prepare a mousse. At least there would be a wonderful dessert!

Andrea focused on preparing a panzanella, a classic tomato and bread salad that doesn't involve the stove, a smart thing to do given the circumstances. "Bread was the first thing I thought about using when I walked in that morning," he said. "You can use bread anywhere. It should never be thrown away. You can use it in a thousand recipes, crushed, soaked and baked."

The gas was finally fixed around 11 a.m. There was a mad rush to the stovetop to prepare Davide's originally planned Panriso. Andrea pureed his panzanella into a creamy tomato sauce to serve with a baked gratin of bread, onion, and Parmigiano. The gratin was a cross between *pappa al pomodoro* (Tuscan tomato and bread soup) and panzanella. He baked layers of bread with cheese and onions and served it over the pureed panzanella—a recipe he had invented on the spot.

We were a little behind schedule when the kids arrived at noon. They sat down and Cristina introduced herself. She often gave lessons about the value of brown bananas and day-old bread to help the kids understand what we were doing. The kids arrived hungry and Cristina began the lesson by passing around some fragrant but bruised bananas. She asked the group, "Is anyone hungry?" The kids looked at the bananas and responded, "Noooo!" in disgust. She proceeded to explain that these bananas could be turned into delicious ice cream, and that they had great flavor, even if they didn't look very good. Then a small sample of ice cream was passed around to encourage the kids to think differently about this common fruit. We learned that if you talk to kids about food when they are hungry, they really pay attention.

The risotto was served first. Risotto is a Milanese classic and the surrounding countryside of Lombardy is dotted with rice paddies. While Andrea was plating his dish, Davide came out of the kitchen to talk to them about his childhood. "In my family pronouncing the world 'waste' was already a waste of breath," he said. "My mother taught me to think before going out for groceries and to weigh everything before cooking. At home we never ate *riso al salto* (a typical Milanese dish made with leftover saffron risotto) because there were never leftovers to make it with."

As the kids ate their last bites of mascarpone mousse, Don Giuliano, who had slipped in to eat lunch, conducted the group in a chant: "Davide! Andrea! Davide! Andrea! Davide! Andrea!!" They clapped until the chefs came out of the kitchen to receive a standing ovation. The two chefs were blushing. The kids had really enjoyed the lunch because the flavors were familiar and tasty, but also because of the stories that were shared with them. After the room settled down, I stood between the chefs and told the kids, "You know, I couldn't have done this project without the help of friends like these. This morning the gas wasn't even working, but these guys didn't walk away. With or without gas, they were going to make lunch no matter what."

I could see that Andrea and Davide were glad they had come. They still had the evening meal ahead of them and the charisma of the kids would keep their spirits lifted for days to come. Don Giuliano joined us again for dinner. He said, "This is a true example of Italian cuisine—simple but delicious. It goes straight to your heart! They got applause from the evening diners as well and afterward came up to me and said: "Thank you, Massimo. We had no idea what this experience would be like. Can we do it again?" And they did. A year later, they flew to Rio de Janeiro to cook at the Refettorio Gastromotiva. That is what friends are for.

Andrea Berton & Davide Oldani

July 1

Andrea Berton & Davide Oldani

BREAD AND ONIONS WITH RAW TOMATO CREAM

Serves 6

TOMATO CREAM
1 lb 2 oz (500 g) datterini or other tomatoes, chopped
1 cup (25 g) fresh basil leaves
4 teaspoons salt
4 tablespoons extra-virgin olive oil

BREAD AND ONIONS
scant ½ cup (110 ml) extra virgin oil, plus more for
    brushing the bread
4½ lb (2 kg) white onions, finely chopped
generous 2 cups (500 ml) chicken stock
½ teaspoon salt
¼ teaspoon freshly ground black pepper
2 loaves (1¾ lb/800 g each) stale bread, cut into slices
    ½ inch (1.5 cm) thick
4 oz (120 g) Parmigiano-Reggiano cheese, grated

MAKE THE TOMATO CREAM

In a medium bowl, combine the tomatoes, basil, salt, and oil and let marinate for 15 minutes. Transfer to a blender and blend until smooth. Strain through a fine-mesh sieve. Reserve at room temperature.

MAKE THE BREAD AND ONIONS

Preheat the oven to 325°F (160°C/Gas Mark 3). Grease an 8-inch (20 cm) square baking dish 2 inches (5 cm) deep.

In a medium saucepan, heat the olive oil over low heat. Add the onions and cook, stirring occasionally, until caramelized, about 20 minutes. Add the chicken stock, salt, and pepper and cook for 10 minutes. Drain the broth into a bowl and reserve the onions.

Arrange half of the bread in the prepared baking dish, covering the entire surface. Sprinkle with some of the onion broth, make a layer of cooked onion, and sprinkle with Parmigiano. Repeat the layering with the remaining bread slices, making a layered bread cake, reserving 2 tablespoons of Parmigiano for the last layer and 2 tablespoons of onions for the garnish, and finishing with a layer of bread. Brush the top layer with olive oil and sprinkle with the reserved Parmigiano.

Transfer to the oven and bake until golden brown, about 20 minutes. Remove from the oven to cool slightly. Set the oven to broil and line a baking sheet with parchment paper. Cut the bread cake into 2- to 2½-inch (5 to 6 cm) squares. Transfer to the lined baking sheet and broil until golden brown, about 5 minutes

TO SERVE

Place a spoonful of the tomato cream on each plate. Top with the bread and onion cake and garnish with the reserved cooked onions.

📷 P. 79

PANRISO

Serves 6

10 oz (300 g) Parmigiano-Reggiano cheese rinds,
    roughly chopped
3 tablespoons extra-virgin olive oil
5 oz (150 g) ground (minced) beef
4 tablespoons white wine
½ cup (60 g) dried breadcrumbs
scant 2¼ cups (420 g) carnaroli or other short-grain rice
1 teaspoon salt
4 tablespoons (60 g) butter
generous 1 cup (100 g) freshly grated Parmigiano-
    Reggiano cheese
2 teaspoons balsamic vinegar

In a large pot, combine the Parmigiano rinds with 6 cups (1.5 liters) water and bring to a boil over medium heat. Simmer for 20 minutes. Strain the Parmigiano stock through a fine-mesh sieve into a clean saucepan and keep warm over low heat.

In a medium frying pan, heat 2 tablespoon of olive oil over medium heat. Add the beef and cook, stirring to break it up as it browns, about 8 minutes. Add the wine and cook until evaporated. Set aside.

In a separate pan, heat the remaining 1 tablespoon of olive oil over medium heat. Add the breadcrumbs and toast until golden brown and crunchy. Set aside.

In a medium saucepan, combine the rice and salt and toast over medium heat, stirring constantly, about 6 minutes. Add a ladleful of the Parmigiano stock and stir. Once absorbed, add another ladleful of stock and continue until all of the stock has been used. Continue to cook, stirring constantly, until al dente, about 20 minutes.

Add the butter, Parmigiano, and balsamic vinegar and stir. Remove from the heat and let rest for 5 minutes.

TO SERVE

Place a ladleful of risotto in each bowl and top with a tablespoon of the minced meat. Garnish with toasted breadcrumbs and serve.

RECIPE NOTES: _____
_____
_____
_____
_____
_____
_____
_____
_____
_____
_____
_____
_____

Andrea Berton & Davide Oldani

MASCARPONE MOUSSE WITH CARAMELIZED APPLES

Serves 6

MASCARPONE MOUSSE
10½ oz (450 g) mascarpone cheese
2 tablespoons heavy (whipping) cream
2 eggs, separated
4 generous tablespoons granulated sugar

CARAMELIZED APPLES
scant ½ cup (90 g) granulated sugar
3 apples, peeled and sliced

MAKE THE MOUSSE

In a medium bowl, whisk the mascarpone with the cream to soften. Set aside.

Bring a medium pot of water to a boil. In a large heatproof bowl, combine the egg yolks and half of the sugar. Place the bowl over the boiling water and whisk until foamy. Remove the bowl from the pot and set aside.

In another bowl, whisk the egg whites with the remaining sugar until stiff peaks form.

Fold the whipped mascarpone into the egg yolks with a spatula. Fold in the beaten egg whites. Form spheres the size of a golf ball. Transfer to a tray lined with parchment paper and refrigerate until ready to serve.

MAKE THE CARAMELIZED APPLES

In a medium frying pan, melt the sugar over medium heat, until bubbling and golden brown. Add the apple and sauté until golden brown and caramelized, about 2 minutes. Keep warm until ready to serve.

TO SERVE

Place 1 sphere of mascarpone mousse in each bowl. Top with 2 pieces of caramelized apple and drizzle with the caramel from the frying pan.

📷 P. 81

RECIPE NOTES:

Andrea Berton & Davide Oldani

Sara Papa & Alberto Calamandrei

A very important day at the Refettorio—perhaps the most important—was when baker Sara Papa visited to host a workshop on breadmaking for the volunteers. A professional bread oven was donated to the Refettorio by Oscar Farinetti of Eataly and placed in the entrance (not the kitchen) to welcome our guests with the smell of fresh bread. The warm, fragrant loaves were baked every day in the late afternoon to represent the value of "breaking bread" together.

Sara began the lesson with the basics. She starred in her own television series about making bread and cooking, so she knew exactly how to chose simple words to explain the composition and methodology behind using a sourdough starter for leavening bread. She is a passionate baker and very knowledgeable about heritage grains, organic flours, and the magic of sourdough starter. Everyone was listening attentively to her fairy tale-like narration. As I watched from afar, I noticed among the group of predominantly female volunteers, a white-haired man with a large white mustache who was writing down every word. Later I learned his name was Alberto Calamandrei.

Alberto was one of the numerous volunteers from the Greco neighborhood who had responded to our call for help. He was a retired computer engineer who was looking for something valuable to do with his free time. When Alberto presented himself at the first volunteer meeting before the Refettorio opened, we asked what he would like to do and he offered himself for the kitchen team. "Can you cook?" Cristina asked. "Cook? Well, I'm not a cook but I did spend a lot of time in the kitchen with my mother because I was the youngest in the family." Little did we know that Alberto would be more of a resource than we could have ever imagined.

When the workshop was over, Alberto stood up and ran after Sara, holding on tightly to his notes scribbled on scraps of paper. They were chatting away and I could see there was a connection. Sara was so impressed by Alberto's passion about breadmaking that she

asked him to join her on the shopping trip to buy the necessary tools needed to begin setting up the bakery. Alberto returned holding bags of different types of organic flour, baskets for leavening, knives for cutting bread, and even a cart to move the dough between the kitchen and the bakery. Sara suddenly looked at her watch and realized she was about to miss her return train to Rome and left in a flurry.

Julien, a French chef hired by Caritas to assist in the kitchen, took on the task of preparing the dough. He had never made bread and was curious to learn. After about a week, I noticed that the loaves were looking flat and tasted acidic. Alberto was in the kitchen chopping vegetables for the mirepoix when he heard me speaking with Alessandra, the head baker at Osteria Francescana, asking her to bring up some of our sourdough starter from Modena. He leaned in toward me and asked politely, "Massimo, can I have a look first? I think I know what to do." He looked at the starter, scratched the surface, took a small piece, smelled it, and then tasted it. "This sourdough is still good. It is just a little bit . . . down. Let me try to cheer it up."

Alberto grabbed some bruised apples, pears, and grapes from the walk-in refrigerator and sliced them. He filled a large bowl of warm water and left the fruit floating in it. He left a note that read "Do not touch" over the bowl and let it sit overnight. Cristina had her doubts, but I had already understood what he was trying to do and it was brilliant. The next day, he took the water that the fruit had been soaking in and kneaded it into the sourdough starter. The sugars from the fruit were the perfect fuel for the weak sourdough starter. "You know, bacteria is a living thing. It needs to be listened to and cared for."

From that day on, Alberto began to share the breadmaking responsibility with Julien and the bakery took on a life of its own. Every morning, Alberto entered the Refettorio with a clean apron and his pockets full of pieces of paper. Guest chefs commented on how beautiful the loaves were, golden brown

and fully shaped, with perfect scoring. Alberto seemed to be standing taller, smiling more. He was proud of his daily bread.

One day I confronted Alberto, "Tell me the truth: You've done this before." He admitted that he used to make bread at home when he had a family around to cook for, but now that he was living alone, he was very happy to have found a place to make bread for people again. Sara returned a few weeks later to give a follow-up lesson. The first thing she did was taste the bread from the day before. She asked, "Who made this bread?" Alberto raised his hand and Sara said to the group, "*Questo ragazzo è fatto della pasta giusta,*" which translates literally as, "This guy is made of the right kind of dough."

Sara Papa & Alberto Calamandrei

July 2

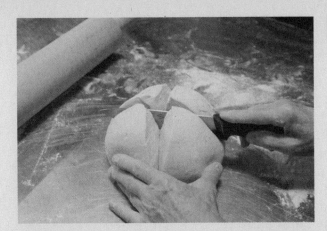

Makes 12 rolls

2 egg yolks (see Note)
¼ cup (60 ml) milk
2 cups (250 g) whole wheat bread (strong) flour
2½ oz (75 g) sourdough starter
5 tablespoons honey
5 teaspoons salt
5¼ teaspoons (25 g) butter, cubed
1 tablespoon plus 1 teaspoon extra-virgin olive oil

In a small bowl, whisk together the egg yolks and 1 tablespoon of the milk. Set the egg wash aside.

In a large bowl, mix together the flour, starter, the remaining milk, and ½ cup (120 ml) plus ½ tablespoon water. When the dough begins to appear grainy and coarse, cover it with a damp tea towel and let it rest for 30 minutes.

Mix in the honey, salt, and butter, then drizzle with the olive oil. In a stand mixer fitted with the dough hook attachment, knead until the dough is elastic and homogeneous. Measure the temperature of the dough: It should be between 75° and 77°F (24° and 25°C). Cover with the damp tea towel and let rest on a floured surface for 15 to 20 minutes.

Preheat the oven to 400°F (200°C/Gas Mark 6). Line a baking sheet with parchment paper.

Divide the dough into twelve 1-ounce (30 g) portions and form into balls. Transfer to the prepared baking sheet. Brush the rolls with the egg wash and let rise until doubled in volume, about 45 minutes.

Transfer the rolls to the oven and place a baking sheet with a few ice cubes on the rack below to create some steam. Bake for 8 to 9 minutes. Reduce the oven temperature to 350°F (180°C/Gas Mark 4) and continue baking until golden brown, about 50 minutes. Transfer to a wire rack to cool.

Note: Save the egg whites to make Meringues (pages 32 or 387).

RECIPE NOTES:

WHOLE WHEAT SOURDOUGH BREAD

Makes 2 loaf

8⅓ cups (1 kg) whole wheat bread flour
9 oz (250 g) sourdough starter
scant 1 tablespoon salt

In a stand mixer fitted with the dough hook attachment, combine the flour and 2¾ cups (650 ml) of 68°F (20°C) water and mix on low speed for 3 minutes. Let rest until the flour begins to absorb the liquid, 20 to 30 minutes.

Mix in the starter, salt, and a scant ½ cup (100 ml) of 68°F (20°C) water and knead with the dough hook attachment until the dough forms strings. Measure the temperature of the dough: It should be between 75° and 77°F (24° and 25°C). Turn the dough out onto a floured surface and divide in half. Cover with a damp tea towel and let rest for 30 minutes.

Transfer to 2 banettons (proofing baskets) or floured bowls and let double in size, about 45 minutes. Measure the temperature of the dough: It should be between 79° and 80°F (26° and 27°C).

Preheat the oven to 450°F (230°C/Gas Mark 8). Line a baking sheet with parchment paper.

Turn the loaf out onto the prepared baking sheet and make a cut in the surface with a sharp knife. Transfer to the oven and place a baking sheet with a few ice cubes on the rack below to create some steam. Bake for 10 minutes. Reduce the oven temperature to 350°F (180°C/Gas Mark 4) and continue baking until golden brown, about 50 minutes. Transfer to a wire rack to cool.

RECIPE NOTES:

REFFETORIO SOURDOUGH BREAD

Makes 2 loaves

1 tablespoon Active Sourdough Starter (recipe follows)
6 cups (775 g) all-purpose (plain) flour or bread (strong white) flour
1 tablespoon salt

In a medium bowl, combine the starter, ½ cup (75 g) of the flour, and 5 tablespoons water and mix thoroughly. Cover and let the sponge rest for 12 hours. When the surface of the sponge is very bubbly, it's ready to use (to check, drop a small spoonful of sponge into a cup of water; if it floats, it's ready).

In a small bowl, combine the salt and 3 tablespoons water, stirring to dissolve. Set aside.

In a large bowl, combine the sponge and 2 cups (475 ml) water. Stir with a spatula or use your hands to dissolve the sponge into the water (it's okay if a few clumps remain). Add the remaining 5½ cups (700 g) flour and stir until a shaggy dough is formed. Cover with plastic wrap and let rest for at least 30 minutes or up to 4 hours.

Pour the dissolved salt over the dough and work it in by pinching and squeezing (the dough will be quite wet and loose). Grab the dough on one side, lift it up, and fold it over on top of itself. Fold the dough 4 times, moving clockwise from the top of the bowl. Let rest for 30 minutes, then repeat this process a total of 6 times (the dough will gradually smooth out and become tighter). Let rise undisturbed until slightly puffed, 30 to 60 minutes (sourdough won't double in size; it should just look larger than when you started).

Turn the dough out onto a floured surface and fold gently to avoid deflating it. Divide the dough in half. Sprinkle with a little flour and shape each piece with a dough scraper into loose rounds by moving the scraper under the edge and around the curve of the dough. Repeat a few times to build surface tension, flouring the dough scraper as needed to keep it from sticking. Let rest for 20 to 30 minutes.

Line two bowls with tea towels and dust heavily with flour, rubbing the flour into the cloth on the bottom and up the sides to form a thin layer (use more flour than you think you'll need). Dust a ball of dough with flour and flip it over so the unfloured, sticky surface is up. Fold the dough: Grab the lip at the bottom, pull it gently up, then fold it over onto the center. Repeat with the right and left sides of the dough, then repeat with the top of the dough, using your thumb to grab the bottom lip and gently roll the dough right side up. If it's not quite round or doesn't seem taut, rotate the dough against the counter to shape it up. Repeat for the second loaf. Dust the shaped loaves generously with flour and transfer to the prepared bowls seam side up. Cover loosely with plastic wrap (clingfilm) and let rise until billowy and poofy, 3 to 4 hours. (Alternatively, place the covered bowls in the refrigerator and let rise slowly overnight, 12 to 15 hours. If rising overnight, bake the loaves straight from the fridge.)

Preheat the oven to 400°F (200°C/Gas Mark 6). Place two Dutch ovens (casseroles) or other heavy-bottomed pots with lids in the oven.

Carefully remove one of the pots from the oven and remove the lid. Tip a loaf out of the bowl into the pot so it lands seam side down. Use a sharp knife to quickly score the surface of the loaf at a slight angle. Repeat with the second pot and loaf. Cover the pots and return to the oven. Bake for 20 minutes. Reduce the oven temperature to 375°F (190°C/Gas Mark 5) and bake for 10 minutes. Remove the lids to release any remaining steam (at this point, the loaves should have a dry surface and be just slightly golden). Bake until the crust is deeply browned and just short of burnt, 15 to 25 minutes.

Lift the loaves out of the pots with a spatula and transfer to a wire rack to cool to room temperature before slicing.

ACTIVE SOURDOUGH STARTER

Makes about 2¾ lb (1.3 kg)

3 cups plus 4 tablespoons (420 g) all-purpose (plain) flour

In a 2 quart (2 liter) container, combine ¾ cup plus 2 tablespoons (105 g) all-purpose (plain) flour and ½ cup (120 ml) filtered water. Stir vigorously until smooth but sticky and thick. Scrape down the sides and loosely cover the container with plastic wrap (cling film) or a clean kitchen towel secured with a rubber band. Let sit for 24 hours in a place with a constant temperature of 70–75°F (21–23°C).

By the second day, the starter should smell fresh, mildly sweet, and yeasty. Feed the starter with ¾ cup plus 2 tablespoons (105 g) all-purpose flour and ½ cup (120 ml) filtered water. Stir vigorously until smooth but sticky and thick. Scrape down the sides and loosely cover the container with plastic wrap or a clean kitchen towel secured with a rubber band. Let sit for 24 hours in a place with a constant temperature of 70–75°F (21–23°C). Continue feeding the starter for two more days. By the third day, it should smell a little sour and musty. By the fourth day, it should taste sour and slightly vinegary. By the fifth day, it should be ready to use. It should have doubled in bulk and should be very bubbly, even frothy. Store in the fridge. Remove 2 to 3 days before baking.

To maintain the starter, use half of the starter and feed the remaining half with equal parts flour and water, stirring vigorously to combine and letting rest in a place with a constant temperature of 70–75°F (21–23°C).

Note: Making sourdough starter takes about 5 days. Each day you feed the starter with equal amounts flour and filtered water. It can take longer depending on the climate.

📷   P. 89

RECIPE NOTES: _____
_____
_____
_____
_____
_____
_____
_____

Sara Papa & Alberto Calamandrei

Antonio, Alberto & Giovanni Santini

Lara and I were at the very start of our journey when we first dined at Dal Pescatore, the restaurant owned and run by the Santini family since 1924. We were a month shy of opening Osteria Francescana, painting the walls and putting the final touches on what would become our life project. Dal Pescatore, on the other hand, was the result of generations of traditional cooking with Michelin stars to boot. Antonio Santini was considered the pillar of Italian gastronomy and Nadia, his wife, the authority on traditional recipes. Soon after our visit, Nadia would become the first female chef to earn three stars in Italy. At the time, my only claim to fame was a six-month stint at the Hôtel de Paris with Alain Ducasse. Fortunately, Antonio was a great fan of French chefs and he took me under his wing.

On our first wedding anniversary, in July 1996, we returned to Dal Pescatore and have returned every July since for the past twenty years. In the fall of 1999, Antonio visited Osteria Francescana along with a delegation of high-profile chefs and restaurateurs, among which were Sirio Maccioni from Le Cirque in New York and Michel Troisgros of the legendary eponymous restaurant in Roanne, France. It was an intimidating table and I still remember the advice Antonio gave me after his visit: "Start looking for a maître d', a real one, you are going to need it." One year later, we found Beppe Palmieri and convinced him to join us at Osteria Francescana. Seventeen years later, he is still here. Thank you, Antonio.

The restaurant Dal Pescatore is named after the fisherman, Antonio Santini senior, whose most famed dish was fried fish. Antonio's son, Giovanni, and his talented wife, Bruna, eventually took over the osteria and then passed it onto their son Antonio. Antonio met Nadia studying political science at the University of Milan and brought her to the tiny town of Canneto sull'Oglio where she would blossom under Bruna's leadership and help bring Dal Pescatore the fame it has today. Dal Pescatore is still a family affair, going into its fourth generation.

Antonio still runs the front of house while he mentors his son Alberto, and Nadia is grooming their second son, Giovanni, to find his place among the stovetops. When I invited them to the Refettorio, I did not expect Giovanni, Antonio, and Alberto to all come— but I should have, because they are, first and foremost, a family.

Giovanni's ability to pull together a cohesive meal out of the oddest ingredients impressed me. Giovanni had a very clear observation about what it means to cook with salvaged ingredients. "Massimo, this is not hard, but it does take time, much more time than it would if we had all of the best ingredients at our fingertips," he said. "It is quicker to make a filet than a meatball or to come up with a new pasta recipe. These ingredients take time and creativity to turn into a good meal."

For the pasta course, he worked frozen broccoli, pomegranate, mozzarella, and smoked tuna into a refreshing and flavorful pasta salad. It looked like an impossible combination, but it was fun and full of bright colors. He called it winter–summer pasta because the pomegranate and broccoli are winter produce that were surprising to find in the hot summer. The hamburgers arrived premade, so they enhanced them with condiments and served them with crisp eggplant, creamy apple puree, and toasted bread. The banana dessert was the highlight of the meal. You would think that we would have been tired of banana ice cream by now, but the caramelized bananas with a touch of lime made old bananas taste brand new.

Antonio and Alberto had kept themselves busy in the kitchen, cleaning, chopping, and tasting, but when the guests arrived, a transformation occurred. They moved effortlessly around the tables interacting with them and making small talk, filling the water glasses and bread baskets, as if they were back at Dal Pescatore. That night Antonio pulled out all of his charms by praising his sons and sharing stories about growing up in the Mantovan countryside. He demonstrated to us all that hospitality is not just skin deep.

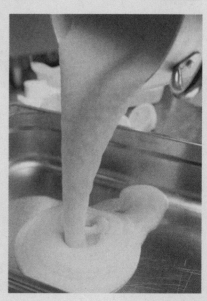

July 7

Serves 4

1 tablespoon extra-virgin olive oil
2 medium heads broccoli, cut into florets
⅔ cup (150 ml) milk
Salt
9 oz (250 g) sedanini rigati or other short tube pasta
¾ cup (70 g) freshly grated Parmigiano-Reggiano cheese
7 oz (200 g) mozzarella cheese, diced
3½ oz (100 g) pomegranate seeds
1 oz (25 g) smoked tuna or other smoked fish, sliced

In a medium pot, heat the olive oil over medium heat. Add the broccoli and sauté for 3 minutes. Add the milk, cover, and simmer until soft, about 15 minutes. Season to taste with salt. Transfer to a blender and blend until smooth. Set aside

Bring a large pot of lightly salted water to a boil over medium heat. Add the pasta and cook until al dente. Drain and transfer to a large bowl. Add the broccoli sauce and Parmigiano and mix to combine.

Divide the pasta among 4 plates and top with the mozzarella. Sprinkle with the pomegranate seeds and garnish with the smoked tuna.

RECIPE NOTES:

Antonio, Alberto & Giovanni Santini

HAMBURGER ALLA PARMIGIANA
WITH EGGPLANT CHIPS AND APPLE PUREE

Serves 4

HAMBURGER

1 lb 2 oz (500 g) ground (minced) beef
1 small white onion, finely diced
3 oz (80 g) Parmigiano-Reggiano cheese, grated
1 egg
1 teaspoon salt
½ teaspoon freshly ground black pepper
1 tablespoon extra-virgin olive oil

APPLE PUREE

3 tart apples, peeled and chopped
1 cup (250 ml) dry white wine
1 tablespoon (15 g) butter
Salt

EGGPLANT CHIPS

1 cup (250 ml) canola (rapeseed) oil
1 eggplant (aubergine), thinly sliced

FOR SERVING

½ cup (120 ml) canned tomato sauce (seasoned passata),
   warmed
4 slices bread, toasted

MAKE THE HAMBURGERS

In a medium bowl, combine the beef, onion, Parmigiano, egg,
salt, and pepper and mix. Divide into 4 portions and carefully
roll into balls. Gently push down to flatten into patties about
1 inch (3 cm) thick. Transfer to a plate, cover with plastic wrap
(clingfilm), and refrigerate until firm, at least 30 minutes.
    In a medium frying pan, heat the olive oil over medium
heat. Add the patties and cook until both sides are golden
brown, about 3 minutes per side.

MAKE THE APPLE PUREE

In a medium pot, combine the apples and white wine and
cook over medium heat for 7 minutes. Add the butter and stir.
Transfer to a blender and blend until smooth. Season to taste
with salt.

MAKE THE EGGPLANT CHIPS

In a medium pot, heat the oil to 338°F (170°C) over medium
heat. Add the eggplant (aubergine) and fry until crispy, about
30 seconds. Transfer to paper towels to absorb excess oil.
Set aside.

>>

TO SERVE

Place 2 tablespoons of the tomato sauce on each plate and top
with a slice of bread, then a hamburger patty. Garnish with
the apple puree and eggplant chips.

P. 96

RECIPE NOTES: _____

BANANA ICE CREAM WITH CARAMELIZED BANANAS

Serves 6

BANANA ICE CREAM
    4 ripe bananas, cut into chunks (see Note)
    1 cup (150 g) granulated sugar
    1 teaspoon fresh lime juice
    2 cups (500 ml) heavy (whipping) cream

CARAMELIZED BANANAS
    1 tablespoon (15 g) butter
    2 bananas, finely diced (see Note)
    ½ cup (100 g) packed light brown sugar
    Juice of 1 lime
    ¾ cup (180 ml) cognac or other brandy

MAKE THE BANANA ICE CREAM

In a blender, combine the bananas, granulated sugar, lime juice, and cream and process until smooth. Transfer to an ice-cream machine and process according to the manufacturer's instructions. (If you don't have an ice-cream machine, freeze the mixture until hard enough to scoop.)

MAKE THE CARAMELIZED BANANA

In a medium frying pan, heat the butter over medium heat. Add the bananas and sauté until the bananas are browned, about 2 minutes. Add the brown sugar and lime juice and simmer for 2 minutes. Add the cognac and cook until evaporated.

TO SERVE

Place a spoonful of the caramelized bananas in each bowl and top with a scoop of the banana ice cream.

Note: Save the peels to make Banana Peel Chutney (page 158).

RECIPE NOTES: _____

Ugo Alciati

Ugo Alciati was raised among the pots and pans of his parents' restaurant in Asti. Founded in 1960, Ristorante Guido turned away from the economic boom model—large quantities of food for large numbers of people—in favor of a fine dinning model with long tablecloths, a well-stocked wine cellar, silverware, and crystal. His parents even made reservations mandatory. The food was classic Piedmontese with a contemporary outlook that offered a focus on local ingredients. Over time, the classic recipes evolved, guests learned to reserve their tables, and this tablecloth restaurant model would eventually come to define modern Italian cuisine.

At the age of fifteen, Ugo started cooking professionally in that same kitchen. To this day, he still follows his mother's approach to cooking. In 2004, he moved Ristorante Guido to Bra, and it became an integral part of the happy bubble of Slow Food in Pollenzo. I dined there shortly thereafter and still remember the *vitello tonnato*. It was unlike any I had ever tasted, and not because it was deconstructed or modern—it was just absolutely delicious. More recently, in a collaboration with Oscar Farinetti, the entrepreneur behind Eataly food markets and restaurants, Ugo and his brother Piero moved Ristorante Guido to Alba.

Piedmontese cuisine is heavily influenced by nearby France and the long reign of the Savoy royal family. The resulting food is full of rich, deep, and luxurious flavors. Perhaps that is why Ugo had such a hard time adjusting to the limits of the Refettorio pantry at first. He admitted that he was discouraged when he found himself in the walk-in refrigerator. "It will take a while to figure out what to serve for dinner!" he exclaimed. "I'm accustomed to choosing my ingredients—the quality and quantity—and I fear that my creativity has been seriously endangered with this sparse selection."

But like many chefs who had cooked at the Refettorio, it only took a few hours of work to find the freedom and creativity that comes with making do with what's available. Ugo came up with tasty and innovative solutions that did not seem at all to compromise his culinary skills. First, he prepared a nontraditional risotto, cooking it as if it were a gratin finished in the oven, rather than on the stovetop. This made it much easier to prepare ahead of time and serve to a large crowd. It was crunchy on top and soft in the middle. He cut it into squares and served it with a creamy turmeric and crescenza cheese sauce. He dehydrated bresaola in the oven, crushed it into bits—similar to bacon bits—and sprinkled it over each square. The guests loved the fact that it looked like lasagna and tasted like risotto. It was the best of both.

For the main course, he reverted to a childhood favorite. It was often childhood memories that led the chefs who cooked at the Refettorio to find the perfect recipe for the ingredients that they found in the pantry—those all-time basic ingredients that are so common we often forget how comforting they can be. He served meatballs with a lemon sauce, the way his grandmother used to do. That evening, he told stories about growing up with his grandparents while his parents worked at the restaurant. It was a tender and endearing moment. Our guests were grateful for the warm meal and the care that was put into cooking it, but more than anything they appreciated listening to Ugo talk about his life and how difficult it could be at times to live in the shadow of his parents' success and dreams. It offered them a rare moment to escape their own hardships.

Seeing everyone laughing and acting like a family around the table was exactly what I had imagined when I began this project. As the pink and orange caramelized peaches with mascarpone were being served, I found an empty seat and sat down next to Giuliano, one of the regulars whom I had met on the very first day. All eyes were on me while I tasted Ugo's dessert. I smiled. The peaches were delicious and I was happy to be eating them at a table with friends.

Ugo Alciati

RICE CUBES
WITH CRESCENZA CREAM AND BRESAOLA CHIPS

Serves 6

RICE CUBES

    Extra-virgin olive oil, for brushing the pan
    2¼ cups (420 g) carnaroli or other short-grain rice
    generous 1 cup (100 g) freshly grated Parmigiano-
       Reggiano cheese
    4 tablespoons (60 g) butter
    4 teaspoons salt

CRESCENZA CREAM

    14 oz (400 g) crescenza cheese or other soft, mild cheese
    1 teaspoon ground turmeric
    ⅓ cup (90 ml) milk
    Salt and freshly ground black pepper

BRESAOLA CHIPS

    5¼ oz (150 g) thinly sliced bresaola or other cured meat

MAKE THE RICE CUBES

Preheat the oven to 450°F (230°C/Gas Mark 8). Line a baking
sheet with parchment paper and brush with the olive oil.
    In a small pot, bring 3 cups (700 ml) water to a boil.
    Meanwhile, in a medium pot, toast the rice over low
heat, without browning, for 8 minutes.
    Add the hot water to the rice little by little, stirring con-
stantly, until creamy, about 12 minutes. Add the Parmigiano,
butter, and salt and mix to combine. Transfer to an 8 x
10-inch (20 x 26 cm) container and spread to thickness
of 2 inches (5 cm). Let cool. Cut into 4 x 3-inch (10 x 8 cm)
cubes and arrange on the prepared baking sheet. Bake
until golden brown, 10 to 12 minutes.

MAKE THE CRESCENZA CREAM

In a blender, combine the cheese, milk, and turmeric and
process until smooth. Season to taste with salt and pepper.

MAKE THE BRESAOLA CHIPS

Preheat the oven to 200°F (100°C) or as low as your oven
can go. Line a baking sheet with parchment paper.
    Arrange the bresaola on the baking sheet and let dry
in the oven for 1 hour. Let cool for 15 minutes. Crush into
small pieces.

TO SERVE

Spoon 3 tablespoons of the crescenza cream at the bottom
of each serving plate and top with a rice cube. Garnish with
the bresaola chips.

P. 103

Serves 6

RATATOUILLE
- 3 tablespoons extra-virgin olive oil
- 1 white onion, slivered
- 3 carrots, diced
- 3 zucchini (courgettes), diced
- 1 eggplant (aubergine), diced
- 1 red bell pepper, diced
- 1⅔ cup (375 g) tomato puree (passata)
- Salt and freshly ground black pepper

MEATBALLS
- Extra-virgin olive oil, for the baking sheet
- 1 lb 5 oz (600 g) ground (minced) beef
- ¾ cup plus 2 tablespoons (90 g) freshly grated Parmigiano-Reggiano cheese
- 4 oz (120 g) stale bread, finely crumbled (1½ cups)
- 4 eggs
- 1 tablespoon salt
- ½ teaspoon freshly ground black pepper
- Flour, for dredging

LEMON SAUCE
- 2 tablespoons (30 g) butter
- 3 tablespoons all-purpose (plain) flour
- Juice of 4 lemons
- Salt and freshly ground black pepper

MAKE THE RATATOUILLE

In a large frying pan, heat the olive oil over medium heat. Add the onion and sauté until translucent, about 4 minutes. Add the carrots and cook for 5 minutes. Add the zucchini (courgettes) and cook for 2 minutes. Add the eggplant (aubergine) and bell pepper and cook for 2 minutes. Add the tomato puree (passata) and cook until the vegetables are tender, about 10 minutes. Season to taste with salt and pepper. Set aside.

MAKE THE MEATBALLS

Preheat the oven to 350°F (180°C/Gas Mark 4). Line a rimmed baking sheet with parchment paper and brush with oil.
   In a bowl, combine the beef, Parmigiano, breadcrumbs, eggs, salt, and pepper and mix. Shape into eighteen ping-pong–size balls and roll in the flour. Arrange on the prepared baking sheet and cover with foil. Bake until golden brown, about 15 minutes. Set aside

MAKE THE LEMON SAUCE

In a medium saucepan, melt the butter over medium heat. Add the flour, whisking constantly for about 1 minute. Add the lemon juice and scant ½ cup (100 ml) water, and bring to a boil over medium heat. Season to taste with salt and pepper.

>>

TO SERVE

Place a spoonful of the ratatouille in each bowl and top with 3 meatballs. Drizzle with the lemon sauce.

RECIPE NOTES: _____
_____
_____
_____
_____
_____
_____
_____
_____
_____
_____
_____
_____
_____
_____
_____
_____
_____
_____
_____
_____
_____
_____
_____
_____
_____
_____
_____
_____
_____
_____
_____
_____
_____
_____
_____
_____
_____
_____
_____
_____
_____
_____

Ugo Alciati

CARAMELIZED PEACHES WITH MASCARPONE

Serves 6

1 cup (200 g) granulated sugar
6 peaches, halved
10 oz (300 g) mascarpone cheese
4 tablespoons milk
3 tablespoons cacao powder
1½ oz (40 g) salted peanuts, roughly chopped

Preheat the oven to 400°F (200°C/Gas Mark 6). Line a baking sheet with parchment paper.

Spread 10 tablespoons of the sugar on a plate. Dip the cut sides of the peaches in the sugar. Arrange on the prepared baking sheet cut side up and bake until the sugar is caramelized, 7 to 8 minutes.

Meanwhile, in a food processor, combine the remaining 6 tablespoons sugar, the mascarpone, milk, and cacao and blend until smooth.

To serve, place two baked peach halves on each plate and top each half with 2 tablespoons of the mascarpone. Garnish with the peanuts.

RECIPE NOTES:

Mitsuharu Tsumura

When I hear people talk about Nikkei cuisine, I think of Mitsuharu Tsumura. I didn't know what Nikkei cuisine was until I ate at his restaurant Maido Mitsuharu in Lima, Peru. In 2009 I began attending the gastronomic conference Mistura and during my annual returns, I had to eat at Maido. I felt like the flavors—the soy and lime, the sweet and sour—had cast a spell on me.

Nikkei cuisine is a mixture of Japanese traditions that over time slowly blended into the Peruvian culinary dialect and took on its own identity—neither Asian nor Latin, but a hybrid of both. Micha, as everyone calls him, often says, "Nikkei is still coming into its own. Many people in Peru eat Nikkei and love it and have no idea about its origin."

There are actually three stages of Nikkei cuisine. The first stage developed after a wave of migrant workers came to Peru in 1889 on two-year contracts working mostly on sugarcane plantations. When the contracts ran out, many stayed in Peru. They began making food for a living, Peruvian food with Japanese touches, such as substituting fish for meat, using citrus in a new way, and subtly changing the original recipes. The second stage of Nikkei developed when Japanese car companies settled in Peru. They brought staff, chefs, and families with them. With that came a demand for more familiar flavors. The third stage developed out of the restaurants like Maido that are taking the cuisine from its popular base to fine dining.

Micha was in Milan that summer to cook for another event, and I borrowed him for one day at the Refettorio. None of our guests had ever heard of Nikkei cuisine, but they fell for the immediacy of the flavors just like me. The first dish he prepared was a variation of *causa rellena*, a traditional Peruvian potato layer cake. It is similar in concept to lasagna, but more decorative and it isn't baked. All the ingredients are cooked before and then assembled and chilled. The dough is a curious blend of mashed potatoes, oil, lime juice, and ají amarillo sauce. Ají amarillo is a chili pepper that is one of the primary ingredients in the Peruvian kitchen and one Micha never travels without. To make the amarillo sauce, he added some of the chili paste to a creamy, fresh cheese base. Micha affectionately calls this dish a potato cake even though it is served as a starter. The one he made had three layers: potato dough on the bottom pressed into the baking pan, a layer of shrimp and fish with red pepper mayonnaise, another layer of potato dough, and a fresh vegetable garnish on top. He chilled it and cut it into squares. More than potato cake, it tasted like a potato salad that had been elevated from being a condiment to becoming a course of its own.

Next he prepared *tacu tacu*, something I had never eaten before but reminded me of a recipe my mother made called *calza gatti* or "cat socks." The name comes from the cat's paw shape of this traditional mixture of leftover polenta and beans, which are fried and eaten as a snack or starter. *Tacu tacu* is similar, made with a mixture of rice and beans that are grilled, but it is served with something else, a fried egg, braised meat, or vegetables. It is soft in the middle and crunchy on the outside. Micha added a red cabbage salad on the side to complete the meal.

That day, Micha cooked everything that was available to him, leaving nothing behind. He even used unexpected ingredients like balsamic vinegar that he would not necessarily use in Peru. Fortunately Gastón Acurio had left behind soy sauce, oyster sauce, sesame oil, and rice vinegar, ingredients that are essential for creating magical Nikkei flavors. Everything he cooked was just as haunting as my first trips to Peru—even the lime ice cream was so tasty I almost licked the bowl.

CAUSA LIMEÑA WITH BELL PEPPER MAYONNAISE

Serves 6

BELL PEPPER MAYONNAISE
  1 red bell pepper
  1 egg
  1¼ cups (300 ml) extra-virgin olive oil
  Juice of 5 limes
  Salt

CAUSA LIMEÑA
  2¼ lb (1 kg) yellow-fleshed potatoes, peeled and quartered
  ⅔ cup (150 ml) extra-virgin olive oil
  scant ½ cup (100 ml) Ají Amarillo Puree (recipe follows)
  scant ½ cup (100 ml) fresh lime juice
  Salt
  1 lb (500 g) smoked trout or other smoked fish, finely chopped
  3 oz (80 g) cooked shrimp, finely chopped

GARNISH
  6 asparagus spears
  1 zucchini (courgette), thinly sliced
  4 cherry tomatoes, halved
  ¾ oz (20 g) thinly sliced prosciutto

MAKE THE BELL PEPPER MAYONNAISE

Char the pepper over the open flame of a stove burner until the skin is completely blackened. (If you don't have a gas stove, char under a hot broiler [grill].) Transfer to a plastic bag and let sit for 5 minutes. Peel and seed the pepper. Transfer to a blender, add the egg, olive oil, and lime juice and blend until smooth. Season to taste with salt. Cover and refrigerate.

MAKE THE CAUSA LIMEÑA

Bring a large pot of water to a boil. Add the potatoes and cook until soft, about 15 minutes. Drain. When cool enough to handle, peel and transfer to a bowl. Using your hands, smash to form a dough. Cover and refrigerate until cold.

Once chilled, add the olive oil, ají amarillo puree, and lime juice. Using your hands, knead until a soft, smooth dough is formed. Season to taste with salt. Cover and refrigerate.

In a medium bowl, combine the smoked trout, shrimp, and three-fourths of the bell pepper mayonnaise and mix with a spatula. Season to taste with salt.

In a deep 8 x 10-inch (20 x 26 cm) baking dish, spread half the dough to form an even layer. Cover with the smoked fish and shrimp filling, then cover with the remaining dough. Cover with plastic wrap (clingfilm) and refrigerate for 30 minutes. Cut into six 4-inch (10 cm) square portions.

>>

MAKE THE GARNISH

Set up a large bowl of ice and water. In a medium pot of boiling water, blanch the asparagus until al dente, about 2 minutes. Drain and transfer to the ice bath to cool. Drain again and cut into 1¼-inch (3 cm) pieces. Repeat this process for the zucchini.

In a medium bowl, combine the asparagus, zucchini, tomatoes, and prosciutto.

TO SERVE

Place squares of the causa limeña on each plate and dress with the remaining bell pepper mayonnaise. Place a spoonful of the garnish on the side.

AJÍ AMARILLO PUREE

Makes about 1¼ cups (300 ml)

  2¼ lb (1 kg) ají amarillo or other fresh yellow chilies, seeded

In a medium pot of boiling water, blanch the chilies for 30 minutes. Repeat this process two more times. Transfer to a blender and process until smooth. Set aside.

📷 P. 111

RECIPE NOTES: _____
_____
_____
_____
_____
_____
_____
_____
_____
_____
_____
_____
_____
_____
_____
_____
_____
_____
_____
_____
_____
_____
_____

Mitsuharu Tsumura

TACU TACU WITH BRAISED PORK AND RED CABBAGE

Serves 6

LENTIL AND RICE CAKE
7 oz (200 g) lentils
1 cup (200 g) rice
4 tablespoons extra-virgin olive oil
1¾ oz (50 g) garlic, chopped
7 oz (200 g) white onion, chopped
3½ oz (100 g) Ají Amarillo Puree (see recipe on 110)

BRAISED PORK
15 garlic cloves
3½ oz (100 g) fresh colorado chilies (see Note)
3½ oz (100 g) fresh mirasol chilies (see Note)
2 tablespoons extra-virgin olive oil
1 lb 2 oz (500 g) boneless pork leg, cut into 1¼-inch
    (3 cm) cubes
½ cup (110 ml) canola (rapeseed) oil
10 oz (300 g) red onion, finely diced
1⅔ cups (400 ml) dark beer
4¼ cups (1 liter) beef stock
Salt and freshly ground black pepper

CABBAGE SALAD
1 red cabbage, finely chopped
½ cup (80 g) finely chopped white onion
3 tablespoons balsamic vinegar
2 tablespoons plus 2 teaspoons extra-virgin olive oil
Salt

MAKE THE LENTIL AND RICE CAKE

In a medium pot, bring 2½ cups (600 ml) water to a boil. Add the lentils and simmer until soft, about 15 minutes. Drain and set aside.

In a medium saucepan, bring 2 cups (500 ml) water to a boil. Add the rice and simmer until tender, about 10 minutes. Drain and set aside.

In a medium frying pan, heat 2 tablespoons of the olive oil over medium heat. Add the garlic and onion and sauté for 1 minute. Add the ají amarillo puree and simmer for 15 minutes over low heat.

In a food processor, combine half the lentils and half the rice and blend for 30 seconds. Transfer to a bowl and add the remaining rice and lentils and the sautéed onions, and mix to combine. Cover and let sit for 1 hour.

Transfer the lentil/rice mixture to a 4 x 8-inch (10 x 20 cm) loaf pan and press until compact. Cut the loaf crosswise into 6 slices 1⅓ inches (3.5 cm) thick.

In a large frying pan, heat the remaining 2 tablespoons olive oil over low heat. Add the slices and sear until golden brown, about 8 minutes on each side.

>>

MAKE THE BRAISED PORK

In a medium pot of boiling water, blanch the garlic for 1 minute. Repeat this process two more times. Transfer to a blender and blend until smooth. Set aside. Repeat this process for the colorado and mirasol chilies, pureeing them separately after blanching.

In a medium frying pan, heat the olive oil over medium heat. Add the pork and sear until a golden brown crust forms, about 8 minutes. Remove from the heat and set aside.

In a large pot, warm the canola (rapeseed) oil over low heat. Add the onion and the garlic puree and sauté until translucent, about 15 minutes. Add the colorado puree and mirasol puree and let simmer for 20 minutes. Add the beer and beef stock and let simmer for 15 minutes. Add the pork and let cook over medium heat until the pork falls apart easily with a fork, about 30 minutes. Season to taste with salt and pepper.

MAKE THE CABBAGE SALAD

In a medium bowl, mix together the cabbage, onion, vinegar, and olive oil. Season to taste with salt.

TO SERVE

Place 1 slice of the lentil and rice cake on each dish and top with the braised pork. Garnish with the cabbage salad.

Note: If you don't have colorado or mirasol chilies, substitute with 3½ oz (100 g) jalapeño chilies.

RECIPE NOTES: _____
_____
_____
_____
_____
_____
_____
_____
_____
_____
_____
_____
_____
_____
_____
_____
_____
_____
_____
_____
_____
_____
_____
_____

Mitsuharu Tsumura

LIME PIE ICE CREAM WITH GOOSEBERRIES

Serves 8

    1 cup (250 ml) evaporated milk
    1 cup (250 ml) heavy (whipping) cream
    scant ½ cup (100 ml) condensed milk
    3 tablespoons whole-milk powder
    4 tablespoons granulated sugar
    5 egg yolks (see Note)
    scant ½ cup (100 ml) fresh lime juice
    ½ cups (15 g) cornflakes
    16 gooseberries or other berry

In a medium pot, warm the evaporated milk, cream, condensed milk, milk powder, and 2 tablespoons of the sugar over medium heat and bring to 149°F (65°C).

In a medium bowl, whisk the egg yolks with the remaining 2 tablespoons sugar until smooth and fluffy. Slowly add one-fourth of the hot milk mixture, stirring constantly. Transfer the warmed eggs to the pot and heat to 176°F (80°C). Set the pot in a large bowl of ice and water to cool. Stir in the lime juice. Transfer to an ice-cream machine and process according to the manufacturer's instructions. (If you don't have an ice-cream machine, freeze the mixture until hard enough to scoop.)

To serve, place a scoop of ice cream in each bowl and garnish with 1 tablespoon of the cornflakes and 2 gooseberries.

Note: Save the egg whites to make Meringues (pages 32 or 387).

RECIPE NOTES: _____

Alain Ducasse

How do I introduce you to Alain Ducasse? He is a legend in the culinary world, like Björn Borg is to tennis; but to me he is much more than that. I was a young, self-taught chef running a roadside restaurant six miles (ten kilometers) from Modena in the early 1990s. I was taking a break from peeling potatoes sitting in the back courtyard of Trattoria del Campazzo and flipping through a magazine when I saw a picture of Alain. It wasn't a food magazine, it was about business, lifestyle, and people. It was love at first sight. This chef was revolutionizing French cuisine and bringing it back to its peasant roots with a deep focus on products, artisans, farmers, and ingredients. He was one of the first farm-to-table chefs not cooking in the countryside or on a farm but in downtown Monte Carlo, at his restaurant Le Louis XV. I decided then and there that I had to meet Alain.

To make a long story short, he came to visit me. A balsamic vinegar producer from Modena brought Ducasse to Trattoria del Campazzo for lunch to close a deal with him and that was the beginning of our beautiful friendship. Two months later I sold the trattoria and moved to Monte Carlo to work at Le Louis XV. The rest is history.

Alain was one of the first chefs that came to mind when I was dreaming about this project. I knew that he would be curious to work in a kitchen so different from the Michelin-starred ones he was used to. We agreed he would cook on July 14—which I forgot was my wedding anniversary. When July came around and Lara asked, "What do you want to do for our twentieth anniversary?" what could I say? So I replied, "Do you want to celebrate at Plaza Athénée, Louis XV, or the Refettorio Ambrosiano?" Lara immediately understood that my question was rhetorical. This would be a once in a lifetime anniversary.

All July was hot but I think the fourteenth was the hottest day of the summer with temperatures hovering at 104°F (40°C). Lara and I arrived in Milan in the late afternoon and I remember walking into an empty kitchen. Ducasse was nowhere to be seen, nor were the chefs from our team who had caught an earlier train to help in the kitchen.

Suddenly, Emmanuelle Perrier, Alain's long-time assistant, waved from the dining room and said, "They are all in the walk-in."

It was a sight to behold. Four chefs standing hunched over a makeshift table (a cardboard box resting on plastic crates), rolling meatballs in the cold walk-in refrigerator. They had tried to make the meatballs in the kitchen, but they wouldn't stick together in the heat.

Ducasse had been there at 9 a.m. sharp when the delivery truck arrived and unloaded his supplies. He took a crate of goat milk and goat cheese. The only vegetables that day were big bruised eggplants (aubergines), which he would puree into a cream. The meat—a combination of chicken, veal, and beef—was mixed with herbs and spices and rolled into the meatballs. And some golden barley in the pantry would become a chilled multigrain velouté with goat cheese. The dessert made the best of the only fruit available, rhubarb and strawberries. It was a balanced, flavorful, and light menu for a hot summer's eve.

Later, after the guests had eaten, Lara, Ducasse, and I talked while we had our meal. Ducasse told us stories about growing up on a farm in the Southwest of France and how a life like that leaves an imprint on you forever. He said, "Virtually nothing was thrown away or lost. Peelings or stale bread, for instance, were given to poultry." This reminded me of my childhood, because (although we didn't have chickens), my grandmother would gather the crumbs from the table and save them all week to make the dough for *passatelli* on Sundays. It was my favorite meal of the week.

Ducasse went on to talk about his grandmother, "When my grandmother was preparing the meals for the family, she would ask me to pick four carrots from the kitchen garden. I never picked five."

We talked about the challenges of food waste and the shocking numbers that you read: Peaks in obesity and hunger and enough wasted food to feed a nation. Off the top of his head he quoted Jacques Cousteau, the pioneer of marine conservation, who said something very true: "People protect and respect what they love." He continued making the parallel, "That is exactly what we, chefs, must do: make the 'no waste' attitude desirable—a happy and delicious way of eating."

Anyone who has had the pleasure of experiencing a Ducassian meal, today or thirty years ago, knows this approach to ingredients has always been part of his culinary philosophy. Leaves of root vegetables or pea pods or even potato skins are used in many recipes. I remember distinctly the fish trimmings that were used for stocks. Ducasse reminded me, "When you use a good product—and ours are exceptional—the entire product is worth being used."

So often chefs both in restaurants and at home do not look at the whole ingredient, the leaves, the stems, the skins, the bones, and the parts that are not necessarily on the desirable list but are essential to any tasty kitchen. Ducasse seemed to think things were changing and I said, "Our young commis realize that using the entire product is not only challenging, but it enriches the end result. The same goes for our clients: When they see what is on their plates, and when they taste it, they realize how good it is. I believe this is the most effective way of making change."

As we were saying goodbye he whispered in my ear, "Massimo, the meal was very, very modest, but we made it with care so I'm sure it is in harmony with this place and its vision. Voilà, simplicity."

It was a good anniversary because Lara and I felt like we had something to celebrate other than our marriage, the restaurant, and our family: We were celebrating the future. We had believed in an impossible dream and it had come true. We both felt we had stumbled onto something that would define the twenty years to come.

Alain Ducasse

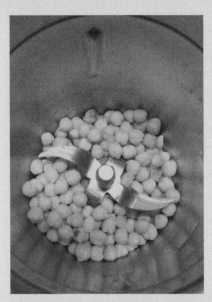
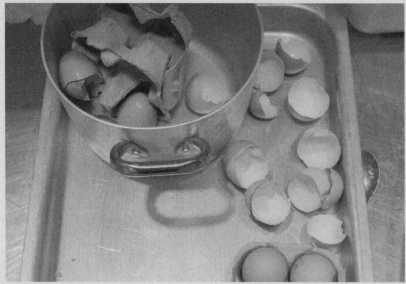

CREAM OF MIXED GRAINS
WITH PUFFED RICE AND GOAT MILK ROYALE

Serves 8

CREAM OF GRAINS
1¾ cups (400 g) wheat berries (whole grain)
1 cup (200 g) pearl barley
⅔ cup (150 ml) extra-virgin olive oil
7 oz (200 g) boneless, skinless chicken breast, chopped
2 small white onions, diced
4 tablespoons (60 g) butter
4¼ cups (1 liter) chicken stock
1 carrot, roughly chopped
8 white button mushrooms, quartered
2 tomatoes, quartered
1 bouquet garni (1 sprig thyme, 1 bay leaf, 3 sprigs parsley)

GOAT MILK ROYALE
2 gelatin sheets
3⅓ cups (800 ml) goat milk
3 garlic cloves
3 sage leaves
2 saffron pistils
¼ teaspoon ground cumin
Salt and freshly ground black pepper

RICE CRACKER
½ cup (100 g) short-grain rice
⅛ teaspoon curry powder

GARNISH
1⅔ cups (400 ml) vegetable stock
1 carrot, very finely diced
1 medium white onion, very finely diced
Extra-virgin olive oil, for drizzling
Balsamic vinegar, for drizzling

MAKE THE CREAM OF GRAINS

Soak the wheat berries (whole grain) and barley in lukewarm water for 1 hour. Drain and rinse thoroughly with clean water.

In a medium pot, warm the olive oil over medium heat. Add the chicken and sear until golden brown on both sides. Reduce the heat to low, add the onions, and caramelize gently until golden brown, about 10 minutes. Add the butter and, once it is golden brown, add the soaked grains, stirring until they abosorb the juice and the oil. Add the chicken stock, carrot, mushrooms, tomatoes, and bouquet garni. Cover the pot and cook over low heat until the grains can be crushed easily, at least 1 hour. Measure out one-fourth of the mixture for the garnish. Transfer the remaining mixture to a blender and process until velvety in texture. Refrigerate to chill.

>>

MAKE THE GOAT MILK ROYALE

In a small bowl, soak the gelatin in cold water until soft, about 10 minutes. Drain and set aside.

Meanwhile, in a saucepan, heat the goat milk over medium heat. Add the garlic, sage, saffron, cumin, and salt and pepper to taste. Simmer until the garlic is soft, about 5 minutes. Pass through a fine-mesh sieve. Add the gelatin sheets and mix until dissolved. Set aside.

MAKE THE RICE CRACKER

Preheat the oven to 325°F (160°C/Gas Mark 3).

Thoroughly rinse the rice under cold running water and drain. Place the rice in a pot, add 1¼ cups (300 ml) cold water and bring to a boil over medium-high heat. Add the curry powder and stir. Reduce the heat to low, cover, and cook until all of the water is absorbed, 15 to 20 minutes. Transfer to a blender and blend until smooth.

Line a rimmed baking sheet with parchment paper. Spread a thin layer of the rice puree on the lined baking sheet. Bake until dry and crispy, about 18 minutes. Remove from the baking sheet and let cool.

MAKE THE GARNISH

Set up a large bowl of ice and water. In a medium pot, bring the vegetable stock to a boil over medium heat. Add the carrot and cook until firm-tender, about 2 minutes. Scoop out the carrot and transfer to the ice bath to cool. Scoop out and set aside. Repeat the process with the onion. Mix the carrot and the onion with the reserved whole grains. Dress the mixture with a drizzle each of olive oil and balsamic vinegar and set aside.

TO SERVE

Ladle the soup into chilled bowls. Top with a good spoonful of the garnish, a shard of the puffed rice, and a dollop of the goat milk royale. Drizzle with olive oil.

📷 P. 119

RECIPE NOTES: _____
_____
_____
_____
_____
_____
_____
_____
_____
_____
_____
_____
_____
_____

Alain Ducasse

SPICED MEATBALLS WITH SMOKED EGGPLANT, TOASTED CHICKPEAS, AND EGGPLANT CONDIMENT

Serves 8

MEATBALLS

2 garlic bulbs
¼ teaspoon freshly grated nutmeg
2½ teaspoons ras el hanout
3½ oz (100 g) stale bread, sliced
1¼ cups (300 ml) heavy (whipping) cream
1 lb 12 oz (800 g) mixed meats (such as 14 oz [400 g] beef, 7 oz [200 g] chicken, and 7 oz [200 g] veal), cut into chunks (see Note)
7 oz (200 g) beef fat and beef trimmings
5¼ teaspoons (25 g) butter
12 white button mushrooms, finely chopped
1 bunch parsley, finely chopped
1 medium head radicchio, finely chopped
3 egg yolks (see Note)
6 oz (150 g) fresh ginger, finely chopped
Extra-virgin olive oil
Freshly ground black pepper
Salt
½ cup (50 g) dried breadcrumbs
2 tablespoons soy sauce

POPCORN

1 tablespoon corn oil
scant ¼ cup (50 g) popcorn kernels

HUMMUS

generous 1¾ cups (300 g) drained canned chickpeas, skins removed
1½ tablespoons extra-virgin olive oil
Salt
2½ tablespoons white miso
1 garlic clove
scant ½ cup (100 ml) lemon juice
3½ tablespoons yogurt

SMOKED EGGPLANT

3 eggplants (aubergines)
Salt and freshly ground black pepper
4 teaspoons soy sauce

CHICKPEAS

1¼ cups (200 g) canned chickpeas, drained (liquid reserved) and skins removed
3 tablespoons plus 1 teaspoon extra-virgin olive oil
5 teaspoons (20 g) butter
1 tablespoon julienned fresh ginger

>>

MAKE THE MEATBALLS

Preheat the oven to 350°F (180°C/Gas Mark 4).

Wrap the garlic bulbs in foil and bake until soft, about 30 minutes. Remove the garlic and remove the cloves. Set aside. Leave the oven on.

Meanwhile, in a bowl, mix together the nutmeg and ras el hanout. Add the sliced bread and soak in the cream for 1 hour at room temperature. Squeeze the extra liquid and set aside.

Run the meats, beef fat, and trimmings through a meat grinder to finely grind.

In a medium frying pan, heat the butter over medium heat. Add the mushrooms and cook until golden brown, about 5 minutes. Set aside.

In a large bowl, combine the ground (minced) meat, baked garlic, parsley, radicchio, mushrooms, soaked bread, egg yolks, ginger, a drizzle of olive oil, and black pepper, and mix until combined. Correct seasoning with salt and add 4 tablespoons of the dried breadcrumbs. Let rest for at least 2 hours in the fridge before forming 1½-ounce (45 g) meatballs, using the remaining 3 tablespoons dried breadcrumbs to help bind the meat so it does not stick to your hand.

Coat a rimmed baking sheet with olive oil, arrange the balls on the sheet, and bake for 15 minutes. Pour the soy sauce over the meatballs and bake until they form a golden brown crust, about 15 minutes longer. Set aside, keeping them warm.

MAKE THE POPCORN

In a medium pot, melt the corn oil over high heat. Just as the oil begins to smoke, add the popcorn and quickly cover with a lid. Vigorously shake the pan while the popcorn begins to pop. Once the popping begins to subside, remove from the heat and continue shaking for about 1 minute. Once cool, remove the popcorn and discard any unpopped kernels. Transfer to a food processor and blend into medium-size bits. Set aside.

MAKE THE HUMMUS

In a food processor, blend the chickpeas with the olive oil and a pinch of salt. Add the miso and garlic and blend until smooth. Add the lemon juice and yogurt and stir until combined. Set aside.

>>

Alain Ducasse

MAKE THE SMOKED EGGPLANT

Preheat the oven to 375°F (190°C/Gas Mark 5).

Bake the eggplant (aubergines) until the skin is lightly burnt, about 15 minutes. Leave the oven on.

Halve the eggplants, scoop out the flesh, and set aside to drain in a colander. Roughly chop the eggplant skins. Measure out half and stir into the hummus. Pat the eggplant flesh dry with paper towels, transfer to a bowl, season with salt and pepper, and stir in the other half of the chopped eggplant skins. Refrigerate until cold.

Add the soy sauce and mix until incorporated. On a sheet of foil, form the mixture into a log ¾ inch (2 cm) in diameter. Remove any air pockets by tightening at the ends. Bake until caramelized, about 30 minutes. When cool enough to handle, slice crosswise with a sharp knife into 1¼ -inch (3 cm) portions. Set aside on a small tray.

MAKE THE CHICKPEAS

In a medium pot, combine the chickpeas, their canning liquid, the olive oil, butter, and half of the ginger and cook over medium heat until the liquid is reduced by half, about 5 minutes. Set aside.

TO SERVE

Place 1 tablespoon of the hummus on each plate and top some smoked eggplant and 4 meatballs. Garnish with the chickpeas, reduced juice, popcorn, and remaining ginger.

Note: Save the egg whites to make Meringues (pages 32 or 387). If you don't have a meat grinder, use ground meat.

RECIPE NOTES: _____
_____
_____
_____
_____
_____
_____
_____
_____
_____
_____
_____
_____
_____
_____
_____
_____
_____
_____
_____
_____
_____

BREAD TART
WITH CARAMELIZED FRUITS

Serves 8

BREAD TART
- 4 egg whites (see Note)
- ¾ cup (150 g) granulated sugar
- 1 cup (100 g) almond flour (ground almonds)
- generous 2 cups (500 ml) milk
- 4 eggs
- 7 oz (200 g) nuts (such as pinenuts or hazelnuts), roughly chopped
- ⅔ cup (150 ml) almond milk
- 10 oz (300 g) stale bread, sliced

CARAMELIZED FRUITS
- 2¼ lb (1 kg) fruits (such as apple or strawberry), diced
- scant ½ cup (90 g) granulated sugar
- 1 vanilla bean, split lengthwise

MAKE THE BREAD TART

In a bowl, whisk the egg whites to soft peaks.

In a large bowl, mix the sugar, almond flour (ground almonds), and milk. Add the eggs, nuts, and almond milk, then fold in the egg whites. Soak the bread in this mixture for 1 to 2 hours.

Preheat the oven to 350°F (180°C/Gas Mark 4). Butter a 7¾ x 10¼ -inch (20 x 26 cm) baking dish. Arrange the bread in the dish. Bake until a wooden pick or tip of a knife comes out dry, about 20 minutes.

MAKE THE CARAMELIZED FRUITS

In a large pot, combine the fruit and sugar. Scrape in the vanilla seeds and add the pod. Simmer over low heat, stirring regularly, until the fruit is soft like a compote, about 15 minutes. Remove the pod and discard. Let cool.

TO SERVE

Place a piece of warm bread tart on the bottom of each plate. Top with a spoonful of the caramelized fruits.

Note: Save the egg yolks to make Zabaione (page 371) or ice cream.

RECIPE NOTES: _____
_____
_____
_____
_____
_____
_____
_____
_____
_____
_____

Viviana Varese

I was taking a nap in the chef's apartment and it was unbearably hot. When I arrived at the Refettorio I was in a bad mood and called out to Cristina, "You really need to get a fan or something for that apartment!" Viviana Varese sensed a dark cloud coming and jumped in to save Cristina. "I know a store that is having a sale on fans. I'll give you a ride. Hop on my Vespa."

Viviana is like that. She's a busy woman. Her restaurant Alice in Milan is booked year round and yet she always has her eye out for others. Here is where she shows her Neapolitan roots: warm, outgoing, and always ready to lend a hand. Throughout this project she has been helpful in any way she can, not just by cooking, which she did on more than one occasion, but also by donating meat and other ingredients that we did not have coming in as frequently as, say, potatoes and onions.

Viviana studied with Gualtiero Marchesi and interned at restaurants including el Celler de Can Roca. In 2007 she met Sandra Ciciriello, her business partner, and opened Alice Restaurant in Milan. Seven years later she moved Alice to Eataly in the former Smeraldo Theater in the center of the city. And that is where Viviana and I got to know each other. In fact, Lara and I were having lunch at Alice when I was beginning to dream up this crazy idea of opening a soup kitchen.

When Viviana talks about food, it is always emotional: "To me food means to feed. It's like a mission; my aim in life is to feed—through food, through love. It's my way of life. I began cooking at seven, because my parents had a restaurant and I started making pizzas. At thirteen I really knew how to make pizza." Before opening her first restaurant, she learned to prepare traditional recipes, family-style cooking. "I grew up in a restaurant, so we fed a lot of people. When you cook it's important to impart a message. My message is a healthy one, to make people feel good."

That day she made almost an entire meal out of two vegetables: zucchini (courgettes) and eggplant (aubergine). Since there was so much mozzarella, she decided to make a baked pasta dish with macaroni, mozzarella, and fried eggplant. Then she began the second course preparing fried zucchini that would be marinated in a *scapece* sauce: a mix of mint, garlic, and vinegar. She explained that the idea is to have a simple menu, "I didn't want to bring my restaurant cooking here. Instead, I wanted to recreate a memory of home. People need that sort of memory." As she worked, she told me that these recipes were her mother's, though she admitted that the meatloaf was not her mother's recipe but something improvised. Viviana wanted to add more flavor to the meatloaf, and push it out of the classic Italian palate. What surprised me was the unexpected sauce made from a loaf of stale bread. She soaked it in milk, garlic, onion, turmeric, salt, and pepper, then blended it until it was creamy. It was an elegant way to use the old bread and keep the meatloaf moist.

When it came to preparing the dessert, she was adamant about using all of the fruit left in the walk-in refrigerator because it wouldn't have lasted one more day. She prepared a plum coulis, a banana ice cream, and a fruit salad of exotic fruits: papaya, passion fruit, and pineapple. She cleverly added a very Italian touch to the fruit salad, with sweetened breadcrumbs used the way Sicilians sprinkle savory breadcrumbs on top of spaghetti instead of grated cheese.

Before the guests arrived, she told us stories about her childhood, in particular a tender reflection about her mother: "When my mother reheated the pasta and bean soup the day after with a crust of bread or cheese on top, she was embarrassed to be serving the same thing twice, but I always thought it was better the day after." I agreed. My mother's pasta and bean soup was always better the day after. Viviana continued to talk about her childhood, "At our house, nothing was wasted. Leftover pasta with ragù was put on pizza as a condiment the day after. You can't imagine how good it is: crunchy on top and flavorful in the middle, but nonetheless, informal and easy to eat without a fork and knife because it's pizza."

I asked her to repeat the story. I couldn't believe that I had never heard of this recipe before. I love pizza almost as much as I love Neapolitans. On the drive back to Modena I couldn't stop thinking about the endless possibilities of that dish . . . leftover pasta as a pizza condiment . . . . Genius!

Viviana Varese

BAKED PASTA ALLA PARMIGIANA

Serves 6

5 medium eggplants (aubergines), cut into medium cubes
½ cup (65 g) all-purpose (plain) flour
4¼ cups (1 liter) sunflower oil
Salt
1 lb (600 g) rigatoni pasta or other short pasta
scant ½ cup (100 ml) extra-virgin olive oil
1 onion, finely diced
2 carrots, finely diced
1 celery stalk, finely diced
1¾ lb (800 g) canned peeled tomatoes, drained
½ tablespoon granulated sugar
Freshly ground black pepper
5 oz (150 g) mozzarella cheese, thinly sliced
12 basil leaves
7 oz (200 g) Parmigiano-Reggiano cheese, grated

Preheat the oven to 325°F (160°C/Gas Mark 3).

Toss the eggplants (aubergines) in the flour. In a medium pot, heat the sunflower oil to 347°F (175°C). Working in batches, add the eggplant and fry until crispy and golden brown, 6 minutes. Transfer to paper towels to drain. Set aside.

Bring a large pot of lightly salted water to a boil over medium heat. Add the pasta and cook until al dente. Drain and set aside.

Meanwhile, in a medium pot, heat 1 tablespoon of the olive oil over medium heat. Add the onion, carrots, and celery and cook until golden, about 15 minutes. Add the tomatoes and sugar and season to taste with salt and pepper. Stir in the pasta and toss to combine.

Transfer one-fourth of the pasta mixture to a deep 8 x 10-inch (20 x 26 cm) baking dish and spread to cover. Top with one-fourth of the mozzarella, one-fourth of the eggplant, and 3 basil leaves. Repeat this layering three more times, omitting the basil leaves on the top layer. Sprinkle the top layer with the Parmigiano.

Bake until golden brown, about 35 minutes. Let cool for 20 minutes before serving.

P. 127

RECIPE NOTES:

Viviana Varese

MEATLOAF WITH BREAD CREAM AND ZUCCHINI SCAPECE

Serves 6

MEATLOAF
2¼ lb (1 kg) ground (minced) chicken, turkey, or beef
   (or a mixture of all three)
5 oz (150 g) stale bread, crumbled
3 eggs
3 tablespoons heavy (whipping) cream
½ cup (50 g) freshly grated Parmigiano-Reggiano cheese
½ cup (50 g) freshly grated Pecorino Romano cheese
¼ teaspoon freshly grated nutmeg
Salt and freshly ground black pepper
2 tablespoons extra-virgin olive oil
½ tablespoon cornstarch (cornflour)
3½ tablespoons (50 g) butter

BREAD CREAM
1 tablespoon extra-virgin olive oil
½ small white onion, chopped
2 garlic cloves, minced
7 oz (200 g) stale bread, torn up
1⅔ cups (400 ml) milk
½ teaspoon ground turmeric
¼ teaspoon ground cumin
Salt and freshly ground black pepper

SCAPECE ZUCCHINI
4 medium zucchini (courgettes), cut into small cubes
Flour, for coating
4¼ cups (1 liter) sunflower oil
Salt
3 tablespoons extra-virgin olive oil
1 garlic clove, minced
3 tablespoons red wine vinegar
½ tablespoon granulated sugar
Leaves of 5 sprigs mint
¼ teaspoon freshly ground black pepper

MAKE THE MEATLOAF

Preheat the oven to 375°F (190°C/Gas Mark 5). Line a rimmed baking sheet with parchment paper.

In a stand mixer, combine the ground (minced) meat, breadcrumbs, eggs, cream, Parmigiano, Pecorino, and nutmeg. Season with salt and pepper and mix until smooth. Transfer to the prepared baking sheet and roll to form a cylinder. Cover with foil and bake until firm, 35 to 40 minutes.

In a medium frying pan, heat the olive oil over medium heat. Add the meatloaf and brown on all sides, about 2 minutes per side. Remove and let cool. Cut into 1 inch (3 cm) thick slices and let rest in a tray to gather the cooking juices.

Transfer the cooking juices to a small pot and warm over low heat. Whisk in the cornstarch and cook, stirring continuously, for 1 minute. Remove from the heat, add the butter, and whisk until melted. Set aside the gravy.

MAKE THE BREAD CREAM

In a medium pot, heat the olive oil over medium heat. Add the onion and garlic and cook until soft, about 3 minutes. Add the bread and milk and cook over low heat until reduced by almost half, about 30 minutes. Using a hand blender, blend until smooth. Add the turmeric and cumin and season to taste with salt and pepper. Set aside.

MAKE THE ZUCCHINI SCAPECE

Toss the zucchini (courgettes) in some flour to coat.

In a medium heavy-bottomed pot, heat the sunflower oil to 347°F (175°C). Working in batches, fry the zucchini until golden brown, about 4 minutes. Transfer to paper towels to drain. Transfer to a shallow bowl and season to taste with salt.

In a medium frying pan, heat the olive oil over medium heat. Add the garlic and fry until golden. Carefully add the vinegar and sugar and cook until evaporated. Add the mint, pepper, and salt to taste. Pour over the zucchini.

TO SERVE

Place a spoonful of the bread cream on each plate and top with 2 slices of the meatloaf. Drizzle with the gravy and garnish with the zucchini *scapece*.

RECIPE NOTES: _____

\>\>

Viviana Varese

BANANA ICE CREAM
WITH PLUM COULIS AND BREAD CRUMBLE

Serves 8

BANANA ICE CREAM
 1½ cups (350 ml) milk
 ¾ cup (180 ml) heavy (whipping) cream
 1¼ cups (260 g) granulated sugar
 5 tablespoons whole-milk powder
 1 lb 2 oz (500 g) ripe bananas, cut into ¾-inch (2 cm)
   chunks (see Note)

PLUM COULIS
 10 oz (300 g) plums, cut into small pieces
 ½ cup (100 g) granulated sugar
 3 tablespoons plus 1 teaspoon lime juice

MARINATED DRAGON FRUIT
 1 dragon fruit, peeled and cut into cubes
 1 teaspoon fresh lemon juice

BREAD CRUMBLE
 1 stick plus 3 tablespoons (150 g) butter
 5 oz (150 g) stale bread, finely crumbled (2⅔ cups)
 ¾ cup (150 g) packed light brown sugar

MAKE THE BANANA ICE CREAM

In a medium saucepan, bring the milk and cream to 86°F
(30°C) over low heat. Add the granulated sugar and milk
powder and bring the mixture to 185°F (85°C) over medium
heat, stirring constantly. Remove from the heat and add the
bananas. Using a hand blender, blend until smooth. Cover
and refrigerate until chilled.

Transfer to an ice-cream machine and process according
to the manufacturer's instructions. (If you don't have an
ice-cream machine, freeze the mixture until hard enough
to scoop.)

MAKE THE PLUM COULIS

In a small pot, combine the plums, granulated sugar, and
lime juice and cook over low heat until the plums are soft but
not falling apart, 15 to 20 minutes. Transfer to a blender and
blend until smooth. Strain through a fine-mesh sieve, cover,
and refrigerate to chill.

MAKE THE MARINATED DRAGON FRUIT

In a small bowl, combine the dragon fruit and lemon juice.
Cover and refrigerate.

>>

MAKE THE BREAD CRUMBLE

In a large frying pan, melt the butter over low heat. Add the
breadcrumbs and cook, stirring constantly, until golden
brown. Add the brown sugar and cook, stirring constantly,
for 1 minute. Set aside to cool.

TO SERVE

Place a tablespoon or so of the plum coulis in each bowl and
top with a scoop of the banana ice cream. Garnish with the
dragon fruit and sprinkle with the bread crumble.

Note: Save the peels to make Banana Peel Chutney (page 158).

RECIPE NOTES: _____
_____
_____
_____
_____
_____
_____
_____
_____
_____
_____
_____
_____
_____
_____
_____
_____
_____
_____
_____
_____
_____
_____
_____
_____
_____
_____
_____
_____
_____
_____
_____
_____

Luca Fantin started his career at the top-ranked restaurants La Pergola in Rome and Mugaritz in San Sebastián, Spain. His life took a radical shift when he moved in 2009 to Japan to open a fine-dining restaurant at the top of the Bulgari tower in Ginza, which has since been awarded a Michelin star. Luca is not planning to leave Japan anytime soon. He married a Japanese woman and intends to raise his family there. The kitchen at Il Ristorante Luca Fantin reflects this marriage of two cultures—Italian and Japanese—and if you ask me, it brings out the best in both. In both cultures there is a shared obsession with quality ingredients, meticulous preparation, and a deep connection to history.

Luca was scheduled to cook two full days at the Refettorio and the first service would be a lunch for a large group of kids. The kids were late and he was pacing. He looked nervous and admitted he was daunted at first by the idea of not knowing what ingredients he would have to work with. But after a few minutes he started to relax and felt like he was cooking at home, for friends. He told me, "Sometimes you don't have anything in the fridge. You need to really look and find something. And it's challenging, but it's a nice idea to create something with food that is going into the rubbish tomorrow."

That day Luca prepared many sophisticated dishes. This lunch did not look like a home-cooked meal but rather something restaurant worthy. There was a bowl of panzanella accompanied with fennel and orange soup, the pasta was served with poached egg, and for dessert there was goat's milk ice cream. These were not easy dishes, that's for sure. If he had wanted to play it safe, pasta with tomato sauce would have been a better choice. I think he was nervous because he wanted to see if complex flavors were appealing to the kids; the tang of goat's milk rather than chocolate, the addition of fennel to the common panzanella, the hybrid pasta with poached egg, something Italian kids rarely see.

The kids came in like a forceful wave. They were hungry and loud. As soon as they started to eat Luca began to relax. I could tell that he was really happy to be there because he was cooking up a storm and the dishes seemed to come out of thin air. It didn't look like there was much to cook with and yet all this amazing food appeared. After lunch he told me, "We all have different situations in life. I remember my grandmother always cooking for me. So I feel at home cooking for them. This is the concept. It comes from the heart."

When dinner came around, he tensed up again. Luca wanted to please. The pasta he had constructed was a combination of whatever he found in the refrigerator. I couldn't believe it worked, but it did. It looked more like a Japanese fish bowl with lots of different ingredients than an Italian pasta, and in fact it was served like a main course with a zucchini (courgette) puree on the bottom, a poached egg on top, penne pasta all around, and speck sautéed with crispy potatoes. It offered textures and flavors that were in contrast to the classic pasta-plus-sauce model. In this plate I saw the two sides of Luca—the Italian and the Japanese—shining through.

He wanted to speak to the guests but he was timid. "I don't know how to talk or how to say something . . . you know because, I cannot ask 'how is your life?' or 'how was yesterday?' You need to be careful about what you want to express. Do I say 'Hi, I'm Luca from Treviso. I am here to cook for you?' "

"Yes," I said. I pushed him out on the floor to talk to the guests and tell them some stories. Many of them spoke Italian and were curious to meet the chefs. I thought Luca's story of emigrating to Japan would be fascinating for them. And it was. Many of them were immigrants. I caught Luca talking about the pasta with one of the young men and he looked perfectly at ease as if he were back in Ginza talking to a guest at his restaurant. And what was the real difference here? One is a paying guest and the other is not. For a chef it really doesn't matter who you are cooking for, you always do your best to make it as good as it can be.

Luca Fantin

July 16 and 17

PANZANELLA WITH FENNEL CREAM

Serves 6

FENNEL CREAM
2 tablespoons extra-virgin olive oil
$1\frac{3}{4}$ oz (50 g) onion, thinly sliced
1 lb 2 oz (500 g) fennel, chopped
7 oz (200 g) potato, cut into medium dice
1 cup (250 ml) milk

CHEESE CREAM
$3\frac{1}{2}$ oz (100 g) cream cheese
1 tablespoon extra-virgin olive oil
2 tablespoons milk
Salt

PANZANELLA
$\frac{1}{2}$ medium red onion, thinly sliced
$\frac{1}{2}$ cup (120 ml) extra-virgin olive oil
$\frac{1}{4}$ cup (60 ml) red wine vinegar
$\frac{1}{2}$ teaspoon salt
Freshly ground black pepper
14 oz (400 g) stale bread, cut into $\frac{3}{4}$-inch (2 cm) cubes
2 heirloom tomatoes, chopped
1 medium red bell pepper, chopped
6 basil leaves, thinly sliced

DILL OIL
scant $\frac{1}{2}$ cup (110 ml) extra-virgin olive oil
5 tablespoons dill fronds

FOR SERVING
7 oz (200 g) fennel, sliced $\frac{1}{3}$ inch (1 cm) thick
2 oranges, segmented

MAKE THE FENNEL CREAM

In a medium pot, heat the olive oil over medium heat. Add the onion, fennel, potato, and milk and simmer for 20 minutes. Transfer to a food processor and process until smooth. Pass through a fine-mesh sieve and set aside.

MAKE THE CHEESE CREAM

In a food processor, combine the cheese, olive oil, and milk and process until smooth. Season to taste with salt and set aside.

MAKE THE PANZANELLA

Soak the onion in a small bowl of cold water for 10 to 15 minutes.

Meanwhile, in a large bowl combine the olive oil, vinegar, salt, and a few grinds of pepper and whisk. Add the bread, tomatoes, and pepper and toss. Let mariante for 30 minutes, stirring occasionally. Stir in the basil just before serving.

>>

MAKE THE DILL OIL

In a food processor, combine the olive oil and dill and blend for 15 minutes. Pass through a cheesecloth and set aside.

TO SERVE

Set up a large bowl of ice and water. Bring a medium pot of water to a boil over high heat. Add the fennel and cook for 5 minutes. Immediately transfer to the ice bath to cool. Drain and set aside.

Put a spoonful of the cheese cream at the bottom of each plate, then cover with the fennel cream. Top with the fennel and orange segments, a spoonful of panzanella, and drizzle with the dill oil.

P. 135

RECIPE NOTES: _____

Luca Fantin

PENNE WITH ZUCCHINI, POACHED EGG, AND SPECK

Serves 6

- 2 tablespoons extra-virgin olive oil, plus more for drizzling
- 1 garlic clove, chopped
- ½ cup (75 g) chopped white onion
- 1½ lb (700 g) zucchini (courgettes), thinly sliced into ribbons
- 4 tablespoons white wine
- 9 oz (150 g) baking potato (such as russet or King Edward)
- 4½ oz (150 g) speck, sliced
- Salt
- 6 eggs
- 13 oz (400 g) penne, sedanini, or other short pasta

In a medium saucepan, heat 1 tablespoon of the olive oil over medium heat. Add the garlic and onion and sauté until golden brown, about 3 minutes. Add the zucchini (courgettes), white wine, and ¼ cup (60 ml) water, and cook for 10 minutes. Transfer to a blender and blend until smooth. Set the zucchini cream aside.

Bring another medium pot of water to a boil over high heat. Add the potatoes and cook until soft, about 12 minutes. Drain and cut into small chunks.

In a frying pan, heat the remaining 1 tablespoon olive oil over medium heat. Add the potatoes and speck and sauté until golden brown, about 2 minutes. Remove from the heat and set aside.

Bring a medium pot of lightly salted water to a boil over medium heat. Crack in the eggs one at a time and poach for 6 minutes. Carefully remove with a slotted spoon.

Bring a large pot of lightly salted water to a boil over medium heat. Add the pasta and cook until al dente. Drain and transfer to a large bowl. Drizzle with olive oil and stir.

To serve, place a spoonful of the zucchini cream in each bowl and top with an egg. Add the pasta around the egg and garnish with crispy potato chunks and speck. Serve immediately.

RECIPE NOTES:

Luca Fantin

GOAT MILK ICE CREAM WITH APPLE AND MERINGUE

Serves 6

CUSTARD CREAM

1 egg

4 tablespoons granulated sugar

1 cup (250 ml) milk

1 cup (250 ml) heavy (whipping) cream

1 vanilla bean, split lengthwise

GOAT MILK ICE CREAM

generous 2 cups (500 ml) goat milk

4 tablespoons granulated sugar

4 tablespoons rice

CARAMELIZED APPLES

3½ tablespoons (50 g) butter

4 tablespoons granulated sugar

¼ lb (250 g) medium apples, peeled and cut into chunks

MERINGUE

6 egg whites (see Note)

½ cup (100 g) granulated sugar

1½ oz (40 g) pistachios, finely chopped

MAKE THE CUSTARD CREAM

In a medium bowl, whisk the egg with the sugar until creamy.

In a medium pot, combine the milk and cream. Scrape in the vanilla seeds. Warm over medium heat until it reaches 176°F (80°C). Stirring constantly, slowly add one-fourth of the hot milk to the eggs. Transfer the warmed eggs to the pot and bring to a boil. Immediately remove and pass through a fine-mesh sieve. Cover and refrigerate.

MAKE THE GOAT MILK ICE CREAM

In a medium pot, bring the goat milk to a boil over medium heat and cook until reduced by half, about 15 minutes. Add the sugar and rice, cover, and cook until the rice is soft, about 15 minutes. Transfer to a food processor and process until smooth. Refrigerate until chilled. Transfer to an ice-cream machine and process according to the manufacturer's instructions. (If you don't have an ice-cream machine, freeze the mixture until hard enough to scoop.)

MAKE THE CARAMELIZED APPLES

In a medium pot, melt the butter over low heat. Add the sugar and cook until golden brown, about 7 minutes. Add the apples and cook until caramelized, about 10 minutes. Set aside to cool.

>>

MAKE THE MERINGUE

Preheat the oven to 200°F (100°C) or as low as your oven can go. Line a baking sheet with parchment paper.

In a medium bowl, beat the egg whites with the sugar until stiff peaks form. Transfer to a pastry (piping) bag and pipe circular mounds onto the prepared baking sheet. Sprinkle with the chopped pistachios. Transfer to the oven and let dry for 6 hours. Let cool, then transfer to an airtight container.

TO SERVE

Place a spoonful of the custard cream in each bowl and top with a scoop of the goat milk ice cream. Garnish with the caramelized apples and meringues.

Note: Save the egg yolks to make Zabaione (page 371) or ice cream.

RECIPE NOTES: _____

_____

_____

_____

_____

_____

_____

_____

_____

_____

_____

_____

_____

_____

_____

_____

_____

_____

_____

_____

_____

_____

_____

_____

_____

_____

_____

_____

_____

_____

_____

_____

_____

_____

_____

_____

_____

_____

Daniel Patterson

Daniel Patterson flew into Milan on an incredibly long flight from San Francisco. That summer he was in the midst of a career change. The chef who had earned two Michelin stars at his San Francisco restaurant Coi was putting himself aside to create a new model for healthy, fast food in one of the most dangerous neighborhoods of Los Angeles. He had placed another chef at the helm of Coi and was working day and night with chef Roy Choi to launch the first Locol. Those who know Daniel understand that he does not make decisions easily, or take matters lightly. This was a well contemplated, important shift and I was honored that he was taking the time to cook here in Milan.

Daniel and I met in 2009 at the first Cook It Raw gathering in Copenhagen. He was a curious yin/yang blend of East Coast intellectual and West Coast hippie. We had talked months earlier about him bringing his family for a proper vacation, but as so often occurs, the trip boiled down to a three-day all-work and no-play deal. Sorry, Daniel.

Not only did Daniel get the short end on his trip to Italy but also the short end of the delivery truck. When the doors opened, it was practically empty. There were four measly zucchini (courgettes), three large bruised eggplants (aubergines), a lot of mint, and lemons. He tried not to look disappointed and took the tray into the kitchen. In the walk-in he did not find summer vegetables but lots of winter greens and a disproportionate amount of ricotta with a threatening expiration date. There was also an oddball collection of tropical fruits—pineapple, passion fruit, and dragon fruit—which puzzled him. I explained that we often had waves of tropical fruit coming in: It seems that although supermarkets want to offer exotic things, not many people actually buy them. I found it ironic that such expensive ingredients were ending up in a soup kitchen.

Nonetheless, despite his sad pickings, Daniel was amazed that the ingredients were considered waste. He said, "In our kitchen, we talk about waste primarily in relation to when food is burned or spilled." I laughed. He was right. I was reminded of all the mistakes I made as a young chef, the burned ragù, the over-cooked rice, and all the waste that can happen daily in a restaurant kitchen. I still go crazy when pasta is overcooked at a staff meal because no one will eat it. Now, that is waste!

I asked him his plans for this less than bountiful basket and he said, "Part of the fine-dining experience is an expectation that the best, most vibrant ingredients will be used. But for everyday cooking, a good cook can make delicious food out of almost anything."

Daniel was preparing an eggplant soup with spices and mint, a vegetarian meatball with a potato and bitter greens salad, and a creamy ricotta ice cream with balsamic vinegar. As we worked together Daniel told me about growing up with his grandmother's cooking and how it has always been a reference. He described it as "Russian peasant food distilled through an American sensibility. Immigrant food, made from humble ingredients, with deep and honest flavors." And then we talked about how important it is to show young chefs that ingredients don't need to be expensive for a meal to be good.

What surprised me about the eggplant soup was its brightness. It was served chilled and had a touch of acidity from the vinegar and lemons. It was very refreshing and clean. Most of all, it had the distinct fragrance of a summer garden. It was hard to believe it came out of that truck. Even the plain, un-seasonal, and nearly undressed salad with potato, radicchio, endive (chicory), and radish had a magical effect on the room. He had boiled the potatoes and chilled them. He had sliced the radishes and let them soak in cold water in the refrigerator. The radicchio and endive were tossed into the bowl, but together these four ingredients, the crisp leaves and chilled radish, transferred another season's memories onto us all. It was as if a breeze had passed through the room. Everyone ate in silence cleaning the plates and asking for seconds.

It was one of the happiest meals we served that summer.

The Montreal-based columnist for *La Presse*, Marie-Claude Lortie, was volunteering in the Refettorio that week. She cleaned and served, took notes and observed. Two months later *La Presse* printed her article "On the Table, Not in the Bin." It didn't surprise me that she opened the article talking about Daniel's eggplant soup: "Quietly seated at the table, Saab smiles. He loves the eggplant cumin soup cooked by the great Californian chef Daniel Patterson. He tastes it one sip at a time. 'Babaganouj,' suddenly the quiet man says. He repeats the name of the Middle-Eastern dish, while nodding with his head. 'When I was a kid, in Egypt, it tasted exactly the same . . .' Saab isn't exactly a gourmet. He didn't know Patterson and he doesn't precisely remember when he came to Italy. 'It's been such a long time ago.' Life hasn't been that easy for him. That's why he lives in a shelter of the charity organization Caritas and eats tonight at Refettorio Ambrosiano."

Saab was just one of our repeat guests whom we greeted nightly by name. His story, like so many others, began with great hopes and spiraled into despair. It was our job, our duty, and our mission to make their meal the best part of their day. Could a bowl of soup that brought back memories of a distant Egypt somehow do more than just fill his empty stomach? We were all helping, but would it ever be enough? Daniel Patterson said, "At the end, we come here to cook with what we have, with other ingredients. This helped me remember why I love to cook: to feed people, in many ways."

Daniel Patterson

Serves 6

⅛ teaspoon cumin seeds
⅛ teaspoon coriander seeds
3 large eggplants (aubergines), thinly sliced
2 tablespoons extra-virgin olive oil, plus more for drizzling
Salt
1 onion, sliced
large pinch of crushed chili flakes
½ teaspoon sherry vinegar
1 tablespoon fresh lemon juice
14 mint leaves
Freshly ground black pepper

Preheat the oven to 325°F (160°C/Gas Mark 3). Line a baking sheet with parchment paper.

In a small dry frying pan, heat the cumin seeds over low heat and toast until fragrant. Transfer to a mortar and grind with a pestle. Repeat the same process for the coriander seeds.

In a large bowl, toss the eggplants with 1 tablespoon of olive oil and season with salt. Transfer to the prepared baking sheet and bake until tender, about 20 minutes. When cool enough to handle, roughly chop. Set aside

In a medium pot, heat the remaining 1 tablespoon of olive oil over medium heat. Add the onion, season with salt, and cook until tender, about 5 minutes. Add the eggplant, cumin, coriander, and chili flakes. Add water to cover and simmer until very tender, about 10 minutes. Transfer to a food processor or blender and blend until smooth. Transfer to a large bowl, cover, and refrigerate to chill. Stir in the sherry vinegar and lemon juice.

To serve, ladle the soup into bowls. Drizzle with olive oil and garnish with mint leaves and black pepper. Serve chilled.

RECIPE NOTES: _____

VEGETABLE LOAF
WITH BITTER GREENS AND POTATO SALAD

Serves 6

VEGETABLE LOAF

2 tablespoons vegetable oil
½ onion, finely chopped
4 garlic cloves, minced
1 yellow bell pepper, finely chopped
1 red bell pepper, finely chopped
4 small squash
7 oz (200 g) shiitake mushroom caps, cut into ¼-inch (6 mm) dice
1¾ cups (200 g) fine dried breadcrumbs
generous 1 cup (100 g) freshly grated Parmigiano-Reggiano cheese
2 teaspoons soy sauce
4 teaspoons chili-garlic sauce (such as Sriracha)
2 tablespoons red miso
4 eggs
1 cup (200 g) cooked lentils
⅔ cup (100 g) cooked pearl barley
Salt and freshly ground black pepper

TOMATO SAUCE

1 tablespoon vegetable oil
2 onions, chopped
1 garlic clove, minced
2 cups (16 oz/500 g) canned tomato sauce (seasoned passata)

BITTER GREENS AND POTATO SALAD

4½ lb (2 kg) new potatoes
Salt
1 head radicchio, sliced
4 Belgian endives (chicory), sliced
1 bunch radishes, sliced
3 tablespoons red wine vinegar
⅓ cup (90 ml) extra-virgin olive oil
Freshly ground black pepper

MAKE THE VEGETABLE LOAF

Preheat the oven to 375°F (190°C/Gas Mark 5). Line a rimmed baking sheet with parchment paper and grease the paper with vegetable oil.

In a medium pan, heat the vegetable oil over medium heat. Add the onion and cook until soft, about 5 minutes. Add the garlic and peppers and cook for 1 minute. Let cool to room temperature, then transfer to a large bowl.

Meanwhile, grate the squash on the large holes of a box grater. Squeeze the grated squash to remove excess liquid.

Add the squash, mushrooms, breadcrumbs, Parmigiano, soy sauce, Sriracha, miso, eggs, lentils, and barley. Mix well (it should feel moist but not overly wet). Season to taste with salt and pepper. Shape a loaf on the prepared baking sheet. Bake until the outside is browned and crisp, about 45 minutes.

MAKE THE TOMATO SAUCE

In a medium pot, heat the oil over medium heat. Add the onions and garlic and sauté until translucent, about 6 minutes. Add the tomato sauce and simmer for 15 minutes. Let cool to room temperature.

MAKE THE BITTER GREENS AND POTATO SALAD

Place the potatoes in a large pot and add water to cover. Season with salt. Bring to a boil over high heat and cook until tender but firm, about 12 minutes. Drain and when cool enough to handle, peel and slice ⅓ inch (1 cm) thick. Transfer to a large bowl and toss with the radicchio, endives (chicory), radishes, vinegar, and olive oil, and season to taste with salt and pepper.

TO SERVE

Slice the vegetable loaf with a bread knife and reheat the slices in the oven at 325°F (160°C/Gas Mark 3). Place a spoonful of the tomato sauce on each plate and top with a slice of the vegetable loaf. Serve with the potato salad on the side.

P. 144

RECIPE NOTES: _____
_____
_____
_____
_____
_____
_____
_____
_____
_____
_____
_____
_____
_____
_____
_____
_____
_____
_____
_____
_____
_____
_____
_____
_____
_____
_____
_____
_____

RICOTTA ICE CREAM WITH TROPICAL FRUIT SAUCE

Serves 6 to 8

RICOTTA ICE CREAM
- 1½ cups (360 ml) milk
- ¾ cup (180 ml) heavy (whipping) cream
- 1 cup (200 g) granulated sugar
- 9 oz (250 g) ricotta cheese

TROPICAL FRUIT SAUCE
- 9 oz (250 g) passion fruits, halved
- 10 oz (300 g) peeled mango, cut into ⅓-inch (1 cm) cubes
- 3½ oz (100 g) chopped fruit (any type) or fruit compote, puree, or fruit juice
- 2 tablespoons superfine (caster) sugar (optional)

FOR SERVING
- 2 tablespoons aged balsamic vinegar or honey

MAKE THE RICOTTA ICE CREAM

In a blender, combine the milk, cream, sugar, and ricotta and blend for 1 minute. Transfer to an ice-cream machine and process according to the manufacturer's instructions. (If you don't have an ice-cream machine, freeze the mixture until hard enough to scoop.)

MAKE THE TROPICAL FRUIT SAUCE

Scoop the passion fruit pulp and strain through a fine-mesh sieve, discarding the seeds. Transfer to a blender, add the mango, and blend until smooth. Transfer to a bowl, add the remaining fruits, and mix. Sweeten with sugar if necessary.

TO SERVE

Place a scoop of ice cream at the bottom of each bowl and drizzle with the tropical fruit sauce. Finish with a drizzle of balsamic vinegar.

RECIPE NOTES:

Daniel Patterson

Mark Moriarty

Mark Moriarty and I met during the S.Pellegrino Young Chef competition in Milan. Twenty finalists from many different countries competed for the award. The judging panel was made up of chefs from around the world: Gastón Acurio, Grant Achatz, Yannick Alléno, Margot Janse, Yoshihiro Narisawa, Joan Roca, and myself. We all agreed that there was one chef who had made a dish that was not only delicious but carried a message and clear identity. This was Mark, a twenty-three-year-old Irish chef who had been cooking in restaurants since he was fifteen and was determined to bring Irish cooking to every corner of the earth. His winning dish was celeriac roasted in Irish pearl barley and fermented hay.

That night I invited Mark to cook at the Refettorio. I learned that although Irish cuisine is very different from Italian cuisine, both developed out of necessity and with humble ingredients that over the centuries have come to define each country. Irish cooking, he explained, is much more than potatoes and alcohol. Today, his spirit and determination to share Ireland's culinary heritage has him running a series of pop-up restaurants around the world.

Mark defines his cooking as simple, recognizable, and basic. At the Refettorio I saw more than basic cooking. I saw a young man bringing together different experiences and techniques to create dishes with a direct and focused message about food. "The Refettorio showed me that food can be a tool to bring people together and create positivity," Mark said. "In fact, sometimes when things get very serious in the restaurant kitchen, I think back to that experience for perspective." As Mark travels, bringing Irish cuisine to every corner of the globe, I am happy to know that this message is traveling with him.

Mark prepared a summer gazpacho with roasted vegetables. This is a great solution when vegetables are no longer their freshest. Roasting tomato, fennel, and eggplant brings out the rich flavors of the vegetables. He then came up with an eggless carbonara—which he playfully called "Marconara"—that was distinctively heartier than the Italian version with the addition of cream, mushrooms, onions, and garlic. His intention was to bring to the Refettorio an Italian dish he often makes for friends at home—and he thought it would be fun for me to see an Irishman try to cook pasta. Pasta was always our guests' favorite part of the meal, and this one went around the room twice. For dessert Mark put together a more sophisticated plate with three different elements of varying temperatures and textures: warm rice pudding with slightly pickled peaches and a pistachio crumble.

I was curious about whether Mark's meal at the Refettorio would be more Irish or more Italian. I always wonder how much of our identity is left when we leave our ingredients at home. But that day Mark did bring a little something from Ireland: his Irish soda bread recipe. I had never been to Ireland and hadn't heard of this bread, but it brought out the Irish in all the other dishes, even the pasta. I later learned that sharing Irish soda bread is part of Irish hospitality, about showing you care.

When I walked into the kitchen I saw Mark talking on the phone and scribbling down some notes on a piece of paper. He was so concentrated he didn't even notice I had arrived. When he finally put his phone down and looked up, he blushed and confessed, "That was my mum. I learned how to make soda bread from her when I was young and I still can't remember the recipe!" Mark told me that Irish soda bread is something all kids learn to make in Ireland, usually from their grandparents. His recipe came from his mother's side of the family and incorporates buttermilk, which would have been a byproduct of churning butter in the home. "The best part," he said, "is that the buttermilk makes the bread and then the butter goes on top!"

IRISH BROWN SODA BREAD

Makes 1 loaf

5¾ cups (700 g) coarsely ground whole wheat
    (wholemeal) flour
2⅔ cups (350 g) cream flour
7 tablespoons wheat germ
2 teaspoons baking soda (bicarbonate of soda)
2½ teaspoons salt
1 scant cup (50 g) wheat bran
6 tablespoons sunflower seeds
3 cups (710 ml) plus 3 tablespoons buttermilk or sour
    cream
3 tablespoons molasses (treacle)

Preheat the oven to 425°F (220°C/Gas Mark 7). Line a baking
sheet with parchment paper.
    In a stand mixer fitted with the dough hook attachment,
mix together the whole wheat (wholemeal) flour, cream flour,
wheat germ, baking soda (bicarbonate of soda), salt, bran,
and sunflower seeds. Slowly add the buttermilk, stirring, until
wet and smooth. Add the molasses (treacle) and mix until
just combined. Shape the dough into a round loaf on a clean,
floured surface. Cut a cross in the top and transfer to the
prepared baking sheet. Let rest for 30 minutes.
    Bake for 10 minutes. Reduce the oven temperature
to 350°F (180°C/Gas Mark 4) and bake until risen and the
loaf sounds hollow when tapped on the bottom, about
40 minutes. Transfer to a wire rack to cool.

RECIPE NOTES: _____
_____
_____
_____
_____
_____
_____
_____
_____
_____
_____
_____
_____
_____
_____
_____
_____
_____
_____
_____
_____
_____
_____
_____
_____

ROAST VEGETABLE GAZPACHO

Serves 6

GAZPACHO
2 garlic bulbs
2 eggplants (aubergines), peeled and sliced ⅓ inch
    (1 cm) thick
4 zucchini (courgettes), sliced ⅓ inch (1 cm) thick
2 red bell peppers
1 fennel bulb, trimmed and thickly sliced
6 canned whole peeled tomatoes
10 basil leaves
2 tablespoons red wine vinegar
4 tablespoons granulated sugar
1 tablespoon salt
½ cup (118 ml) extra-virgin olive oil

FOR SERVING
2 cups (50 g) arugula (rocket)
2 cups (50 g) baby spinach
1 tablespoon mint
2 tablespoons extra-virgin olive oil, plus more for drizzling
Salt
20 crostini

MAKE THE GAZPACHO

Preheat the oven to 350°F (180°C/Gas Mark 4). Line two
baking sheets with parchment paper.
    Wrap the garlic in foil and bake until soft, about
30 minutes. Let cool, then squeeze out the garlic and
set aside.
    Meanwhile, arrange the eggplants (aubergines) on a pre-
pared baking sheet and bake until soft, about 20 minutes.
Set aside.
    Arrange the zucchini (courgettes) on the second lined
baking sheet and bake until soft, about 15 minutes. Set aside.
    Char the peppers over the open flame of a stove burner
until the skin is completely blackened. (If you don't have a
gas stove, char under a hot broiler [grill].) Transfer to a bowl,
cover, and let sit for 5 minutes. Peel, seed, and roughly chop.
Set aside.
    In a food processor, combine the eggplant, zucchini,
peppers, fennel, tomatoes, basil, garlic, vinegar, sugar, and
salt and pulse until smooth. With the machine running,
stream in the olive oil. Season to taste with more salt.
Transfer to a bowl, cover, and refrigerate to chill.
    In a medium bowl, toss the arugula (rocket), spinach,
and mint with the olive oil. Season to taste with salt.

TO SERVE

Ladle the gazpacho into soup bowls, drizzle with extra-
virgin olive oil, and garnish with crostini. Serve with the
mixed greens.

Mark Moriarty

"MARCONARA"

Serves 8

2 lb (1 kg) Parmigiano-Reggiano cheese rinds
Salt
1¾ lb (800 g) spaghetti
2 tablespoons extra-virgin olive oil
2 onions, finely diced
4 garlic cloves, chopped
7 oz (200 g) smoked bacon (streaky), diced
12 white button mushrooms, diced
generous ¾ cup (200 ml) white wine
generous 2 cups (500 ml) heavy (whipping) cream
1 teaspoon freshly ground black pepper
Juice of 1 lemon
1 lb 2 oz (500 g) Parmigiano-Reggiano cheese, grated

In a large pot, combine the Parmigiano rinds with 2 quarts (2 liters) water. Bring to a boil over medium heat and cook for 30 minutes. Reduce the heat to low and cook for 20 minutes. Let cool, then strain through a fine-mesh sieve into a bowl and set aside.

Meanwhile, bring a large pot of lightly salted water to a boil over medium heat. Add the spaghetti and cook until al dente. Drain and set aside.

In a large saucepan, warm the olive oil over medium heat. Add the onions, garlic, and bacon and cook for 2 minutes. Add the mushrooms and cook until soft, 6 minutes. Increase the heat to medium-high, add the white wine, and cook to reduce by half, about 10 minutes. Add 4¼ cups (1 liter) of the Parmigiano stock and reduce by a quarter, about 12 minutes. Add the cream and black pepper and cook until the sauce has reduced to the consistency of heavy cream, about 10 minutes.

Add the spaghetti, lemon juice, salt to taste, and grated Parmigiano and toss to combine. Serve immediately.

P. 152

RECIPE NOTES:

Mark Moriarty

RICE PUDDING
WITH PICKLED PEACHES AND PISTACHIO CRUMBLE

Serves 6

RICE PUDDING
8½ cups (2 liters) milk
3 vanilla beans, split lengthwise
12 egg yolks (see Note)
1¼ cups (250 g) granulated sugar
1 cup (200 g) short-grain rice, rinsed
1⅔ cups (200 g) powdered (icing) sugar

PICKLED PEACHES
3 tablespoons plus 1 teaspoon balsamic vinegar
3 tablespoons plus 1 teaspoon red wine vinegar
4 tablespoons granulated sugar
1 orange, zested
1 whole star anise
2 vanilla beans, split lengthwise
5 peaches, quartered

PISTACHIO CRUMBLE
¾ cup (100 g) all-purpose (plain) flour
¾ cup (100 g) pistachios
2 tablespoons plus 1 teaspoon granulated sugar
5 tablespoons plus 2 teaspoon (80 g) cold butter

FOR SERVING
24 basil leaves

MAKE THE RICE PUDDING

Place 4¼ cups (1 liter) of the milk in a medium pot. Scrape in the seeds from 1 vanilla bean. Warm the milk over medium heat.

In a medium bowl, whisk together the egg yolks and sugar until creamy. Stir in one-fourth of the hot milk, stirring constantly. Transfer the warmed egg mixture to the pot and bring to 181°F (83°C). Pass the egg mixture through a fine-mesh sieve into a bowl and let cool.

In a medium pot, combine the rice, remaining 4¼ cups (1 liter) milk, and powdered (icing) sugar. Scrape in the seeds from the remaining 2 vanilla beans and add the pods. Bring to a boil over medium heat. Simmer until softened, about 20 minutes. Drain the rice in a sieve set over a bowl and reserve the milk. (Fish out the vanilla pods and save for another use.)

Return the rice to the pot and cover with the egg mixture. Bring to a simmer over medium-low heat. Loosen with some of the reserved milk if necessary. Let cool, then cover and refrigerate to chill.

>>

MAKE THE PICKLED PEACHES

In a medium saucepan, combine the vinegars, sugar, orange zest, and star anise. Scrape in the vanilla seeds and add the pods. Add 3 tablespoons water and bring to a boil over medium heat. Let cool, then add the peaches and marinate for 20 minutes.

PISTACHIO CRUMBLE

Preheat the oven to 350°F (180°C/Gas Mark 4). Line a baking sheet with parchment paper.

In a food processor, pulse the flour and pistachios. Add the sugar and butter and pulse until the consistency of a crumble. Transfer to the prepared baking sheet and bake until golden brown, about 15 minutes, mixing every 3 minutes. Remove from the oven and set aside.

TO SERVE

Place a spoonful of the rice pudding in each bowl and top with the pickled peaches. Sprinkle with the pistachio crumble and garnish with 4 basil leaves.

Note: Save the egg whites to make Meringues (pages 32 or 387).

RECIPE NOTES: _____
_____
_____
_____
_____
_____
_____
_____
_____
_____
_____
_____
_____
_____
_____
_____
_____
_____
_____
_____
_____
_____
_____
_____
_____
_____
_____
_____

Gastromotiva

David Hertz is a chef and social activist. "Social gastronomy" is his mission. He founded a nonprofit organization, Gastromotiva, in Brazil to train people with economic needs for the hospitality industry. We met in August 2014 at the MAD food camp in Copenhagen when David presented a project in collaboration with chef Alex Atala training women in Brazilian prisons to cook. I remember David saying, "Let us use the power and the potential and the responsibility of gastronomy to transform lives; to create bridges between different social realities. Food is the perfect tool." After his presentation, I introduced myself and said, "One year from now I want to see you in Milan cooking at the Refettorio." He didn't understand what I was talking about, but he knew the project had something to do with social gastronomy and so he came.

David brought along Katia and Bianca Barbosa, a mother-daughter team who had helped him expand Gastromotiva from São Paolo to Rio de Janeiro. Katia told me the unbelievable story of how she became a chef. She was cleaning floors in the restaurant where her brother worked as a cook. He had to leave suddenly and she offered to take his place. She found her calling and shortly thereafter Claude Troisgros, a well-known chef in Rio, praised her cooking and launched her career. The Barbosa family now runs several successful restaurants in Rio. With them were Alexandra Forbes, a Brazilian journalist who organizes fundraising events for Gastromotiva, and Diego Silva Dos Santos, a graduate of the Gastromotiva culinary program, who had come down from Torino where he was studying at the Slow Food University.

The Gastromotiva team had packed their suitcases with lots of Brazilian ingredients and the rest they would improvise. They wanted to cook very traditional dishes that carry Brazilian flavors and tell stories about the culture. Alexandra gave me the backstory to some of the dishes, such as *xinxim*, a recipe brought to Brazil by slaves from Africa. She explained to me that David always cooks this recipe when he

travels as a way of creating a network of people who are using food as a tool for empowerment and cross-cultural understanding. David said, "For me it's all about people. Gastromotiva is about employing people, giving them an opportunity." He began sautéing the chicken and explained the *xinxim de galinha*, "We marinate chicken with spring onions, garlic, ginger, and saffron root. Then we sauté it with *dendê* (palm oil) to bring the taste of Brazil to Milan. This dish represents the influence of Africans in Brazil. Brazilians eat this once a year for health and prosperity. It's yellow and shines like gold."

While the *xinxim* was a traditional dish that had a symbolic meaning for David, the *moqueca* was the perfect recipe for "no waste." Several chefs had made versions of goulash or stew with mixed meat, fish, and vegetables, but no one had made a vegetarian version. *Moqueca* is a traditional fish stew from Bahia. Katia informed me that the vegetarian version is only served in a few restaurants. She and her sister serve it with banana and heart of palms at their restaurant in Rio, but there are other varieties made with sweet potato or okra. You can use any vegetables and it will turn into an outstanding meal. They had also brought tapioca to make the dessert and a potato bread recipe that Diego was preparing.

There was one more thing that stuck with me from those two days: the banana peel chutney recipe. We had been working with brown bananas since the opening, often not knowing what to do next with them. I felt that we had exhausted every banana recipe on the planet until I saw Alexandra chopping banana peels. I never would have thought about using the banana peels. This was absolutely brilliant. I tasted it and couldn't believe how rich and tasty a banana peel could be. This recipe is the perfect example of how much learning can happen in a kitchen like this one. If you open your mind and start thinking differently about ingredients, then you no longer have to throw away a banana peel ever again.

They cooked for two days and prepared numerous dishes. The smells and the

sounds of Brazilian language filled the kitchen. I always think that when people are happy, they cook a lot of food. The energy was contagious. I was learning about Brazilian traditions and also learning to fight food waste through cooking. The first day, I found twenty packages of presliced cold cuts that were about to expire. I shouted out, "Someone come back here and help me!" Alexandra came running and I filled her arms with packages of prosciutto. I ordered her to open them and throw them into the pot. I was a bit overzealous and she looked at me like I had gone mad. I didn't even know at that point if I was making pasta, ragù, rice, or soup, but not long after we were all sitting down to a civilized lunch of prosciutto and frozen broccoli florets risotto. The atmosphere created in the kitchen most likely influenced my response to the voicemail David left me only a few months later. The message was: "Massimo, I think we should open a Refettorio in Rio during the Olympics." And one year later, we did.

BANANA PEEL CHUTNEY

Makes about 1¾ cups (600 g)

1 tablespoon mustard seeds
2 tablespoons (30 g) butter
1 tablespoon vegetable oil
9 oz (250 g) red onions, diced
2 teaspoons grated fresh ginger
2 malagueta or habanero chilies, chopped
¼ teaspoon ground cinnamon
2½ teaspoons coriander seeds
1½ teaspoons whole cloves
1½ teaspoons cardamom pods
2 whole star anise
Peels from 5 overripe bananas, finely diced
1 teaspoon salt
5 tablespoons packed light brown sugar
Juice of 2 oranges, plus more if needed
⅓ cup (50 g) whole green grapes
Juice of 2 limes

In a saucepan, heat the mustard seeds over medium heat until they start to pop. Add the butter, oil, and onions and sauté until golden. Add the ginger, chilies, and spices and cook until fragrant, about 15 seconds. Add the banana peels, salt, brown sugar, and orange juice and let cook for 15 minutes, or until a thick chutney consistency is obtained. Add the grapes and cook for 5 minutes more. Remove from the heat and add more orange juice or filtered water if necessary to obtain a jammy consistency. Season to taste with salt and sweeten with sugar if necessary. Add the lime juice and stir. Transfer to a sterilized jar and store in the fridge for up to 1 week.

 P. 159

RECIPE NOTES: _____
_____
_____
_____
_____
_____
_____
_____
_____
_____
_____
_____
_____
_____
_____
_____
_____
_____
_____

VEGETARIAN MOQUECA

Serves 6

3 tablespoons plus 1 teaspoon palm oil
1 onion, sliced
1 red bell pepper, cut into medium squares
1 yellow bell pepper, cut into medium squares
1 green bell pepper, cut into medium squares
2 tomatoes, sliced and seeds reserved
2 zucchini (courgettes), sliced
1 eggplant (aubergine), cut into medium cubes
generous 2 cups (500 ml) coconut milk
Salt
¾ cup (50 g) chopped parsley
1 malagueta or habanero chili, minced
Juice of 1 lime

In a medium frying pan, heat the palm oil over low heat. Add the onion and cook until translucent, about 6 minutes. Add the bell peppers and cook for 2 minutes. Add the tomatoes, zucchini (courgettes), eggplant (aubergine), and coconut milk and simmer for 10 minutes. Season to taste with salt. Cover and continue to cook until the vegetables are tender, about 5 minutes. Add the parsley, chili, and lime juice. Taste for seasoning and add more salt if needed.

To serve, ladle into soup bowls.

 P. 160

POTATO BUNS

Makes 12 buns

3½ oz (100 g) yellow-fleshed potatoes, peeled
5 tablespoons (70 g) butter
generous ¼ cup (70 g) whole-milk yogurt
½ tablespoon plus ½ teaspoon granulated sugar
1 teaspoon baking soda (bicarbonate of soda)
2⅓ cups (300 g) all-purpose (plain) flour
1 teaspoon salt
generous ½ cup (135 ml) milk

Preheat the oven to 325°F (160°C/Gas Mark 3). Line 2 baking sheets with parchment paper.

Place the potatoes in a large pot and cover with water. Bring to a boil and cook until soft, about 12 minutes. Drain and let cool. Puree with a potato masher and add the butter. Set aside.

In a large bowl, stir together the yogurt, sugar, and baking soda (bicarbonate of soda). Add the flour, salt, milk, and potato puree and knead until homogeneous. Divide into twelve 1¾-ounce (50 g) portions and shape into balls. Transfer to the prepared baking sheet and bake until golden brown, about 25 minutes. Serve warm.

CHICKEN XINXIM

Serves 6

BRAZILIAN SPICE SEASONING
  2 onions, peeled and quartered
  3 garlic cloves, chopped
  4 teaspoons grated fresh ginger
  1 bunch cilantro (coriander), with the roots, chopped
  1 bunch parsley, chopped
  1 bunch chives, chopped
  Extra-virgin olive oil

XINXIM
  1 oz (30 g) smoked salted dried shrimp
  2¼ lb (1 kg) boneless, skinless chicken thighs
  Salt
  2 garlic cloves, chopped
  generous ½ cup (75 g) cashews
  ½ cup (75 g) unsalted roasted peanuts
  2 tablespoons palm oil
  4 teaspoons extra-virgin olive oil
  10 oz (300 g) tomatoes
  2 small chilies (such as dedo de moça or habanero), chopped
  2 tablespoons fresh lime juice
  3½ oz (100 g) cilantro (coriander), chopped

MAKE THE BRAZILIAN SPICE SEASONING

In a blender, combine the onions, garlic, ginger, cilantro (coriander), parsley, and chives. Add enough olive oil or water to blend into a thick sauce.

MAKE THE XINXIM

Soak the shrimp in a medium bowl of cold water for 30 minutes. Drain and repeat 3 times. Peel and set aside.

In a medium bowl, season the chicken with salt and garlic. Add half of the Brazilian spice seasoning, cover, and let marinate for 1 hour in the fridge.

Meanwhile, grind the cashews and peanuts to a paste in a blender. Set the nut paste aside.

In a frying pan, heat the palm oil and olive oil over medium heat. Add the chicken and cook until browned, about 12 minutes. Add the tomatoes, shrimp, and a scant ½ cup (100 ml) warm water and cook until the chicken is tender, about 20 minutes.

And the chilies and season to taste with salt. Season to taste with the remaining Brazilian spice mixture. Stir in the nut paste and cook for 10 minutes more. Remove from the heat and add the lime juice and cilantro. Serve alone or with rice.

RECIPE NOTES: _____
_____
_____
_____
_____

TAPIOCA CRISPS
WITH CARAMELIZED BANANAS AND PASSION FRUIT SYRUP

Serves 6

TAPIOCA CRISPS
  3⅓ cups (400 g) hydrated tapioca flour

CARAMELIZED BANANAS
  4 bananas, sliced ¼ inch (0.5 cm) thick (see Note)
  4 tablespoons granulated sugar
  ¾ teaspoon ground cinnamon

PASSION FRUIT JELLY
  4 passion fruits, halved
  1 cup (200 g) granulated sugar

MAKE THE TAPIOCA CRISPS

Heat a medium frying pan over medium heat. Sprinkle the bottom of the pan with 2 tablespoons of tapioca flour and cook until a thin disk forms. Flip and cook the other side. Remove from the pan and let cool. Repeat to make 6 disks. Set aside.

MAKE THE CARAMELIZED BANANAS

In a medium frying pan, heat the bananas, sugar, and cinnamon over low heat, stirring well, until the sugar melts and the bananas begin to caramelize. Remove from the heat and set aside to cool.

MAKE THE PASSION FRUIT JELLY

Scoop the passion fruit pulp into a medium saucepan and add the sugar and 1 cup (250 ml) water. Cook over low heat until reduced by half and the sauce is the consistency of a syrup, about 8 minutes. Set aside to cool.

TO SERVE

Place a tapioca crisp on each plate. Top with a spoonful of caramelized bananas and drizzle with the passion fruit syrup.

Note: Save the peels to make Banana Peel Chutney (page 158).

RECIPE NOTES: _____
_____
_____
_____
_____
_____
_____
_____
_____
_____
_____

Joan Roca

Just months earlier, I was hugging Joan Roca in London before he and his brothers jumped on stage to claim once again the number one position on the World's 50 Best Restaurant list. El Cellar de Can Roca located in Girona, Spain, is run by the three Roca brothers: Joan, Josep, and Jordi. Their passion and hard work to the development of avant-garde cuisine is recognized all over the world.

There were a lot of Catalan speakers in the kitchen that day. Joan, his wife, Anna, and his sous-chef, Nacho, were making lunch for a group of kids in addition to dinner for the evening guests. They seemed genuinely moved and excited to be serving a group of schoolchildren and decided to make something fun and approachable. "The idea," Joan said, "is a quick exercise in creative thinking by using what's available."

That morning what was available turned out to be a truck full of *piadine*. A *piadina* is a flat bread from Romagna, a cross between a very flat pita and a flour tortilla. Blue-and-white-striped shacks line the Romagnola coast, selling slight variations of *piadina* from Ravenna to Rimini. Thirty-one miles (fifty kilometers) north or south of these towns, the shacks disappear but the tradition continues in the supermarket version (like the ones that arrived in the truck) to prepare at home. A *piadina* is cooked like a crêpe on a hot round cast-iron surface and then filled with cheese, cold cuts, or vegetables— and occasionally even Nutella—and folded over like a half-moon. It is street food and something you don't need a fork and knife to eat.

Joan looked quizzically at the packaged *piadina* and Cristina quickly explained how they were used customarily. He stood there for half a minute processing the information, and eventually decided to make wraps.

The *piadine* were filled with a meat and vegetable stew, then rolled up and cut at an angle and served with a creamy sauce. These were the most elegant and radical *piadina* I had ever seen. Looking at this recipe, it became very clear to me

why I asked these chefs to come here to cook. Not because I wanted or expected them to re-create the food from their restaurants, not because we needed fancy meals with siphoned foams and sous-vide, but because I knew that they possessed the technique, knowledge, and creativity to see these ingredients from another point of view. The transformation of the ingredients was of course physical, but it was above all intellectual. Working in the kitchen of the Refettorio was like working on a math problem, except that the chefs reasoned with ingredients and proved their theories with recipes. The other difference was that these solutions were not mathematical; they were emotional.

The lunch project ran in tandem with the soup kitchen. From the beginning we invited different school programs and summer camps around the city to visit the space and eat meals made with what would have otherwise been thrown away. Lunch always came with a lesson and lots of questions: We would show them a crate of brown bananas and old bread, or the ingredients used that day, and would ask them: What is this? And then we would tell them how we were transforming ugly and old food into nice and tasty food. "I think cooking is in fact a very powerful tool," Joan said. "Through the kitchen we can help, but we can also make people think about what and why they eat, where these products come from."

Lunch service meant about ninety hungry kids racing into the Refettorio at 12 p.m. sharp, excited and full of energy. But on that day, when noon came around, there were no kids to be seen. Cristina waited half an hour and then got on the phone to see if the bus was lost. She found out that someone had made a terrible mistake and the kids were not coming. She took me aside and whispered the bad news in my ear. I started freaking out. I ran over to the nursery school next door and begged. I counted thirty little kids from ages three to six years old with six teachers. They would have to do or this day would go down as the worst case of No Show in history.

Fortunately Joan and Anna didn't notice. The kids were really cute and ate everything. Joan and Anna had worked hard all morning and were very gracious with them. The highlight came with dessert when the kids were so excited they screamed. Joan's brother and pastry chef at El Celler de Can Roca, Jordi Roca, had provided chocolates and a recipe for chocolate ice cream. The kids may have been too young to understand that one of the best chefs in the world was making their lunch that day, but it didn't really mater because they were happily covered in chocolate ice cream. Later that evening when our guests arrived, to my relief, there wasn't an empty seat in the house. We served the same menu with the addition of an exquisite *salmorejo* soup and I couldn't stop laughing when I saw the guests as covered in chocolate ice cream as the kids had been earlier that day.

Joan Roca

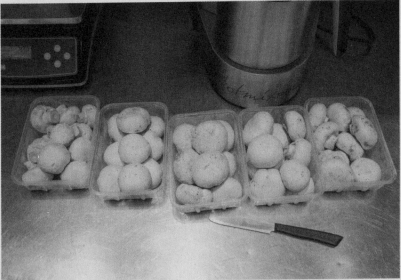

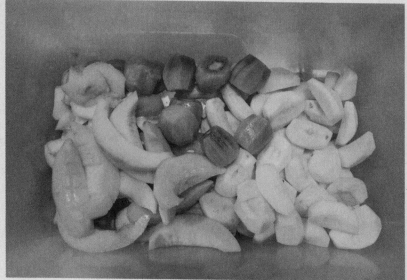

SALMOREJO

Serves 6 to 8

1 slice stale bread, diced, plus 3 oz (90 g) stale bread,
    torn into pieces
2¼ lb (1 kg) tomatoes, quartered
2½ teaspoons sherry vinegar
4½ tablespoons extra-virgin olive oil, plus more
    for drizzling
1 garlic clove
2 teaspoons salt
4 eggs
3½ oz (100 g) prosciutto, sliced paper thin
15 basil leaves, slivered

Preheat the oven to 325°F (160°C/Gas Mark 3). Line a baking
sheet with parchment paper.

Place the diced bread on the prepared baking sheet
and bake until golden brown, about 10 minutes. Set the
croutons aside.

In a food processor or blender, combine the tomatoes,
torn bread, vinegar, olive oil, garlic, and salt and process until
smooth, about 10 minutes. Pass through a fine-mesh sieve
into a bowl, cover, and refrigerate to chill.

In a medium pot, combine the eggs with water to cover.
Bring to a boil over medium heat and cook for 11 minutes.
Drain and when cool enough to handle, peel and finely chop.

To serve, ladle the chilled soup into bowls and top with the
prosciutto, chopped eggs, and croutons. Drizzle with olive oil
and garnish with basil leaves.

📷   P. 167

PIADINA WRAPS WITH BEEF
AND PARMIGIANO BÉCHAMEL

Serves 8

BEEF
1 lb 2 oz (500 g) tomatoes
3½ tablespoons extra-virgin olive oil
1 garlic clove, chopped
¼ lb (120 g) white onions, chopped
8 oz (240 g) white button mushrooms, chopped
7 oz (200 g) zucchini (courgettes), finely diced
Salt and freshly ground black pepper
14 oz (400 g) ground (minced) beef (you can also use
    turkey, chicken, or pork)

>>

PARMIGIANO BÉCHAMEL
generous 1 cup (250 ml) milk
1 tablespoon all-purpose (plain) flour
5¼ teaspoons (25 g) butter
½ teaspoon salt
3½ oz (100 g) Parmigiano-Reggiano cheese, grated

FOR SERVING
8 piadinas or 9½-inch (24 cm) flour tortillas
scant ½ cup (40 g) freshly grated Parmigiano-
    Reggiano cheese
Rosemary sprigs, for garnish

MAKE THE BEEF

Set up a large bowl of ice and water. Bring a medium pot
of water to a boil over medium heat. Add the tomatoes and
blanch for 10 seconds. Transfer to the ice bath. Peel and scoop
the seeds into a bowl; reserve the seeds. Dice the tomato.

In a medium frying pan, heat 1 tablespoon of the olive oil
over medium heat. Add the garlic and onions and sauté until
golden brown, about 4 minutes. Transfer to a plate.

In the same pan, heat ½ tablespoon of the olive oil over
medium heat. Add the mushrooms and sauté for 1 minute,
or until golden brown. Add to the garlic and onions.

In the same pan, heat 1 tablespoon of the olive oil over
medium heat. Add the zucchini (courgettes) and sauté until
golden brown, about 3 minutes. Combine with the garlic,
onions, and mushrooms.

In the same pan, heat the remaining 1 tablespoon of the
oil over medium heat. Add the beef and sauté until browned,
about 8 minutes. Combine with the zucchini mixture and add
the diced tomatoes. Season to taste with salt and pepper. Let
sit for 10 minutes, then drain the juices.

MAKE THE PARMIGIANO BÉCHAMEL

In a medium pot, warm the milk over medium heat.

In a medium saucepan, toast the flour over low heat,
stirring with a spatula until light brown. Add the butter and
stir until melted. Add the warm milk, stir, and let simmer for
3 minutes. Add the salt. Pass the sauce through a fine-mesh
sieve into a clean pan. Stir in the Parmigiano and keep the
béchamel warm.

TO SERVE

Mix the beef mixture with half the béchamel. Fill each
piadina with 2 spoonfuls of the mixture, then tightly wrap
and cut each in thirds. Place 3 pieces of the *piadina* wrap on
each dish. Garnish with rosemary and pass the remaining
béchamel and the grated Parmigiano at the table.

📷   P. 168

RECIPE NOTES: _____
_____
_____
_____

Joan Roca

CHOCOLATE ICE CREAM WITH FRUIT SALAD

Serves 8

CHOCOLATE SAUCE
5 tablespoons plus 1 teaspoon heavy (whipping) cream
1 cup (200 g) granulated sugar
5 tablespoons plus 1 teaspoon unsweetened cocoa powder

CHOCOLATE ICE CREAM
7 oz (200 g) dark chocolate (60% cacao), chopped
generous 2¾ cups (680 ml) milk
5 tablespoons heavy (whipping) cream
5 tablespoons plus 1 teaspoon unsweetened cocoa powder
⅓ cup (40 g) whole-milk powder
4½ tablespoons granulated sugar

CHOCOLATE CRISPS
3½ oz (100 g) dark chocolate (70% cacao), coarsely
    chopped
1 tablespoon fine dried breadcrumbs, for sprinkling

FRUIT SALAD
4 tablespoons granulated sugar
1 lb (500 g) apples, diced
1 lb (500 g) pears, diced
generous 2 cups (500 ml) orange juice

MAKE THE CHOCOLATE SAUCE

In a medium pot, combine the cream, sugar, and scant
⅔ cup (140 ml) water and bring to boil over medium heat.
Cook for 2 minutes, then remove from the heat and add
the cocoa. Use a hand blender to blend until smooth. Pass
through fine-mesh sieve into a bowl, cover, and refrigerate
to chill.

MAKE THE CHOCOLATE ICE CREAM

Place the chopped chocolate in a heatproof medium bowl.
    In a medium pot, heat the milk, cream, cocoa, and
1⅔ cups (390 ml) water and heat to 104°F (40°C). Add the
powdered milk and sugar and heat to 185°F (85°C).
    Pour the hot milk mixture over the chopped chocolate,
stirring with a spatula. Use a hand blender to blend until
smooth. Pass through a fine-mesh sieve into a bowl, cover,
and refrigerate for 4 hours.
    Transfer to an ice-cream machine and process according
to the manufacturer's instructions. (If you don't have an
ice-cream machine, freeze the mixture until hard enough
to scoop.)

>>

MAKE THE CHOCOLATE CRISPS

Line a baking sheet with parchment paper.
    In a heatproof bowl set over a pan of simmering water,
stir the chocolate until melted. Place a spoonful of the melted
chocolate onto the parchment paper and gently flatten with
the back of the spoon to make circular decorations. Repeat
to make 8 disks. Sprinkle with breadcrumbs and refrigerate
to set.

MAKE THE FRUIT SALAD

In a medium pot, combine the sugar and 3 tablespoons water,
bring to a boil over medium heat, and cook until syrupy,
about 8 minutes. Set aside to cool.
    In a medium bowl, combine the apples, pears, orange
juice, and sugar syrup and toss to combine. Cover and refrigerate to chill.

TO SERVE

Place a spoonful of the fruit salad in each bowl and top with
the chocolate ice cream. Drizzle with the chocolate sauce and
garnish with a chocolate crisp.

RECIPE NOTES: _____
_____
_____
_____
_____
_____
_____
_____
_____
_____
_____
_____
_____
_____
_____
_____
_____
_____
_____
_____
_____
_____
_____
_____
_____
_____
_____
_____

ALMA
International School of Italian Cuisine

The ALMA International School of Italian Cuinsine is located in Colorno, Italy, in a monumental setting, la Reggia di Colorno—the Ducal Palace where the dukes of Parma summered in the Versailles-like palace. The seat of the school was once used as a hospital for mental illness, an art gallery, and finally in 2003 became the headquarters of ALMA with Gualtiero Marchesi, a pillar of Italian gastronomy, as the dean. ALMA is known for its remarkable culinary library with over 12,000 books and the constant flow of international students thanks to its outreach program with a network of schools around the world—Japan, Turkey, Korea, India, Brazil, Mexico, UK, USA, and Canada, to name a few. In fact, the George Brown College, whose deans cooked at the Refettorio in September, as well as the MSA from Istanbul, who also cooked in September, are both part of this network.

When the Refettorio was still in its planning stage, I knew I would invite students from ALMA to be part of the project. Over the years, students from ALMA have interned in the kitchen and the front of house of Osteria Francescana. I believe when you have a real experience, not just through lectures, but through cooking, even in the extreme conditions of the Refettorio, students understand the value of food not as an abstract concept. When I called Giovanni Ciresa, the coordinator of ALMA at that time, he didn't hesitate for a second. He personally wanted to join us and cook for the guests.

That morning even before the truck arrived, students were emptying the refrigerator and taking out ingredients from the pantry in preparation for the day's work ahead. I saw them carrying bags of stale bread, which they turned into bread pudding and served with coconut ice cream. They also did a great job of emptying the fridge by taking out tons of packaged hamburger meat that were turned into spiced meatballs served with two condiments: garlic cream and parsley cream. There was not a single leaf of parsley that day, but Giovanni really wanted that special touch and so without even taking off his apron, he left the Refettorio seeking parsley. He returned with a box full of mixed aromatic herbs in his arms. Actually, they were not the best looking but the fragrance was intense. Giovanni was ecstatic. "The Indian grocer at the corner gave these to me for free," he said. "He has heard about the Refettorio and wanted to contribute as much as he could." It was good to know that we had an ambassador in the neighborhood.

The starter course was a creamy risotto with endive, orange, and mustard. The broth was enriched with Parmgiano Reggiano cheese rinds. I was taken aback by the daring combination of bitter endive, sweet orange juice, and pungent mustard. However, it worked and the guests were asking for seconds.

As Giovanni walked around the room, he was surprised when certain guests shared their opinions—mostly good, but even a few critical observations—about the dinner. "It is so rare to have people tell you what they really think. I have never had such interesting and free dialogue," he told me. "Both critiques and praises were well reasoned and founded. And they were spontaneous. One gentleman praised us for the refined garlic cream. Do we ever hear words like that from food bloggers? Never!"

The students who came that day shared their experience at school and soon enough word got around that cooking at the Refettorio was really cool. Giovanni returned several times not just with students but with teachers as well. Our guests thrived not only on delicious meals but the vibrant atmosphere the young students created in the dining room. Back in June we didn't know the future of the Refettorio. Before Expo was over on October 31, Caritas confirmed that they would continue running the project as we had created it. When I shared this news with Giovanni he was almost in tears. Only then did I understand how attached he was to the project. Not only had he become a regular visitor, but he later cooked a New Year's Eve dinner that was unforgettable!

Serves 6

10 oz (300 g) Parmigiano-Reggiano cheese rinds
5 medium Belgian endives (chicory)
Salt and freshly ground black pepper
7 tablespoons (105 g) butter
generous ¾ cup (200 ml) orange juice
1 tablespoon mustard seeds
scant 2¼ cups (420 g) carnaroli or other short-grain rice
2 shallots, minced
7 oz (200 g) Parmigiano-Reggiano cheese, grated

In a large pot, combine the Parmigiano rinds with 6 cups (1.5 liters) water and bring to a boil over medium heat. Simmer for 1 hour. Strain the Parmigiano stock through a fine-mesh sieve into a clean saucepan and keep warm over low heat.

Meanwhile, season the endives (chicory) with salt and pepper. In a medium frying pan, melt 3 tablespoons (45 g) of the butter over low heat. Add the orange juice, mustard seeds, and endives. Cover and cook until the endives are soft but firm, about 8 minutes. Remove the endives and carefully separate the external leaves from the hearts. Return the external leaves to the pan and caramelize over high heat for 3 minutes. Set aside.

Add the endive hearts to a food processor or blender and process until smooth.

In a medium frying pan, melt 2 tablespoons (30 g) of butter over medium heat. Add the rice and shallots and cook until the rice is toasted, about 2 minutes. Add a ladleful of the Parmigiano stock and stir. Once absorbed, add another ladleful of stock and continue until all of the stock has been used. Continue to cook, stirring constantly, until al dente, about 15 minutes.

Add the endive puree, half of the caramelized endives, the grated Parmigiano, and the remaining 2 tablespoons (30 g) of butter and stir to combine. Serve immediately and garnish with the remaining caramelized endives.

P. 175

RECIPE NOTES:

SPICED MEATBALLS WITH GARLIC AND PARSLEY SAUCES

Serves 6

MEATBALLS
2¼ lb (1 kg) mixed ground (minced) meat (such as chicken, turkey, beef, and/or pork)
5 oz (150 g) Parmigiano-Reggiano cheese, grated
½ teaspoon ground cardamom
¼ teaspoon freshly ground black pepper
¼ teaspoon ground white pepper
¼ teaspoon ground fennel
¼ teaspoon ground coriander
½ teaspoon salt
All-purpose (plain) flour, for dredging
1¼ cups (300 ml) canola (rapeseed) oil

GARLIC AND PARSLEY SAUCES
3 garlic bulbs, separated into cloves
generous 2 cups (500 ml) milk
5 oz (150 g) parsley
5 tablespoons extra-virgin olive oil

MAKE THE MEATBALLS

In a medium bowl, combine the meat, Parmigiano, cardamom, peppers, fennel, coriander, and salt and mix well. Form into meatballs the size of ping-pong balls, then roll each one in flour.

In a medium frying pan, heat the canola (rapeseed) oil over medium heat to 338°F (170°C). Working in batches, fry the meatballs until an even crust has formed, about 6 minutes. Drain on paper towels.

MAKE THE GARLIC AND PARSLEY SAUCES

Bring a small pot of water to a boil over high heat. Add the garlic and blanch for 1 minute. Remove, change the water, and blanch again. Repeat 3 more times. Peel the garlic and remove the central germs.

In a small pot, heat milk over medium heat. Add the garlic and cook until soft, at least 40 minutes. Let cool, then transfer to a blender and blend until smooth. Set aside

Set up a bowl of ice and water. Bring a small pot of salted water to a boil over high heat. Add the parsley and blanch for 5 seconds. Reserving some of the cooking water, drain and transfer the parsley to the ice bath. Transfer to a blender and blend with the olive oil and 2 tablespoons of the reserved cooking water until smooth.

TO SERVE

Serve the meatballs with the garlic and parsley sauces on the side.

RECIPE NOTES:

BREAD PUDDING WITH COCONUT ICE CREAM

Serves 6

COCONUT ICE CREAM
- ½ cup (120 ml) milk
- 1⅔ cups (400 ml) coconut cream
- 3 tablespoons plus 1 teaspoon heavy (whipping) cream
- ½ cup (40 g) sweetened coconut flakes

BREAD PUDDING
- Butter, for the pan
- generous 1 cup (250 ml) milk
- generous 1 cup (250 ml) heavy (whipping) cream
- 1 teaspoon vanilla extract
- ½ cup (100 g) granulated sugar
- 4 egg yolks (see Note)
- 1 lb (500 g) stale bread, sliced

MAKE THE COCONUT ICE CREAM

In a food processor or blender, combine the milk and coconut cream and process until smooth. Add the heavy (whipping) cream and coconut flakes and stir to combine. Transfer to an ice-cream machine and process according to the manufacturer's instructions. (If you don't have an ice-cream machine, freeze the mixture until hard enough to scoop.)

MAKE THE BREAD PUDDING

Preheat the oven to 325°F (160°C/Gas Mark 3). Butter an 8 x 12-inch (20 x 30 cm) loaf pan.

In a medium pot, warm the milk, cream, and vanilla over medium heat. Add the sugar and cook until dissolved. Let cool to room temperature.

In a medium bowl, whisk the egg yolks. Slowly add the milk mixture in a steady stream and whisk to combine.

Layer the bread in the prepared loaf pan and pour over the egg and milk mixture. Let sit for 10 minutes. Transfer to the oven and bake for 40 minutes. Let cool completely at room temperature before slicing.

TO SERVE

Place a slice of the bread pudding on each plate and top with a scoop of the coconut ice cream.

Note: Save the egg whites to make Meringues (pages 32 or 387).

RECIPE NOTES:

Antonia Klugmann & Fabrizio Mantovani

Sometimes the calendar of the Refettorio was full of surprises. When we called Antonia Klugmann, at her restaurant on the northeastern border of Italy, and Fabrizio Mantovani, at his restaurant in central Italy, both were only available on the same day: August 3. Of course, we said yes to both, and thankfully they seemed excited to cook together, albeit for the very first time. I was curious to see what would happen.

Antonia comes from Trieste, in the Friuli-Venezia Giulia region, near the border between Italy and Slovenia. The area still has echoes of past Austrian domination, German and Yugoslav occupation, and all the invasions from those who passed through Northern Italy for the past 1,500 years. No matter which empire was reigning, Trieste still kept its identity as a frontier city. Due to this peculiar concoction, locals define themselves as Mitteleuropean. And so does Antonia, who decided to open her restaurant, l'Argine a Vencò (literally, the bank in Vencò), less than a mile (1.6 kilometers) from the Slovenian border. Her cuisine is representative of the region, where ingredients, local products, game, and wild herbs tell the story of her land.

Fabrizio, on the other hand, is a pure Romagnolo and hails from Emilia-Romagna's eastern coast. Before becoming a chef, Fabrizio was a diehard rock musician and the bass player for Alex Baroni, an Italian pop star from the 1990s. He never let go of that passion and when he opened his restaurant, FM, he named it not only for his initials but also FM radio, with the tag line "tune into taste." The restaurant is in Faenza, a city of Roman origins, known for majolica ceramics. The first factories for the glazed earthenware were founded in the first century BC and reached their height of fame during the Renaissance. This rich history defined Faenza as a place where art and culture flourished.

When two chefs cook together you can't always count on intuitive synergy. Luckily, Antonia and Fabrizio worked together brilliantly and created every aspect of the menu unanimously. They chose the ingredients and decided on the dishes they would serve: bread gnocchi, typical of Antonia's region; meatloaf with roasted vegetables to recover all of the ground meat Fabrizio found in the fridge; and finally a milk ice cream with *sbrisolona,* a cake typical of Lombardy. As they cooked, Antonia and Fabrizio chatted the entire time, sharing kitchen stories and tips, as if they were old friends.

"Bread gnocchi are typical from Trieste, both served in broth and sautéed with butter and sage," said Antonia. "When I was a young girl, we used to eat them with spinach, ham, and Parmigiano, because my father's mother was from Emilia. My mother's family, on the other hand, was from Puglia and her father loved fish, so it was commonplace to serve it at every meal. In this recipe I combined the two traditions in one."

Because the weather was so hot, Fabrizio wanted to make ice cream for dessert. Strangely, the fridge was lacking any fruit or any interesting dairy other than milk, and the pantry didn't provide a single dried fruit or nut. Fabrizio said it would have been so sad to serve plain milk ice cream, and that is when he thought about making *sbrisolona* (whose name translates as "crumbly"), a typical cake from Mantova in Northern Italy. It is an easy cake to make. He grabbed flour, butter, and eggs and once it was baked and chilled, he crumbled it on top of the ice cream. I thought I would be nostalgic eating this dessert because my mother always made *sbrisolona*, which she learned from living with her in-laws in Mantova; but Fabrizio's *sbrisolona* had so many interesting twists, like orange zest and anise seeds, that it tasted like a brand new recipe.

On that night, the jovial atmosphere trickled out of the kitchen and into the dining hall. Antonia and Fabrizio were serving the guests as if they had been working together in the same kitchen for ages. At the end of the night before saying goodbye, I saw Antonia placing a piece of paper in Fabrizio's hands. "What kind of secret messages are being passed around here?" I said. Both started laughing. "No secrets, just the recipe for bread gnocchi," explained a blushing Antonia. Fabrizio chipped in, "Antonia has given me the perfect solution to all the surplus bread. I can't wait to make them at the restaurant." Antonia responded with a grin, "We'll just have to see if a Romagnolo guy can make them properly!"

Antonia Klugmann & Fabrizio Mantovani

Antonia Klugmann & Fabrizio Mantovani

FISH SOUP WITH BREAD GNOCCHI

Serves 6

BREAD GNOCCHI

1 lb 2 oz (500 g) stale bread, chopped
1¼ cups (300 ml) milk
2 eggs
¾ cup (100 g) all-purpose (plain) flour
1 teaspoon salt
¼ teaspoon freshly ground black pepper
Extra-virgin olive oil, for drizzling
½ cup (50 g) freshly grated Parmigiano-Reggiano cheese

FISH SOUP

3 tablespoons extra-virgin olive oil
1 garlic bulb, separated into cloves and peeled
1 can (14 oz/400 g) whole peeled tomatoes
2 fresh tomatoes, chopped
4 small mullets or other white fish, cleaned and boned, heads and bones reserved
5 anchovy fillets
2 pepperoncini or other mild chilies, chopped
2 tablespoons capers
2 onions, chopped
2 carrots, finely chopped
3 celery stalks, finely chopped
2 hake fillets or other white fish (about 5 oz/140 g each)
2 tablespoons chopped parsley, for serving

MAKE THE BREAD GNOCCHI

In a large bowl, soak the bread in the milk for 30 minutes.

Preheat the oven to 350°F (180°C/Gas Mark 4). Line a baking sheet with parchment paper.

Squeeze the excess liquid out of the soaked bread. Discard the liquid and return the bread to the bowl. Add the eggs, flour, salt, and pepper and mix thoroughly to form a dough. Shape the dough with your hands to form gnocchi.

In a medium pot of boiling water, cook the bread gnocchi until they float to the surface, about 5 minutes. Drain. Transfer to the prepared baking sheet and drizzle with olive oil and sprinkle with the Parmigiano. Bake until golden brown, about 40 minutes.

>>

MAKE THE FISH SOUP

In a medium pot, heat the 2 tablespoons of the olive oil over medium heat. Add the garlic and brown. Add the canned and fresh tomatoes, mullets, fish heads and bones, anchovies, pepperoncini, capers, and onions and simmer for 3 minutes. Add the carrots, celery, and ¼ cup (60 ml) water, and cook over low heat for 15 minutes. Discard the fish bones and heads and set aside the mullets. Transfer to a food processor or blender and blend until smooth. Strain through a colander.

In a medium frying pan, heat the remaining tablespoon of olive oil over medium heat. Add the hake fillets skin side down and sear until just firm, about 3 minutes.

TO SERVE

Ladle the soup into each bowl and top with 5 gnocchi. Divide the mullets and hake fillets among the bowls and garnish with the parsley.

📷 P. 183

RECIPE NOTES: _____
_____
_____
_____
_____
_____
_____
_____
_____
_____
_____
_____
_____
_____
_____
_____
_____
_____
_____
_____
_____
_____
_____
_____
_____
_____
_____
_____
_____
_____
_____
_____

Antonia Klugmann & Fabrizio Mantovani

MEATLOAF WITH ROASTED VEGETABLES

Serves 6 to 8

> 3 heads radicchio, quartered
> 1 lb 5 oz (600 g) potatoes, diced
> 1½ onions, 1 quartered and ½ finely chopped
> Extra-virgin olive oil, for brushing
> Salt
> 5 oz (150 g) stale bread
> generous ¾ cup (200 ml) milk
> 1 lb 2 oz (500 g) ground (minced) meat (such as pork
>   and/or beef)
> 1 cotechino sausage or other mild sausage (about
>   5 oz/150 g), chopped
> ½ cup (50 g) freshly grated Parmigiano-Reggiano cheese
> ½ cup (30 g) chopped parsley
> 1½ tablespoons oregano, chopped
> 2 eggs
> 1 garlic clove, smashed
> Freshly ground black pepper
> All-purpose (plain) flour, for dredging
> scant ½ cup (100 ml) white wine

Preheat the oven to 350°F (180°C/Gas Mark 4). Line two rimmed baking sheets with parchment paper.

Place the radicchio, potatoes, and the quartered onion on one of the prepared baking sheets. Brush with olive oil and season with salt. Bake until softened, about 20 minutes. Remove from the oven but leave the oven on for the meatloaf.

In a medium bowl, soak the bread in the milk for 30 minutes. Squeeze the excess liquid out of the soaked bread and discard the liquid. In a separate medium bowl, mix the ground (minced) meat, sausage, and Parmigiano by hand. Add the soaked bread, parsley, oregano, eggs, garlic, and finely chopped onion. Season with salt and pepper. Shape the mixture into a loaf and sprinkle lightly with flour.

In a medium pan, heat 1 tablespoon of the olive oil over medium heat. Add the meatloaf and brown on all sides. Transfer to the other prepared baking sheet and bake until golden brown, about 20 minutes. Add the wine to the baking sheet to deglaze, cover the baking sheet with foil, and return to the oven. Bake until evenly cooked through and a thermometer reads 176°F (80°C) in the center, about 40 minutes.

To serve, slice the meatloaf and serve with the roasted vegetables on the side.

RECIPE NOTES: _____
_____
_____
_____
_____
_____
_____
_____
_____
_____
_____
_____

MILK ICE CREAM WITH SBRISOLONA CAKE

Serves 6 to 8

MILK ICE CREAM
> 2½ cups (600 ml) milk
> scant ½ cup (100 ml) heavy (whipping) cream
> ¾ cup (150 g) granulated sugar

SBRISOLONA CAKE
> 2 sticks (225 g) butter, at room temperature
> 7 oz (200 g) peeled raw almonds
> 1⅓ cups (180 g) all-purpose (plain) flour
> 2 cups (170 g) semolina
> 1 cup (200 g) granulated sugar
> ½ teaspoon salt
> Grated zest of 1 large navel orange
> 1 teaspoon anise seeds, plus more for topping
> 2 egg yolks (see Note)
> Powdered (icing) sugar, for dusting

MAKE THE MILK ICE CREAM

In a medium pot, bring the milk, cream, and sugar to 158°F (70°C) over medium heat and cook for 5 minutes, whisking constantly. Let cool, then cover and refrigerate for 1 hour to chill. Transfer to an ice-cream machine and process according to the manufacturer's instructions. (If you don't have an ice-cream machine, freeze the mixture until hard enough to scoop.)

MAKE THE SBRISOLONA CAKE

Preheat the oven to 350°F (180°C/Gas Mark 4). Line a 10-inch (25 cm) tart pan with a removable bottom with a round of parchment paper. Grease the paper with butter.

Set aside a handful of almonds. In a food processor, finely crush the remaining almonds.

In a large bowl, mix together the finely crushed almonds, flour, semolina, sugar, salt, orange zest, and anise seeds. Add the butter and egg yolks and mix with a spatula until combined (the dough shouldn't be uniformly smooth). Transfer to the prepared pan. Top with the reserved almonds and some anise seeds. Bake until golden brown, about 30 minutes. Let cool in the pan. Dust with powdered (icing) sugar.

TO SERVE

Place a slice of *sbrisolona* cake on each plate and top with a scoop of the milk ice cream.

Note: Save the egg whites to make Meringues (pages 32 or 387).

📷   P. 185

RECIPE NOTES: _____
_____
_____
_____

Antonia Klugmann & Fabrizio Mantovani

Charity Dinner

During the six months of Expo we held two dinners that were open to the public, turning the Refettorio into a restaurant. The dinners were organized to raise funds for the soup kitchen and communicate our mission to fight food waste. That singular objective created a rare atmosphere that was unlike any other culinary event.

For the first charity dinner, Cristina had the brilliant idea of inviting four Latin American chefs: Matías Perdomo, Enrique Olvera, Carlos García, and Rodolfo Guzmán. Each of these chefs is an iconoclast, breaking ground and evolving their national kitchens. They all have a keen sense of civic responsibility and were eager to take on the challenge. That evening, four chefs, eleven sous-chefs, and an army of volunteers turned a gala dinner into a family affair.

Everyone arrived at the Refettorio on Saturday afternoon. But this was not only a group of chefs, there were also other familiar faces: friends like Nidal Barake, Sasha Correa, and Luciana Bianchi; sous-chefs, ex-chefs, and interns. Everyone was curious to find out what kind of ingredients they had to work with for Sunday's feast. To their delight, the pantry was stuffed. Cristina had stocked it with a surplus of ingredients: fish, meat, cold cuts, vegetables, dairy products, grains, pasta, you name it. There was a lot to do, but as the chefs got started, they just looked like a group of friends who had decided to make a nice meal by opening the fridge and working with whatever was available— like most people do on any given day.

The next morning, only Matías and his sous-chef Simon Press showed up early; everyone else was still asleep. Matías, who is from Uruguay, has been working and living in Milan for over ten years and becomes more Italian every day. He is playful with his cooking and language, turning things upside down and revealing the unexpected in every bite he serves at his restaurant Contraste. By the time everyone else arrived, Matías and Simon were way ahead. They had prepped two starters, a fresh coconut salad with balsamic vinegar and rasp-berries, and a Mediterranean-inspired chilled tomato salad with watermelon sorbet, passion fruit, crescenza cheese, fried capers, and almond crumble.

Enrique is a Mexican chef who, over the past ten years, has taken on Mexican culinary traditions as no one has done before. His Mexico City restaurant Pujol has redefined Mexican culinary heritage, while his New York outpost Cosme, lead by the talented chef Daniela Soto-Innes, is taking on contemporary Mexican cuisine. Enrique and Daniela made a *mole dell'orto*, an improvised version of the traditional *mole verde*. Daniela even went out behind the Refettorio looking for wild greens to create this unexpectedly fresh *mole*.

Enrique talked a lot about his research into Mexico's pre-Hispanic period, when the Incas began to see the potential in garbage: "For the Incas," he explained, "waste became a resource that could be recovered, reused, recycled, and used productively in manufacturing and agriculture. Necessity helped them discover self-sufficiency."

Carlos is the chef at Alto in Caracas. He is a symbol of courage in the face of uncertainty. Due to the political situation in Venezuela, Alto struggles to have fresh water, as well as basic ingredients like sugar, flour, and milk. My respect for Carlos's resourceful kitchen and his determination to fight the system with good food and ethical practices is only one of the reasons I invited him to Milan. Carlos is a team player, and someone who is accustomed to hard work. He seemed to be cooking with everyone and I don't know how he found the time to make his dishes. For the staff lunch that day, Carlos made Venezuelan arepas. That is how he got the idea to serve an arepa-inspired dish for dinner. Carlos served a beef and horseradish broth with chickpeas, a poached egg, crispy salami—and the crispest corn chips made with an arepa dough. For one of the desserts, Carlos took bananas and collaborated with Daniela on Plátano Balsamico, a banana dessert with balsamic vinegar and crescenza cheese.

The Chilean chef Rodolfo is at the helm of Boragó in Santiago. He is an innovator passionate about exploring indigenous ingredients, rare plants, herbs, and flowers. His kitchen is extremely seasonal with attention to the diversity of native Chilean ingredients. In fact, he secretly packed some native ingredients in his suitcase, such as fragrant wood for smoking. Rodolfo was intent on smoking various things: first the broth for his chilled pulmay soup and then the mushrooms for his mushroom ice cream. Prepared with a smoked broth of squid, shellfish, and pisco, it was the transition between the savory courses and the sweet ones—somewhere between a salad and a sorbet. He followed with three types of rice pudding.

As the dinner approached, there were volunteer waiters, line cooks, and runners everywhere. After fifteen minutes, Thomas Piras—who runs the front of house at Matías's restaurant Contraste—took control of the army of volunteers, setting the guidelines that would keep the chaos of eighty guests and thirty-odd waiters (plus fifteen chefs) to a minimum.

That night, there was contagious energy in the room and everybody wanted to help. To get everyone settled and in their seats, I grabbed the microphone and introduced the chefs one by one. As each of them described their dish, I looked out over the dining room. The Refettorio looked more like a college dining hall than a restaurant. There were unfamiliar faces and others I recognized. I saw a table with chefs from Osteria Francescana. I saw several journalists who were witness to the evening's activities. I even saw Luca Fantin who had cooked at the Refettorio the month before and tonight was dining with his wife and son.

Actually, the camaraderie that I was feeling that evening had begun two days earlier, when everyone first arrived in Modena. I couldn't have imagined a better start to this gala than the pick-up soccer game we played on the cobblestones in front of Modena's eleventh-century cathedral at 3 a.m. that Saturday morning. Naturally, the teams were Italy versus Latin America. I'll let you guess who won.

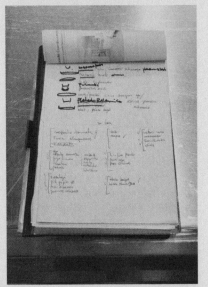

MOLE DELL'ORTO

Serves 8

3 yellow squash, cut into rounds
2 tablespoons extra-virgin olive oil, plus more for drizzling
3 cucumbers, peeled into ribbons
1 lb 2 oz (500 g) purslane or mâche (lamb's lettuce)
Salt
2 cups Mole (recipe follows)
40 chickweed or baby spinach leaves, for garnish
8 geranium leaves

Preheat the oven to 350°F (180°C/Gas Mark 4). Line a baking sheet with parchment paper.

Place the squash on the prepared baking sheet and toss with the olive oil. Bake until soft, about 10 minutes.

In a medium bowl, combine the cucumbers, purslane, and squash. Drizzle with olive oil and toss to combine. Season to taste with salt. Set aside.

To serve, ladle ¼ cup (60 ml) of the *mole* into each plate. Top with the salad and garnish with the chickweed and geranium leaves.

MOLE

Makes about 2 quarts (2 liters)

⅓ cup (80 g) pumpkin seeds
5 tablespoons pine nuts
¼ cup (40 g) raw almonds
¼ cup (40 g) white sesame seeds
3 tablespoons peanuts
scant ½ cup (110 ml) grapeseed oil
1 small white onion, chopped
6 garlic cloves, sliced
1½ oz (40 g) cilantro (coriander) stems
2⅔ cups (350 g) green peas
3½ oz (100 g) serrano chilies, sliced
¾ cup (20 g) shiso (see Note)
⅔ cup (15 g) basil
¾ cup (15 g) epazote (see Note)
3⅓ cups (800 ml) ice water
Salt
Juice of 2 limes

>>

In a medium dry frying pan, toast the pumpkin seeds, pine nuts, almonds, sesame seeds, and peanuts over medium heat until golden brown, about 5 minutes. Transfer to a plate to cool. Set aside.

In a large pot, heat the grapeseed oil over medium heat. Add the onion and garlic and cook until translucent, about 6 minutes. Add the toasted seeds and nuts and cilantro (coriander) stems and cook for 2 minutes. Remove from the heat and let cool.

Set up a large bowl of ice and water. Bring a medium pot of salted water to a boil. Add the peas and cook for 4 minutes. Scoop out the peas and immediately transfer to the ice bath. Blanch and cool the serrano chilies, shiso, basil, and epazote in the same manner for 4 seconds each.

In a food processor, combine the peas, serranos, shiso, basil, epazote, nuts and seeds, and ice water and blend until smooth. Pass through a fine-mesh sieve into a bowl and let cool. Stir in the lime juice and set aside. Season to taste with salt when ready to serve.

Note: If you don't have shiso or epazote, subsitute with mint.

📷   P. 191

RECIPE NOTES: _____
_____
_____
_____
_____
_____
_____
_____
_____
_____
_____
_____
_____
_____
_____
_____
_____
_____
_____
_____
_____
_____
_____
_____
_____
_____
_____
_____
_____
_____
_____
_____
_____
_____
_____
_____
_____

TOMATO SALAD WITH TOMATO-WATERMELON SORBET

Serves 6

ALMOND CRUMBLE

3½ oz (100 g) blanched almonds
½ cup (100 g) granulated sugar
¾ cup (100 g) all-purpose (plain) flour
6 tablespoons plus 1 teaspoon (90 g) butter
2 teaspoons extra-virgin olive oil
½ teaspoon fresh oregano
1 teaspoon salt

TOMATO-WATERMELON SORBET

⅓ cup (50 g) mesquite pod flour
¼ teaspoon salt
1¼ cups (300 ml) watermelon juice
1¼ cups (300 ml) tomato juice

FRIED CAPERS

¾ cup (180 ml) extra-virgin olive oil
2 tablespoons capers

MARINATED TOMATOES

2 oxheart or heirloom tomatoes (about 5 oz/150 g each),
    sliced ¼ inch (6 mm) thick
1 passion fruit, halved
2 tablespoons extra-virgin olive oil
Salt
3½ oz (100 g) crescenza cheese or other soft, mild cheese
4 teaspoons heavy (whipping) cream

MAKE THE ALMOND CRUMBLE

Preheat the oven to 300°F (150°C/Gas Mark 2). Line a baking sheet with parchment paper.

In a food processor, process the almonds to a fine powder. Transfer to a medium bowl and add the sugar, flour, butter, olive oil, oregano, and salt and mix to combine.

On a floured surface, roll out the dough to a ¾-inch (2 cm) thickness. Transfer to the prepared baking sheet and bake until crunchy, about 20 minutes. Let cool, then transfer to a food processor and process until a fine powder is obtained.

MAKE THE TOMATO-WATERMELON SORBET

In a medium pot, bring 1¼ cups (300 ml) water to 185°F (85°C) over medium heat. Add the mesquite pod flour and salt, and stir for 4 minutes, until the salt is dissolved. Remove from the heat and let cool. Cover and refrigerate to chill.

Stir in the watermelon and tomato juices, cover, and refrigerate for 2 hours. Transfer to an ice-cream machine and process according to the manufacturer's instructions. (If you don't have an ice-cream machine, freeze the mixture, then grate with a fork and serve as a granita.)

>>

MAKE THE FRIED CAPERS

In a small pot, heat the olive oil over medium heat to 330°F (165°C). Add the capers and fry until crispy, about 40 seconds. Transfer to a tray lined with paper towels and set aside.

MAKE THE MARINATED TOMATOES

Place the tomatoes in a medium bowl. Scoop the passion fruit pulp over the tomatoes, drizzle with the olive oil, and season to taste with salt. Cover and let marinate in the fridge for 10 minutes.

Meanwhile, in a medium bowl, whisk the cheese and cream until smooth and creamy. Dress the tomatoes with the crescenza cream.

TO SERVE

Place a spoonful of the tomatoes on each plate and top with the tomato-watermelon sorbet. Sprinkle with the fried capers and almond crumble.

RECIPE NOTES:

COLD PULMAY

Serves 6

SQUID
1 tablespoon extra-virgin olive oil
7 oz (200 g) fresh or frozen squid, cut into ⅓ x 1¼ -inch
   (1 x 3 cm) julienne
Salt

MARINATED APPLES
7 oz (200 g) green apples, cut into ⅓ x 1¼ -inch (1 x 3 cm)
   julienne
generous ¾ cup (200 ml) fresh lime juice

PULMAY
24 mussels
24 small hardshell clams
3½ oz (100 g) tepú wood, firewood (such as apple, cherry,
   maple, juniper, oak, hickory), or store-bought wood
   chips for home smokers (such as Green Egg)
1 small white onion, finely diced
2 small green chilies, finely diced
½ cup (10 g) cilantro (coriander)
scant ½ cup (100 ml) fresh lime juice
2 tablespoons extra-virgin olive oil
4 teaspoons pisco

FOR SERVING
1 teaspoon extra-virgin olive oil
6 lemon verbena leaves, plus more for garnish
Lemon balm leaves, for garnish
Parsley and Lemon Verbena Oil (recipe follows), for serving

COOK THE SQUID

In a medium frying pan, heat the olive oil over medium
heat. Add the squid and sauté until tender, about 2 minutes.
Season to taste with salt.

PREPARE THE MARINATED APPLES

In a small bowl, combine the apples and lime juice and
let marinate for 10 minutes. Drain, cover, and refrigerate.

>>

MAKE THE PULMAY

Set up a large bowl of ice and water. Bring a medium pot of
water to a boil over medium heat. Add the mussels, reduce
the heat to low, cover, and cook for 2 minutes. Scoop out the
mussels (discard any unopened shells) and transfer to the ice
bath to cool for 3 minutes. Pull the meat from the shells and
set aside. Repeat the cooking and chilling for the clams.
   Light the wood. When it begins to smoke, place it in a large
pot over high heat. Suspend a sieve in the pot over the smold-
ering wood and add the onion, chilies, mussel meats, and
clam meats. Cover with foil and let smoke for 10 minutes.
   Transfer to a food processer and blend at maximum speed
for 8 minutes. Add the cilantro (coriander), lime juice, olive
oil, pisco, and 3 tablespoons water and process for 3 minutes.
Pass through a fine-mesh sieve and refrigerate.

TO SERVE

Brush a grill (griddle) pan over low heat with the oil.
Place the 6 lemon verbena leaves on the hot pan and cook
for 1 minute on one side only. Set aside until ready to serve.
   Ladle the pulmay soup into each bowl and top with the
squid. Garnish with the marinated apples, lemon balm,
grilled lemon verbena, and fresh lemon verbena. Drizzle
with a few drops of the parsley and lemon verbena oil.

PARSLEY AND LEMON VERBENA OIL

Makes a generous ¾ cup (200 ml)

7 oz (200 g) parsley
generous ¾ cup (200 ml) canola (rapeseed) oil
2¾ cups (70 g) lemon verbena

Preheat the oven to 275°F (140°C/Gas Mark 1).
   Place the parsley on a baking sheet and brush with
1 tablespoon of the canola (rapeseed) oil. Let dry in the
oven for 6 minutes.
   Transfer the parsley to a food processor, add the remaining canola oil, and blend for 5 minutes. Add the lemon
verbena and blend for 5 minutes more. Pass through a sieve
lined with cheesecloth and refrigerate.

RECIPE NOTES: _____
_____
_____
_____
_____
_____
_____
_____
_____
_____
_____
_____
_____
_____

CHICKPEA RAGOUT
WITH POACHED EGG AND CORN CRISPS

Serves 8

CORN CRISPS
1¾ cups (300 g) precooked white cornmeal
2 tablespoons salt

BEEF STOCK
1 tablespoon extra-virgin olive oil
8¾ lb (4 kg) beef bones
2 medium white onions, roughly chopped
3 garlic cloves, roughly chopped
3½ oz (100 g) chives, roughly chopped
generous 2 cups (500 ml) red wine
4 tablespoons grated fresh horseradish
1 teaspoon grated fresh ginger
½ teaspoon freshly ground black pepper
Grated zest of 1 lime

CHICKPEA RAGOUT
⅓ cup (90 ml) extra-virgin olive oil
2 white onions, diced
3 garlic cloves, minced
5 carrots, diced
1 lb (500 kg) tomatoes, diced
½ teaspoon granulated sugar
2½ tablespoons balsamic vinegar
2¼ lb (1 kg) mixed meat (such as beef, pork, and chicken),
    cut into ¾-inch (2 cm) cubes
generous 1 cup (250 ml) red wine
½ tablespoon salt
½ teaspoon freshly ground black pepper
1 can (14 oz/400 g) chickpeas, drained and rinsed

SALAMI CRISPS
8 thin slices salami

POACHED EGGS
8 eggs

MAKE THE CORN CRISPS

Preheat the oven to 325°F (160°C/Gas Mark 3). Line a baking sheet with parchment paper.

In a medium bowl, mix together the cornmeal and salt. Add scant 1 cup (230 ml) water and mix with a spatula until a homogeneous dough forms.

Heat a medium nonstick pan over medium heat. Add a ladleful of the batter and spread thinly with a spatula. Cook until dried, about 3 minutes. Transfer to the prepared baking sheet and bake until crispy and golden brown, about 40 minutes.

>>

MAKE THE BEEF STOCK

In a large pot, heat the olive oil over high heat. Add the beef bones and cook until browned, about 35 minutes. Reduce the heat to medium and add the onions, garlic, and chives and cook until the onions are soft, about 5 minutes. Add the red wine and cook for 10 minutes to reduce slightly. Add the horseradish, ginger, black pepper, lime zest, and 3 quarts (3 liters) water and bring to a boil over medium heat. Reduce the heat to low and cook until reduced by half, about 4 hours. Remove from the heat and let cool for 15 minutes. Skim the fat from the top with a ladle, then strain through a fine-mesh sieve into a medium pot. Cook over medium heat until reduced by half, about 15 minutes. Set aside.

MAKE THE CHICKPEA RAGOUT

In a medium pot, heat 2 tablespoons of the olive oil over medium heat. Add the onions, garlic, and carrots and cook, stirring occasionally, until the onions are translucent, about 10 minutes. Add the tomatoes and simmer over low heat for 5 minutes. Add the sugar and cook until the tomatoes are very soft, about 12 minutes. Add the vinegar and cook until evaporated. Set aside.

In a large pot, heat the remaining 4 tablespoons olive oil over medium heat. Add the meat and cook until browned, about 10 minutes. Add the wine and cook until evaporated, about 6 minutes. Season with the salt and pepper. Add the beef stock, tomato mixture, and chickpeas. Cover and cook over medium heat for 5 hours. Remove from the heat, skim the fat from the top with a ladle, and let cool.

MAKE THE SALAMI CRISPS

Preheat the oven to 250°F (120°C/Gas Mark ½). Arrange the salami on a tray lined with parchment paper and bake until crispy, 2 hours.

MAKE THE POACHED EGGS

Bring a medium pot of lightly salted water to a boil over medium heat. Reduce the heat to a simmer over low heat and gently crack and slip each egg into the water one at a time and cook until the egg white is opaque but soft, about 6 minutes. Carefully remove with a slotted spoon and transfer to a warm water bath until ready to serve.

TO SERVE

Place a ladleful of the chickpea ragout in each bowl and top with a poached egg. Garnish with the salami crisps and the corn crisps.

RECIPE NOTES: _____
_____
_____
_____
_____
_____

THREE RICE PUDDINGS WITH MUSHROOM ICE CREAM

Serves 8

MUSHROOM ICE CREAM
  2½ oz (75 g) matsutake mushrooms (pine mushrooms)
  3 cups plus 3 tablespoons (750 ml) milk
  scant 1 cup (225 ml) heavy (whipping) cream
  ½ cup plus 1½ tablespoons (75 g) whole-milk powder
  ⅓ cup (75 g) granulated sugar
  2 gelatin sheets

GOAT MILK RICE PUDDING
  generous 2 cups (500 ml) goat milk
  ⅓ cup (125 g) rice
  2 teaspoons grated lime zest
  ⅓ cup (75 g) granulated sugar
  8 rose petals

SMOKED RICE PUDDING
  scant ¾ cup (125 g) wild rice
  ½ cinnamon stick
  3⅓ cups (800 ml) milk
  6 tablespoons packed light brown sugar

HORSERADISH RICE PUDDING
  generous 2 cups (500 ml) milk
  ½ cup (125 g) rice
  6 tablespoons packed light brown sugar
  1 tablespoon finely grated fresh horseradish

MAKE THE MUSHROOM ICE CREAM

Preheat the oven to 200°F (100°C) or as low as your oven can go. Line a baking sheet with parchment paper.

Arrange the mushrooms on the lined baking sheet and bake until dehydrated, about 1 hour. Remove from the baking sheet and let cool completely. Crush and pass through a sieve to obtain a fine powder.

In a medium pot, warm the milk and cream over medium heat for 6 minutes. Add the mushroom powder and mix well. Bring the temperature of the milk mixture to 176°F (80°C) and simmer for 8 minutes. Strain through a fine-mesh sieve into a bowl and set into a large bowl of ice and water. Let cool until the mixture reaches 122°F (50°C). Stir in the milk powder and sugar.

While the milk mixture is cooling, soften the gelatin in cold water until hydrated, about 10 minutes. Drain and set aside.

Return the milk mixture to the pot and heat to 185°F (85°C), stirring constantly. When the mixture reaches 185°F (85°C), add the softened gelatin and stir until melted. Let cool, then cover and refrigerate for 1 hour to chill. Transfer to an ice-cream machine and process according to the manufacturer's instructions. (If you don't have an ice-cream machine, freeze the mixture until hard enough to scoop.)

>>

MAKE THE GOAT MILK RICE PUDDING

In a medium pot, combine the goat milk, rice, lime zest, and sugar and cook over medium heat until the rice is soft, about 20 minutes. Remove from the heat and add the rose petals. Let cool, then cover and refrigerate to chill.

MAKE THE SMOKED MILK RICE PUDDING

Arrange the wild rice on a perforated baking sheet and cover with foil. Place the cinnamon in a deep roasting pan and light it on fire. When the cinnamon begins to smoke, place the baking sheet with the wild rice on top, and smoke for 5 minutes. Remove the baking sheet from the roasting pan and set aside.

In a medium pot, combine the milk, smoked wild rice, and brown sugar and cook over medium heat, stirring constantly, until the rice is soft, about 30 minutes. Let cool, then cover and refrigerate to chill.

MAKE THE HORSERADISH RICE PUDDING

In a medium pot, combine the milk, rice, and brown sugar and cook over medium heat until the rice is soft, about 20 minutes. Let cool, then cover and refrigerate to chill. Stir in the horseradish just before serving.

TO SERVE

Place a spoonful of each rice pudding in each bowl and top with a scoop of the mushroom ice cream.

RECIPE NOTES: _____
_____
_____
_____
_____
_____
_____
_____
_____
_____
_____
_____
_____
_____
_____
_____
_____
_____
_____
_____
_____
_____
_____

CARAMELIZED BANANAS WITH CRESCENZA CHEESE

Serves 8

3½ tablespoons (50g) butter
8 baby bananas, peeled but whole (see Note)
½ cup plus 1½ tablespoons (120 g) granulated sugar
scant ½ cup (100 ml) balsamic vinegar
7½ oz (210 g) crescenza cheese or other soft, mild cheese
Flower petals (such as white pansy petals, chamomile
	petals, or other edible flower)
Lemon verbena leaves

In a medium saucepan, heat the butter over low heat until melted. Remove from the heat and let sit for 2 minutes. Scrape the foam and pass the melted butter through a fine-mesh sieve.

In a large frying pan, heat the clarified butter over medium heat. Add the bananas and cook until soft and caramelized, about 7 minutes. Transfer to a tray lined with paper towels and set aside.

In a medium pot, heat the sugar and vinegar over medium heat and cook until reduced by half, about 7 minutes. Let cool at room temperature.

To serve, place a spoonful of crescenza cheese in each bowl. Top with a banana and drizzle with balsamic reduction. Garnish with the white pansy petals and verbena leaves.

Note: Save the peels to make Banana Peel Chutney (page 158).

📷 P. 197

RECIPE NOTES: _____

Cristina Bowerman

When I walked into the Refettorio, I saw a pink halo and knew it couldn't be anyone but Cristina Bowerman. Cristina followed an unconventional path to arrive at her culinary destination. After law school in 1992, she left her hometown in Puglia to continue her studies in San Francisco. There she shifted gears from law to graphic design. It was only after moving to Austin, Texas, that she found her calling in the culinary arts. In 2004, she returned to Italy to run Glass Hostaria in Rome, which has become an acclaimed Michelin-starred restaurant.

She admitted from the start that she was a daughter of the postwar generation where there was economic security and with that, a culture of waste. "Salvaging food is not a concept that I grew up with," she confessed, "even if my family always tried to make me aware of the value of things." She then went on to talk about her experience living in the United States where she learned more about the philosophy of "second hand." She said, "Second hand is a common practice and reaches every aspect of lifestyle, from clothes to furniture." Her reflection brought me back to the hours spent rummaging through plastic crates in search of used vinyl records for my collection, or a perfectly worn-in pair of cowboy boots. I too had grown up with plenty and yet here I was working to reclaim food rather than let it go to waste. And I realized how much this project was changing me day after day, and making me realize that something recovered is something gained, whether it be a handknit sweater bought at a garage sale or a crate of brown bananas. The secret was seeing the potential.

The food delivery had not been particularly generous that morning. There was salt cod, cherry tomatoes, carrots, couscous, millet, polenta, and lots of eggs. After Cristina's initial shock, she shifted gears and got herself into a pragmatic state of mind. She laid everything out on the table and in an instant she knew what she was going to cook. She began transforming the ingredients one by one into better versions of themselves. First, she marinated the fish in a mixture of chopped cucumber, kefir, and lime juice to make a quick ceviche-tzatziki sauce. She served the fish with couscous seasoned with lime juice and salt. Second, she sliced tomatoes and placed them on a baking sheet to confit in the oven. Then she chopped a mound of carrots and sautéed them with onions and deglazed them with orange juice. To that, she added a vegetable broth and blended it all into a puree. Next she was preparing the batter for a sweet cornbread that she would make for dessert. There was so much cooking happening all at once that in no time the kitchen filled up with the smells of deliciousness.

Cristina knew how to get the most out of humble and simple ingredients, and talked about how she reduces food waste at Glass Hostaria. For instance, she uses the outer leaves of vegetables—the ones that are usually discarded because they are tough—and dries them into intense edible powders that are great flavors enhancers. I liked the idea that something of apparently no use could become a secret weapon in the kitchen, a super power that could magically transform a dull dish into a vibrant one.

As Cristina topped each bowl of carrot puree with a poached egg, she looked up at me and confessed, "You know how in our work we get used to having everything at our disposal? Now I am starting to think that such abundance of possibilities and ingredients can actually block our creative process. By having too much, we risk forgetting one of the most important elements: simplicity."

She returned to handling the delicate poached eggs and placing the puffed millet on the side of the bowl. It was one of the nicest looking dishes I had seen at the Refettorio and it was made with only three ingredients—and humble ones at that. Cristina was talking about simplicity, but I was witnessing a complete transformation through creativity and imagination. She had never made this recipe before and would probably never make it again, and yet she was laboring over it as if her life depended on it. I was already imagining what it would look like when the poached egg broke and flowed into the carrot puree—and I couldn't wait to try it.

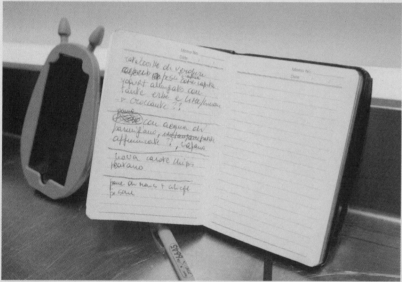

CARROT PUREE, POACHED EGG, AND PUFFED MILLET

Serves 4

CARROT PUREE
1 tablespoon extra-virgin olive oil
1 white onion, roughly chopped
8 carrots, roughly chopped
Juice of 2 oranges
2½ cups (600 ml) vegetable stock
¼ teaspoon ground cinnamon
¼ teaspoon ground cumin
1 teaspoon apple cider vinegar

POACHED EGG
4 eggs
1 teaspoon apple cider vinegar

PUFFED MILLET
1⅔ cups (400 ml) sunflower oil
3 tablespoons millet
Salt

FOR SERVING
4 geranium leaves

MAKE THE CARROT PUREE

In a medium saucepan, heat the olive oil over medium heat. Add the onion and sauté until translucent, 6 minutes. Add the carrots and cook for 6 minutes. Add the orange juice and cook to reduce by half, about 7 minutes. Add the stock and cook until the carrots are soft, about 15 minutes. Add the cinnamon and cumin. Transfer to a blender, add the vinegar, and blend until smooth. Set aside.

MAKE THE POACHED EGGS

Crack the eggs into individual ramekins or cups.
In a medium pot, bring a generous 2 cups (500 ml) water to 158°F (70°C) over medium heat. Add the vinegar and whisk the water to create a gentle whirlpool. Slowly tip the eggs into the water, one at a time, adding the whites first. Cook for 3 minutes. Remove with a slotted spoon, cutting off any wispy edges, and transfer to a bowl of warm water.

MAKE THE PUFFED MILLET

In a medium pan, heat the sunflower oil to 350°F (175°C). Slowly add the millet and fry for a few seconds until it pops. Transfer to paper towels to drain. Season to taste with salt.

TO SERVE

Place a spoonful of the carrot puree in each plate and top with a poached egg. Sprinkle with the puffed millet and garnish with a geranium leaf.

P. 202

WHITE FISH CEVICHE WITH LEMON-PEPPER COUSCOUS

Serves 4

CONFIT TOMATOES
2 tomatoes, chopped
4 teaspoons extra-virgin olive oil
Grated zest of 1 orange
Grated zest of 1 lemon
2 sprigs thyme
1 teaspoon salt
5 tablespoons powdered (icing) sugar

LEMON-PEPPER COUSCOUS
generous ¾ cup (200 ml) vegetable stock
¼ teaspoon ground Sichuan pepper
½ cup (100 g) couscous
Juice of 3 lemons

WHITE FISH CEVICHE
2 garlic cloves, thinly sliced
14 oz (400 g) white fish (such as sea bass), cut like sashimi
scant ½ cup (100 ml) labne or plain Greek yogurt
2 cucumbers, seeded and thinly sliced
Juice of 6 limes

FOR SERVING
Lettuce leaves

MAKE THE CONFIT TOMATOES

Preheat the oven to 200°F (100°C) or as low as your oven can go. Line a baking sheet with parchment paper.
In a medium bowl, combine the tomatoes, olive oil, orange zest, lemon zest, thyme, salt, and sugar. Transfer to the prepared baking sheet and bake until dried but still slightly juicy, about 6 hours.

MAKE THE LEMON-PEPPER COUSCOUS

In a medium pot, combine the stock and pepper and simmer over medium heat for 15 minutes. Strain through a fine-mesh sieve into a medium bowl. Add the couscous and let rest until the liquid is absorbed, about 20 minutes. Add the lemon juice and fluff with a fork.

MAKE THE WHITE FISH CEVICHE

Spread the garlic evenly over the surface of a medium bowl. Add the fish, labne, cucumbers, and lime juice and let marinate for 15 minutes.

TO SERVE

Place a spoonful of the couscous on each plate and top with the confit tomatoes and the white fish ceviche. Garnish with the lettuce leaves.

P. 204

CORNBREAD WITH VANILLA ICE CREAM

Serves 6

CORNBREAD
7½ tablespoons (140 g) butter
scant ¾ cup (165 ml) milk
½ teaspoon salt
2 eggs
1¼ cups (165 g) yellow cornmeal, fine or medium-coarse grind
½ cup (50 g) all-purpose (plain) flour
1½ teaspoons baking powder

VANILLA ICE CREAM
3 gelatin sheets
1⅔ cups (400 ml) heavy (whipping) cream
1 vanilla bean, split lengthwise
scant ½ cup (100 ml) milk
3 generous tablespoons granulated sugar

FRUIT SALAD
1 cup (200 g) granulated sugar
4 peaches, peeled and diced
1 small pineapple, peeled and diced
4 mandarins, peeled and diced

MAKE THE CORNBREAD

Preheat the oven to 350 (180°C/Gas Mark 3 to 4). Butter a deep 8-inch (20 cm) square cake pan.

In a medium pot, combine the milk, butter, and salt and cook over low heat until the butter is melted. Transfer to a medium bowl and let cool to room temperature. Whisk in the eggs.

In another medium bowl, whisk together the cornmeal, flour, and baking powder until well combined. Add to the milk/egg mixture and stir until smooth. Transfer to the prepared cake pan and bake until a wooden pick inserted in the center comes out dry, about 25 minutes. Let cool in the pan.

MAKE THE VANILLA ICE CREAM

In a small bowl, soak the gelatin in cold water until soft, about 10 minutes. Drain and set aside.

Place the cream in a medium pot and scrape in the vanilla seeds. Bring to a boil over medium heat, then add the milk, sugar, and softened gelatin and simmer for 6 minutes. Let cool. Transfer to an ice-cream machine and process according to the manufacturer's instructions. (If you don't have an ice-cream machine, freeze the mixture until hard enough to scoop).

>>

PREPARE THE FRUIT SALAD

In a medium pot, combine the sugar and ¾ cup (180 ml) plus 2 tablespoons water and cook over medium heat for 1 minute. Let the simple syrup cool.

In a medium bowl, combine the peaches, pineapple, mandarins, and simple syrup. Cover and refrigerate to chill.

TO SERVE

Place a slice of the cornbread on each plate and top with a scoop of the vanilla ice cream. Garnish with the fruit salad.

Note: You can use any fruits you have on hand for the fruit.

RECIPE NOTES: _____
_____
_____
_____
_____
_____
_____
_____
_____
_____
_____
_____
_____
_____
_____
_____
_____
_____
_____
_____
_____
_____
_____
_____
_____
_____
_____
_____
_____
_____
_____
_____
_____
_____

Cristina Bowerman

Alessandro Negrini & Fabio Pisani

It is unusual for two chefs to share a kitchen equally, but that is the case with Alessandro Negrini and Fabio Pisani. Alessandro comes from Valtellina, in Northern Italy. Fabio is from Puglia at the southern tip of the boot. Together, they express the best of Northern and Southern Italy in the shared kitchen of a historical restaurant called Il Luogo di Aimo e Nadia in Milan. Since opening in 1962, Il Luogo has always been ingredient driven and today works with eighty-two different providers from farmers to fishermen to butchers. Alessandro and Fabio actually met at Dal Pescatore, a Michelin three-star restaurant in the Mantovan countryside, in 2003. They went their separate ways, but later found themselves working side by side at Il Luogo di Aimo e Nadia. When Aimo Morini turned eighty, he and his daughter Stefania offered the two chefs a partnership in the restaurant.

It only made sense for them to cook together at the Refettorio. Fabio said that the first moment was difficult because they are so accustomed to having only the best ingredients: "It was a challenge for me. I arrived empty handed and was faced with a totally new cupboard of ingredients compared to what we have at the restaurant. I think we are all more creative when faced with difficulties than when we are at ease. Missing things in the kitchen is actually a good stimulation for creating something new."

As Alessandro opened cans of borlotti beans and cleaned the Parmigiano rinds, he said with pride, "Salvaging food is really part of the history of Italian cuisine, and many cuisines around the world. Think about dishes like ribollita, or panzanella, or the preserves that are in every cupboard. Nothing was ever thrown away in the kitchens of our grandmothers. Today we are trying to return to this ethos."

They made a humble and delicious pasta and bean soup with rosemary, Parmigiano rinds and *pasta mista*. *Pasta mista* is an Italian tradition in which a variety of pasta shapes such as curved macaroni, fusilli, farfalle, and even broken linguini come together in one dish. Italians are very precise about preparing the exact amount of pasta— never too much, never too little—which can often lead to several bags of pasta in the cupboard, each with only enough for one serving. *Pasta mista* is a way of making due with what you have. This pasta and beans soup is a beautiful expression of the Italian pantry. When you think there is nothing there, you look harder. The more you look, the more you find. A can of beans, a few tomatoes, some anchovies, a random combination of pasta shapes, and all of a sudden there is an improvised meal. To me that is what emotional cooking is all about.

The real surprise came with dessert— a surprise not only for the guests but for the chefs as well. Alessandro told me the story: "The ice cream we made with Actimel—a kind of drinkable yogurt— in a little bottle. We found lots of them in the refrigerator and they needed to be used that same day. This forced us to make space for creativity, while putting aside our egos because the most important thing was giving the guests something delicious to eat."

The more they talked, the more I saw what a great team they make. Chefs who work with only the finest products and the most dedicated artisans were not only making do but also having fun with little more than their imagination. Fabio explained how they work hard at the restaurant not to throw anything away. "Recently we have been cleaning and blanching the artichoke stems and dipping them in chocolate for a total transformation." Then Alessandro added, "And what about the 'Couscous of Trash Spaghetti' recipe?" I jumped in, "Did you say trash spaghetti?" He explained, "Basically we used the trimmings from the vegetables we cook for our classic Etruscan soup and we juiced them. Then we finely ground up spaghetti and cooked it like couscous. And we added deep-fried onion roots and potato skins for garnish." They showed me the video of the recipe on YouTube and I scolded them, "Guys, you really should have made trash spaghetti here today!"

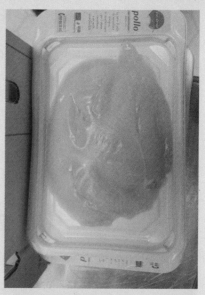

August 24

Serves 6

2 tablespoons extra-virgin olive oil, plus more for drizzling
1 garlic clove, chopped
1 sprig rosemary
1¾ cups (300 g) mixed canned legumes (such as borlotti
    beans, lentils, and chickpeas), drained and rinsed
scant ½ cup (100 ml) vegetable stock
Salt and freshly ground black pepper
7 oz (200 g) Parmigiano-Reggiano cheese rinds, cut into
    small chunks
generous ¾ cup (200 ml) milk
10 oz (300 g) mixed short pasta (such as penne, macaroni,
    farfalle, dadini, sedanini, and even broken linguini)

In a medium saucepan, heat the 2 tablespoons olive oil over medium heat. Add the garlic and rosemary and cook until the garlic is golden brown, about 2 minutes. Add the beans and cook for 5 minutes. Add the vegetable stock and cook for 30 minutes. Remove from the heat and let cool. Discard the rosemary, transfer to a blender, and blend until smooth. Season to taste with salt and pepper. Set aside.

In a medium pot, combine the Parmigiano rinds, milk, and a generous ¾ cup (200 ml) water. Heat to 194°F (90°C) over medium heat and simmer for 1 hour. Remove the Parmigiano rinds and set aside.

Bring a large pot of lightly salted water to a boil over medium heat. Add the pasta and cook until al dente. Drain and transfer to a medium pan. Add a generous ¾ cup (200 ml) of the Parmigiano broth and cook until completely absorbed, about 12 minutes.

To serve, place 1 tablespoon of the Parmigiano rind chunks at the bottom of each plate and cover with the bean puree. Top with the pasta and drizzle with olive oil.

RECIPE NOTES:

Alessandro Negrini & Fabio Pisani

CARAMELIZED CHICKEN WITH BREAD PUREE

Serves 6

CONFIT TOMATOES

3 tomatoes, quartered
1 tablespoon extra-virgin olive oil
Leaves from 1 sprig thyme, finely chopped
Leaves from 1 sprig rosemary, finely chopped
1 teaspoon granulated sugar
1 teaspoon salt

BREAD PUREE

1 lb 2 oz (500 g) stale bread, torn into pieces
1⅔ cups (400 ml) vegetable stock
5 teaspoons (20 g) butter
2 teaspoons freshly ground black pepper
Salt

CARAMELIZED CHICKEN

8 dried prunes, pitted
1 tablespoon plus 4 teaspoons extra-virgin olive oil
6 boneless, skinless chicken breasts
2 teaspoons honey
3 teaspoons balsamic vinegar

MAKE THE CONFIT TOMATOES

Preheat the oven to 350°F (180°C/Gas Mark 4). Line a baking
sheet with parchment paper.
   Arrange the tomato quarters on the baking sheet and
sprinkle with the olive oil, thyme, rosemary, sugar, and salt.
Bake until almost dry, about 1 hour.

MAKE THE BREAD PUREE

In a food processor, blend the bread until finely chopped
   In a medium pot, bring the stock to a boil over medium
heat. Add the bread and whisk. Cook until thick, about
7 minutes. Stir in the butter and pepper. Season to taste
with salt. Set aside.

MAKE THE CARAMELIZED CHICKEN

Preheat the oven to 350°F (180°C/Gas Mark 4).
   In a blender, combine the prunes and 1 tablespoon water
and blend until smooth.
   In a medium frying pan, heat 1 tablespoon of the olive oil.
Add the chicken and cook for 2 minutes on each side. Spread
one side of the chicken with the prune paste and transfer to
the oven. Cook for 7 minutes. Let rest for 10 minutes before
slicing ⅓ inch (1 cm) thick.
   Meanwhile, in a small bowl, whisk together the honey,
vinegar, and remaining 4 teaspoons olive oil.

>>

TO SERVE

Place the chicken on each plate and dress with the honey-
vinegar sauce. Garnish with confit tomatoes and serve with
the bread puree on the side.

RECIPE NOTES: _____

_____

_____

_____

_____

_____

_____

_____

_____

_____

_____

_____

_____

_____

_____

_____

_____

_____

_____

_____

_____

_____

_____

_____

_____

_____

_____

_____

_____

_____

_____

_____

_____

CHOCOLATE AND PEAR CAKE
WITH YOGURT ICE CREAM AND POPCORN

Serves 6

CHOCOLATE AND PEAR CAKE

6 tablespoons (90 g) butter

1 cup (130 g) all-purpose (plain) flour

⅓ cup (80 g) unsweetened cocoa powder

¾ teaspoon baking soda (bicarbonate of soda)

⅛ teaspoon salt

4 oz (115 g) dark chocolate, chopped

1¾ cups (350 g) granulated sugar

2 eggs

½ cup (120 ml) milk

5 ripe pears, peeled, cored, and chopped into large chunks

YOGURT ICE CREAM

scant 3 cups (700 ml) probiotic yogurt drink
(such as DanActive or Actimel), chilled

CARAMELIZED POPCORN

1 tablespoon corn oil

scant ¼ cup (50 g) popcorn kernels

2 tablespoons plus 1 teaspoon granulated sugar

2 tablespoons plus 2 teaspoons heavy (whipping) cream

5¼ teaspoons (25 g) butter

Pinch of salt

MAKE THE CHOCOLATE AND PEAR CAKE

Preheat the oven to 350°F (180°C/Gas Mark 4). Butter a 9-inch (23 cm) square baking pan and dust with flour.

In a medium bowl, sift together the flour, cocoa powder, baking soda (bicarbonate of soda), and salt. Set aside.

In a heatproof bowl set over a pan of simmering water, melt 4 tablespoons (60 g) of the butter and the chocolate. Transfer to a large bowl and add ¾ cup (150 g) of the sugar. With an electric mixer, beat on medium-high until light in color, about 4 minutes. Add the eggs and continue beating until combined. Stir in half the flour mixture, then half the milk, alternating between the two until combined. Fold in three of the pears. Transfer to the prepared pan and bake until a wooden pick inserted in the center of the cake comes out clean, about 45 minutes. Let cool in the pan on a wire rack for 30 minutes.

Meanwhile, in a medium pan, heat the remaining 2 table-spoons (30 g) butter over medium heat. Add the remaining pears and 1 cup (250 g) sugar and cook until soft and syrupy, about 5 minutes. Set aside.

MAKE THE YOGURT ICE CREAM

Pour the yogurt drink in an ice-cream machine and process according to the manufacturer's instructions. (If you don't have an ice-cream machine, freeze the mixture until hard enough to scoop).

>>

MAKE THE POPCORN

In a medium pot, warm the corn oil over medium heat. Add the popcorn kernels and quickly cover with a lid. Once the popcorn begins to pop, vigorously shake the pot. Once the popping begins to subside, remove from the heat and continue shaking for about 1 minute. Remove the lid and let cool. Discard any unpopped kernels. Spread out on a baking sheet lined with parchment paper.

In a small saucepan, heat the sugar over medium heat until melted and golden brown, about 2 minutes. Add the cream, butter, and salt and stir until combined. Pour the caramel over the popcorn and let sit until hardened. Break into chunks.

TO SERVE

Place 1 tablespoon of the pears and syrup on each plate and top with a square of the chocolate and pear cake. Garnish with the caramelized popcorn and a scoop of the yogurt ice cream.

📷   P. 213

RECIPE NOTES: _____

_____
_____
_____
_____
_____
_____
_____
_____
_____
_____
_____
_____
_____
_____
_____
_____
_____
_____
_____
_____
_____
_____
_____
_____
_____
_____
_____
_____
_____

Alessandro Negrini & Fabio Pisani

Giuseppe Palmieri

Giuseppe Palmieri has been the manager, maître d', and sommelier of Osteria Francescana since 2000. Beppe, as he is affectionately called, was a skinny waiter from southern Italy with a lot of ambition. He had left his hometown of Matera in May 1995 to work at the Grand Hotel Diplomat in Cattolica on the Adriatic Riviera for a long summer season. He then worked for several years at Michelin restaurants in Italy before departing for London. He returned to Italy six months later with a job at the Locanda Solarola in Bologna. That is where Lara and I met him. At 9:45 a.m. on September 12, 2000, he started working at Osteria Francescana and has never left.

Osteria Francescana was at a crossroads when we met Beppe: Either we were going to invest in a dining room or remain an osteria forever. What I saw in Beppe was that he was even more determined than me. He was, and is, stubborn, focused, and unforgiving. Hospitality is not improvisation, nor can a dining room come together overnight. It takes experience, daily practice, and rigorous routine.

Several years ago he began a crusade to bring back the art of hospitality called Noi di Sala ("we, front of house"). Beppe was one of the first people to talk about the early warning signs of a crisis in the restaurant business. "In the near future we will see an army of chefs with no one to serve." Those of us who run restaurants know that 51 percent of the job is the front of house. Without competent and dedicated professionals serving, chefs can hang up their aprons.

Actually, a detail that differentiates the Refettorio from many other soup kitchens is that there is no self-service counter. We styled the soup kitchen like a restaurant, not a cafeteria. When we explained the idea to Caritas—which runs many soup kitchens in Italy and would be taking care of the daily operations at the Refettorio in Milan—they said it was impossible. They did not believe we could find enough volunteers to serve guests at the table and they insisted on building a self-service

counter anyway. It has never been used, at least not yet. Volunteers put on their aprons at 6 p.m., set the tables, explain the menu, serve the guests, and clear the tables. At the end of the evening they are invited to sit down to a family-style meal.

Why was table service so important to us? We imagined it would work the way the front of house works in a restaurant, acting as the bridge between the kitchen and the diners. We felt that this was important for involving the community in the project. The volunteers who served nightly made the biggest difference of all, maybe more than the chefs, because they were the real hosts, welcoming our guests by name.

That morning Beppe drove to Milan with his wife, Gabriela. I brought along Taka, Giulio, and Daniele from Osteria Francescana. Preparing a meal for one hundred guests is not a job for one. I had warned Beppe that ingredients were great some days, less so others. He said, "Massimo, I am from Matera where people have faced poverty and bare pantries for ages. I know how to make pasta with olive oil and nothing else and still make it taste good." Actually, I wasn't worried at all, because I know that deep down Beppe's dream is to be a chef. He is obsessed with cooking. We have a ritual at Osteria Francescana where every New Year's Eve the staff writes anonymous wishes on paper and we read them out loud. I pulled out one a couple of years ago: "When I grow up, I want to be a chef." I knew it could have only been written by Beppe.

When we arrived there were lots of cherry tomatoes, bread, and bananas. Beppe decided to make a panzanella, a classic Italian dish but with many regional variations. I told Beppe I didn't grow up eating panzanella even if it is a classic. Beppe laughed and told me he didn't grow up eating it either. "Panzanella," he said, "was from my parents' generation more than mine. They were much poorer and grew up eating old bread with whatever there was to dress it up a bit. A meal out of almost nothing." The panzanella Beppe made was a far cry from almost nothing. It was made with ripe cherry

tomatoes, capers, onions, and basil. It was fragrant and delicious.

The main course was pasta, which is Beppe's specialty. He has dedicated years to getting it right and experiments every weekend. Often he will call me on Sunday to ask me a question or, more often, to brag about what a great pasta he just made. At the Refettorio, instead of preparing an elaborate dish, he prepared *spaghetti all'aglio, olio e pepperoncino*. The classic combination of garlic, olive oil, and chili pepper is a poor man's feast because it can bring flavor to even the bleakest table. Some recipes add parsley to dress it up a bit, but Beppe chose to add a very personal combination of southern Italian flair to make it sing. Actually, his recipe reveals some of the coveted secrets he has learned over the years. First, he flavors the oil with crushed garlic, not chopped, and a whole pepper, both of which are removed from the oil before dressing the spaghetti. Second, he garnishes the pasta with an abundant amount of toasted garlic breadcrumbs. This is a southern Italian replacement for grated Parmigiano cheese, a northern Italian luxury. He knew this dish would resonate with the guests, and everyone asked for a second helping.

For dessert, Taka prepared a batch of his extraordinary banana ice cream, which had become a symbol of the Refettorio that summer. He had made the recipe back in June on one of his first visits to the Refettorio and shared the recipe with everyone. Since there was never a shortage of overripe bananas—or neighborhood kids who happily accepted ice cream—a fresh batch was prepared nearly every day.

Beppe added a treat from Modena to make this dessert unique. He asked the Gollini pastry shop in the nearby town of Vignola if they would donate a few boxes of their speciality chocolate cake called Torta Barozzi. Happily, they did. He served the banana gelato and added crushed Torta Barozzi, like a crumble, on top. The food was honest, tasty, and filling. The service was excellent, but it was the chef, Beppe, who had made the difference that day.

PANZANELLA

Serves 6

½ red onion, thinly sliced
Salt
8 plum tomatoes or other tomato of similar size, sliced
5 cherry tomatoes, sliced
7 oz (200 g) stale bread, torn into chunks
4 tablespoons white wine vinegar
1 yellow bell pepper, chopped
1 tablespoon capers
1 small garlic clove, minced
⅓ cup (90 ml) extra-virgin olive oil
15 basil leaves

Put the onion slices in a bowl of cold water with a pinch of salt and leave to soak for 1 hour.

Place the tomatoes in a colander set over a bowl. Sprinkle with ½ teaspoon salt and let drain.

Place the bread in a large bowl and moisten with the vinegar. Drain the onion and add to the bowl, along with the bell pepper and capers. Gently press the tomatoes with your hands to squeeze the juice into a small bowl. Reserve the juice and transfer the tomatoes to the bowl with the bread.

Add the garlic to the tomato juice, then whisk in the olive oil. Season to taste. Pour the dressing over the salad and toss thoroughly. Roughly tear half of the basil leaves and sprinkle on top. Let sit for 30 minutes to 1 hour.

Serve in bowls and garnish with the remaining basil leaves.

📷   P. 219

RECIPE NOTES: _____
_____
_____
_____
_____
_____
_____
_____
_____
_____
_____
_____
_____
_____
_____
_____
_____
_____
_____
_____
_____
_____
_____
_____

SPAGHETTI WITH GARLIC, OLIVE OIL, AND CHILI PEPPER

Serves 6

TOASTED BREADCRUMBS
2 tablespoons extra-virgin olive oil
2 garlic cloves, crushed
7 oz (200 g) stale bread, coarsely crumbled (about 2 cups)

PASTA
⅓ cup (90 ml) extra-virgin olive oil
3 garlic cloves, crushed
1 small fresh red chili
1½ lb (700 g) spaghetti
Salt

MAKE THE TOASTED BREADCRUMBS

In a medium pan, warm the olive oil and garlic over low heat for 1 minute. Add the breadcrumbs and cook until crunchy and golden, about 2 minutes. Remove the garlic and set aside.

PREPARE THE PASTA

Bring a large pot of lightly salted water to a boil over medium heat.

Meanwhile, in a small saucepan, combine the olive oil, garlic, and chili and heat over medium heat. Warm until the oil begins to sizzle and the garlic begins to turn golden brown, about 2 minutes. Remove from the heat and let sit. Remove the garlic and chili before tossing with the pasta.

Add the pasta to the boiling water and cook until al dente. Reserving some of the cooking liquid, drain the pasta well, and return to the cooking pot. Add the flavored oil and 2 tablespoons of the reserved cooking liquid and toss to coat. Garnish with the toasted breadcrumbs and serve immediately.

RECIPE NOTES: _____
_____
_____
_____
_____
_____
_____
_____
_____
_____
_____
_____
_____
_____
_____
_____
_____
_____
_____
_____
_____
_____

BANANA ICE CREAM WITH BAROZZI CAKE

Serves 6

BANANA ICE CREAM

2 cups (500 ml) milk
¾ cup (150 g) granulated sugar
Pinch of salt
2 eggs
½ cup (125 ml) evaporated milk
generous 1 cup (250 ml) heavy (whipping) cream
2 to 3 medium overripe bananas (about 7 oz/200 g), peeled (see Note)
1 teaspoon fresh lemon juice

BAROZZI CAKE

1 cup (90 g) sliced (flaked) almonds
7 tablespoons (100 g) butter
9 oz (255 g) dark chocolate, finely chopped
4 eggs, separated
1 cup (200 g) granulated sugar
2 tablespoons rum, orange liqueur, or balsamic vinegar
¼ cup (60 ml) brewed coffee
2 tablespoons powdered (icing) sugar

MAKE THE BANANA ICE CREAM

In a large saucepan, heat the milk to 167°F (75°C) over low heat. Add the sugar and salt and stir until dissolved.

In a medium bowl, lightly beat the eggs. Whisk a small amount of the hot milk into the eggs. Transfer the warmed eggs to the saucepan, whisking constantly. Cook over low heat, stirring occasionally until the mixture reaches 149°F (65°C) and coats the back of a metal spoon. Remove from the heat and set in a large bowl of ice and water to cool quickly, stirring for 2 minutes. Stir in the evaporated milk and cream and mix. Line the surface of the custard with plastic wrap (clingfilm) and refrigerate until cold, about 2 hours.

Meanwhile, mash the bananas with the lemon juice.

Remove the custard from the refrigerator and stir in the bananas. Transfer to an ice-cream machine and process according to the manufacturer's instructions. (If you don't have an ice-cream machine, freeze the mixture until hard enough to scoop.)

>>

MAKE THE BAROZZI CAKE

Preheat the oven to 350°F (180°C/Gas Mark 4). Line a baking sheet with parchment paper and butter an 8-inch (20 cm) round cake pan.

Arrange the almonds on the lined baking sheet and toast in the oven until golden brown, about 5 minutes. Reduce the oven temperature to 325°F (175°C/Gas Mark 3).

In a food processor, grind the almonds to a fine powder. Set aside.

In a heatproof bowl set over a pan of simmering water, melt the butter and chocolate. Set aside.

In a medium bowl, with an electric mixer, beat the egg yolks and granulated sugar until thick and light yellow, 4 to 5 minutes. Add the ground almonds, melted chocolate mixture, rum, and coffee and stir to combine. Set aside.

In a medium bowl, with an electric mixer, beat the egg whites until soft peaks form.

Fold the egg whites into the batter. Transfer to the prepared pan and bake until a wooden pick inserted in the center comes out clean, 35 to 40 minutes. Let cool completely on a wire rack, then carefully remove from the pan. Dust with the powdered (icing) sugar.

TO SERVE

Serve a big scoop of banana ice cream with the chopped Barozzi cake.

Note: Save the peels to make Banana Peel Chutney (page 158).

P. 221

RECIPE NOTES: _____

_____
_____
_____
_____
_____
_____
_____
_____
_____
_____
_____
_____
_____
_____
_____
_____
_____
_____
_____
_____
_____

Giuseppe Palmieri

Andreas Caminada

An old man knocked on the door of the Refettorio with a huge zucchini (courgette) wrapped around his neck. He introduced himself as Gino. He occasionally offered vegetables and aromatic herbs to the chefs from his garden behind the train tracks. Many chefs were looking for fresh herbs and most of the ones that arrived in the truck were wilted and brown. He gave Cristina his cell phone number and told her to call him. He said he would deliver any time of the day or night. This was good timing because Andreas Caminada was arriving the next day from Switzerland.

Andreas cooks in a castle but he doesn't come from royalty. Andreas grew up twenty minutes from his restaurant Schloss Schauenstein. While working as a young chef in Vancouver, Canada, he decided that he would return to Switzerland someday and open a restaurant of his own. When he found the property in Schauenstein, he knew it was the right place. He started in 2003 with four employees and occupied only a few rooms of the castle in the sunny Graubünden valley. Today Schloss Schauenstein has three Michelin stars in what Andreas calls "the smallest town in the world."

Andreas arrived early. Tied to the door of the kitchen, waiting for him, was a plastic bag with flowering rosemary, fresh mint, and thyme. It was a gift from Gino and a good omen because the truck was more bountiful than ever before: summer tomatoes, ricotta, whole chickens, and packages of ground meat. Andreas told me later that he was nervous about the challenge of improvising with unknown quantities and quality of ingredients. As a back up, he brought Swiss chocolate and some pastries from the restaurant as well as a few staff members to guarantee the guests would have a great meal. The menu was extensive with two bread recipes, a complex chilled tomato soup with ricotta, a main course with succulent chicken and vegetables, and two desserts. Birgit, the pastry chef, made the chocolate dessert, Patrick was in charge of freshly baked breads, and

a young woman named Zineb Hattab took care of the garnishes.

Zineb knew her way around the Refettorio kitchen. She had begun cooking professionally in Andreas's kitchen after a radical career shift from engineer to cook, and then interned at Osteria Francescana in 2014 for six months. She witnessed firsthand the beginnings of the Refettorio project, and through her close relationship with Cristina arranged to join us periodically at the Refettorio. Her language skills—Arabic, English, German, and Spanish—as well as her abilities in the kitchen served as a great support to many chefs.

Andreas is very Swiss. He is good looking, energetic, and precise. He is also full of surprises. I'll never forget the silly face he made coming out of the truck with a crate full of packaged pizza dough in his arms. He looked at the expiration date and said, "September 1 is today!" Patrick, who was making dough for freshly baked rolls with Alberto, the volunteer charged with baking bread, looked over at him in dismay. It was clear that Andreas wanted to take on the challenge of working with this store-bought, packaged, nearly expired pizza dough. He rolled it out very, very thin, did not let it rise, brushed it with olive oil, and dusted it with salt. He called them "pizza chips" even if they did not look or taste like pizza.

As he was planning the menu, he decided to serve the pizza chips as a starter with three vegetable dips: curry, herb, and red pepper. Though making dips was a great way to clean out the refrigerator (which was thrifty and also thoughtful), Andreas was thinking more about creating a social moment for the guests. He was the first chef who had considered serving a communal plate for everyone at the table to share. He searched for serving bowls for the dips and found nothing except for aluminium cups typically used for baking flan. He arranged the chips on a plate, put the dips around them, and took a hard look. He wasn't happy with what he saw.

This was a curious moment. I was about to see a side of Andreas that I didn't

know. I watched him leave the kitchen and pace the courtyard in front of the church. He came back inside and asked me, "Massimo, what do you think if I cut off some olive branches from the tree outside?" I said, "Are you crazy?"

Back in Switzerland he is accustomed to walking out into his garden and cutting herbs and flowers around the grounds of the castle. We were in the heart of Milan, surrounded by concrete and train tracks. The only green thing in the plaza was the olive tree. He ran outside and went looking for Don Giuliano. Andreas found him playing soccer with some kids in the inner courtyard. He explained to Don Giuliano that he wanted this moment to be special and decorative. He was looking for a few olive branches to decorate the plate; otherwise it just wasn't going to be right.

Five minutes later he was beneath the olive tree carefully cutting off some small branches. He arranged them on the plate with the pizza chips and the dips. It was a small gesture, a detail, but the detail that transformed the table into a celebration. I later watched the guests share the chips and complimented Andreas for the idea. He said, "No waste means we have to be creative. That is what I teach my chefs: Make the best of it and make a very good meal to share."

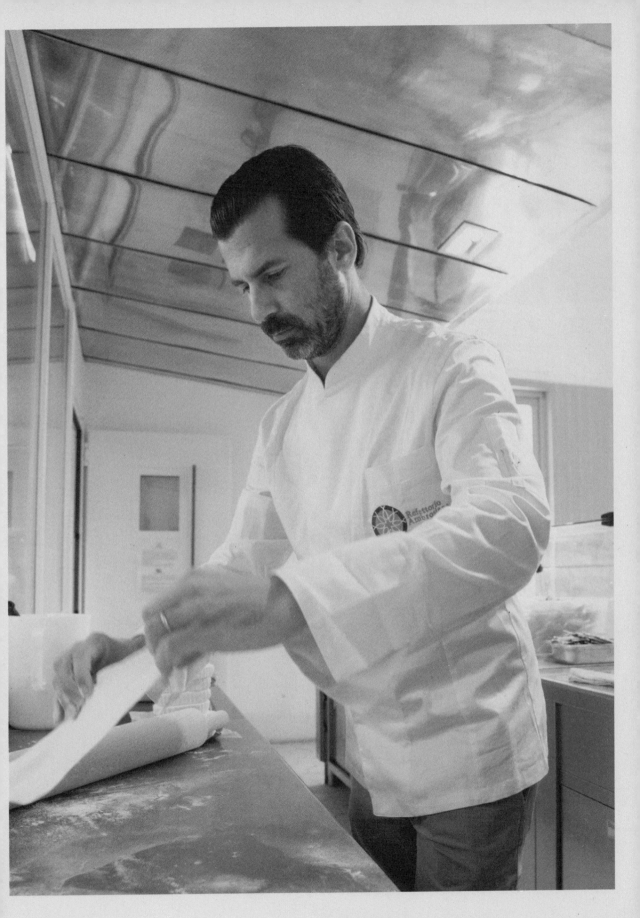

Andreas Caminada

September 1

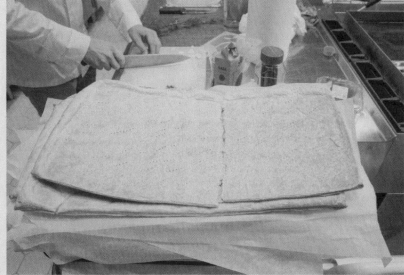

Serves 8

CURRY DIP

5 oz (150 g) quark cheese or cream cheese
1 teaspoon paprika
1 teaspoon curry powder
1 cup (250 ml) sunflower oil
Salt

HERB DIP

1¾ oz (50 g) dill, finely chopped
1¾ oz (50 g) tarragon, finely chopped
1¾ oz (50 g) parsley, finely chopped
1 lb 2 oz (500 g) ricotta cheese or other fresh cheese
Salt and freshly ground black pepper

REP PEPPER DIP

4 red bell peppers
2 tablespoons extra-virgin olive oil
1 garlic clove, chopped
1 pepperoncino or other chili, seeded and finely sliced
1 teaspoon ground cumin
5 oz (150 g) quark cheese or cream cheese
Salt and freshly ground black pepper

PIZZA CHIPS

All-purpose (plain) flour, for sprinkling
10 oz (300 g) store-bought refrigerated pizza dough
3 tablespoons extra-virgin olive oil, for brushing
Coarse salt, for sprinkling

MAKE THE CURRY DIP

In a medium bowl, whisk together the cheese, paprika, and curry powder. Slowly add the oil, whisking constantly. Season to taste with salt.

MAKE THE HERB DIP

In a medium bowl, mix together the dill, tarragon, parsley, and fresh cheese. Season to taste with salt and pepper.

MAKE THE RED PEPPER DIP

Preheat the oven to 325°F (160°C/Gas Mark 3). Line a baking sheet with parchment paper.

Arrange the bell peppers on the baking sheet and bake until soft, about 35 minutes. When cool enough to handle, peel and seed the peppers. Transfer to a blender and set aside.

In a medium saucepan, heat the olive oil over high heat. Add the garlic and chili and cook until browned, about 10 minutes. Add to the blender along with the cumin and blend until smooth. Add the cheese and pulse to combine. Season to taste with salt and pepper. Cover and refrigerate.

>>

MAKE THE PIZZA CHIPS

Preheat the oven to 350°F (180°C/Gas Mark 4). Line a baking sheet with parchment paper.

Dust a clean surface with flour. Divide the dough into 4 portions and roll each one as thinly as possible, until almost transparent. Transfer the dough to the prepared baking sheet, brush with olive oil, and sprinkle with salt. Bake until golden and crispy, about 10 minutes. Remove and let cool. Break into smaller pieces.

TO SERVE

Serve the pizza chips with the curry, herb, and red pepper dips.

P. 227

RECIPE NOTES: _____

_____
_____
_____
_____
_____
_____
_____
_____
_____
_____
_____
_____
_____
_____
_____
_____
_____
_____
_____
_____
_____
_____
_____
_____
_____
_____
_____
_____
_____
_____
_____
_____
_____

Andreas Caminada

WHITE ROLLS

Makes 12 rolls

    2½ cups (325 g) all-purpose (plain) flour
    ½ tablespoon salt
    1 tablespoon plus ½ teaspoon granulated sugar
    ⅓ cup (90 ml) plus 1 tablespoon milk, at room temperature
    ⅓ cup (90 ml) plus 1 tablespoon water, at room
        temperature
    2 tablespoons extra-virgin olive oil
    1 packet (7 g) active dry yeast

Preheat the oven to 400°F (200°C/Gas Mark 6). Place a deep baking dish filled with water on the bottom rack. Line a baking sheet with parchment paper.

In a stand mixer fitted with the dough hook attachment, mix together the flour, salt, and sugar. Beat in the milk, water, olive oil, and yeast and knead for 16 minutes at medium speed.

Divide the dough into twelve ½-ounce (45 g) portions and form into rolls. Transfer to the prepared baking sheet. Cover with a thin dampened tea towel and let rise until doubled in size, about 1 hour.

Dust the tops with flour and bake for 8 minutes. Reduce the oven temperature to 350°F (180°C/Gas Mark 4) and bake until a golden crust forms, about 17 minutes. Transfer to a wire rack to cool.

RECIPE NOTES: _____
_____
_____
_____
_____
_____
_____
_____
_____
_____
_____
_____
_____
_____
_____
_____
_____
_____
_____
_____
_____
_____
_____

CHILLED TOMATO ASPIC WITH RICOTTA AND COUSCOUS

Serves 6

COUSCOUS SALAD
    1⅔ cups (400 ml) chicken stock
    3 slices fresh ginger, chopped
    ½ tablespoon mild curry powder
    1½ stalks lemongrass, chopped
    generous ¾ cup (150 g) couscous
    5 oz (150 g) pineapple, finely diced
    1 apple, chopped
    1 fennel frond, finely chopped
    1 tablespoon red wine vinegar
    2 tablespoons extra-virgin olive oil
    Salt

TOMATO WATER
    6⅔ lb (3 kg) tomatoes, chopped
    3 tablespoons powdered (icing) sugar
    1 teaspoon salt
    Leaves from 1 bunch fresh basil, roughly chopped

TOMATO ASPIC
    2 gelatin sheets
    5 basil leaves
    1 sprig tarragon
    2 sprigs cilantro (coriander)
    ½ teaspoon salt
    ¼ teaspoon freshly ground black pepper

RICOTTA-STUFFED ZUCCHINI
    ⅔ cup (150 ml) heavy (whipping) cream
    3 tablespoons ricotta cheese
    3 tablespoons sour cream
    ½ tablespoon white wine vinegar
    Salt and ground white pepper
    2 zucchini (courgettes), sliced into wide ribbons
    Extra-virgin olive oil, for drizzling
    Salt

DRIED TOMATOES
    4 tomatoes, peeled and finely diced
    Leaves from 4 sprigs rosemary, chopped
    Salt and freshly ground black pepper

MARINATED CUCUMBER
    1 medium cucumber, sliced into thin ribbons
    1 tablespoon extra-virgin olive oil
    1 teaspoon balsamic vinegar
    Salt and freshly ground black pepper

>>

Andreas Caminada

MAKE THE COUSCOUS SALAD

In a small pot, warm the chicken stock, ginger, curry and lemongrass over medium heat and simmer for 8 minutes. Strain into a bowl.

Meanwhile, in a medium saucepan, toast the couscous over medium heat until golden brown, about 2 minutes. Remove from the heat, add the hot broth, and let rest until completely absorbed, about 15 minutes. Add the pineapple, apple, and fennel frond and toss to combine. Add the vinegar and olive oil and season to taste with salt.

MAKE THE TOMATO WATER

Working in batches if necessary, in a blender, combine the tomatoes, sugar, and salt and process for just a few seconds, until coarsely ground. Transfer to a bowl, stir in the basil, and let marinate for 15 minutes. Line a large sieve or colander with cheesecloth and set over a bowl. Add the chopped tomatoes and let drain for 5 hours or overnight, discarding the first few red drops (do not press the tomatoes). Set the clear tomato water aside (it will be used in the tomato aspic as well as the stuffed zucchini). (Save the tomato mixture to make a tomato sauce for pasta.)

MAKE THE TOMATO ASPIC

In a small bowl, soak the gelatin in cold water until soft, about 10 minutes. Drain and set aside.

Meanwhile, measure out 1⅔ cups (400 ml) of the clear tomato water and transfer to a small saucepan. Add the basil, tarragon, cilantro (coriander), salt, and black pepper and cook over low heat for 5 minutes. Strain through a fine-mesh sieve. Return to the pot and cook over medium heat for 5 minutes. Add the gelatin and stir to dissolve. Divide among 6 bowls and refrigerate until firm, about 1 hour.

MAKE THE RICOTTA-STUFFED ZUCCHINI

In a medium bowl, mix together 3 tablespoons tomato water, the cream, ricotta, and sour cream. Stir in the white wine vinegar. Season to taste with salt and white pepper. Transfer to a pastry (piping) bag and set aside.

Set up a large bowl of ice and water. Bring a medium pot of lightly salted water to a boil. Add the zucchini (courgettes) and blanch for 3 seconds. Transfer to the ice bath to cool.

Roll into cylinders and pipe the ricotta mixture into the center of each. Drizzle with olive oil and sprinkle with salt.

MAKE THE DRIED TOMATOES

Preheat the oven to 200°F (100°C) or as low as your oven can go.

In a medium bowl, season the tomatoes with the rosemary and salt and pepper to taste. Transfer to the prepared baking sheet and let dry for 1 hour.

>>

MAKE THE MARINATED CUCUMBER

In a medium bowl, combine the cucumber, olive oil, and vinegar. Season to taste with salt and pepper and let rest for 10 minutes. Roll into cylinders.

TO SERVE

Remove the chilled bowls of tomato aspic from the fridge and top with 1 stuffed zucchini roll, 1 cucumber roll, and a spoonful of the couscous salad. Garnish with the dried tomatoes.

RECIPE NOTES: _____
_____
_____
_____
_____
_____
_____
_____
_____
_____
_____
_____
_____
_____
_____
_____
_____
_____
_____
_____
_____
_____
_____
_____
_____
_____
_____
_____
_____
_____
_____
_____
_____
_____
_____
_____
_____
_____
_____
_____

CHICKEN WITH CARROTS AND BREAD DUMPLINGS

Serves 6

ROAST CHICKEN
6 boneless, skinless chicken breasts
Salt and freshly ground black pepper
1 tablespoon extra-virgin olive oil

CARAMELIZED ONIONS
1 tablespoon butter
2 onions, roughly chopped
Salt

GLAZED CARROTS
4 tablespoons (60 g) butter
2 shallots, finely diced
6 carrots, peeled (see Note)
½ teaspoon powdered (icing) sugar
Salt and freshly ground black pepper
scant ½ cup (100 ml) chicken stock

CARROT PUREE
3 teaspoons (20 g) butter
9 oz (250 g) carrots peels and/or roughly chopped carrots
1 teaspoon powdered (icing) sugar
Salt and freshly ground black pepper
3 tablespoons chicken stock

BREAD DUMPLINGS
9 oz (250 g) stale bread, cubed
⅓ cup (75 ml) milk
½ teaspoon salt
¼ teaspoon freshly grated nutmeg
1 small onion, finely diced
2 slices bacon (streaky), finely diced
1 sprig parsley, finely chopped
1 egg
Freshly ground black pepper
½ cup (25 g) grated stale bread (optional)
½ tablespoon butter

FOR SERVING
6 teaspoons Lemon Confit (recipe follows)

MAKE THE ROAST CHICKEN

Preheat the oven to 325°F (160°C/Gas Mark 3).
Season the chicken with salt and pepper. In a large frying pan, heat the oil over medium heat. Add the chicken and brown, 1 minute per side. Transfer to a baking sheet and bake until the internal temperature reaches 149°F (65°C), 10 minutes.

MAKE THE CARAMELIZED ONIONS

In a medium frying pan, melt the butter over medium heat. Add the onions, season with salt, and cook over low heat until soft and caramelized, 15 minutes.

MAKE THE GLAZED CARROTS

In a medium pot, melt 2 tablespoons of the butter over medium heat. Add the shallots and sauté until translucent, 5 minutes. Add the carrots and powdered (icing) sugar and season to taste with salt and pepper. Add the stock and cook until the carrots are al dente, 3 minutes. Add the remaining 2 tablespoons butter and cook until golden brown, 4 minutes.

MAKE THE CARROT PUREE

In a medium pot, melt 2 tablespoons of the butter over medium heat. Add the carrot peels and cook until soft, 10 minutes. Add the powdered sugar and season to taste with salt and pepper. Add the stock and cook, partially covered, until soft, 10 minutes. Transfer to a food processor and blend to a puree. Add the remaining 1 tablespoon butter and blend.

MAKE THE BREAD DUMPLINGS

Place the bread in a large bowl. In a medium pot, warm the milk, salt, and nutmeg over medium heat for 10 minutes. Pour over the bread and refrigerate for 2 hours.
In a medium frying pan, sauté the onion and bacon over medium heat until golden brown, 2 minutes. Transfer to the soaked bread. Mix in the parsley and egg.
Bring a medium pot of lightly salted water to a boil. Cook a test dumpling: Form the mixture into a ⅓-inch (1 cm) ball. Cook until it rises to the surface, 4 minutes. If it doesn't hold its shape, add enough grated bread to firm up the mixture and try another test. Form and cook the remaining dumplings.
In a medium pan, heat the butter over medium heat. Add the dumplings and sauté until golden brown, 5 minutes.

TO SERVE

Place 1 chicken breast on each plate and top with the onions, carrots, bread dumplings, lemon confit, and carrot puree.

Note: Save the carrot peelings for the carrot puree. Supplement with coarsely chopped carrots, if necessary.

LEMON CONFIT

Makes about 1 lb (400 g)

Rinds from 10 lemons
1½ cups (300 g) granulated sugar
1 whole star anise
1 whole clove

Set up a large bowl of ice and water. Bring a medium pot of water to a boil. Add the lemon rinds and blanch for 2 minutes. Transfer to the ice bath. Repeat this process 2 more times. Finely dice and transfer to a medium saucepan. Add the sugar, star anise, and clove, and cook over medium heat for 15 minutes without browning. Set aside.

Andreas Caminada

RECIPE P. 232

CHOCOLATE CAKE WITH CARAMEL ICE CREAM

Serves 8

DULCE DE LECHE
  1 can (14 oz/400 g) condensed milk

CHOCOLATE CAKE
  5 eggs, separated
  Pinch of salt
  7 oz (200 g) dark chocolate
  7 tablespoons (100 g) butter
  generous ¾ cup (100 g) powdered (icing) sugar

CHOCOLATE MOUSSE
  ½ cup (125 ml) heavy (whipping) cream
  1¾ oz (50 g) dark chocolate
  ½ gelatin sheet
  4 teaspoons Grand Marnier or other orange liqueur
  1 egg yolk (see Note)
  ½ tablespoon powdered (icing) sugar

CARAMELIZED APPLES
  ½ cup (100 g) granulated sugar
  generous ¾ cup (200 ml) white wine
  3 tablespoons plus 1 teaspoon orange juice
  4 Fuji apples or other apples, peeled and quartered
  2 whole star anise
  2 bay leaves
  2 whole cloves
  1 cinnamon stick

CHOCOLATE CRUMBLE
  ¾ cup plus 3 tablespoons (180 g) packed light brown sugar
  1¾ cups plus 2 tablespoons (185 g) almond flour
    (ground almonds)
  1¼ cups (165 g) all-purpose (plain) flour
  2 tablespoons unsweetened cocoa powder
  1½ teaspoons salt
  1 stick plus 5 tablespoons (180 g) butter, at room
    temperature

CARAMEL-CINNAMON ICE CREAM
  2⅓ cups (550 ml) heavy (whipping) cream
  2⅓ cups (500 ml) milk
  3 cinnamon sticks
  1 vanilla bean, split lengthwise
  5 egg yolks (see Note)
  1 cup (200 g) granulated sugar

CHOCOLATE GANACHE
  3½ oz (100 g) dark chocolate (70% cacao), chopped
  scant ½ cup (100 ml) heavy (whipping) cream

>>

MAKE THE DULCE DE LECHE

Place the can of condensed milk in a medium pot and cover with water. Bring to a boil over high heat. Reduce heat to a simmer and cook for 2 hours, checking the pot every 30 minutes to ensure the water level stays above the can. Remove and let cool. Open and pour into a small bowl.

MAKE THE CHOCOLATE CAKE

Preheat the oven to 350°F (180°C/Gas Mark 4). Butter a 9-inch (23 cm) cake pan.

In a medium bowl, whisk the egg whites and salt until stiff peaks form. Set aside.

In a heatproof bowl set over a pan of simmering water, melt the chocolate. Set aside.

In a stand mixer fitted with the paddle attachment, cream the butter at medium speed until creamy. Slowly beat in the powdered (icing) sugar. Add the egg yolks one at a time, mixing well after each. Mix in the melted chocolate at low speed. By hand, fold in the egg whites. Transfer to the prepared cake pan and bake until the top is puffed and starting to crack, about 40 minutes. Let cool.

MAKE THE CHOCOLATE MOUSSE

In a stand mixer fitted with the whisk attachment, whisk the cream until stiff peaks form. Set aside.

In a small heatproof bowl set over a pan of simmering water, melt the dark chocolate. Set aside.

In a small bowl, soak the gelatin in cold water until soft, about 10 minutes. Drain and set aside.

In a heatproof bowl set over a pan of simmering water, whisk together the Grand Marnier, egg yolk, and powdered sugar until creamy. Stir in the gelatin and melted chocolate. Let cool, then fold in the whipped cream. Spread over the top of the chocolate cake. Refrigerate until firm, at least 2 hours.

MAKE THE CARAMELIZED APPLES

In a medium saucepan, melt the sugar over medium heat until caramelized, about 7 minutes. Add the white wine and orange juice and cook until syrupy, about 6 minutes. Add the apples, star anise, bay leaves, cloves, and cinnamon and cook until soft, about 10 minutes.

MAKE THE CHOCOLATE CRUMBLE

Preheat the oven to 350°F (180°C/Gas Mark 4). Line a baking sheet with parchment paper.

In a large bowl, combine the brown sugar, almond flour (ground almonds), all-purpose (plain) flour, cocoa, and salt. With your hands, work in the butter until large, moist clumps form. Transfer to the prepared baking sheet and press down. Bake until golden brown, about 20 minutes. Let cool on the baking sheet, then break into smaller pieces.

>>

Andreas Caminada

MAKE THE CARAMEL-CINNAMON ICE CREAM

In a medium pot, combine the cream, milk, and cinnamon sticks. Scrape in the vanilla seeds and add the pod. Bring to a simmer over medium heat and cook for 10 minutes.

In a medium bowl, whisk together the egg yolks and half the sugar until creamy.

In a medium saucepan, heat the remaining sugar over medium heat until caramelized, about 7 minutes. Transfer to the pot of cream mixture and mix to combine. Slowly add one-fourth of the hot cream mixture to the eggs, stirring constantly. Return the warmed eggs to the pot and cook for 6 minutes over medium heat, stirring constantly. Remove the cinnamon sticks and vanilla pod and let cool. Transfer to an ice-cream machine and process according to the manufacturer's instructions. (If you don't have an ice-cream machine, freeze the mixture until hard enough to scoop.)

MAKE THE CHOCOLATE GANACHE

Place the chocolate in a medium heatproof bowl.

In a small saucepan, bring the cream to a boil over medium heat. Remove and pour over the chocolate. Let rest for 5 minutes. Using a hand blender, blend the mixture to ensure there are no lumps. Cover and refrigerate. Transfer to a pastry (piping) bag.

TO SERVE

Place a slice of chocolate cake on each plate, top with a spoonful of the dulce de leche, and sprinkle with the chocolate crumble. Serve with a spoonful of the caramelized apples, a scoop of the caramel-cinnamon ice cream, and a spoonful of the chocolate ganache.

Note: Save the egg whites to make Meringues (pages 32 or 387).

P. 231

RECIPE NOTES:

Ferran & Albert Adrià

Ferran Adrià is a Catalonian chef who was the creative force behind elBulli. He joined the restaurant in 1984 and took over the kitchen in 1987. He was a pioneer of new techniques, celebrated everyday ingredients, and changed the perception of fine dining forever. His younger brother Albert Adrià worked alongside him. Since closing elBuli, Albert has opened his own restaurants in Barcelona. Ferran and Albert are among the most influential chefs in the world and they had not cooked together for years before cooking at the Refettorio.

The brothers came straight from the airport on the first flight from Barcelona wearing jeans and sneakers. They would return to Barcelona on the last flight out after dinner. They were like two mischievous kids, out to tag a wall or stir up some trouble, who would then slip back into their daily lives as if nothing had happened.

Cristina went over the program of the day and explained how the other chefs had proceeded. Then Ferran asked Zineb, who had cooked the day before with Andreas Caminada, "Do you have the product list?" She said, "I didn't know what he was talking about. All the other chefs just went through the fridges and the truck and decided what to cook with what they found, but Ferran wanted a list of leftovers from the previous chefs." She searched and found chicken and milk chips from Caminada's meal the day before and they ended up using everything.

From that moment on they got straight to work, barely taking the time to take off their backpacks. Lunch was for ninety kids at noon and there would be another ninety guests for dinner at 6 p.m. I hadn't seen Ferran in a kitchen cooking since the last night at elBulli in 2011. A few lucky chefs were there for the "Last Waltz," as Ferran had nicknamed that event, including René Redzepi, Grant Achatz, José Andrés, and myself. ElBulli has been for many of us the place where we learned how to put our passions, our terroir, and ourselves into our cooking. It was a message of freedom.

Ferran took on the savory courses, as he had always done, and handed over the dessert making to Albert. He used chicken and stale bread to reinvent a classic Spanish chicken croquette in the form of a soup. For the second course, Ferran made a dish with eggplant (aubergine) and potatoes and added a ragù that he found in the refrigerator.

Once a week at the Refettorio, while guest chefs prepared their dishes, I would take on the task of cleaning out the refrigerator. I found it incredibly satisfying to turn all the leftovers of the previous chefs into something edible and useful, a process I called the Exercise of Everything. At times "everything" became a soup or a broth; other times "everything" became a ragù I called it an exercise because it wasn't just throwing things into a pot; I had to think about which ingredients would taste good together and how to bring out the most flavor. Just the day before, while Andreas was cooking I made a ragù with defrosted turkey breasts; a variety of ground meat (including chicken, beef, and veal); a mirepoix of onions and carrots seasoned with pancetta in place of salt; a case of overripe tomatoes; and speck for extra flavor. Ferran asked, "What is it made of?" I answered, "EVERYTHING."

Albert, who hadn't made a dessert since elBulli closed, was making rice pudding with roasted apple and honey ice cream together with Riccardo Forapani, better known as Pippo, a chef at Osteria Francescana. The apples were very ripe, but that didn't stop him from making a magnificent ice cream. He said, "If a product is about to expire that doesn't mean that it is bad. It's true that the older the fruit and vegetables, the worse they are, but in the end a good chef can extract the best out of all this produce."

After lunch service we were starving and I made a simple pasta dish for everyone. The chefs were thrilled to be sitting at a table with Ferran and Albert. For them it was like sitting at a table with demigods. I was happy to have them here cooking together after so many years and bringing new ideas to the project. Looking around the table Ferran said, "See, we chefs don't always eat caviar and foie gras. This is the family meal. And this is very interesting for me. We wrote a book called *The Family Meal*, and we spent three years making menus with the cheapest possible ingredients—without freezing anything and very fast preparations." It is true. If you care, you can make delicious food with the simplest ingredients. The meal they prepared that day was made with care, even if the ingredients had come from the supermarket surplus or were left over from the night before.

At every service there was always a guest or two who did not appreciate the food. That night was no exception. A woman kept sending the plates back without eating them. I watched the exchange from a distance and tried to hide the situation from Ferran until he caught me, "What's going on Massimo? What is wrong?" I was embarrassed, but Ferran said, "What is the problem? She needs something to eat." There during the rush of service, I watched Ferran push aside the other plates to make a delicate little salad with sliced tomatoes and pesto. A volunteer brought it to the woman but the plate returned untouched again. It turned out she didn't eat cheese.

Ferran & Albert Adrià

THE CHICKEN CROQUETTE
THAT DREAMS ABOUT BECOMING A CREAM

Serves 8

7 oz (200 g) stale bread, finely crumbled (3½ cups)
1½ cups (200 g) all-purpose (plain) flour
1 stick plus 6 tablespoons (200 g) butter
4¼ cups (1 liter) chicken stock
4¼ cups (1 liter) milk
1 lb 2 oz (500 g) chicken parts, cut into ⅓-inch (1 cm) dice
Salt and freshly ground black pepper

Preheat the oven to 350°F (180°C/Gas Mark 4). Line a baking sheet with parchment paper.

Place the bread on the baking sheet and bake until it golden, about 3 minutes. Set aside.

In a medium saucepan, toast the flour over medium heat until light brown, about 2 minutes. Add the butter and cook over medium heat, stirring constantly, until golden brown, about 6 minutes.

In another medium saucepan, heat the chicken stock and milk to 158°F (70°C.) Add the flour mixture little by little, stirring constantly, until creamy. Add the chicken and cook over low heat for 15 minutes, stirring regularly so the bottom doesn't burn or stick. Transfer to a blender and blend until smooth. Season to taste with salt and pepper. Ladle the cream into each bowl and garnish with the breadcrumbs.

📷   P. 239

RAGÙ WITH MASHED POTATOES

Serves 8

10 medium potatoes
7 tablespoons (100 g) butter
7 oz (200 g) Parmigiano-Reggiano cheese, grated
Salt and freshly ground black pepper
7 oz (200 g) green beans, trimmed and halved
3 to 4 cups (710 to 945 ml) Ragù of Everything
    (recipe follows)

MAKE THE MASHED POTATOES

Bring a medium pot of water to a boil. Add the potatoes and cook until fork-tender, about 15 minutes. Drain and when cool enough to handle, peel and pass through a fine-mesh sieve. Add the butter and Parmigiano and gently mix to combine. Season with salt and pepper to taste and set aside.

Set up a large bowl of ice and water. Bring a medium pot of salted water to a boil over high heat. Add the green beans and cook until they are crisp-tender, about 4 minutes. Drain and transfer to the ice bath to cool. When cold, drain and set aside.

>>

TO SERVE

Place a spoonful of the hot ragù in each bowl. Top with a spoonful of the mashed potatoes and garnish with the green beans.

RAGÙ OF EVERYTHING

Serves 12

3 tablespoons extra-virgin olive oil
9 oz (250 g) pancetta, chopped
2 large onions, diced
6 carrots, diced
1 celery stalk, diced
1 lb 2 oz (500 g) turkey breast, cut into 1-inch (3 cm)
    chunks
2¼ lb (1 kg) ground (minced) chicken, beef, and veal
9 oz (250 g) speck, chopped
1 lb 2 oz (500 g) fresh tomatoes
1 cup (250 ml) canned whole peeled tomatoes
5 bay leaves
1 sprig thyme
Salt

In a large saucepan, heat the olive oil over medium heat. Add the pancetta and cook until browned, about 10 minutes. Next, add the onions and sauté until translucent, about 10 minutes. Add the carrots and celery and sauté for another 10 minutes. Add the turkey and the ground (minced) meat in batches, stirring constantly until browned, about 15 minutes. Reduce the heat to low and cook, stirring occasionally, for 15 minutes. Add the speck and cook until browned, about 15 minutes. Add the fresh tomatoes, canned tomatoes, bay leaves, and thyme and simmer until thick and reduced, about 1½ hours. Remove the bay leaves and thyme. Season to taste with salt. Let cool in the saucepan for 2 hours before serving or refrigerating. Reheat over low heat before serving.

RECIPE NOTES: _____
_____
_____
_____
_____
_____
_____
_____
_____
_____
_____
_____
_____
_____
_____
_____
_____

Ferran & Albert Adrià

RICE PUDDING WITH APPLE-HONEY ICE CREAM

Serves 8

RICE PUDDING
4¼ cups (1 liter) milk
½ cinnamon stick
Strips of zest from 1 lemon
1¼ cups (250 g) rice
¾ cup (150 g) granulated sugar
1 tablespoon ground cinnamon

APPLE-HONEY ICE CREAM
¾ cup (150 g) granulated sugar
4 golden apples
1⅔ cups (400 ml) heavy (whipping) cream
1¼ cups (300 ml) milk
5 tablespoons dark honey

FOR SERVING
10 fan wafers, roughly crushed

MAKE THE RICE PUDDING

In a medium pot, bring the milk, cinnamon, and lemon zest to a simmer over medium heat and cook for 10 minutes.

In a medium pot, heat 1 cup (250 ml) water and the rice over medium heat. Once the water has evaporated, reduce the heat to medium, add the boiled milk little by little, and cook until tender, about 15 minutes. Remove the cinnamon stick and lemon zest. Add the sugar and stir to combine. Let cool to room temperature. Sprinkle with the ground cinnamon, cover, and refrigerate to chill.

MAKE THE APPLE-HONEY ICE CREAM

In a small pot, heat the sugar and ⅔ cup (150 ml) water over medium heat and cook until dissolved. Remove from the heat and set the simple syrup aside.

Preheat the oven to 350°F (180°C/Gas Mark 4). Line a baking sheet with parchment paper.

Place the whole apples on the baking sheet and bake until soft, about 20 minutes. When cool enough to handle, peel, core, and seed. Transfer to a food processor or blender, add the cream, milk, honey, and 2½ tablespoons of the simple syrup, and blend until smooth. Transfer to an ice-cream machine and process according to the manufacturer's instructions. (If you don't have an ice-cream machine, freeze the mixture until hard enough to scoop.)

TO SERVE

Place ⅓ cup (85 g) of rice pudding in each bowl. Top with a scoop of the apple-honey ice cream and garnish with the crushed fan wafers.

P. 241

Ferran & Albert Adrià

Petter Nilsson

Petter Nilsson and I met at an event called Gelinaz! organized by Andrea Petrini at the seminal culinary festival Lo Mejor de la Gastronomía in San Sebastián, Spain. The year was 2005 and the group comprised five chefs who did not know each other very well: Fulvio Pierangelini, Andoni Luis Aduriz, Thierry Marx, Petter, and me. Those were the golden years of Lo Mejor when so many of the ideas of the past two decades were first demonstrated, discussed, talked about, and tasted. Petter and I crossed paths again in Copenhagen for Cook It Raw, a chef-driven event that was launched in 2009, also by the notorious Petrini. Petter was cooking at La Gazzetta in Paris. He had taken over the small bistro near the Marché d'Aligre in 2007 at about the same time that Iñaki Aiziparte opened Le Chateaubriand. Iñaki, originally from the Basque country, and Petter were both key figures in the launch of the Parisian gastro-bistro trend and curiously neither of them was French.

Petter returned to Stockholm several years ago to open the restaurant in the Spritmuseum, a museum dedicated to spirits and the art of distillery. He moved cautiously to transform a museum restaurant into an innovative one where he would be able to express himself. During his years in France he cooked French food with Nordic influences, from the seaweed and small herbs to his minimalist approach to plating. Back in Sweden, at the Spiritmuseum, he is playing just the opposite: a distinctly Swedish cuisine that employs French classicism and technique. Petter is a chef whom I will always put on the A list. He is dedicated, ethical, whimsical, and knows how to cook. There was no doubt in my mind he needed to be here at the Refettorio.

When Petter arrived, he took a good look at the pantry and refrigerators and offered his thoughts about the ingredients that were available. "When I saw the produce I thought, 'Do they really throw away all this?' It's such a shame. How can we be so careless with the produce in stores and markets? I mean, there are people employed to manage the food that is brought into stores and markets, so how can we possibly waste so much?" I shared the same sentiment. By then I had seen every kind of vegetable and fruit, meat, fish, poultry, dairy product, and luxury item come into our kitchen. I asked myself on a weekly basis if these items were really destined for the trash or if someone was playing a joke on us. Naturally we were working mostly with onions, potatoes, stale bread, cheese rinds, and rotting vegetables, but the repeat event of asparagus, porcini, lobster tails, and rare cheeses continued to take me by surprise.

Petter insists on giving everything in the kitchen value, not only to avoid waste but also to increase flavor. He said, "To me 'no waste' is first and foremost about using everything to the last bit, and we also have to think about making sure that every preparation adds value to the product." So if the stalks and stems, leaves and bones, are used properly, they add value. Adding value to the product was exactly what the chefs were doing here everyday. They were not only finding clever ways to use celery leaves or potato skins, but enhancing flavor through the creation of broths, ragùs, and concentrated sauces, often with unwanted trimmings and offcuts of meat.

Pumpkins and winter squash were in season and we already had a few around, so Petter made a butternut squash risotto. He knew that my Mantovan culinary heritage was inclined to question if a squash was savory or sweet. He worked with this idea and added sage and pomegranate to an otherwise classic risotto. This small touch enhanced the risotto and brought it closer to Turkey and the Baltic Sea than to Italy. Our guests, many of whom were from Eastern Europe, could not get enough of it. He followed with a vegetarian main course of grilled zucchini (courgette), eggplant (aubergine) puree, and capers. And he finished with a lovely fall apple and plum dessert. With absolutely no control over the ingredients in the pantry, remarkably Petter was able to prepare a meal that was perfectly aligned with the late summer/early fall season. This, above all, demonstrated to me a masterful ability to pull a recipe out of thin air.

Petter often acknowledges that his childhood had a great influence on the way he handles ingredients. The fact that he was raised by his older relatives taught him about being prudent. "My grandparents were used to harder times than the ones Sweden provided me and my brother in the early seventies. So they really enforced restraint and respect," he said. "Everything was used to the last bit. The idea of not finishing a plate never occurred."

Our time together in Milan was grounding and civilized in comparison to some of the more wild days in our past. Petter reminded me (I had totally forgotten) that at the Gelinaz! event back in 2005, he was the only one who showed up in the morning to prep for the big event on stage. The rest of us were still in bed after a night of gin and tonics. We laughed about it now, but at the time I'm sure he thought, *What the hell have I gotten myself into?* It's a good thing that friends are forgiving.

September 7

Petter Nilsson

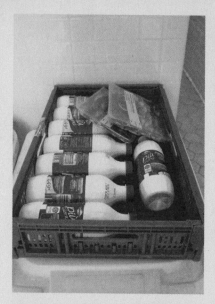

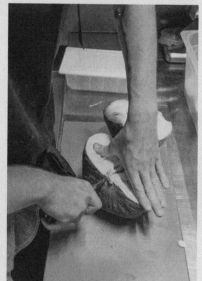

September 7

Serves 4

1 lb 2 oz (500 g) eggplant (aubergine)
1 garlic clove
2 tablespoons extra-virgin olive oil
Salt and freshly ground black pepper
8 plums, pitted and cut into medium pieces (see Note)
2 tablespoons sherry vinegar
1 tablespoon salt-packed capers, rinsed
3 tablespoons blanched almonds, coarsely chopped
¾ oz (20 g) pancetta, diced
4 small zucchini (courgettes), halved lengthwise
2 tablespoons corn oil

Char the eggplant (aubergine) over the open flame of a stove burner all over until the skin is completely blackened. (If you don't have a gas stove, char under a hot broiler [grill].) Peel the skin. Transfer to a blender, add the garlic and olive oil, and process until smooth. Add a little water to loosen if necessary. Pass through a fine-mesh sieve. Season to taste with salt and pepper and set aside.

In a medium bowl, combine the plums, vinegar, and capers and mix. Let marinate for 15 minutes.

Meanwhile, in a medium frying pan, cook the almonds and pancetta over medium heat until golden brown, about 6 minutes. Transfer to the plum mixture and stir to combine. Set aside.

Lightly salt the zucchini (courgettes) and set aside in a colander to drain for 10 minutes. Dry with paper towels.

In a medium frying pan, heat the corn oil over high heat. Add the zucchini cut side down, reduce the heat to medium-low, and cook for 5 minutes. Remove and transfer to paper towels to absorb any excess oil. Season to taste with salt and pepper.

To serve, place a spoonful of the eggplant puree on each plate and top with the zucchini. Garnish with the plum mixture.

Note: Save the plum pits for the Plum Ice Cream (page 249).

RECIPE NOTES:

Petter Nilsson

SQUASH RISOTTO WITH POMEGRANATE BUTTER

Serves 4

POMEGRANATE BUTTER

Seeds (arils) of 1 pomegranate
5 tablespoons plus 2 teaspoons (80 g) butter
1 sprig sage
1 tablespoon white wine vinegar

SQUASH RISOTTO

5 teaspoons (20 g) butter
7 oz (200 g) winter squash (such as pumpkin, kabocha, Hokkaido, or red kuri), peeled and cut into medium chunks
1 bay leaf
Salt and freshly ground black pepper
generous ¾ cup (160 g) carnaroli or other short-grain rice
scant ½ cup (40 g) freshly grated Parmigiano-Reggiano cheese
Juice of ½ lemon

MAKE THE POMEGRANATE BUTTER

Spread the pomegranate seeds on a dehydrator tray and dehydrate at 113°F (45°C) until dry, at least 6 hour or overnight. (If you don't have a dehydrator, microwave on medium for 30 seconds, stir, then return to the microwave for another 30 seconds. Continue until the pomegranate seeds are completely dry.)

In a medium saucepan, warm the butter over low heat and cook until light brown, about 5 minutes. Add the sprig sage and fry. Remove the sage and add the pomegranate seeds and vinegar. Set aside.

MAKE THE SQUASH RISOTTO

In a medium saucepan, warm the butter over medium heat. Add the squash, bay leaf, and a generous ¾ cup (200 ml) water. Cover and cook until soft, about 15 minutes. Transfer to a blender and blend until smooth. Season to taste with salt and pepper. Measure out 1¾ cups (200 g) of the puree and set aside. (Save any remainder for another use.)

In a small pot, bring 1½ cups (350 ml) water to a boil.

Meanwhile, in a medium pot, toast the rice over medium heat without browning. Add the boiling water little by little, stirring constantly, until creamy, about 15 minutes. Add the reserved squash puree and the Parmigiano and cook for 3 minutes. Remove from the heat and let rest for 3 minutes. Add the lemon juice and stir to combine. Season to taste with salt and pepper.

TO SERVE

Place a generous spoonful of the squash risotto in each bowl and drizzle with the pomegranate butter.

P. 248

APPLE SORBET AND PLUM ICE CREAM

Serves 4

APPLE SORBET
10 oz (300 g) Fuji apples or other apples, diced
4½ tablespoons granulated sugar
1 cinnamon stick

PLUM ICE CREAM
1 oz (30 g) plum pits (about 2)
generous ¾ cup (200 ml) milk
scant ½ cup (100 ml) heavy (whipping) cream
3 egg yolks (see Note)
3 generous tablespoons granulated sugar

BREADCRUMB GARNISH
1 tablespoon butter
7 oz (200 g) stale bread, finely chopped
1 tablespoon superfine (caster) sugar

MAKE THE APPLE SORBET

In a medium pot, combine the apples, sugar, cinnamon stick, and 1¼ cups (300 ml) water and cook over medium heat until soft, about 10 minutes. Remove the cinnamon stick. Transfer to a blender and blend until smooth. Pass through a fine-mesh sieve and refrigerate to chill. Transfer to an ice-cream machine and process according to the manufacturer's instructions. (If you don't have an ice-cream machine, freeze the mixture until hard enough to scoop.)

MAKE THE PLUM ICE CREAM

In a food processor, process the plum pits until finely crushed.

In a medium pot, combine the milk, cream, and plum pits and bring to a boil over low heat. Remove from the heat and let infuse for 10 minutes. Strain through a fine-mesh sieve.

Bring a medium pot of water to a simmer over medium heat. In a medium heatproof bowl, whisk together the egg yolks and sugar until creamy. Whisk some of the hot milk/cream into the egg yolks to warm them, then whisk in the remaining milk/cream. Place the bowl over the pot of simmering water and cook, stirring constantly, for 7 minutes. Strain the custard through a fine-mesh sieve and refrigerate to chill. Transfer to an ice-cream machine and process according to the manufacturer's instructions. (If you don't have an ice-cream machine, freeze the mixture until hard enough to scoop.)

MAKE THE BREADCRUMB GARNISH

In a medium frying pan, heat the butter over low heat. Add the bread and cook until golden brown, about 5 minutes. Add the sugar and continue to cook, stirring, for another 5 minutes.

>>

TO SERVE

Place a spoonful of the apple sorbet in each bowl and top with a scoop of the plum ice cream. Garnish with the breadcrumbs.

Note: Save the egg whites to make Meringues (pages 32 or 387).

RECIPE NOTES: _____

Carlo Cracco

On the Milanese culinary scene, Carlo Cracco is one of the most respected chefs because of an avant-garde approach he established early in his career. Over the years he has been an influencer, known by other chefs, food journalists, and gourmet travelers; but since the very first episode of *MasterChef Italia*, in 2011, he emerged as a the most well-loved and famous chef in all of Italy.

When tracing a family tree of the new generation of Italian chefs, Carlo belongs to the prestigious branch of Gualtiero Marchesi, the father of modern Italian cuisine. In fact, he took his first steps in the kitchen of the restaurant named after Gualtiero himself, and then traveled all over France and back to Italy to work in some of the most prestigious restaurants. Once back in his hometown of Milan, in 2001, he accepted an invitation by the Stoppani family, owner of Milan's famous gourmet shop Peck, to open Cracco Peck. It was awarded two Michelin stars and in 2007, Carlo took over to become the sole owner of Ristorante Cracco.

The thing about Carlo is that no matter how famous he is, he is a friend. He has always supported me in good times and bad. During the summer of 2015, he was busier than ever with commitments with the opening of a second restaurant in Milan called Carlo e Camilla in Segheria, and simultaneously filming *MasterChef* and *Hell's Kitchen Italia*. Nonetheless, he found the time to cook one evening in early September.

Carlo was extremely motivated and excited to share the experience with his kitchen staff and brought several of them along. He asked Cristina for detailed information about the past menus and the guests' preferences. That morning he pulled asparagus, eggplants (aubergines), tomatoes, and veal shoulder from the truck and set out to work on a deeply Italian meal, enriched by his signature touch. The only problem was dessert. Carlo closed his eyes and smiled. Suddenly he said out loud, "Chocolate cake! That's what we'll make." I would have never imagined that Carlo's most desired comfort food was a simple chocolate cake. He found enough eggs, flour, sugar, and butter in the pantry but there was no trace of chocolate—not even cocoa powder. There was no way to change Carlo's mind: He jumped in his car and drove away. One hour later he came back from the restaurant with a box full of dark chocolate.

Everything was set and ready to go, but something strange was in the air; something I hadn't felt before at the Refettorio. All the volunteers were whispering to each other. They kept coming through the kitchen to get odds and ends. At a certain point I came out of the kitchen and asked one of our volunteers, an older gentleman named Carlo, "What's going on in here?" Carlo took two steps toward me, "We are so excited that Chef Cracco is here. He looks even better in real life than on TV! Can we ask him for an autograph?" I wanted to laugh but I decided to be serious and told him, "Not now. We are about to serve dinner. Afterward, if you have done a good job, you can even take a picture with him."

He had prepared a perfectly balanced menu, in proper Cracco-style, one that I would happily repeat at home for a Sunday meal: The pasta served with asparagus, almonds and a turmeric béchamel was in keeping with his nontraditionalist approach to Italian cuisine; a flavorful end of summer stew announced the changing seasons; and an impossible to resist chocolate cake closed the meal. The pasta was light enough for a warm September night and offered a flavor change from the tomato excess that often happens at the end of the growing season. It was sweet, savory, and spicy at the same time. The stew was full of late-summer vegetables and cooked down like a caponata, only that Carlo had added many unconventional ingredients like soy sauce, ginger, and orange zest. The chocolate cake was no frills and simply delicious. After the very first bite, I clearly understood why that chocolate dessert was so important to Carlo.

Despite the incredible meal, that evening our guests were far too starstruck to pay attention to the food. The fact that Carlo was there, cooking for them in person, standing there in front of them, really struck a chord. The truth is, Carlo was the only chef that our guests knew by name or recognized. He was the center of attention and spent most of service weaving from table to table because everyone wanted a picture with him or at least to shake his hand, and that is when I got an idea: what if Carlo brought *Hell's Kitchen* to the Refettorio?

After dinner, I asked him, "What do you think about filming an episode of *Hell's Kitchen* here at the Refettorio?" He got a pensive look on his face and kept me in suspense for a few seconds, then looked at me and said, "Let's do it!" I would never have imagined that the semi-finale of *Hell's Kitchen* would take place right here in this kitchen. The show was aired a year later and it turned out to be an unforgettable experience for everyone, above all for the competitors who asked to volunteer in the kitchen after the show ended. I cannot thank Carlo enough for having shared the message of the Refettorio with such a broad audience, and for showing that there is more to cooking shows than competition.

September 8

Carlo Cracco

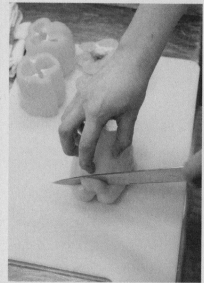

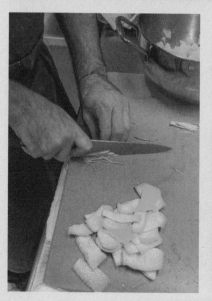

September 8

CONCHIGLIONI PASTA
WITH ASPARAGUS, ALMOND, AND TURMERIC BÉCHAMEL

Serves 6

¼ cup (30 g) whole almonds
6 oz (180 g) asparagus, peeled and cut into 2-inch
   (5 cm) pieces
Salt and freshly ground black pepper
5 teaspoons (20 g) butter
2½ tablespoons all-purpose (plain) flour
1½ cups (350 ml) milk
1 teaspoon salt
½ teaspoon ground turmeric
1 lb 5 oz (600 g) conchiglioni rigati or other shell-like pasta
1 tablespoon extra virgin oil

Preheat the oven to 325°F (160°C/Gas Mark 3). Line a baking
sheet with parchment paper.

Arrange the almonds on the lined baking sheet and toast
in the oven until golden brown, about 6 minutes. Roughly
chop and set aside.

In a medium frying pan, heat 5 tablespoons water over
medium heat. Add the asparagus and cook until al dente,
about 10 minutes. Remove from the heat and season with
salt and pepper.

Meanwhile, in a medium saucepan, melt the butter over
medium-high heat until foaming. Add the flour and cook,
stirring with a wooden spoon or spatula until bubbling, 1 to
2 minutes. Remove from the heat and slowly add the milk,
whisking constantly, until the mixture is smooth. Return to
the heat and cook, stirring with a wooden spoon or spatula,
until the sauce begins to boil and is thick enough to coat the
back of a wooden spoon, 10 to 12 minutes. Remove from the
heat and stir in the salt and turmeric.

Bring a large pot of lightly salted water to a boil over
medium heat. Add the pasta and cook until al dente. Drain
well. Toss with the asparagus and béchamel sauce. Divide
among 6 bowls and garnish with the toasted almonds.

📷   P. 255

RECIPE NOTES:

Serves 6

VEAL

1 lb 2 oz (500 g) veal shoulder, cut into 1-inch
    (3 cm) chunks
5 garlic cloves, chopped
2 tablespoons grated fresh ginger
Grated zest of 1 orange
scant ½ cup (100 ml) fresh lemon juice
generous ¾ cup (200 ml) soy sauce
1 teaspoon freshly ground black pepper
3 tablespoons extra-virgin olive oil
3 sage leaves
Salt

VEGETABLES

4 tablespoons extra-virgin olive oil
2 eggplants (aubergines), cut into ¾-inch (2 cm) cubes
3 zucchini (courgettes), cut into ¾-inch (2 cm) cubes
2 celery stalks, chopped
2 red bell peppers, cut into ¾-inch (2 cm) squares
1 onion, chopped
generous 2 tablespoons pine nuts, toasted
1 tablespoon salt-packed capers, rinsed
1 tablespoon raisins
½ cup (20 g) finely chopped fresh basil (about 2½ cups)
1½ tablespoons red wine vinegar
1½ tablespoons white wine vinegar
2 tablespoons granulated sugar

MAKE THE VEAL STEW

Place the veal in a container. Sprinkle with the garlic, ginger, orange zest, lemon juice, soy sauce, and pepper and rub into the veal. Cover with plastic wrap (clingfilm) and refrigerate for 1 hour. Reserving the marinade, drain the veal.

In a large sauté pan, heat the olive oil and sage over high heat. Add the veal and brown all sides until a golden brown crust forms, about 4 minutes. Add the reserved marinade and cook over low heat until tender and reduced by half, about 30 minutes. Season to taste with salt and set aside.

MAKE THE VEGETABLES

In a Dutch oven (casserole), heat 2 tablespoons of the olive oil over high heat. Add the eggplant (aubergines) and cook, stirring occasionally, until firm-tender, about 3 minutes. Set aside. Repeat the same process for the zucchini (courgettes), celery, peppers, and onion. Toss the eggplant, zucchini, celery, peppers, and onion with the pine nuts, capers, raisins, and basil and set aside.

In a small saucepan, heat the vinegars, sugar, and scant ½ cup (100 ml) water over medium heat until it reaches (185°F (85°C). Simmer until the liquid reduces by half, about 20 minutes.

>>

TO SERVE

Divide the vegetables among 6 plates and drizzle with a spoonful of the reduced vinegar sauce. Serve alongside the stewed veal.

RECIPE NOTES: _____
_____
_____
_____
_____
_____
_____
_____
_____
_____
_____
_____
_____
_____
_____
_____
_____
_____
_____
_____
_____
_____
_____
_____
_____
_____
_____
_____
_____
_____
_____
_____
_____
_____
_____
_____
_____
_____
_____

CHOCOLATE CAKE

Serves 6

CHOCOLATE CAKE

5 tablespoons (70 g) butter
¾ cup (70 g) all-purpose (plain) flour
9 oz (250 g) dark chocolate (65% cacao)
¼ teaspoon salt
4 eggs
generous ⅓ cup (80 g) granulated sugar
1 vanilla bean, split lengthwise

CARAMELIZED APPLES

5¼ teaspoons (25 g) butter
3 apples, diced
2 tablespoons honey
1 teaspoon fresh lemon juice
¼ teaspoon poppy seeds

CANDIED LEMON PEELS

Peels from 5 lemons, cut into thin strips
¾ cup plus 2 tablespoons (175 g) granulated sugar

MAKE THE CHOCOLATE CAKE

Preheat the oven to 425°F (220°C/Gas Mark 7). Line an 8-inch (20 cm) round cake pan with parchment paper. Grease the paper with butter and dust with flour

Bring a medium pot of water to a simmer. Combine the butter and 7 ounces (200 g) of the chocolate in a heatproof bowl and set over the simmering water. Stir until melted. Remove the bowl from the pot and add the salt.

In a medium bowl, whisk the eggs with the sugar until it becomes a light and fluffy cream. Place the flour in a sifter or sieve and scrape in the vanilla seeds. Sift the mixture into a medium bowl. Slowly add the flour mixture to the egg/sugar mixture, stirring to combine. Add the melted chocolate and stir until smooth.

Roughly chop the remaining 2 ounces (50 g) chocolate.

Pour half of the batter into the prepared cake pan. Cover with the chopped chocolate, then cover with the remaining batter. Transfer to the oven and bake until just set, about 10 minutes. Let cool in the pan.

MAKE THE CARAMELIZED APPLES

In a medium saucepan, heat the butter over high heat. Add the apples, honey, lemon juice, and poppy seeds and cook until the apples are soft, about 8 minutes. Set aside.

>>

MAKE THE CANDIED LEMON PEEL

In a small pot, bring 1⅔ cups (400 ml) water to a boil. Add the lemon peel and boil for 2 minutes. Remove. Repeat at least 3 times, or until soft and the bitterness is gone. Drain. In a small pan, heat a generous ¾ cup (200 ml) water over medium heat. Add the sugar and peel and cook for 10 minutes, or until reduced by half. Drain and set aside to cool. Reserve at room temperature until ready to serve.

TO SERVE

Slice the cake and garnish with the caramelized apples and the candied lemon peel.

RECIPE NOTES: _____
_____
_____
_____
_____
_____
_____
_____
_____
_____
_____
_____
_____
_____
_____
_____
_____
_____
_____
_____
_____
_____
_____
_____
_____
_____
_____
_____
_____
_____
_____
_____
_____
_____

Basque Culinary Center & Juan Mari Arzak

San Sebastián, Spain, is a place that I have come to love after repeat visits to the annual food conference Gastronomika. The Basque Culinary Center, or BCC, is a collaboration between Mondragon University and a group of prominent Basque chefs, including Juan Mari Arzak, Martín Berasategui, Andoni Luis Aduriz, and Eneko Atxa. It is unlike any other culinary school in that the aim from the beginning was to create a training, research, and innovation project focused not only on the culinary sector (chefs), but also on management, science, and other culinary disciplines. The contemporary campus, inaugurated in 2011, sits on a sloping hillside above the town of San Sebastián.

I became involved with the BCC project from the laying of the first brick. In 2009, two years before the opening of the BCC, I was in Madrid for a food festival and I caught Juan Mari watching my presentation. As soon as I got off the stage, I heard him calling my name, "Massimo, Massimo, Massimo!" Juan Mari, as I have always referred to him, does not waste time with small talk. He dove straight into a monologue about a totally new concept for a culinary university in the Basque country. "This will be a unique university focusing on theory, practice, and research," he said, adding that Ferran Adrià would be president of the International Advisory Board and chefs like Gastón Acurio, René Redzepi, and Yoshihiro Narisawa would act as advisers. Without even a breath between his first sentence and his last, he blurted out the question, "So, will you join us too?" I blushed. This was not just any person standing in front of me. It was Juan Mari Arzak.

Juan Mari took over the kitchen of his family restaurant in 1966 and quickly rose to become a culinary star. The tavern, which had served traditional Basque food up until his arrival, received its first Michelin star in 1972. At that time, Basque chefs, which included Juan Mari, were influenced by the nouvelle cuisine of France and in turn created the *nouvelle cuisine basque*, firmly Basque in substance, but with less rustic versions of traditional dishes. Juan Mari became the most famous exponent and one of the first Michelin three-star restaurants in Spain. In a few years the movement swept across Spain, becoming the country's default haute cuisine.

I had met Juan Mari a couple of times before I joined the board of the BCC. The first time we met was during the summer of 2000. He was at elBulli presenting the book *Celebrar el milenio*, co-authored by Ferran and Juan Mari. While Juan Mari was talking, Ferran looked over at me and said, "If it weren't for Juan Mari Arzak, you know, I wouldn't be here." This confirmation solidified Juan Mari's position as the father of the Spanish culinary movement.

I knew that Joxe Mari Aizega, the director of the BCC, and Fernando Bárcena, the head chef, would be cooking to represent the school, but I didn't know that Juan Mari was coming along, too, until he called me in the afternoon. "Massimo, where are you?" he asked. I jumped in the car with my mother-in-law and in less than two hours we were in Piazza Greco.

When I arrived, Joxe Mari and Fernando were preparing *tortillas* (Spanish omelets) with a chilled lentil salad. The second course was a meat and vegetable stew. The meal concluded with fruit salad and vanilla ice cream. It was a very Spanish meal with humble ingredients and strong flavors. Often these were the meals that our guests appreciated the most. Arzak had developed the menu with Fernando, and he diligently watched over the kitchen to insure that everything was running smoothly.

I introduced Juan Mari, who is in his mid-seventies, to my mother-in-law, Janet, who is eighty-two. Who knew they would light up like teenagers? She doesn't speak Spanish and he speaks only a few words of English, but they did not need to converse. Janet put on an apron and started setting the tables for dinner. Arzak watched her through the kitchen window. Every time she passed him she smiled and he blushed. Their exchange charged the kitchen with flirtatious energy. During the meal, Juan Mari walked among the tables and patted the gentlemen guests on the back speaking in Spanish regardless of whether they understood the language. He asked them if they liked the food and offered them second servings. That night he was there to please.

Juan Mari's biography is entitled, *A Teacher with the Eyes of a Child*. That night, I saw how fitting this title is. He was watching us all and looking over our shoulders, but not in the role of a judge or a critic—he was there because he was first and foremost curious to see what would happen. Even at his age, after having changed the history of Spanish gastronomy, he wanted to live this experience, too. That simple meal in Milan confirmed what I already knew: This man believes in culture and the power of food to change the way we see the world—he believes in the future.

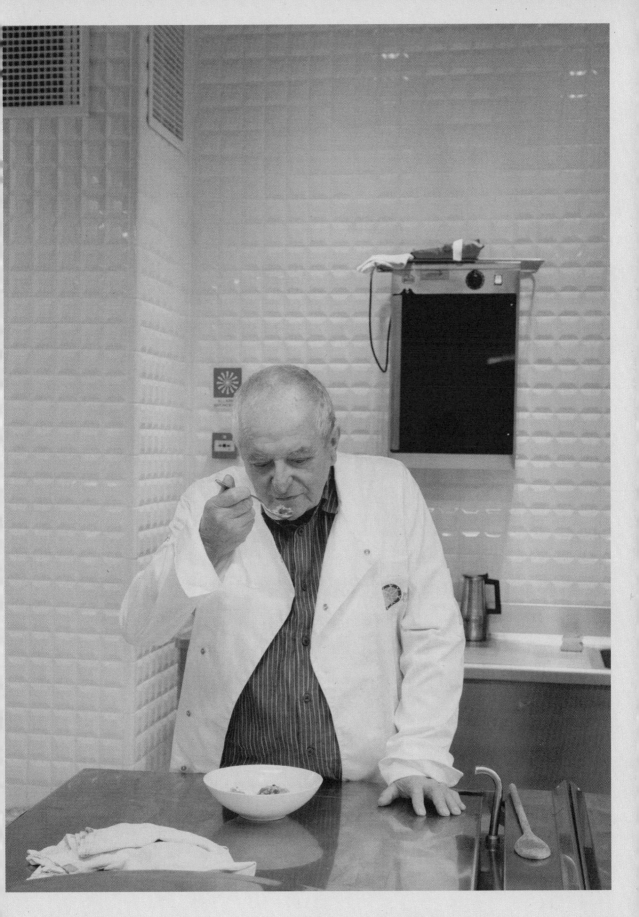

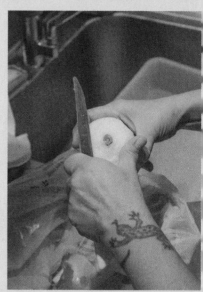

SPANISH TORTILLA WITH COLD LENTIL SALAD

Serves 8

SPANISH TORTILLA

    2¼ lb (1 kg) potatoes, peeled and cut into ⅓-inch
       (8 mm) dice
    1 quart (1 liter) extra-virgin olive oil
    2 medium onions, finely diced
    16 eggs
    1 teaspoon salt

COLD LENTIL SALAD

    1 can (15 oz/425g) cooked lentils, drained and rinsed
    1 red bell pepper, finely chopped
    1 green bell pepper, finely chopped
    1 onion, finely chopped
    ⅓ cup (90 ml) extra-virgin olive oil
    3 tablespoons red wine vinegar
    Salt

MAKE THE SPANISH TORTILLA

Place the potatoes in a large bowl and cover with water.
Set aside until ready to cook.

In a medium pot, heat the olive oil over medium heat.
Add the potatoes and slowly cook, taking care that they do not
change color, until soft, about 10 minutes. Reserving the oil,
transfer the potatoes to a colander to drain. Repeat the same
process with the onions.

In a large bowl, lightly beat the eggs. Stir in the potatoes,
onions, and salt.

In a small nonstick pan, heat 2 tablespoons of the reserved
cooking oil over medium heat. Add 1 cup (240 ml) of the egg
and potato mixture and cook until both sides are firm, but
the inside is still soft, about 5 minutes per side. Repeat this
process to make 8 tortillas.

MAKE THE COLD LENTIL SALAD

In a large bowl, combine the lentils, bell peppers, onion, olive
oil, and vinegar. Season to taste with salt.

TO SERVE

Place a tortilla on each plate and serve a spoonful of the lentil
salad alongside.

📷   P. 263

RECIPE NOTES: _____

STEWED MEAT WITH RICE

Serves 6

RICE
2 cups (400 g) rice
1 bay leaf
2 garlic cloves, roughly chopped

STEWED MEAT
14 oz (400 g) beef, lamb, or pork shoulder, cut into
    1½-inch (4 cm) chunks
Salt and freshly ground black pepper
All-purpose (plain) flour, for dredging
4 tablespoons extra-virgin olive oil
2 onions, cut into 1¼-inch (3 cm) chunks
2 garlic cloves, chopped
2 tomatoes, diced
1 green apple, cut into 1¼-inch (3 cm) chunks
1 bay leaf
generous 2 cups (500 ml) red wine
1 quart (1 liter) beef stock
1 green bell pepper, roughly chopped

FOR SERVING
½ cup (50 g) freshly grated Parmigiano-Reggiano cheese

MAKE THE RICE

In a medium pot, bring 4¼ cups (1 liter) water to a boil over high heat. Add the rice, bay leaf, and the garlic. Reduce the heat to low and cook for 12 minutes. Drain and refresh with cold water.

MAKE THE STEWED MEAT

Season the meat with salt and pepper and dredge in flour. In a large frying pan, heat 1 tablespoon of the olive oil over medium heat. Add the meat and brown all over, about 2 minutes.

In a medium pot, heat 1 tablespoon of the olive oil over medium heat. Add the onions, garlic, tomatoes, green apple, and bay leaf and sauté until golden brown, about 3 minutes. Stir in the meat. Add the wine and stock and let simmer over medium heat until the meat is cooked through and tender, about 8 minutes. Remove the meat using tongs and strain the liquid through a fine-mesh sieve (discard the solids). Add the meat to the strained liquid and let cool down at room temperature.

In a medium saucepan, heat the remaining 2 tablespoons of the olive oil over medium heat. Add the bell pepper, and sauté until lightly browned, about 2 minutes. Add the meat with the strained liquid and boil for 20 minutes. Add the rice, reduce the heat to low, and simmer for 30 minutes. Set aside.

TO SERVE

Serve the stewed meat and rice in bowls and sprinkle with the Parmigiano.

Basque Culinary Center & Juan Mari Arzak

VANILLA ICE CREAM WITH FRUIT SALAD

Serves 6

VANILLA ICE CREAM
    scant ½ cup (100 ml) milk
    1⅔ cups (385 ml) heavy (whipping) cream
    1 vanilla bean, split lengthwise
    2 eggs
    3 generous tablespoons granulated sugar

FRUIT SALAD
    ½ pineapple, cut into ¾-inch (2 cm) dice
    1 small melon, and cut into ¾-inch (2 cm) dice
    2 mangoes, cut into ¾-inch (2 cm) dice
    2 oranges, cut into ¾-inch (2 cm) dice
    1 apples, cut into ¾-inch (2 cm) dice
    2 kiwis, peeled and cut into ¾-inch (2 cm) dice
    2 peaches, cut into ¾-inch (2 cm) dice
    1 banana, sliced (see Note)
    4¼ cups (1 liter) orange juice
    1 cup (250 ml) Moscato or other sparkling sweet wine
    1¾ cups (350 g) granulated sugar
    Mint leaves, for garnish

MAKE THE VANILLA ICE CREAM

In a medium saucepan, combine the milk and cream. Scrape in the vanilla seeds and add the pod. Bring to a simmer over medium heat and simmer for 10 minutes. Remove from the heat and let cool.

In a medium bowl, whisk the eggs with the sugar. Slowly add one-fourth of the hot milk mixture, whisking constantly. Return the warmed eggs to the pan and cook over low heat until creamy, about 10 minutes. Cover and refrigerate to chill. Discard the vanilla pod, transfer to an ice-cream machine, and process according to the manufacturer's instructions. (If you don't have an ice-cream machine, freeze the mixture until hard enough to scoop.)

MAKE THE FRUIT SALAD

In a large bowl, combine the fruit, orange juice, Moscato, and sugar and stir to combine. Garnish with the mint.

TO SERVE

Place 2 spoonfuls of fruit salad in each bowl and top with a scoop of ice cream.

Note: Save the peels to make Banana Peel Chutney (page 158). You can use any fruits for the fruit salad.

RECIPE NOTES:

Michel Troigros

Michel Troigros and I met almost twenty years ago, but only during the past ten years have we become friends. We met for the first time in the fall of 1999 at Osteria Francescana when we were a little restaurant with big dreams and no Michelin stars. He was sitting at the most intimidating table I had served so far, one with some iconic Italian chefs and restaurateurs including Fulvio Pierangelini, Sirio Maccioni, and Antonio Santini. We met again in 2004 while I was on a road trip with the journalist Andrea Petrini to film a program called *Guess Who Is Coming to Dinner?* We took a detour on the way to Jacques Decoret's restaurant in Vichy to eat in Roanne at the legendary Troigros family restaurant. Michel had become head chef and I was curious about how he was balancing the family restaurant and his own culinary voice. But it wasn't until 2007, on a trip to Modena, that we finally got to know each other and discovered our mutual passions for contemporary art, fast cars, and lyrical food.

When Michel came to Milan, he brought with him two Italian chefs that work with him in Roanne. That morning the truck offered spectacular asparagus. But apart from that there was a random selection of ingredients, including sausages, Squacqerone di Romagna cheese, eggs, lemons, and bananas. We went to the walk-in refrigerator to see what else we could find. Michel was so quiet, so I asked him, "*Michel, tutto bene?*" He replied, "Si, Massimo. Tutto bene. I was just thinking we need to remember how to cook with very little, as it was in the past when local resources had to be enough to nourish and amaze the palate." He talked about his thrifty grandmother, an Italian immigrant in France. Her fear of uncertainty drove her to consider all food sacred. Sacred was the right word and described not only his grandmother but also mine, and even my mother who was a young woman during World War II. Michel said poignantly, "I always have her in mind to guide me in the kitchen."

Michel is a mixture of Italian ancestry and deep French traditions. Italian flavors are in his blood from family holidays in Italy. He knew instinctively that with the few ingredients he had available, he could make a very nice Réconfort Soup. The name of the soup comes from the French word to comfort and restore the body and soul. This soup was everything I imagined from a chef like Michel. It was traditional and full of bright flavors and even brighter colors. It was a mixture of France and Italy, but most of all, it was a vibrant way to open a meal in the true spirit of "Bon appétit!"

The next dish was a logistical nightmare to prepare and plate, so much so that it united everyone in the kitchen to help. There wasn't enough meat for a main course, so he used eggs instead, re-creating a tripe recipe in a clever way. He boiled eggs, sliced them as if they were tripe, and served them in a rich sauce. This dish, Boiled Eggs Like Tripe, was one of the finest examples of making do with what you have. He noticed how carefully everyone worked in that kitchen to use the whole ingredient and everything available in the pantry. To this Michel added, "In my kitchen, I try to raise awareness about waste. I ask the team to respect ingredients, even when they're ugly, and to be careful about what they are going to throw away that could actually be saved."

Rarely do you see a chef so obsessed with the presentation of a dish as Michel was that night. One at a time, he layered the sliced eggs like a fan in the bowl, placed them over the tomato sauce, poured the béchamel sauce, and sprinkled chopped tomatoes and grated Parmigiano cheese.

The dessert drew the biggest smiles. Squacquerone is a fresh cheese from Romagna, like cottage cheese, but it has the disadvantage of quickly turning sour. We had a constant supply of this cheese at the Refettorio. Michel treated it like sour cream instead of a cheese, and with the addition of sugar and lemon zest, it tasted like lemon cream pie.

Since May we had been working with overripe brown bananas. By September 15, I felt like I had bananas coming out of my ears. Chefs had transformed these bananas into ice creams, banana breads, cakes, and chutney. Michel wanted to keep the banana in its natural shape, even if was bruised, because the curve simulated a smile. The plate was decorated like a face with a caramelized banana smile, caramelized pineapple eyes, and Squacqerone and lemon zest ice cream for hair.

Michel had lifted our spirits with his good humor and playfulness. He closed the evening with a story as valid and vitalizing for home cooks as restaurants. "Every Thursday, we make a bouillon in the biggest pot we have with all the peels, leaves, stems, and pits left from fresh vegetables," he said. "We let it cook very slowly for four days, during which we add ingredients left from different preparations. We filter this broth on the fifth day and it is very clear and tasty, like a consommé. We serve it as it is. The flavor is never the same, the proportions are never the same, but it always tastes very good."

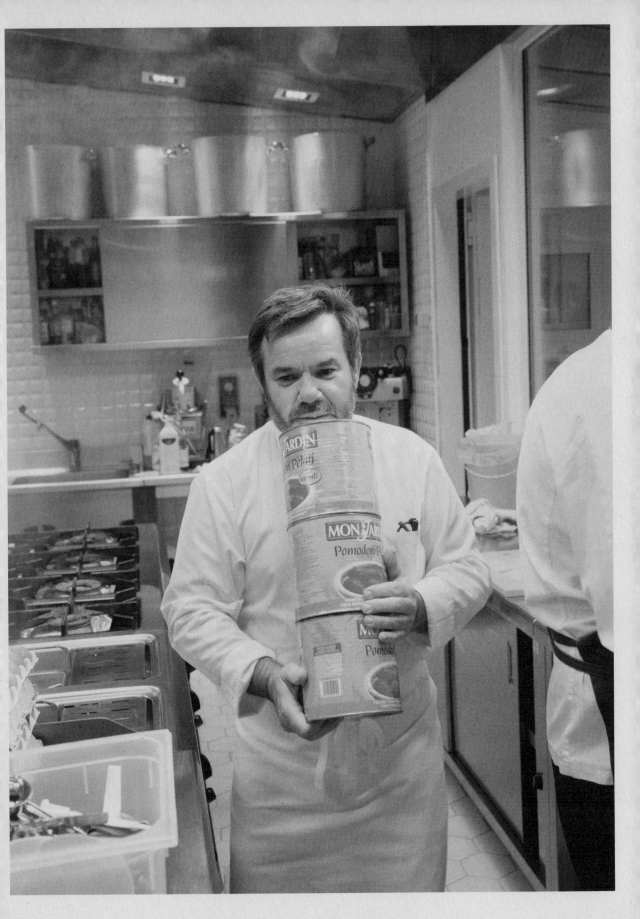

Michel Troisgros

BOILED EGGS LIKE TRIPE

Serves 6

9 eggs
5 teaspoons (20 g) butter
4 sweet onions, sliced
Salt and freshly ground black pepper
3 tablespoons all-purpose (plain) flour
1½ cups (375 ml) milk
1½ cups (375 g) canned whole peeled tomatoes, seeded and drained
⅔ cup (60 g) freshly grated Parmigiano-Reggiano cheese
2½ teaspoons curry powder

In a medium pot of water, combine the eggs and water to cover. Bring to a boil over medium heat and cook for 10 minutes. Cool, peel, slice, and set aside.

In a medium saucepan, melt the butter over low heat. Add the onions, cover, and cook until translucent, about 15 minutes. Season to taste with salt and pepper. Add the flour and cook for 3 minutes, stirring occasionally. Add the milk and cook for 5 minutes. Season to taste with salt and pepper. Set aside.

In a small saucepan, cook the tomatoes over medium heat until thick, about 15 minutes. Season to taste with salt and pepper.

To serve, place a spoonful of the tomato sauce in each bowl. Cover with slices of the hard-boiled eggs and dress with the béchamel sauce. Sprinkle with the Parmigiano and a pinch of curry.

RECIPE NOTES: _____
_____
_____
_____
_____
_____
_____
_____
_____
_____
_____
_____
_____
_____
_____
_____
_____
_____
_____
_____
_____
_____
_____
_____
_____

RÉCONFORT SOUP

Serves 6

2 white onions, peeled and halved
4 carrots
2 celery stalks, halved
5 garlic cloves
7 oz (200 g) Parmigiano-Reggiano rinds
8 asparagus spears, halved
Salt
5 oz (140 g) orecchiette pasta or other short pasta
9 oz (250 g) stale bread, cut into large cubes
generous ¾ cup (200 ml) milk
1 lb 2 oz (500 g) ground (minced) veal
Freshly ground black pepper

In a large pot, combine the onions, carrots, celery, garlic, Parmigiano rinds, and 2 quarts (2 liters) water. Cook over low heat for 30 minutes. Fish out the carrots and celery, slice, and set aside. Continue cooking for 2 hours. Strain through a fine-mesh sieve and return to the pot. Cook over medium heat until reduced by one third, about 10 minutes. Add the sliced carrots and celery and the asparagus. Season to taste with salt and set aside.

Bring a large pot of lightly salted water to a boil over medium heat. Add the orecchiette and cook until al dente. Drain and set aside.

In a medium bowl, combine the bread and milk and let soak until soft, about 5 minutes. Drain and squeeze out the extra liquid. Return to the bowl, add the veal, and mix until combined. Season with salt and pepper and mix. Form twenty ¾-inch (2 cm) meatballs.

Bring the broth to a simmer over medium heat. Add the meatballs and cook for 10 minutes. Add the pasta. Ladle the soup into bowls and serve.

📷   P. 271

RECIPE NOTES: _____
_____
_____
_____
_____
_____
_____
_____
_____
_____
_____
_____
_____
_____
_____
_____
_____

Michel Troisgros

BANANA SMILE

Serves 6

COCONUT CRUMBLE
3½ tablespoons (50 g) butter, at room temperature
½ cup (50 g) all-purpose (plain) flour
2 tablespoons plus 1 teaspoon granulated sugar
½ cup (50 g) unsweetened shredded coconut (dessicated)

SQUACQUERONE ICE CREAM
scant ½ cup (100 ml) heavy (whipping) cream
1⅔ cups (400 ml) milk
Grated zest of 2 limes
7 oz (200 g) Squacquerone di Romagna cheese or other soft, mild cheese
¾ cup (150 g) granulated sugar

CARAMELIZED BANANA AND PINEAPPLE
2 tablespoons raisins
1 tablespoon rum
½ lemon
3 bananas, halved lengthwise (see Note)
5 tablespoons (75 g) butter
½ pineapple, peeled and quartered
2 tablespoons granulated sugar

MAKE THE COCONUT CRUMBLE

Preheat the oven to 325°F (160°C/Gas Mark 3). Line a baking sheet with parchment paper.

In a medium bowl, combine the butter, flour, sugar, and coconut and mix until a dough is formed. Spread the mixture on the prepared baking sheet and bake until crisp, about 15 minutes.

MAKE THE SQUACQUERONE ICE CREAM

In a medium pot, combine the cream, milk, and lime zest and bring to a boil over medium heat. Let cool, then strain through a fine-mesh sieve.

In a large bowl, combine the cheese and sugar. Add the milk mixture and stir to combine. Cover and refrigerate to chill. Transfer to an ice-cream machine and process according to the manufacturer's instructions. (If you don't have an ice-cream machine, freeze the mixture until hard enough to scoop.)

MAKE THE CARAMELIZED BANANA AND PINEAPPLE

In a small bowl, soak the raisins in the rum until soft.

In a medium bowl, squeeze the lemon juice over the bananas to avoid browning.

In a medium frying pan, melt the butter over medium heat. Add the bananas and pineapple and cook until golden brown, about 6 minutes. Add the raisins and sugar and cook until caramelized, about 3 minutes.

>>

TO SERVE

Place the bananas and pineapple on each plate and sprinkle with the coconut crumble. Top with a scoop of the squacquerone ice cream.

Note: Save the peels to make Banana Peel Chutney (page 158).

📷   P. 273

RECIPE NOTES: _____

Michel Troisgros

MSA Culinary Arts Academy of Istanbul

The MSA Culinary Arts Academy of Istanbul is Turkey's leading cooking school. I was introduced to the school through a travel and food writer named Cemre Narin. I will never forget meeting Cemre at Osteria Francescana on a warm summer day at lunch. She had come to dine with her husband and two boys, ages three and five. What I remember most is how curious and enthusiastic her older son was about food. He ordered the same tasting menu as his parents and ignored the fact that his younger brother was eating pasta with ragù. He stuck with it, plate after plate, to try new flavors he wasn't familiar with.

Cemre and I ran into each other annually at the World's 50 Best awards in London, which over the past years has become more than an awards ceremony; it is the best chance to catch up with friends from around the world that I might only see once a year. It was there, in May 2015, while talking to friends about the pending opening of the Refettorio that was only weeks away, that Cemre found out about the project. She jumped at the chance to get involved. "The minute I heard about it, I thought Turkish chefs should definitely be a part of it," she said. "Turkish cuisine, like other ancient, traditional cuisines, is filled with smart solutions for food waste and humble yet delicious recipes that make the most of every ingredient."

Cemre suggested that we invite the MSA. She thought the school was "a natural match since it is the leading Turkish culinary school, and more important, one that has always been a pioneer in raising the quality of life through gastronomy." When she said the last sentence, I shouted out, "Yes!" and nearly knocked her socks off. "That is exactly what we need at the Refettorio," I said, "Raising the quality of life through gastronomy."

The cooks from MSA were quite surprised when the truck arrived at the back door. They expected to find a variety of protein and colorful produce, but as they looked into the almost empty truck, they started to wonder what they were going to cook. There were only two racks of ingredients with three packages of fresh mozzarella, a couple of kilos of cucumbers, eggplants (aubergines), and some bread. So Cristina took them to the dry, cold, and frozen storage areas. The first thing they found was vegetable stock—*brodo di tutto*—that I had made the day before with all the vegetable trimmings and a couple of Parmigiano rinds. Immediately they started thinking about how they could use that to make an *ayran aşı*, a traditional chilled soup with yogurt and herbs. They had brought Turkish yogurt with them in their suitcases to make it as authentic as possible.

In keeping with Turkish traditional dining, they made lots of small courses: a soup, a couple of appetizers (or *mezze*), a protein with a vegetable, and a dessert. They found plenty of ground turkey meat in the freezer, which was perfect for preparing *köfte*, a very typical Turkish meatball. The eggplants were charred and pureed. The soggy zucchini (courgette) became a mezze called *saksuka*.

I could tell they were in shock to work this way. Their roles as leaders— an administrator and a teacher—had been turned upside down. They were the students now, learning to cook in a completely new environment. But all their experience would help them navigate their way through this maze to arrive at a delicious meal.

Later, Cem Erol, the school's headmaster, expanded on the idea of working with waste, "I look at the issue of waste not only from a culinary perspective. It is a way of living and appreciating the goods you consume. It is a way of changing the form, or utilizing the product in different ways or functions. After you are done with its initial function, with a little bit of creativity, you benefit from its secondary or other functions."

This was exactly what we were doing with stale bread, cheese rinds, and trimmings, with the leftovers that accumulated in our refrigerators. We were trying to turn them into something else, not a shadow of their former selves, but a brand new thing that had value. They were able to bring age-old Turkish recipes into an exchange with ideas about how to prepare dishes with ingredients that many people consider waste. They did this not as teachers but as students, and in that state of play and discovery they were brought to a place of learning.

September 17

CHILLED YOGURT SOUP

Serves 8

1 quart (1 liter) yogurt
1 quart (1 liter) vegetable stock
1¼ cups (200 g) canned chickpeas, drained and rinsed
½ cup (100 g) canned lentils, drained rinsed
Crushed sea salt and freshly ground black pepper
Chili Oil (recipe follows), for drizzling
Herb Oil (recipe follows), for drizzling

In a medium bowl, whisk together the yogurt and vegetable stock. Add the chickpeas and lentils and season to taste with salt and pepper. Refrigerate until cold, at least 1 hour.

Ladle the soup into bowls and drizzle with the chili and herb oils.

CHILI OIL

Makes 2 cups (500 ml)

generous 2 cups (500 ml) vegetable oil
1¾ oz (50 g) fresh red chilies
½ teaspoon ground allspice
1 clove garlic
5 teaspoons fennel seeds
2 whole star anise
4 cinnamon sticks
1 teaspoon salt

In a blender, combine all the ingredients and process at high speed for 4 minutes. Pass through cheesecloth two times.

HERB OIL

Makes 2 cups (500 ml)

generous 2 cups (500 ml) vegetable oil
7 oz (200 g) parsley
2 tablespoons thyme
½ oz (10 g) chives
1 teaspoon sea salt

In a blender, combine all the ingredients and process at high speed for 4 minutes. Pass through cheesecloth two times.

RECIPE NOTES: _____
_____
_____
_____
_____
_____
_____
_____
_____
_____
_____

SAKSUKA WITH ZUCCHINI AND POTATOES

Serves 8

TOMATO SAUCE
3 tablespoons plus 1 teaspoon extra-virgin olive oil
1 small onion, chopped
5 garlic cloves, sliced
4 cups (950 ml) canned tomato sauce (seasoned passata)
7 oz (200 g) parsley, chopped
Salt and freshly ground black pepper

VEGETABLES
2 tablespoons plus a generous 2 cups (500 ml) corn oil
2 onions, sliced
4 medium potatoes, cut into 1-inch (3 cm) chunks
5 zucchini (courgettes), cubed
All-purpose (plain) flour, for dredging
Sea salt

GARNISH
generous ¾ cup (100 g) freshly made breadcrumbs
1 tablespoon chopped parsley

MAKE THE TOMATO SAUCE

In a medium pot, warm the oil over medium heat. Add the onion and garlic and cook, stirring, until translucent, 6 minutes. Add the tomato sauce and simmer until thick, 20 to 30 minutes. Using a hand blender, blend until smooth. Add the parsley and season to taste with salt and pepper. Set aside.

COOK THE VEGETABLES

In a medium pot, warm 2 tablespoons of the oil over medium heat. Add the onions and cook, stirring, until dark brown and caramelized, 10 minutes. Set aside

In another medium pot, heat the remaining generous 2 cups (500 ml) of the oil over medium heat. Add the potatoes and fry until soft and golden brown, 12 minutes. Transfer to paper towels to drain.

Dust the zucchini (courgettes) with the flour. Add the zucchini to the same pot of hot oil and fry until golden brown, 3 minutes. Transfer to paper towels to drain.

In a medium bowl, combine the onions, potatoes, zucchini, and tomato sauce .

MAKE THE GARNISH

Preheat the oven to 350°F (180°C/Gas Mark 4). Line a baking sheet with parchment paper.

Spread the breadcrumbs on the baking sheet and bake until golden brown, 10 minutes

TO SERVE

Divide the vegetables and top with breadcumbs and parsley.

    P. 279

TURKISH MEATBALLS WITH EGGPLANT

Serves 8

EGGPLANT

2¼ lb (1 kg) eggplants (aubergines)
½ cup (50 g) all-purpose (plain) flour
3½ tablespoons (50 g) butter
1 cup (250 ml) milk
3½ oz (100 g) mozzarella cheese, chopped
4 tablespoons freshly grated Parmigiano-Reggiano cheese
Pinch of freshly grated nutmeg
Sea salt and freshly ground black pepper

TURKISH MEATBALLS

1 lb 2 oz (500 g) ground (minced) turkey
3½ oz (100 g) diced fatty sausage
2 egg yolks (see Note)
generous ¾ cup (50 g) finely crumbled stale bread
6 tablespoons chopped parsley
½ tablespoon crushed chili flakes
½ tablespoon ground cumin
Sea salt and freshly ground black pepper
1 stick plus 6 tablespoons (200 g) butter

FOR SERVING

Extra-virgin olive oil, for drizzling
3½ oz (100 g) parsley, chopped

MAKE THE EGGPLANT

Char the eggplants (aubergines) over the open flame of a stove burner all over until soft. (If you don't have a gas stove, run under a hot broiler [grill].) When cool enough to handle, peel and chop.

In a medium pan, toast the flour over low heat until lightly browned. Add the butter and stir to combine. Stir in the milk and cook until thick, about 3 minutes. Add the eggplant, mix well, and cook for another 10 minutes. Add the mozzarella, Parmigiano, and nutmeg and stir to combine. Season to taste with salt and pepper. Set aside.

MAKE THE TURKISH MEATBALLS

In a medium bowl, combine the turkey, sausage, egg yolks, breadcrumbs, parsley, chili flakes, and cumin. Season with salt and pepper and mix to combine. Cover with plastic wrap (clingfilm) and refrigerate for 30 minutes.

Preheat the oven to 350°F (180°C/Gas Mark 4). Line a baking sheet with parchment paper.

Form the meat mixture into 1-ounce (30 g) balls and transfer to the prepared baking sheet. Bake until golden and cooked through, 10 to 15 minutes.

Meanwhile, in a medium pan, melt the butter over low heat.

When the meatballs are cooked, transfer them to the pan with the melted butter and gently toss to coat.

>>

TO SERVE

Place a spoonful of the eggplant on each plate and top with 3 meatballs. Drizzle with olive oil and garnish with the parsley.

Note: Save the egg whites to make Meringues (pages 32 or 387).

RECIPE NOTES:

DEMIR TATLISI WITH SALEP ICE CREAM

Serves 8

DEMIR TATLISI
    ½ cup (100 g) granulated sugar
    ⅓ cup (175 g) all-purpose (plain) flour
    1 egg
    ½ teaspoon baking powder
    ¼ teaspoon salt
    1 quart (1 liter) vegetable oil, for deep-frying

SALEP ICE CREAM
    1 quart (1 liter) milk
    scant 2 cups (400 g) granulated sugar
    1 tablespoon salep (powdered orchid root) or cinnamon

MAKE THE DEMIR TATLISI

In a medium pot, combine the sugar and a scant ½ cup (100 ml) water over medium heat. Simmer for 10 minutes until the sugar dissolves and becomes a syrup. Let cool.

In a medium bowl, whisk together the flour, egg, baking powder, salt, and ¾ cup (175 ml) water to form a slightly thick batter.

In a medium pot, heat the vegetable oil to 347°F (175°C) over medium heat. Dip a rosette iron into the hot oil to preheat it, about 2 minutes. Shake off the excess oil and dip into the batter about three-fourths of the way down, then immediately plunge the iron into the hot oil. Fry the rosette until golden brown, about 30 seconds. Immediately transfer to the syrup and let soak for 30 seconds. Transfer to a tray lined with parchment paper and set aside. Repeat to make more rosettes.

MAKE THE SALEP ICE CREAM

In a medium pot, bring the milk and sugar to a boil over medium heat. Reduce the heat to low, add the salep, and simmer until slightly thickened, about 6 minutes. Transfer the pot to a large bowl of ice and water to quick-chill. Transfer to an ice-cream machine and process according to the manufacturer's instructions. (If you don't have an ice-cream machine, freeze the mixture until hard enough to scoop.)

TO SERVE

Place a scoop of the salep ice cream in each bowl and top with 1 demir tatlisi.

RECIPE NOTES:

Andoni Luiz Aduriz

Andoni Luiz Aduriz is like a brother to me. Back in 2010, less than a month after an electrical fire had burned down the kitchen of his restaurant Mugaritz, we shared a stage in Melbourne in front of an audience of five hundred. Andoni and I had crossed paths at festivals here and there, but we really didn't know each other. We became close in front of that audience, perhaps because this time we were not cooking. We were just talking about our ideas, the madness and the motivations behind our kitchens and our recipes. We have been brothers ever since.

Andoni is Basque in every possible way. He is an intellectual, a stubborn and delirious thinker who never seems to turn off his batteries. His passions bring his cooking into the theater, the science lab, and nature. In 1998 he opened Mugaritz, a restaurant on a rural property thirty minutes outside of San Sebastián where he established himself as a naturalist with an obsessive attention to local ingredients. Whenever we get together the chemistry is disarming and ideas fly like ping-pong balls. What I like most about Andoni is that he is just as crazy as me, if not more so.

I had invited Andoni to Milan when we were together at the Gastronomica food conference in Madrid. Almost one year later, he was here. The truck was late that morning and so was I. Andoni and his sous-chef, Llorenç Sagarra, took a good look around the kitchen. There was a lot of bread and rice in the pantry and mixed cheeses, milk, and eggs in the walk-in refrigerator. After a quick analysis of the situation, it seemed clear that they would be making *migas* for the main course and rice pudding for dessert. Anything else that arrived would be considered a bonus.

Migas is a Spanish recipe made with finely minced bread and it is dressed according to the region of Spain. It is a humble dish that was traditionally made with whatever people had on hand. Andoni didn't know what kind of migas they would be making until the truck showed up. When it did, there were lots of onions, hamburger meat,

and individually packaged balls of mozzarella. They unloaded everything.

When I arrived, it was almost lunchtime. Llorenç was in a trance, totally and utterly focused on getting the work done. Andoni was stirring the meat sauce and I caught him by surprise. We hugged as if ten years had gone by. "My brother," I said, "what are you cooking, ragù?" "No, no, no, no, no!" he shouted, "Migas! But these will be different from the migas we typically make. A traditionalist would say 'you're crazy to put in ground beef or veal,' but that's what we have here today."

It did not surprise me that Andoni would be serving something nontraditional. Then he said, "Did you know that rice pudding was originally a Jewish recipe?" He had changed the subject so quickly that I didn't understand what he was talking about. I told him that I didn't know anything about rice pudding. He continued on his train of thought, "We want to celebrate coexistence, so a menu with multicultural origins is perfect."

Here was the Andoni I knew: the poet, the intellect, the historian weaving lyrical stories into his recipes while he browned the beef. Andoni, the naturalist, had found this kitchen, with its random ingredients—the beautiful and the ugly, the fresh and the not so fresh—a foreign landscape to explore with enthusiasm. In that moment it was clear why having chefs like Andoni was so important to the project. Anyone can make a good meal, even with so-so ingredients, but how many chefs are curious enough to find beauty and flavor in expired mozzarella, stale bread, and some rice?

That day we were hosting the Fratelli di San Francesco for lunch, an association that takes care of orphaned refugees under eighteen. All we knew about the boys was that they came from different parts of the world. Minutes before they arrived we looked at each other and shared a mutual thought, "Oh, how nice, we are giving them a meal." But as soon as they walked in, we realized that we had oversimplified the situation. Many did not speak Italian or English

and we could read the anxiety on their faces. First we served a simple bowl with mozzarella, tomato sauce, and some parsley powder on top, and gradually we noticed that the eating broke the silence. They had a hard time trusting the migas, but relief came with the rice pudding. Rice means many things to many people. It is universal and self-explanatory.

Lunch was over. As the boys left, the tension dropped. Even though we had done our best, we felt we had failed. No meal could fill the emptiness inside those boys. Andoni finally sat down and said: "If you have a difficult, complicated life, sometimes the only pleasure you get is sitting down to a meal. If we gave these kids a moment of peace, well, that's what food is about."

Andoni Luiz Aduriz

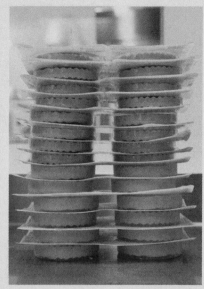

MIGAS A LA EXTREMEÑA

Serves 6

1 lb 5 oz (600 g) stale bread, cut into slices ¼ inch
    (5 mm) thick
6 eggs
10 oz (300 g) ground (minced) beef
Salt
scant ½ cup (100 ml) extra-virgin olive oil, plus more
    for serving
6 garlic cloves, crushed with the side of a knife
1¾ teaspoons smoked paprika

Place the bread slices on a tray and cover with a wet towel.

Bring a medium pot of lightly salted water to a boil over medium heat. Crack the eggs one by one into the water and cook for 6 minutes. Carefully remove with a slotted spoon.

Season the beef with salt. In a medium pot, heat the olive oil over medium heat. Add the beef and sauté until golden brown, about 10 minutes. Add the garlic and sauté until golden brown. Remove from the heat and stir in the paprika. Return to the heat and add the sliced bread, stirring constantly. Add ¼ cup (60 ml) water and continue stirring until a homogenous mixture is obtained. Remove from the heat and season to taste with salt. Set aside, reserving the garlic.

To serve, place 2 spoonfuls of migas in the center of each plate. Make a hole in the center and top with a warm egg. Drizzle with olive oil and top with the reserved garlic.

📷   P. 287

RECIPE NOTES:

Andoni Luiz Aduriz

Serves 6

1 lb 2 oz (500 g) canned crushed (finely chopped) tomatoes
scant ½ cup (3½ oz/100 g) tomato paste (puree)
2 teaspoons minced garlic plus 2 whole garlic cloves
1 teaspoon dried oregano
1 tablespoon granulated sugar
1¼ teaspoons freshly ground black pepper
¼ teaspoon salt
1 lb 10 oz (750 g) mozzarella cheese
3½ oz (100 g) stale bread, finely crumbled (1¾ cups)
1¾ oz (50 g) parsley
5 tablespoons grated Parmigiano-Reggiano cheese rinds

In a medium pot, combine the crushed tomatoes, tomato paste (puree), minced garlic, oregano, sugar, pepper, and salt and cook over medium heat, stirring constantly, until creamy, about 40 minutes.

Slice the mozzarella cheese and transfer to a plate. Cover with plastic wrap (clingfilm) and refrigerate until ready to serve.

In a blender, combine the breadcrumbs, whole garlic, parsley, and grated Parmigiano rinds and blend into a paste. Set aside.

Preheat the oven to 350°F (180°C/Gas Mark 4). Line a baking sheet with parchment paper

Place the mozzarella slices on the prepared baking sheet and bake until bubbling, about 10 minutes.

To serve, place a spoonful of the tomato sauce in each dish and top with a slice of mozzarella. Sprinkle with the parsley-cheese paste and serve.

RECIPE NOTES:

Andoni Luiz Aduriz

RICE PUDDING WITH CINNAMON AND CHOCOLATE

Serves 6

3 cups plus 3 tablespoons (750 ml) milk
1 cinnamon stick
1½ cups (300 g) rice, rinsed
scant ½ cup (90 g) granulated sugar
generous ¾ cup (150 g) bittersweet chocolate chips

In a medium pot, combine the milk and cinnamon stick and simmer over low heat for 10 minutes.

When the milk begins to boil, add the rice and gently stir constantly for 20 minutes. When the rice is almost cooked, add the sugar and stir until soft, about 10 minutes. Remove the cinamon stick and let cool. Cover and refrigerate.

To serve, place a scoop of rice pudding in a dessert bowl and garnish with chocolate chips.

RECIPE NOTES: _____

_____
_____
_____
_____
_____
_____
_____
_____
_____
_____
_____
_____
_____
_____
_____
_____
_____

Jessica Murphy

My wife, Lara, and Cristina met Jessica Murphy in Bilbao at the first Parabere Forum, a conference on women working in gastronomy. They came back from the conference with a list of names of women who were working to make the industry more equally represented. One of the people they were excited about was Jessica, a chef originally from New Zealand and now living on the western coast of Ireland. She and her husband David own Kai Café. We were pleased to find out she was traveling to Italy during the Refettorio project and asked her to join us to cook lunch and dinner.

Jess grew up in rural New Zealand. Her family went to town every six months, so they utilized everything they had. "We didn't waste anything because there was nothing to waste," she said, adding, "My mum always says that sell and use-by dates are bullshit anyway!"

At Kai Café, Jess works with local farmers and fishermen. She told me that they prepare their grow lists with farmers in January or, as she so aptly stated, "We guesstimate how much veg we will need. This is also helpful for the farmers who can then divide up their fields accordingly for their crops, which in turn is better for the soil and crop rotation."

Although we had explained the setup to Jess, she later admitted she was pretty shocked by the situation. "I didn't realize that we had to literally grab from the truck," she said, "and while grabbing we needed to think about a menu and what we would cook. You couldn't be greedy and really had to think on your feet. It was a real 'get on with it' moment." She handled it quite well and I never would have known that she had a minute of doubt. She is a very confident young chef who trusts her instincts and her abilities. She was cooking with her husband, David, for one hundred kids for lunch in a matter of hours and another one hundred adults that night.

Jess and David prepared a multicultural menu starting with *kosheri*, a Middle Eastern dish. She made it with lentils, caramelized onions, rice, macaroni, and spices like cinnamon, nutmeg, and turmeric. A dish like this can feed an army at very low cost. The fact that a New Zealander, living in Ireland was cooking an Egyptian dish, which happens to be part of Peruvian food culture, in a context of a soup kitchen in Italy, boggled my mind. It was a perfect storm; a literal collision of cultures, techniques, and culinary history.

Jess had taken all the packages of preformed hamburgers off the truck that morning. She mixed the meat with grated Parmigiano, eggs, breadcrumbs, garlic, and black pepper for savory and soft meatballs. Many chefs had made meatballs during the past months. It was an easy and appetizing solution for the variety of mixed meats that were delivered almost every morning. What is interesting is that each recipe was slightly different, and how the chefs accompanied the meatballs says a lot about them. The element that defined these meatballs actually was the sauce. Jess made a playful recipe that she called "burnt bread dip." She literally burned slices of bread and then proceeded to char chilies, red bell peppers, garlic, and onions. Everything was blended into a creamy sauce that replicated and condensed the flavors of a toasted bun with ketchup. The meatballs were in sauce, but the taste was classic American hamburger with all the fixings on a grilled bun. I loved this. And now I understood why Lara and Cristina had been so excited to meet her.

Cooking at the Refettorio brought out the resourcefulness in everyone, and at times the chefs seemed more like magicians pulling bunnies and bouquets out of their hats. Out of necessity creative solutions come to the surface. This was also the case with dessert, where so many chefs turned to the professional ice-cream maker to salvage ingredients, resulting in many unusual flavors. One discovery for me was that soft cheeses like ricotta and *squacquerone* made excellent ice creams; also yogurt drinks and packaged snacks were perfect. The obvious and most common ingredient was overripe fruit. Nearly every day we had fruit to work with. Every time we made a fruit-based ice cream I thought, "Where was all this fruit going if it wasn't being turned into ice cream?" Jess came out with another "burnt" flavor for her original ice cream. This time she browned honey into a dark sap and added it to a cream and salt mixture and blended it with toasted millet. It tasted like breakfast oatmeal with honey and we were all transported to Galway, the wild coast of Ireland.

Serves 6 to 8

½ cup (120 ml) extra-virgin olive oil
2 white onions, thinly sliced
2 garlic cloves, chopped
2 pepperoncini or other mild chilies, chopped
2 cans (28 oz/795 g) peeled whole tomatoes, drained
    and chopped
4 tablespoons apple cider vinegar
½ cup (20 g) chopped cilantro (coriander)
10 basil leaves
Leaves of 4 sprigs oregano
2 teaspoons ground cumin
2 tablespoons plus 1½ teaspoons salt
1 tablespoon tomato paste (puree)
Freshly ground black pepper
1½ cups (300 g) lentils, rinsed
2 tablespoons butter
7 oz (200 g) vermicelli (broken into smaller pieces)
    and elbow macaroni or other short pasta
1 cup (200 g) basmati or other long-grain rice, rinsed
1½ teaspoons freshly grated nutmeg
1½ teaspoons ground cinnamon

In a large frying pan, heat 4 tablespoons of the olive oil over medium heat. Add the onions and cook until well caramelized, about 20 minutes. Remove from the pan and drain on paper towels. Wipe out the pan.

In the same pan, heat the remaining 4 tablespoons olive oil over medium heat. Add the garlic and chilies and sauté for 2 minutes. Add the tomatoes, vinegar, cilantro (coriander), basil, oregano, cumin, and 1 tablespoon of salt and bring to a boil over medium heat. Reduce the heat to low and simmer until slightly thickened, about 20 minutes. Add the tomato paste (puree) and stir. Season to taste with salt and pepper. Set the tomato sauce aside.

Meanwhile, in a medium saucepan, combine the lentils and 1 tablespoon of salt with water to cover. Cover and bring to a boil over high heat. Reduce to medium-low and simmer until tender but intact, about 25 minutes. Drain and set aside. Clean the saucepan.

In the same saucepan, melt the butter over medium heat. Add the vermicelli and macaroni and sauté until golden brown, about 2 minutes. Add the rice and stir until the entire mixture is well coated. Add 2 cups (475 ml) water, the nutmeg, cinnamon, 1½ teaspoons salt, and ½ teaspoon black pepper. Cover, reduce the heat to low, and simmer for 12 minutes. Remove from the heat, remove the lid, cover the pan with a clean tea towel, and replace the lid. Let sit for 5 minutes to allow the towel to absorb extra moisture.

In a large bowl, toss together the lentils, rice/vermicelli mixture, and three-fourths of the onions. Season to taste with salt and pepper.

To serve, transfer to a large serving platter and garnish with the remaining onions. Serve with the tomato sauce.

MEATBALLS WITH BURNT BREAD DIP

Serves 6

MEATBALLS

3 tablespoons extra-virgin olive oil
5 cups (1.2 liters) tomato sauce (seasoned passata)
2¼ lb (1 kg) ground (minced) beef, turkey, pork, or chicken
⅔ (60 g) freshly grated Parmigiano-Reggiano cheese
4 large eggs
3½ oz (100 g) stale bread, finely crumbled (about 1¾ cups)
3 large garlic cloves, minced
4 tablespoons chopped parsley
1 teaspoon dried oregano
2 teaspoons salt
1 teaspoon freshly ground black pepper
1 teaspoon minced pepperoncino

BURNT BREAD DIP

9 oz (250 g) stale bread (sourdough or focaccia)
½ onion
1 red bell pepper
1 pepperoncini or other mild chili, seeded
5 garlic cloves, peeled but whole
1 tablespoon honey
1 tomato, roughly chopped
1 bunch parsley, roughly chopped
2 teaspoons celery powder
Juice of 2 lemons
scant ½ cup (100 ml) almond milk
scant ½ cup (100 ml) extra-virgin olive oil
Salt and freshly ground black pepper

MAKE THE MEATBALLS

Preheat the oven to 450°F (230°C/Gas Mark 8). Grease a 9 x 13-inch (23 x 33 cm) baking dish with olive oil.

In a small saucepan, heat the tomato sauce over medium-high heat, stirring often.

In a large bowl, combine the beef, Parmigiano, eggs, breadcrumbs, olive oil, garlic, parsley, oregano, salt, pepper, and pepperoncino and mix by hand until thoroughly combined. Form meatballs the size of golf balls, making sure to pack the meat firmly. Transfer to the prepared baking dish, being careful to line the meatballs up snugly (they should be touching one another).

Bake until the internal temperature of a meatball reaches 165°F (74°C), about 20 minutes. Drain the excess grease out of the baking dish. Pour the tomato sauce over the meatballs, return to the oven, and bake until the sauce is bubbling, about 15 minutes.

>>

MAKE THE BURNT BREAD DIP

In a dry frying pan, burn the bread over high heat until black. Repeat with the onion, bell pepper, chili, and garlic. Transfer to a food processor or blender and blend until smooth. Add the honey, tomato, parsley, celery powder, lemon juice, almond milk, and olive oil and blend until smooth. Season to taste with salt and pepper.

TO SERVE

Serve the meatballs topped with a spoonful of the burnt bread dip.

RECIPE NOTES: _____
_____
_____
_____
_____
_____
_____
_____
_____
_____
_____
_____
_____
_____
_____
_____
_____
_____
_____
_____
_____
_____
_____
_____
_____
_____
_____
_____
_____
_____
_____
_____
_____
_____

Serves 6 to 8

½ cup (100 g) millet
1⅔ cups (400 ml) milk
1¼ cups (300 ml) heavy (whipping) cream
¼ teaspoon flaky sea salt
9½ tablespoons (200 g) orange blossom honey or any local
    honey, plus more for serving
3 egg yolks (see Note)

In a medium frying pan, toast the millet over low heat until golden brown, about 6 minutes.

In a medium pot, bring the milk, cream, and salt to a boil over medium heat. Immediately remove from the heat and let rest for 20 minutes. Pass through a fine-mesh sieve into a clean pot. Stir in half the toasted millet and set aside.

In a medium saucepan, heat the honey over medium heat until it bubbles and darkens, about 10 minutes. Set aside to cool completely.

In a large bowl, whisk the egg yolks for a few minutes until thick, pale, and fluffy.

Return the milk mixture to the stove over low heat. Slowly add one-fourth of the hot milk mixture to the eggs, stirring constantly so as not to cook the eggs. Return the warmed eggs to the pot and cook until the mixture is slightly thick and coats the back of a spoon, about 10 minutes. Let cool, cover, and transfer to the fridge to chill. Transfer to an ice-cream machine and process according the manufacturer's instructions. (If you don't have an ice-cream machine, freeze the mixture until hard enough to scoop.)

To serve, place a tablespoon of the reserved toasted millet in each bowl and top with a scoop of the ice cream. Drizzle with honey.

Note: Save the egg whites to make Meringues (page 32).

📷   P. 297

RECIPE NOTES:

Manuel and Christian Costardi are brothers who run a restaurant in a hotel named after their mother, Cinzia, in the small town of Vercelli on the eastern border of Piedmont. Growing up with Mamma Cinzia at the helm of the fourth-generation family business sounds like a heavy cross to bear, but Manuel and Christian, with their spirited personalities, not only carry this cross, but also wave it proudly.

The restaurant's success and recent Michelin star, is due to the brothers' ability to balance respect for traditional recipes with a touch of pop-art sensibility. The most iconic dish at the restaurant is a risotto served in a soup can with a label that references Campbell's and Andy Warhol's reinterpretation of the classic American brand. From this dish, it would be easy to assume that the Costardis are just about fun and games, but I found out while cooking with them that there is more to a book than its cover.

The bearded and tattooed chefs served their infamous Costardi's canned risotto at the Refettorio. It was easy to see that they wanted to serve the guests some fun with this dish. As the red tins left the kitchen the contagious cheerfulness of Manuel and Christian spread to the volunteers and the guests.

I was more interested in how the rice had been prepared. They had made a rich broth with Parmigiano rinds that simmered for half a day. Then they used the zucchini (courgette) trimmings to garnish the risotto before serving the rice in the cans. Every step of the way they had worked with discarded ingredients and transformed them into something new. This was something they were accustomed to. Back at their restaurant, they toast potato peels to make starchy and smoky broths for risotto, for instance. Manuel explained their way of working: "When that peculiar mix of consciousness and whimsical creativity takes over, you can see waste as a resource. Ingredients can change shape, consistency, and texture, and produce flavors that are different from those we are accustomed to."

For the main course, they prepared comfort food: mashed potatoes with meatballs, chunks of porcini mushrooms, and a clear mushroom broth. It wasn't a decorative plate or served in a fancy container, and it certainly wasn't conceptual, but it was really satisfying and good. They liked to have fun but could also play it straight.

I asked Manuel what was for dessert. He pointed to the refrigerator. When I opened it, I found one hundred glasses of panna cotta. Manuel looked over at me and put his thumbs up just like my sixteen-year-old son, Charlie, does for approval. He showed me a baking tray covered with slices of toasted bread and explained that the dessert would be served with a piece of toast sunk into the panna cotta, as if was being dipped in a glass of milk. This image reminded me of the bowls of hot milk with sugar and breadcrumbs that I loved as a kid. While I was telling them about my childhood memories, I thought, *Are these guys even going to understand what I am talking about?* But Manuel suddenly stopped me and said: "You know, Massimo, one of our fondest memories we have is with our grandmother. She was the one who taught us everything we know about food. Do you know how many nights she would make dinner with a few slices of toasted bread served with a broth of vegetable peels and cheese rinds?" And then it was clear to me that, under those hipster beards, there were two kids remembering their grandmother, just like me.

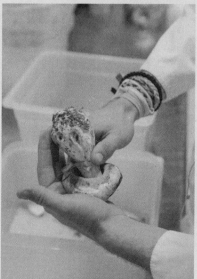

September 24

Serves 6

CONFIT TOMATOES
    4 medium tomatoes, halved
    1½ tablespoons granulated sugar

TOASTED BREADCRUMBS
    1 tablespoon extra-virgin olive oil
    5 oz (150 g) stale bread, finely crumbled (3½ cups)
    1 tablespoon grated fresh ginger
    ½ tablespoon granulated sugar

RISOTTO
    5 zucchini (courgettes), cut into ⅓-inch (1 cm) dice, ends
        trimmed and reserved
    10 oz (300 g) Parmigiano-Reggiano cheese rinds, chopped
    2¼ cups (420 g) carnaroli or other short-grain rice
    Salt and freshly ground black pepper
    7 oz (200 g) crescenza cheese or other soft, mild cheese,
        chopped
    3½ tablespoons (50 g) butter
    ¾ cup plus 2 tablespoons (80 g) freshly grated Parmigiano-
        Reggiano cheese
    1 tablespoon extra-virgin olive oil

MAKE THE CONFIT TOMATOES

Preheat the oven to 275°F (140°C/Gas Mark 1). Line a baking
sheet with parchment paper.
    Arrange the tomatoes on the lined baking sheet and
sprinkle with the sugar. Bake until almost dry, about
30 minutes.

MAKE THE TOASTED BREADCRUMBS

In a medium frying pan, heat the olive oil over medium heat.
Add the breadcrumbs, ginger, and sugar and sauté until golden
brown, about 7 minutes. Remove from the pan and set aside.

>>

MAKE THE RISOTTO

Set up a large bowl of ice and water. Fill a medium pot with
1½ quarts (1.5 liters) water and bring to a boil over medium
heat. Add the zucchini (courgettes) and cook for 1 minute.
Keeping the cooking water in the pot, scoop out the zucchini
and transfer to the ice bath to cool. Drain and set aside.
    Add the reserved zucchini trimmings and the Parmigiano
rinds to the pot of cooking water. Bring to a boil over medium
heat and cook for 20 minutes. Strain the broth through a sieve
into a bowl.
    In a large saucepan, toast the rice over medium heat, about
3 minutes. Add 4 cups (1 liter) of the Parmigiano broth and
simmer for 5 minutes. Add the zucchini. Season with salt and
pepper and continue simmering until the rice is al dente, about
12 minutes. Remove from the heat, add the crescenza cheese
and butter, and stir to combine. Stir in the grated Parmigiano.

TO SERVE

Place a spoonful of the risotto in each bowl and drizzle with
the olive oil. Sprinkle with the toasted breadcrumbs and
garnish with the confit tomatoes.

RECIPE NOTES: _____
_____
_____
_____
_____
_____
_____
_____
_____
_____
_____
_____
_____
_____
_____
_____
_____
_____
_____
_____
_____
_____
_____
_____
_____
_____
_____
_____
_____
_____
_____
_____

Manuel & Christian Costardi

MEATBALLS WITH PORCINI MUSHROOMS AND MASHED POTATOES

Serves 6

MEATBALLS

2¼ lb (1 kg) ground (minced) beef, chicken, pork, or turkey
1 tablespoon salt
1 teaspoon freshly ground black pepper
1¼ cups (300 ml) extra-virgin olive oil
Leaves from 2 sprigs thyme, finely chopped

MUSHROOMS AND MUSHROOM BROTH

1 tablespoon extra-virgin olive oil
1 lb 5 oz (600 g) fresh porcini mushrooms or other mushroom, quartered, trimmings reserved
Salt

PARSLEY WATER

10 sprigs parsley

MASHED POTATOES

4 baking potatoes, peeled and cut into medium dice, trimmings scraps reserved
generous 2 cups (500 ml) milk
2 tablespoons (30 g) butter
Salt and freshly ground black pepper

MAKE THE MEATBALLS

In a medium bowl, combine the meat, salt, and pepper and mix. Shape into 1½-ounce (40 g) meatballs.

In a large frying pan, heat the olive oil over medium heat. Add the meatballs and cook until golden brown, about 8 minutes. Remove and toss with the thyme. Set aside and keep warm.

MAKE THE MUSHROOMS AND MUSHROOM BROTH

In a medium frying pan, heat the olive oil over medium heat. Add the quartered mushrooms and cook until golden brown, about 4 minutes. Set aside.

In a medium pot, combine the porcini trimmings and a generous 2 cups (500 ml) water and bring to a boil over medium heat. Cook, covered, for 15 minutes. Uncover and simmer over low heat for 10 minutes. Season to taste with salt.

MAKE THE PARSLEY WATER

Combine the parsley and a scant ½ cup (100 ml) cold water in a blender and process until smooth. Strain through a fine-mesh sieve. Set aside.

>>

MAKE THE MASHED POTATOES

In a medium pot, combine the potatoes and milk and cook over medium heat until soft, about 20 minutes. Reserving the milk, drain the potatoes and return to the pot. Using a potato masher, mash the potatoes, slowly adding the reserved milk, until fluffy. Add the butter and gently mix. Season to taste with salt and pepper.

TO SERVE

Place a spoonful of the mashed potato on each plate and top with the meatballs and mushrooms. Pour in the porcini broth and finish with the parsley water.

P. 304

RECIPE NOTES: _____
_____
_____
_____
_____
_____
_____
_____
_____
_____
_____
_____
_____
_____
_____
_____
_____
_____
_____
_____
_____
_____
_____
_____
_____
_____
_____
_____
_____
_____
_____
_____
_____
_____

PANNA COTTA WITH TROPICAL FRUIT SAUCE

Serves 6

PANNA COTTA
    3 gelatin sheets
    10 oz (300 g) fresh mozzarella cheese
    1½ cups (350 ml) heavy (whipping) cream
    ½ cup plus 1½ tablespoons (120 g) granulated sugar

TROPICAL FRUIT SAUCE
    10 oz (300 g) papaya, peeled, seeded, and chopped
    2 mangoes, chopped
    2 passion fruits, halved
    Juice of 1 lemon

SUGAR TOASTS
    6 thin slices stale bread
    4 tablespoons (60 g) butter, melted
    ½ cup (100 g) packed light brown sugar

FOR SERVING
    Chocolate chips

MAKE THE PANNA COTTA

In a small bowl, soak the gelatin in cold water until soft, about 10 minutes. Drain and set aside.

In a blender, process the mozzarella until smooth, adding some water to loosen if necessary (there shouldn't be any lumps). Transfer to a medium saucepan, add the cream and sugar, and bring to 158°F (70°C) over medium heat. Remove from the heat and stir in the gelatin until melted.

Divide the mixture among six 4-ounce (120 ml) ramekins and refrigerate until firm about 2 hours.

MAKE THE TROPICAL FRUIT SAUCE

In a blender, combine the papaya and mangoes. Scoop out the passion fruit pulp and strain through a fine-mesh sieve, discarding the seeds. Add the strained passion fruit to the blender and process until smooth. Blend in the lemon juice and set aside.

MAKE THE SUGAR TOASTS

Preheat the oven to 325°F (160°C/Gas Mark 3). Line a baking sheet with parchment paper.

Arrange the bread on the lined baking sheet. Spread with the butter and dust with the sugar. Bake until the sugar is bubbling, about 3 minutes. Remove and let cool. Set aside.

TO SERVE

Drizzle each panna cotta with 2 tablespoons of the fruit sauce, sprinkle with chocolate chips, and garnish with a sugar toast.

RECIPE P. 303

Alex Atala

During the 2004 edition of the annual culinary conference in San Sebastián, Spain, called Lo Mejor de la Gastronomia, a man named Jacques Trefois, a well-traveled gourmet living in Brazil introduced me to Alex Atala. Jacques had been coming to Osteria Francescana since we opened in 1995. When he told me that Alex was working with Brazilian traditions the way I was working with Italian ones, I paid attention. Two years later I received an invitation from Alex to cook at his restaurant D.O.M. in São Paolo. I feel lucky to have seen the beginnings of a deep and soul-searching mission to explore the Amazon and document the native products and culinary traditions, from eating ants to cooking with rare plants. Alex was sending out a message to Brazilian chefs and the world about the importance of culinary identity.

I invited Alex to Milan for the weekend to cook at the Refettorio and help me with a charity dinner. The day before the charity dinner, he prepared lunch for a group of teenagers. I remember the day not because of what he cooked but what he talked about. His Italian was good enough to communicate directly and he spoke to the teenagers as if they were adults. He asked them important food questions and got them thinking about more than their rumbling stomachs.

The first dish he served was Mediterranean-style pasta with tomato sauce. There were no traces of his Brazilian cuisine, but there was a story that he wanted to tell. As the volunteers served the tables, he asked the kids: "Do you like anchovies?" Some of them raised their hands but most of them said, NO. He paced and talked the way I remember my professors used to do. He said, "I have an important story to tell you about anchovies. People like eating fish, but scientists say we have fished too much and for this reason the oceans are poor in fish. There are types of fish that can survive industrial fishing and there are types of fish that cannot survive. Take a look at tuna. They need a long time to grow. If we all eat tuna every day the species will disappear because tuna only reproduce once in a year. On the other hand there are lots of anchovies. Why?" Alex got up real close to a table and said, "Anytime an anchovy finds a little space, they reproduce." Everyone laughed. Alex was having fun. He has a son about their age so he knew exactly how to get their attention. Their eyes were glued to him. He stood perfectly still and waited until everyone had a bowl of pasta in front of them and said, "That's why I made this pasta with tomatoes, capers, olives, and anchovies. Not just because it tastes good. Now, let's all give the anchovies a try." There was total silence. At first, the kids picked at their pasta, trying the tiniest bites, but little by little their appetites opened and they cleaned their plates. Nobody moved and everyone ate the pasta. Alex knew how to make even anchovies appealing to teenagers.

As he introduced the next course, he said, "Our job as chefs is to make sitting at a table a pleasure. It isn't just about eating, but about sharing. Today, you are going to share and have fun." He proceeded to place a tray of chicken skewers on each table with two bowls of sauce and two bowls of crushed popcorn. The kids were instructed to roll the skewer in the sauce and then roll it in the popcorn. The idea that they could assemble their own meal thrilled them. Popcorn was flying everywhere and they were so eager it looked like they hadn't been fed in months. He saw that they were having fun, so he continued with his lesson.

Alex began with a description of the food that arrived on that truck that morning, "Do you know that 30 percent of the food we produce on the Earth ends in the garbage? When I arrived this morning there was a lot of meat: pork, chicken, beef. Do you know where it came from? I didn't buy it and it didn't come from the butcher shop." He ran back to the kitchen to grab an armful of coloured Styrofoam trays from the packaged meat. Holding them up, he said, "See these? Today we like to buy veal or beef or chicken that is packaged and prepared, like these ones from the supermarket; but it wasn't always this way." He put down the packages, walked closer to the tables, and got a very serious look on his face.

"What if I arrived here with a nice little pig and I killed it in front of you? Would that be terrible? You don't like to think about it, right? What if I came back the next day with a chicken and killed it too? Terrible. But you just ate some chicken, right?"

The kids started responding: "But we don't live on a farm with animals!" "We don't want to see animals killed!" Alex said, "But your grandmothers and grandfathers did, so are you saying they were tougher than you? I didn't know what to do with all this meat this morning but I knew it couldn't be thrown away. So we made a meat sauce that we will serve tonight."

He tried to explain to the kids that in order to show respect for the animals we eat, we should act as our grandmothers did by using every part of the animal. He said, "If they made a soup, they didn't use just the breast or legs of the chicken, they also used the necks, wings, and even parts that don't have a lot of meat, but are tasty. You kids have to learn to eat everything."

Watching this interaction I was reminded of how important it is to reach out to younger generations who are just beginning to form their ideas about food, culture, and their role in society. Alex saw the opportunity to plant some seeds in their minds; seeds that someday we all hope will grow into trees.

Alex Atala

September 25

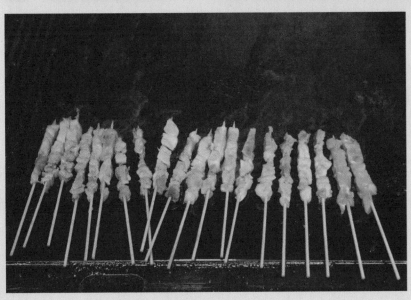

Serves 8

> 3 tablespoons corn oil
> ¾ cup (150 g) popcorn kernels
> ½ cup (120 ml) soy sauce
> ½ cup (120 ml) mirin (sweet rice wine)
> ½ cup (170 g) honey
> 1 lb 5 oz (600 g) boneless, skinless chicken thighs or breast, cut into 2 x ¼ -inch (5 cm x 6 mm) pieces
> 18 bamboo skewers, soaked in water for at least 20 minutes

In a large pot, heat the oil over medium heat. Just as the oil begins to smoke, add the popcorn and quickly cover with a lid. Vigorously shake the pan while the popcorn begins to pop. Once the popping begins to subside, remove from the heat and continue shaking for about 1 minute. Uncover and let cool. Discard any unpopped kernels. Transfer to a food processor and pulse until crushed into medium pieces.

In a medium bowl, whisk together the soy sauce, mirin, and honey. Add the chicken and toss to coat. Refrigerate for 20 minutes.

Remove the chicken from the marinade and transfer the marinade to a small saucepan. Heat the marinade over low heat and cook to reduce by half, until thick enough to coat the chicken, about 6 minutes.

Meanwhile, thread 6 pieces of chicken onto each skewer. On a grill (griddle) pan over medium-high heat, sear the skewers, turning occasionally and brushing with half the reduced marinade, until browned and cooked through, but not dry, about 10 minutes.

To serve, arrange the skewers on a serving dish and serve with bowls of the remaining sauce and crushed popcorn for dipping.

P. 311

RECIPE NOTES:

PASTA WITH ANCHOVY, CAPER, AND TOMATO SAUCE

Serves 8

    4 tablespoons extra-virgin olive oil
    2 garlic cloves, chopped
    10 anchovy fillets, chopped
    2 tablespoons white wine
    1½ tablespoons capers
    1⅔ cups (400 g) canned whole tomatoes, chopped
    3 fillets striped bass or other other white fish (about 4 oz/
        120 g each)
    Salt
    1 lb 3 oz (750 g) penne pasta or other short pasta
    6 basil leaves, for serving

In a large saucepan, heat 2 tablespoons of the olive oil over medium heat. Add the garlic and cook until golden brown, about 1 minute. Add the anchovies, stir, and cook for 2 minutes. Add the wine and let reduce slightly. Add the capers, tomatoes, and a scant ½ cup (100 ml) water and simmer for 20 minutes, stirring occasionally.

In a medium pan, heat the remaining 2 tablespoons olive oil over medium heat. Add the fish skin-side down and cook until cooked through and the skin is crispy, about 3 minutes. Set aside.

Bring a large pot of lightly salted water to a boil over medium heat. Add the penne and cook until al dente. Drain and transfer to the large saucepan with the sauce. Gently toss to combine and season to taste with salt.

To serve, divide the pasta and fish among 8 bowls and garnish with the basil.

RECIPE NOTES: _____
_____
_____
_____
_____
_____
_____
_____
_____
_____
_____
_____
_____
_____
_____
_____
_____
_____
_____
_____
_____
_____
_____

BANANA AND STRAWBERRY SALAD WITH YOGURT ICE CREAM

Serves 6

YOGURT ICE CREAM
    4¼ cups (1 liter) whole-milk yogurt, chilled
    1 cup (200 g) superfine (caster) sugar
    ¼ teaspoon salt
    Juice of 1 lemon

BANANA AND STRAWBERRY SALAD
    3 bananas, sliced (see Note)
    15 strawberries, cut into medium dice
    Juice of 2 oranges

MAKE THE YOGURT ICE CREAM

In a medium bowl, whisk together the yogurt, sugar, and salt. Stir in the lemon juice. Cover and refrigerate for 1 hour to chill. Transfer to an ice-cream machine and process according to the manufacturer's instructions. (If you don't have an ice-cream machine, freeze the mixture until hard enough to scoop.)

MAKE THE BANANA AND STRAWBERRY SALAD

In a medium bowl, combine the bananas, strawberries, and orange juice.

TO SERVE

Divide the banana and strawberry salad among 6 bowls and top with a scoop of yogurt ice cream.

Note: Save the peels to make Banana Peel Chutney (page 158).

📷   P. 313

RECIPE NOTES: _____
_____
_____
_____
_____
_____
_____
_____
_____
_____
_____
_____
_____
_____
_____
_____
_____

Alex Atala

Charity Dinner

Alex Atala was at the counter with a hacksaw, desperately opening coconuts. It looked like a scene from a bad movie. "What is going on?" I asked. He looked up and explained, "All these coconuts were in the refrigerator and no one was using them, so I'm going to make pasta with fresh coconut milk." I must have looked worried because Alex gave me a reassuring thumbs up gesture.

We were holding our second charity dinner over the weekend. The objective was to raise funds and invite the public to experience how chefs were creating unique flavors using ordinary or less than ordinary ingredients. Four chefs would be cooking dinner: Alex Atala, Matt Orlando, Niko Romito, and me. And my sous-chef, Takahiko Kondo, offered to come along and help. Eighty paying guests were arriving at 8 p.m., and dinner was only six hours away.

There were so many coconuts lying around the kitchen that I almost missed Matt quietly working in a corner. "What is that?" I asked pointing to some black stringy looking things in a vacuum-sealed bag. Matt told me that he had been fermenting leek tops for this dinner since May. Matt is a hybrid chef who was raised in California and has been cooking for over a decade in Scandinavia. The difference in climate and landscape couldn't be greater, and yet he has managed to find his identity there. Since opening Amass in Copenhagen in 2011, Matt has been finding creative ways to keep waste to a minimum.

That day, Matt prepared two dishes, a starter and a savory ice cream. For the starter of roasted grains, black rice, pickled fennel, egg yolk, and black leeks, he had put aside the green leafy tops of the leeks that he was not using at Amass and fermented them, transforming their texture and flavor. They became black, sculptural elements with pungent flavor. He pickled fennel and added black Venetian rice to create a starter with the colors of an autumn landscape. The dessert, a green peppercorn ice cream with mushroom vinaigrette and crispy day-old bread was a curious intersection of savory and sweet.

Suddenly, Alex stormed over. "The coconuts are no good. Not a single one. But they make great bowls for pasta, don't you think?" So he got to work on a delicious sauce with sautéed clams and squid in garlic, olive oil, and canned coconut milk, which he would toss with orecchiette and serve in the coconut shells. It was tropical and Mediterranean, decorative and utilitarian. And the bowls told their own story about not wasting.

Taka and I drove up from Modena that morning and we already knew we would be making the main course. Hamburgers seemed like the best solution to the excess quantity of meat that Cristina had warned me about on Friday. We mixed everything that was available, mostly beef and veal, and added grated Parmigiano cheese and a little known sausage called cotechino, which lent a unique flavor to the burgers. Cotechino is what I call an emergency sausage because it is made from ground pork, mostly the tendons and skin—the very last and least desirable parts of the pig. To go with the burgers, instead of French fries we fried a single round slice of potato to sit between the homemade bun, the meat, and two condiments: a *salsa verde* and a balsamic mayonnaise.

Matt, Alex, Taka, and I had been working in the kitchen all day, but Niko Romito was nowhere to be seen. He called at 7 p.m. to say he was stuck in traffic, but now it was almost 8 p.m. and guests were already seated. We were going to have to begin without him. Fortunately, he had everything he needed already prepared in his car. When he arrived, everyone pitched in to help him assemble his dish at the last minute.

Niko is not a classically trained chef and actually was working as an accountant in Rome until he and his sister Cristiana found an ex-monastery on a hilltop in Abruzzo, which seemed to be the perfect location for their dream project. Today, Reale is a Michelin three-star restaurant complete with guest rooms and a culinary school. Despite the remote location, Niko and Cristiana receive visitors from around the world.

Like Matt, Niko had put aside leftovers from his restaurant the month before the dinner. He saved ham bones and pork skin to create an intense broth. He added salvaged outer leaves from late-summer cabbage, the ones that are often worm-holed and discarded. The broth was savory and sweet, intense and rustic, clarified and golden. It was deeply Italian; traditional and contemporary all at once.

Back in July, the journalist Ryan King wrote an article in *Fine Dining Lovers* about the Refettorio saying: "Quite possibly the best restaurant in Milan right now and the only one that's not accepting bookings ever!" Feverish rumors about the exuberant first charity dinner in August fed the fire and when we announced the second charity dinner in early September, seats sold out in twenty minutes. That is just how big the expectations were.

The evening was a celebration of imperfections, but even more memorable because of them. Often we chefs get so lost in our desire to perform and perfect that we lose sight of why we do what we do. That night, every detail from the squiggly leek tops to the worm-eaten cabbage leaves to the bad coconuts connected us to our audience and our mission. The room swelled with excitement. There were journalists waiting tables, chefs on the other side of the kitchen, and many unfamiliar faces from Milan and beyond. As soon as I introduced the chefs, the room became silent. Only then did I realize how eager people were to experience the transformation of ordinary ingredients into an extraordinary meal.

September 26

SALAD OF TOASTED GRAINS, PICKLED FENNEL, AND FERMENTED LEEKS

Serves 4

FERMENTED LEEKS
4 large leeks, sliced into rounds ¼ inch (6 mm) thick
2 tablespoons salt
3 tablespoons thyme

PICKLED FENNEL
5 tablespoons white wine vinegar
1½ tablespoons granulated sugar
1 fennel bulb, trimmed and cut into ⅓-inch (1 cm) dice

EGG YOLK PUREE
4 eggs
3 tablespoons grapeseed oil
2 teaspoons Dijon mustard

TOASTED GRAINS
generous ⅓ cup (75 g) pearl barley
generous ⅓ cup (75 g) spelt berries
generous ¼ cup (60 g) black rice
⅔ cup (150 ml) grapeseed oil
3 tablespoons plus 1 teaspoon extra-virgin olive oil
Salt

FOR SERVING
4 tablespoons sliced black olives

MAKE THE FERMENTED LEEKS

Arrange the leeks in a 32 oz (1 liter) jar.
In a separate jar, combine the salt, thyme, and 3 cups (700 ml) water and shake until the salt dissolves. Pour the brine over the leeks to submerge. Let stand at room temperature, away from direct sunlight, until fermented, at least 3 weeks. Remove from the brine after 3 weeks, transfer to an airtight container, and refrigerate.

MAKE THE PICKLED FENNEL

In a small saucepan, bring the vinegar, sugar, and ⅔ cup (150 ml) water to a boil. Add the fennel and cook until tender, 6 minutes. Let cool. Cover and refrigerate for 20 minutes.

MAKE THE EGG YOLK PUREE

Set up a bowl of ice and water. Bring a medium pot of water to a boil over medium heat. Add the eggs and boil for 14 minutes. Transfer the eggs to the ice bath to cool. Peel and separate the yolks from the whites. Roughly chop the whites and refrigerate. Transfer the yolks to a blender and add 3 tablespoons water, the grapeseed oil, and mustard and blend until smooth. Refrigerate.

>>

MAKE THE TOASTED GRAINS

In a medium pot, bring a generous 2 cups (500 ml) water to a boil over medium heat. Add the barley and cook for 8 minutes. Drain.
In another medium pot, bring a generous 2 cups (500 ml) water to a boil over medium heat. Add the spelt and cook for 10 minutes. Drain.
In a third medium pot, bring a generous 2 cups (500 ml) water to a boil over medium heat. Add the black rice and cook for 10 minutes. Drain.
Transfer the grains to a baking sheet lined with paper towels and refrigerate until slightly dehydrated, 2 hours.
In a medium frying pan, heat the grapeseed oil over medium heat. Working in small batches, add the cooked grains and sauté until chewy, about 2 minutes per batch.
Transfer the grains to a large bowl and toss with the pickled fennel, olive oil, and 3 tablespoons of the fennel pickling liquid. Season to taste with salt.

TO SERVE

Place 1 tablespoon of the egg yolk puree in each bowl. Top with 1 tablespoon of the chopped egg whites and one-fourth of the grain mixture. Garnish with the fermented leeks.

 P. 319

PORK, HAM BONE, AND CABBAGE BROTH

Serves 4

5 oz (150 g) pork rind (pork skin)
1½ tablespoons white wine vinegar
7 oz (200 g) celery, chopped
5 oz (150 g) onion, chopped
1 bay leaf
1 garlic clove, chopped
20 sage leaves
1 prosciutto or ham bone (9 oz/250 g) or a chunk of ham, prosciutto, or other cured meat
Salt
1 lb (500 g) savoy cabbage

Bring a large pot of water to a boil. Add the pork rind and cook until soft, 6 hours. Drain and cut into ⅓-inch (1 cm) dice.
Meanwhile, in another medium pot, combine the vinegar, celery, onion, bay leaf, garlic, sage, ham bone, and 3 quarts (3 liters) water and simmer over low heat for 3 hours. Strain through a colander lined with cheesecloth and season the broth with salt.
Line a steamer insert/basket and place the cabbage in it. Bring the water in the steamer bottom to a boil. Add the steamer basket, cover, and steam until tender, about 50 minutes. Cut into 1½ inch (4 cm) pieces and set aside.
To serve, divide the cabbage among 4 bowls. Ladle the broth over the cabbage and garnish with the diced pork rind.

HAMBURGER OF EVERYTHING

Serves 4

FRIED POTATO
1 large potato
1 cup (250 ml) canola (rapeseed) oil

HAMBURGERS
10 oz (300 g) ground (minced) veal, pork, or chicken
5 oz (150 g) cotechino sausage or other mild sausage, minced
¾ cup plus 2 tablespoons (80 g) freshly grated Parmigiano-
   Reggiano cheese
½ teaspoon salt
¼ teaspoon freshly ground black pepper
2 tablespoons extra-virgin olive oil

FOR SERVING
4 Hamburger Buns (recipe follows)
2 tablespoons Salsa Verde (recipe follows)
4 teaspoons Balsamic Mayonnaise (recipe follows)

MAKE THE FRIED POTATO

Peel the potato and cut it crosswise into slices ¾ inch (2 cm) thick. Using a round cutter, cut four 2⅓-inch (6 cm) rounds (save the potato scraps for another use).

In a medium saucepan, heat the canola (rapeseed) oil over medium-low heat. Add the potatoes and fry until soft in the inside and crispy on the outside, about 4 minutes per side. Transfer to paper towels to absorb any excess oil.

MAKE THE HAMBURGERS

In a medium bowl, combine the veal, sausage, Parmigiano, salt, and pepper and mix well. Form into 4½ ounce (125 g) patties and transfer to a baking sheet. Let rest for 15 minutes.

In a medium frying pan, heat the olive oil over medium heat. Add the patties and cook until golden brown, 3 minutes per side, depending on the doneness you prefer. Set aside.

TO SERVE

Halve the hamburger buns horizontally. Spread ½ tablespoon of the salsa verde on the bottom half of each bun. Top with a hamburger, then the fried potato, and finally 1 teaspoon balsamic mayonnaise. Top with the other half of the hamburger bun and serve.

HAMBURGER BUNS

Makes 25 buns

2⅔ cups (625 ml) milk
2 sticks plus 1½ tablespoons (250 g) butter
generous 3¾ cups (1.25 kg) all-purpose (plain) flour
4 tablespoons fresh yeast

4¼ teaspoons granulated sugar
2½ teaspoons honey
2¾ teaspoons salt
2 eggs, lightly beaten

In a small pot, heat the milk and butter to 120°F (50°C) over medium heat.

In a large bowl, mix together half of the flour, the yeast, sugar, honey, and salt. Add the milk mixture and mix. Add the eggs and mix. Stir in the remaining flour, beating well after each addition. When the dough has pulled together, turn it out onto a lightly floured surface, and knead until smooth and elastic, about 8 minutes. Divide into 12 equal pieces, shape into smooth balls, and arrange on the prepared baking sheet. Flatten slightly, cover with plastic wrap (clingfilm), and let rise for 30 to 35 minutes.

Preheat the oven to 400°F (200°C/Gas Mark 6). Grease a baking sheet with butter.

Bake until golden brown, 10 to 12 minutes. Let cool on a wire rack.

SALSA VERDE

Makes 1¼ cups (300 ml)

4 anchovy fillets
2 garlic cloves
2 tablespoons capers
1½ oz (40 g) stale bread, finely crumbled (scant ¾ cup)
4 tablespoons white wine vinegar
generous ¾ cup (200 ml) extra-virgin olive oil
1 oz (30 g) parsley
Salt

In a blender, combine the anchovies, garlic, capers, bread-crumbs, vinegar, olive oil, parsley, and salt to taste and process until creamy. Strain through a fine-mesh sieve. Cover and refrigerate until ready to use.

BALSAMIC MAYONNAISE

Makes about 1⅓ cups (315 ml)

2 large egg yolks (see Note)
Juice of ½ lemon, or to taste
1 to 2 tablespoons balsamic vinegar, to taste
1 cup (250 ml) canola (rapeseed) oil
Salt

In a blender, combine the egg yolks, lemon juice, vinegar, canola (rapeseed) oil, and salt to taste and process until creamy. Cover and refrigerate until ready to use.

Note: Save the egg whites to make Meringues (pages 32 or 387).

📷 P. 321

Charity Dinner

ORECCHIETTE WITH SQUID, CLAMS, AND COCONUT

Serves 4

2 coconuts, halved, water reserved, flesh scraped and finely chopped, shells cleaned
2 teaspoons coconut oil
7 oz (200 g) squid, body cut into ¾-inch (2 cm) squares
2 garlic cloves, minced, plus 1 tablespoon chopped garlic
⅛ teaspoon salt
½ tablespoon plus 1 teaspoon chopped parsley, plus more for garnish
¼ teaspoon cayenne pepper
9 oz (250 g) orecchiette pasta or other short pasta
7 oz (200 g) Parmigiano-Reggiano cheese, grated
1 can (14.5 oz/440 ml) coconut milk
1 teaspoon fresh lemon juice
16 clams
Salt and freshly ground black pepper

Preheat the oven to 350°C (180°C/Gas Mark 4). Line a baking sheet with parchment paper.

Arrange the coconut shells on the lined baking sheet and bake until light brown and dry, about 20 minutes. Set aside to cool.

In a medium saucepan, heat 1 teaspoon of the coconut oil over medium-high heat. Add the squid and sauté for 1 minute. Add the remaining 1 teaspoon coconut oil, the minced garlic, salt, ½ tablesoon of the parsley, and the cayenne and stir well to coat. Add the coconut flesh and sauté for 1 minute. Remove from the heat and set aside.

Bring a medium pot of lightly salted water to a boil over medium heat. Add the orecchiette and cook until almost al dente. Drain and return to the pot. Add the Parmigiano, coconut milk, lemon juice, remaining 1 teaspoon parsley, and the 1 tablespoon chopped garlic and stir constantly over medium-low heat until the sauce thickens, about 6 minutes. Add half of the squid and coconut mixture and stir, then add the clams, cover, and cook until the clams open, about 3 minutes. Add the remaining squid and coconut mixture and stir to combine. Season to taste with salt and pepper.

Serve in the baked coconuts and sprinkle with parsley.

RECIPE NOTES: _____
_____
_____
_____
_____
_____
_____
_____
_____
_____
_____
_____
_____
_____
_____
_____

BASIL ICE CREAM
WITH APRICOT JAM AND STREUSEL CRUMBS

Serves 6 to 8

BASIL ICE CREAM
1⅔ cups (400 ml) milk
4 egg yolks (see Note)
¾ cup (150 g) superfine (caster) sugar
1 large bunch basil, leaves and stems roughly chopped
1¼ cups (300 ml) heavy (whipping) cream

STREUSEL CRUMBS
6 tablespoons plus 1 teaspoon (90 g) butter
1½ cups (200 g) all-purpose (plain) flour
⅓ cup (35 g) oats
½ cup (100 g) packed light brown sugar
Zested of 1 lemon
1 teaspoons ground cinnamon
¼ teaspoon salt

CARAMELIZED PEPPERONCINO
1 pepperoncino, thinly sliced
½ cup (100 g) granulated sugar

FOR SERVING
6 to 8 tablespoons Apricot Jam (recipe follows)

MAKE THE BASIL ICE CREAM

In a medium pot, warm the milk to 140°F (60°C) over medium heat until just scalded.

In a medium bowl, whisk the egg yolks and sugar until light and fluffy. Slowly add one-fourth of the hot milk, stirring constantly. Transfer the warmed eggs to the pot and add the basil. Cook over low heat, stirring constantly, until the mixture reaches 185°F (85°C) and has slightly thickened (do not let boil). Pour into a bowl and let cool for 2 minutes. Add the cream and stir to combine. Let cool completely, cover, and refrigerate for at least 2 hours to chill.

Strain through a fine-mesh sieve into a clean bowl. Transfer to an ice-cream machine and freeze according to the manufacturer's instructions. (If you don't have an ice-cream machine, freeze the mixture until hard enough to scoop.)

MAKE THE STREUSEL CRUMBS

Preheat the oven to 325°F (160°C/Gas Mark 3). Line a baking sheet with parchment paper.

In a small pot, heat the butter over medium-low heat until melted. Stir in the flour, oats, sugar, lemon zest, cinnamon, and salt with a fork until combined. Transfer to the prepared baking sheet and spread out in an even layer. Bake until golden brown, about 10 minutes. Let cool and set aside.

>>

MAKE THE CARAMELIZED PEPPERONCINO

In a medium pot of boiling water, blanch the pepperoncino for 3 minutes. Repeat this process once more. Set aside.

In a medium pot, combine the sugar and 3 tablespoons water over medium heat. Cook until syrupy, about 6 minutes. Add the blanched pepperoncino and cook for 3 minutes. Fish out the pepperoncino and transfer to a tray lined with parchment paper. Set aside in a dry place until ready to serve.

TO SERVE

Place a scoop of the basil ice cream in each bowl and top with 1 tablespoon of the apricot jam, 1 tablespoon of the streusel crumbs, and 2 caramelized pepperoncini slices.

Note: Save the egg whites to make Meringues (pages 32 or 387).

APRICOT JAM

Makes about 3 cups (1 kg)

2¼ lb (1 kg) fresh apricots, halved
Juice of 1 small lemon
1½ cups (300 g) superfine (caster) sugar
2 tablespoons (30 g) butter

In a medium nonreactive saucepan, combine the apricots, lemon juice, and 3 tablespoons water and bring to a boil over medium heat, stirring occasionally. Reduce the heat to low heat and simmer until the apricots are soft, about 15 minutes. Remove from the heat, add the sugar, and stir until completely dissolved. Return to the heat, add the butter, and stir until melted. Bring to a boil and cook for 15 minutes. Test the thickness by chilling a small spoonful of jam for 3 minutes; if the jam wrinkles when you push it with your finger, it is ready. If the desired thickness has not been reached, boil for 5 minutes more, then test again. Pour into sterilized jars and cover immediately.

GREEN PEPPERCORN ICE CREAM
WITH MUSHROOM VINAIGRETTE AND CROUTONS

Serves 4

MUSHROOM OIL AND REDUCTION

2¼ lb (1 kg) button mushrooms, sliced
scant ½ cup (100 ml) grapeseed oil
1 tablespoon extra-virgin olive oil
4 tablespoons packed light brown sugar
4 teaspoons balsamic vinegar

>>

GREEN PEPPERCORN ICE CREAM

scant ½ cup (100 ml) heavy (whipping) cream
scant ½ cup (100 ml) milk
2 egg yolks (see Note)
4 tablespoons granulated sugar
3 tablespoons dried green peppercorns

CROUTONS

1 loaf (1 lb 2 oz/500 g) stale bread, sliced ⅜ inch (1 cm) thick and cubed
5 tablespoons powdered (icing) sugar, plus more for serving

MAKE THE MUSHROOM OIL AND REDUCTION

In a small pot, combine one-fourth of the mushrooms with the grapeseed oil and cook over medium heat until crispy, about 3 minutes. Strain the oil through a fine-mesh sieve into a bowl (discard the mushrooms). Set aside.

In a large pot, cook the remaining mushrooms with the olive oil over medium heat until browned, about 4 minutes. When the mushrooms start to brown, add the brown sugar and barely cover with water. Continue to cook over medium heat until the broth has strong mushroom flavor, about 30 minutes. Strain through a fine-mesh sieve into a bowl. Return the broth to the pot and cook to reduce to one-fourth its original volume, about 10 minutes. Stir in the vinegar. Let cool, then cover and refrigerate to chill.

MAKE THE GREEN PEPPERCORN ICE CREAM

In a medium pot, heat the cream and milk to 194°F (90°C) over medium heat.

In a medium bowl, whisk the egg yolks with the sugar. Add one-fourth of the hot cream and milk mixture, whisking constantly. Return the warmed eggs to the pot and bring to 181°F (83°C). Transfer to a blender, add the green peppercorns, and blend until smooth. Refrigerate until chilled.

Transfer to an ice-cream machine and process according to the manufacturer's instructions. (If you don't have an ice-cream machine, freeze the mixture until hard enough to scoop.)

MAKE THE CROUTONS

Preheat the oven to 325°F (160°C/Gas Mark 3). Line a baking sheet with parchment paper.

Arrange the bread cubes on the lined baking sheet and sprinkle with the powdered (icing) sugar. Bake until crispy, about 12 minutes

TO SERVE

Place a large scoop of the green peppercorn ice cream in each bowl and drizzle with the mushroom oil and a spoonful of the mushroom reduction. Top with the croutons and dust with more powdered sugar.

Note: Save the egg whites to make Meringues (pages 32 or 387).

Matt Orlando

I met Matt Orlando when he was still cooking at Noma. He always struck me as a typical Southern Californian guy with good manners and a nice smile, but I didn't know more about him until I was in Copenhagen and dined at his restaurant Amass in August 2014. Lara and I had flown in from New York that morning. We were jet lagged and yet we remember the details: local tomatoes (yes, from Denmark), a mushroom as big as a hat—nuances that blended American farm to table with Nordic preservation techniques and Matt's Southern Californian upbeat energy.

We met up again only a few months later in Western Australia at the Gourmet Escape festival in the wine-making region of Margaret River. There, Lara and I told him about the Refettorio project. He lit up and explained how his team at Amass is focused on finding more sustainable solutions for the fine-dining restaurant model: "We use old bread, used coffee grinds, and used tea leaves. We save all the leftover water from the water bottles on the tables to run our immersion circulators and to water our garden. We save all of our green kitchen waste for the chickens that produce our eggs. All gelatinous fish parts are made into stock. All vegetable trimmings are fermented and dried to make seasonings for sauces and stocks. All stems are saved to ferment and dry."

I was impressed that the team had become obsessed with the leftovers, even to the point that they felt guilty if they couldn't find a use for something. We wrote to Matt asking him if he would cook a charity dinner at the Refettorio, and of course he said yes.

We held the charity dinner over the weekend. We were raising funds for the Refettorio and we also wanted to invite the public to see and understand what we were doing, and how the creativity of chefs could bring out unique flavors in ordinary or less than ordinary ingredients.

On Monday, when the party was over, Matt stayed on to prepare a meal for our guests. When I arrived, he was cleaning out the refrigerator. After a weekend of cooking, he wanted to use up everything to insure that nothing went to waste. There were peas, cabbage, tomatoes, fresh cheeses, packages of beef, pasta, anchovies, and some sad looking fruit. With such variety of ingredients, he could have taken this meal in any direction.

He began with a cooked and raw salad as a starter. Boiled green beans and sautéed cabbage were mixed with ricotta, mozzarella, and Parmigiano cheese. Then he prepared a goulash, or stew, for the main course. The stock was made with cooked down Parmigiano rinds, to which he added the meat. He finished it with a pea-anchovy emulsion and toasted breadcrumbs. I closed my eyes, pushed my mental palate to get around the idea of anchovies in goulash, and tasted it. And then I got it. The anchovy balanced the sweetness of the peas and the Parmigiano cheese and rounded out all the flavors. The first signs of fall were just appearing and this soft and savory dish was very satisfying. Our guests loved it. It offered everything they looked forward to in a meal: warm and enveloping with just enough flavor but not too much surprise.

When it came to the dessert, Matt worked with all the fruit that he found in the walk-in refrigerator—an odd combination of strawberries, pineapple, apple, grapes, and pears. Most of the fruit had lost its flavor and texture, but he gave it life through a speedy pickling process with ginger, cinnamon, and sugar. In only a few hours, a brightness that harkened back to fresher times had been resurrected. He served the pickled fruit with custard and ripped bread sautéed in olive oil. This creamy, gingery, savory, and sweet combination was more alive than most "fresh" desserts I encounter.

I cringed when I thought about my home refrigerator. How often did I notice fruit forgotten or lost in a drawer and how sadly familiar was this routine. The fruit Matt pickled could easily be substituted with any fruit combination and the pickling was easy enough for an everyday meal. I liked the remedy and the results. It showed that all the effort Matt and the Amass team were making could be easily applied to a home kitchen as well. I had a recipe and a challenge I would bring back to Modena that night for Lara and the kids. There would be no excuses for sad looking fruit ever again.

September 28

Matt Orlando

September 28

SALAD OF BEANS, FRESH CHEESES, CHARRED CABBAGE, AND HERBS

Serves 4

scant 1 cup (200 ml) plus 3 tablespoons extra-virgin
    olive oil
1 small head savoy cabbage (about 1¾ lb/800 g),
    quartered through the core
2 tablespoons balsamic vinegar
Salt
7 oz (200 g) green beans
2½ cups (60 g) basil leaves
1 cup (30 g) mint leaves
4 tablespoons freshly grated Parmigiano-Reggiano cheese
7 oz (200 g) ricotta cheese
10½ oz (300 g) fresh mozzarella cheese, cut into ⅓-inch
    (1 cm) dice
Salt and freshly ground black pepper

In a large frying pan, heat a scant ½ cup (100 ml) of the olive
oil over high heat. Add the cabbage and char on both sides
until dark brown, about 10 minutes. Remove and roughly cut
into ¾-inch (2 cm) squares. Transfer to a large bowl and toss
with the vinegar. Season to taste with salt. Set aside.

Set up a large bowl of ice and water. In a large pot, bring
a generous 2 cups (500 ml) water with 2 tablespoons salt to
a boil over medium heat. Add the green beans and cook until
just tender, about 4 minutes. Drain and transfer to the ice
bath to cool. Drain and cut into ¾-inch (2 cm) pieces. Cover,
and refrigerate to chill.

In a blender, combine the basil, mint, Parmigiano, and
scant ½ cup (100 ml) olive oil and blend until smooth. Season
with salt. Cover the herb-Parmigiano dressing and refrigerate
until serving time.

In a medium bowl, mix together the ricotta and mozzarella. Season to taste with salt and pepper.

Add the green beans and remaining 3 tablespoons olive oil
to the bowl of cabbage and toss to combine. Season to taste
with salt.

To serve, distribute the cabbage mixture evenly among
4 plates. Top with a spoonful of the cheese mixture and
drizzle with the herb-Parmigiano dressing.

RECIPE NOTES:

Matt Orlando

GOULASH WITH PASTA AND PEAS

Serves 6

PARMIGIANO STOCK
  10 oz (300 g) Parmigiano-Reggiano rinds

GOULASH
  2 tablespoons extra-virgin olive oil
  4 beef short ribs (about 1 lb 2 oz/500 g)
  1 small white onion, chopped
  1 tablespoon sweet paprika
  1 teaspoon hot paprika
  2 cans (14.5 oz/400 g each) chopped tomatoes
  1 bay leaf
  1 red bell pepper, diced
  1 green pepperoncino or other green chili, diced
  Salt

PEA PUREE
  ¾ cup (100 g) frozen green peas
  1 egg yolk (see Note)
  6 anchovies fillets
  2 tablespoons extra-virgin olive oil
  1 teaspoon capers
  Juice of 2 lemons

PARMIGIANO BREADCRUMBS
  5 oz (150 g) stale white bread, finely crumbled (2⅔ cups)
  Freshly ground black pepper
  7 oz (200 g) Parmigiano-Reggiano cheese, finely grated

PASTA
  1 lb 5 oz (600 g) cavatappi pasta or other short pasta

MAKE THE PARMIGIANO STOCK

In a large pot, combine the Parmigiano rinds and cover with 2 quarts (2 liters) water. Bring to boil over medium heat, then reduce the heat and simmer for 1 hour. Strain and set aside.

>>

MAKE THE GOULASH

In a large heavy-bottomed pot, heat the olive oil over medium-high heat. Add the beef and sear until golden brown on both sides, about 10 minutes. Transfer to a plate and set aside. Reduce the heat to medium, add the onion, and sauté until translucent, about 5 minutes. Add both paprikas, the tomatoes, and bay leaf and bring to a simmer. Return the beef to the pot and add enough Parmigiano stock to almost completely submerge the beef. Cover and simmer until the beef is tender and easily pulls apart, about 2 hours. Remove the beef from the broth and when cool enough to handle, shred into bite-size chunks and return to the pot. Set aside.

MAKE THE PEA PUREE

In a blender, combine the peas, egg yolk, anchovies, olive oil, and capers and blend. Add just enough Parmigiano stock to loosen the mixture and form a thick puree. Pass through a fine mesh sieve. Stir in the lemon juice and season to taste with salt.

MAKE THE BREADCRUMBS

Preheat the oven to 350°F (180°C/Gas Mark 4). Line a baking sheet with parchment paper.
  Arrange the breadcrumbs on the baking sheet and toast for 15 minutes. Season generously with black pepper and let cool. Transfer to a medium bowl and toss with the Parmigiano.

COOK THE PASTA

Bring a large pot of lightly salted water to a boil over medium heat. Add the pasta and cook until al dente. Drain and let cool.

FOR ASSEMBLY AND SERVING

Add the bell pepper, pepperoncino, and cooked pasta to the goulash and gently stir to combine over medium heat. Season to taste with salt.
  Place a spoonful of the pea emulsion in the middle of each bowl and top with a few big spoonfuls of the goulash. Garnish with the Parmigiano breadcrumbs.

Note: Save the egg whites to make Meringues (pages 32 or 387).

RECIPE NOTES: _____
_____
_____
_____
_____
_____
_____
_____
_____
_____
_____

GINGER-PICKLED FRUIT
WITH VANILLA CUSTARD AND MINT

Serves 4

PICKLED FRUIT
    12 green grapes, halved
    1 apple, cut into ⅓-inch (1 cm) dice
    4 strawberries, cut into ⅓-inch (1 cm) dice
    1 small pineapple, cut into ⅓-inch (1 cm) dice
    1 pear, cut into ⅓-inch (1 cm) dice
    2 oz (50 g) fresh ginger, peeled and thinly sliced
    1 cup (200 g) granulated sugar
    1 cinnamon stick

VANILLA CUSTARD
    scant ½ cup (100 ml) heavy (whipping) cream
    scant ½ cup (100 ml) milk
    2 egg yolks (see Note)
    scant 3 tablespoons granulated sugar

TOASTED BREAD
    ⅔ cup (150 ml) extra-virgin olive oil
    3½ oz (100 g) stale bread, crusts removed and torn
        into ⅓-inch (1 cm) pieces

GARNISH
    Extra-virgin olive oil
    40 small mint leaves

MAKE THE PICKLED FRUIT

In a heatproof medium bowl, toss together the grapes, apple, strawberries, pineapple, and pear. Set aside.

In a saucepan, combine the ginger, sugar, cinnamon stick, and 1⅔ cups (400 ml) water. Bring to a boil over medium heat and cook for 5 minutes. Refrigerate to chill, then pour the mixture over the fruit and let marinate for 3 hours. Cover and refrigerate. Drain before serving.

MAKE THE VANILLA CUSTARD

In a saucepan, warm the cream and milk to 194°F (90°C). Remove from the heat.

In a medium bowl, whisk the egg yolks and sugar to combine. Slowly add one-fourth of the hot cream mixture, whisking constantly. Transfer the warmed eggs to the pan, whisking constantly. Return the pan to the heat and bring to 181°F (83°C). Remove from the heat. Cover the surface directly with plastic wrap (clingfilm) and refrigerate to chill.

MAKE THE TOASTED BREAD

In a frying pan, heat the olive oil over medium heat. Add the bread and toast lightly. Set aside.

>>

TO SERVE

Place a spoonful of the vanilla custard in the bottom of each bowl and top with the pickled fruit and toasted bread. Drizzle with olive oil and garnish with 10 pieces of mint.

Note: Save the egg whites to make Meringues (pages 32 or 387). You can use any fruits you have on hand for the pickled fruit.

📷   P. 331

RECIPE NOTES:

Matt Orlando

George Brown Canada Cooking School

Osteria Francescana was invited to Toronto in March 2015 to give a master class at the Centre for Hospitality & Culinary Arts at George Brown College, while the Refettorio was under renovation. When we arrived, we were overwhelmed by the warm welcome from more than two hundred students who were lined up on the stairs outside the school. We felt like rock stars. We were swept up in the energy and enthusiasm of the students and their engaging headmaster, Scottish chef John Higgins. The GBC, as it is known, has always been a French-oriented culinary arts program until a few years ago, when a masters program in Italian cuisine was started under the leadership of the Italian chef Dario Tomaselli. It was Dario who had visited Osteria Francescana a year earlier through a program with ALMA (the Italian culinary school), and he had invited me to come to Toronto. It was not unusual to be invited to a culinary school, but what distinguished Dario's request from the others was that he insisted again and again that I talk to the students about the culture of ideas more than the culture of cooking.

I shared with the students a lesson I had learned back in 2012 when a series of earthquakes hit Emilia-Romagna. Parmigiano-Reggiano dairy farmers had over 450,000 wheels of damaged cheese. A broken wheel of cheese has to be sold, and quickly. Our team came up with a recipe called Riso Cacio e Pepe, a risotto that uses a lot of cheese. We shared the recipe during Slow Food's biannual Terre Madre Salone del Gusto conference and invited people to cook the recipe at home, in a kind of virtual dinner party. All the cheese was sold in a couple of weeks and not a single dairy farm closed. What I discovered is that a recipe can be an act of solidarity. From there I talked to the students about Expo and shared with them the origins of the Refettorio.

Among other activities during that week in Toronto, I sat on a panel of judges for a culinary prize. The competition was between six students in the Italian postgraduate program. Each candidate had the opportunity to present a dish along with an explanation of the origin of the idea before it was tasted by each of the panelists. Out of all the students, there was only one who stood out of the crowd. It was not only for his agility in the kitchen and the distinct flavors achieved by the recipe, but more important for his ability to think transversally. Allen Huynh is of Vietnamese descent, born and raised in Canada. He was older than he looked and wiser too. Allen named his dish "A Cod Fish Lost in the Woods," and he invented a magical image to describe the dish, which started out with the rebirth of the Canadian forest in the springtime. To quote Allen, ". . . dead leaves peek out of the melting snow and the earthy odor of sweet humus permeates . . . ." He made a nutty, sweet, and acidic chestnut puree, on top of which were dried crunchy leaves, spring vegetables, and a pure white desalted cod peeking like leaves under the snow. It was poetic and tasted good: a combination I always praise.

The prize was a six-month fully paid internship at Osteria Francescana through a joint program with ALMA. After I announced he had won, I asked him in a very serious and scary tone, "Are you ready?" Allen didn't even wince. His enthusiasm overruled any fear or apprehension, and he has been cooking in our kitchen ever since.

John and Dario said they would be visiting Expo in September. When that date came around I was thrilled to have them come into the kitchen. John, since becoming director of the GBC in 2002, has steered the school through an expansion in response to the explosive demand in enrollment. He never misses a chance to remind students that being a chef is hard work that requires passion and dedication. Dario was born and raised in Milan. He moved to Canada in the 1990s and was the executive chef at ORO restaurant in Toronto for ten years before joining George Brown College. Today he is the coordinator of the Italian postgraduate program.

They ended up cooking at the Refettorio for two full days. They considered it a learning experience. I found this role reversal, from teacher to student, a sign of humility. John later told me that when it was time to cook, "We threw the playbook out the window. Taste and learning would be the main ingredient as the day unfolded." Dario added, "The limitations of the Refettorio kitchen pushed me to reconsider my own kitchen and to use each ingredient to its fullest potential."

The dishes they prepared came from Italian, French, Scottish, and Canadian culinary traditions. Among the many dishes they cooked, the recipes I remember most fondly were: the risotto with braised radicchio and beef; a colorful chicken stew with al dente vegetables and a light touch of citrus; and a maple syrup ice cream—my favorite dessert.

One year after their experience at the Refettorio, John and Dario were still talking about it. In fact, they brought their culinary students to cook at the Devour! food film festival to accompany a screening of *Theater of Life*, a moving documentary about the Refettorio filmed by Canadian filmmaker Peter Svatek. In keeping with the theme of the Refettorio, John and Dario entitled the evening, "Turn Stale Bread into Gold." They sent me a photo of the gnocchi recipe they made combining Scottish savory pudding and stale Italian bread. Their enthusiasm animated everything they touched, exactly as I remembered when they were dancing around the kitchen at the Refettorio singing, "The soul train of food is . . . no waste, no waste, no waste!"

September 29 and 30

Serves 6

4 tablespoons all-purpose (plain) flour
Salt and freshly ground black pepper
1¾ (800 g) boneless chicken thigh, cut into 1-inch
    (2.5 cm) cubes
1 tablespoon extra-virgin olive oil
¾ lb (350 g) onions, finely chopped
¾ lb (300 g) carrots, sliced
2 leeks, finely diced
5 oz (150 g) green beans, halved
5 oz (150 g) peas
12 pearl onions
4 garlic cloves, roughly chopped
2 tablespoons plus 1 teaspoon white balsamic vinegar
    or apple cider vinegar
generous 2 cups (500 ml) chicken stock
2 bay leaves
1½ tablespoons rosemary leaves
4 tablespoons thyme leaves
1¼ cups (300 ml) heavy (whipping) cream
Juice of 2 lemons
16 basil leaves

In a medium bowl, combine the flour, 1 teaspoon salt,
and ¼ teaspoon pepper and set aside.

Season the chicken with salt and pepper. In a medium
saucepan, heat the olive oil over medium heat. Add the
chicken and sauté for 5 minutes without browning the
meat. Add the onions, carrots, leeks, green beans, peas,
pearl onions, and garlic and cook for 3 minutes, turning the
chicken often. Sprinkle the flour mixture over the chicken,
turning to coat evenly, and cook for another 3 minutes. Add
the balsamic vinegar to deglaze the pan. Add the chicken
stock gradually, then add the bay leaves, rosemary, and
thyme. Cover the pan and cook over low heat until the chicken
is cooked through, about 15 minutes. Add the cream and
lemon juice and simmer for 5 minutes. Season to taste with
salt and pepper. Serve garnished with basil.

P. 337

RECIPE NOTES:

RISOTTO WITH RADICCHIO AND BEEF

Serves 6

BRAISED BEEF

2 tablespoons extra-virgin olive oil

10 oz (300 g) beef top round (topside)

1 onion, finely diced

2 celery stalks, finely diced

1 carrot, finely diced

3⅓ cups (800 ml) red wine

2¼ oz (65g) dried porcini, soaked in water

scant ½ cup (90 g) chopped plum tomatoes

1 bay leaf

2 sprigs thyme

2 garlic cloves, chopped

½ cinnamon stick

BRAISED RADICCHIO

4¼ teaspoons (20 g) butter

1 tablespoon extra-virgin olive oil

6 oz (180 g) radicchio, julienned

1 teaspoon granulated sugar

1 tablespoon plus 1 teaspoon balsamic vinegar

Salt and freshly ground black pepper

RISOTTO

4¼ cups (1 liter) vegetable stock

4 teaspoons (20 g) butter

1 shallot, finely chopped

1⅔ cups (320 g) short-grain rice

1 cup (250 ml) red wine

5 oz (150 g) Parmigiano-Reggiano cheese, grated

scant 1 cup (50 g) chopped parsley

Leaves from 3 sprigs marjoram

MAKE THE BRAISED BEEF

In a medium Dutch oven (casserole), heat the olive oil over medium heat. Add the beef and brown all over, about 7 minutes. Add the onion, celery, and carrot and cook until golden brown. Add the wine and deglaze. Add the porcini and cook for 2 minutes. Add the tomatoes, bay leaf, thyme, garlic, and cinnamon stick. Add water to cover and cook over medium heat until the meat is soft and easily falls apart, 4 to 5 hours. Remove the beef and set aside. Strain the cooking liquid (discard the solids). Return the liquid to the pot and cook over medium heat until reduced by half, about 30 minutes. Set the beef braising liquid aside, and pull the meat apart with a fork.

>>

MAKE THE BRAISED RADICCHIO

In a medium saucepan, heat the butter and olive oil over medium heat. Add the radicchio and sugar and cook until lightly caramelized and soft, about 5 minutes. Add the balsamic vinegar and a touch of the beef braising liquid and cook for 5 minutes to reduce slightly. Season to taste with salt and pepper and set aside.

MAKE THE RISOTTO

In a medium heavy-bottomed pot, heat the vegetable stock over low heat. Keep warm.

In a Dutch oven (casserole), heat 2 teaspoons (10 g) of the butter over medium heat. Add the shallot and cook until translucent, about 3 minutes. Add the rice and toast (but don't brown), about 6 minutes. Add the red wine and cook until evaporated. Add the warm vegetable stock, bring to a boil over medium heat, and cook for 7 minutes. Stir in the radicchio and beef, reduce the heat to low, and cook until the rice is soft 17 to 19 minutes. Remove from the heat, add the remaining 2 teaspoons (10 g) butter and the Parmigiano, and stir to combine. Stir in the herbs.

TO SERVE

Place a large spoonful of risotto on each plate and drizzle with the reduced braising liquid. Serve immediately.

RECIPE NOTES: _____

_____

_____

_____

_____

_____

_____

_____

_____

_____

_____

_____

_____

_____

_____

_____

_____

_____

_____

_____

_____

_____

_____

_____

_____

BANANA BREAD WITH BERRY-MAPLE ICE CREAM

Serves 8

BANANA BREAD

3½ tablespoons (50 g) butter
4 tablespoons packed light brown sugar
3 tablespoons milk
½ cup (50 g) pecans, finely chopped
1 cup (300 g) mashed ripe bananas (see Note)
scant 1 cup (200 g) granulated sugar
4 tablespoons canola (rapeseed) oil
½ cup (120 ml) sour cream
2 eggs
1⅔ cups (210 g) all-purpose (plain) flour
1 teaspoons baking powder
1 teaspoons baking soda (bicarbonate of soda)
½ teaspoon salt

BERRY-MAPLE ICE CREAM

1¾ lb (800 g) Saskatoon berries, blueberries, raspberries,
    or other berry
2 eggs
½ cup (125 g) granulated sugar
1½ cups (375 ml) half-and-half (single cream)
1 cup (250 ml) heavy (whipping) cream
½ cup (125 ml) maple syrup

MAKE THE BANANA BREAD

Preheat the oven to 350°F (180°C/Gas Mark 4). Line the bottom of an 8 x 12-inch (20 x 30 cm) baking pan with parchment paper.

In a medium saucepan, melt the butter over medium heat. Add the brown sugar and stir to combine. Add the milk and cook until creamy, about 4 minutes. Stir in the pecans. Set the pecan icing aside.

In a medium bowl, add the bananas and stir in the sugar, canola (rapeseed) oil, sour cream, and eggs. In another bowl, whisk together the flour, baking powder, baking soda (bicarbonate of soda), and salt. Add the flour mixture to the banana mixture and stir to combine; do not overmix. Pour the batter in the prepared baking pan. Bake until a wooden pick inserted in the center comes out clean, about 1 hour. Remove from the oven and cover with the pecan icing. Return to the oven and bake for 5 minutes more. Let cool in the pan.

>>

MAKE THE BERRY-MAPLE ICE CREAM

In a large bowl, mash the berries into a puree. Push through a fine-mesh sieve to remove the seeds.

In a medium bowl, with an electric mixer, beat the eggs and granulated sugar until thick and light yellow, 4 to 5 minutes. Add the berry puree, half-and-half (single cream), heavy (whipping) cream, and maple syrup and stir to combine. Transfer to an ice-cream machine and process according to the manufacturer's instructions. (If you don't have an ice-cream machine, freeze the mixture until hard enough to scoop.)

TO SERVE

Place a slice of the warm banana bread on each plate and top with a scoop of the berry-maple ice cream.

Note: Save the peels to make Banana Peel Chutney (page 158).

RECIPE NOTES: _____
_____
_____
_____
_____
_____
_____
_____
_____
_____
_____
_____
_____
_____
_____
_____
_____
_____
_____
_____
_____
_____
_____
_____
_____
_____
_____
_____
_____
_____
_____
_____
_____
_____

Virgilio Martínez

Virgilio Martínez is passionate about food but he is even more passionate about his country. His mission is to share Peru's diversity with the world through cooking. Over the past five years, his restaurant Central in Lima has become a destination for travelers to discover the many flavors of Peru. A meal at Central focuses on microclimates and extreme terroir, while expressing the diversity of landscapes, altitudes, and cultures from the Pacific Ocean to the Andes to the Amazon, all within one country. Guests have the chance to eat unusual ingredients that Peruvians have been cooking with for centuries. Virgilio works with indigenous communities to learn about their ingredients and techniques. He then applies it to his mission. "It is all about looking for creative alternatives, and innovative solutions," he says. "There are so many hidden products in my country, perceived as unimportant and often forgotten. Now we are telling the stories of our people and communities through these ingredients."

He came to the Refettorio with two chefs: Juan Luis, who was working at Central, and Paulo Rivas, currently head of communications at Central and at the time studying for a master's degree in Milan. Virgilio seemed to be everywhere all at once with his hands in everything. He has the lithe body of an ex-skateboarder and still moves around a room like a teenager. He poured sugar on the radicchio, soaked big pieces of bread in a milk bath, and seemed to play with the ingredients more than cook them. He made the work look fun as he orchestrated things magically into becoming a meal.

"To me, thinking about waste means respecting the integrity of every product. Every part of it is equally special, even more so when you look at it creatively. I don't think there is anything that creativity cannot accomplish. So now we are in this position to take advantage of every single scrap, of every single leaf, every single piece of potato, what is often discarded are actually our most important ingredients."

The most interesting part was watching how Virgilio worked traditional Italian ingredients, like mozzarella and rice, into new versions of themselves. Like the rebel kid he used to be, he was breaking the rules. He tore the mozzarella into small irregular bite-size pieces, like tearing off pieces of bread. He added this to a grilled radicchio and fennel starter, a kind of grilled vegetable salad with a lovely dressing. Then I saw him looking at a jar of specialty black rice, which the Italian journalist Paolo Marchi had recently brought from Veneto. Virgilio was immediately attracted to it, but he had no intention of using it to make risotto. He fried it instead and sprinkled it over the radicchio and fennel for another layer of texture and taste.

When it came to the main course, he was preparing a kind of meat stew that looked very ordinary, only it wasn't. It was Peruvian through and through. He called it *anticucho* veal stew. Anticucho is a kind of street food, usually made with beef heart on a skewer that has been marinated in anticucho sauce. The marinade is made with chilies, vinegar, and garlic. It is probably the most popular street food in Peru.

At the Refettorio, Virgilio sautéed the veal. He put the biggest pot on the stovetop and added tomatoes, potatoes, some water, and the meat. Then he added the anticucho sauce and let everything simmer into a stew. He didn't stop there. He made a *uchucuta*, a salsa that is traditionally raw, but in this case he sautéed the chilies and mixed them with minced garlic, parsley, cheese, and olive oil. This mixture went on top of the stew to complete the dish. It was smokey and acidic with a satisfying kick. I was taken aback: it tasted like the streets of Peru. The stew looked anonymous but tasted completely unique.

When the guests were about to arrive, I caught Virgilio in a corner of the dining room with a pile of white napkins. "What are you doing?" I asked. He was writing little notes to put on top of glasses of fresh juice that he had prepared earlier in the day. He told me the juice is called *refresco* and that in Peru drinking water with a meal is sad and that most people drink refresco. He put a glass of refresco next to each fork and placed a napkin over it that read: "From Peru with love."

October 6 and 7

Serves 6

3 tablespoons extra-virgin olive oil
1 fennel bulb, sliced ⅓ inch (1 cm) thick
Salt
2 heads radicchio, halved through the core
2 tablespoond granulated sugar
1½ cups (350 ml) vegetable oil, for deep-frying
generous ½ cup (100 g) black rice
scant ½ cups (100 ml) Yellow Chili Vinaigrette
    (recipe follows)
9 oz (250 g) mozzarella cheese, torn into
    tablespoon-size pieces

In a medium frying pan, heat 2 tablespoons of olive oil over medium heat. Add the fennel and cook until lightly browned, about 5 minutes. Season to taste with salt. Transfer to paper towels to drain and set aside.

In the same pan, heat the remaining olive oil over medium heat. Add the radicchio, sprinkle with the sugar, and sear on both sides, about 2 minutes. Season to taste with salt and roughly chop. Transfer to paper towels to drain and set aside.

In a medium pot, heat the vegetable oil to 482°F (250°C). Add the rice and cook until it puffs, about 1 minute. Season to taste with salt and transfer to paper towels to drain. Set aside.

To serve, divide the fennel and radicchio among 6 plates and dress with the yellow chili vinaigrette. Sprinkle with the puffed black rice and top with pieces of mozzarella.

YELLOW CHILI VINAIGRETTE

Makes about 3 cups (700 ml)

9 oz (250 g) fresh yellow chilies, seeded
scant ½ cup (100 ml) fresh lemon juice
2 tablespoons plus 1 teaspoon granulated sugar
4 garlic cloves, peeled but whole
1 cup (240 ml) extra-virgin olive oil
Salt

Set up a large bowl of ice and water. Bring a medium pot of water to a boil. Add the chilies and blanch for 5 minutes. Repeat this process 2 more times. Transfer to the ice bath to cool, then transfer to a blender and blend. Add the lemon juice, sugar, and garlic cloves and continue to process until smooth. Add the olive oil and process. Strain through a fine-mesh sieve and season to taste with salt.

📷 P. 345

RECIPE NOTES: _____

Virgilio Martínez

VEAL AND POTATO STEW WITH UCHUCUTA SAUCE

Serves 6

VEAL AND POTATO STEW
    2¼ lb (1 kg) baking potatoes, peeled an cut into
        1¼-inch (3 cm) cubes
    1 lb 5 oz (600 g) veal, cut into ¾-inch (2 cm) cubes
    Salt and freshly ground black pepper
    1 tablespoon extra-virgin olive oil
    3 cloves garlic, minced
    1 lb 2 oz (500 g) tomatoes, peeled
    3 tablespoons ají panca paste or other chili paste
    ¼ teaspoon ground cumin
    generous ¾ cup (200 ml) white wine vinegar

UCHUCUTA SAUCE
    scant ½ cup (100 ml) extra-virgin olive oil
    3 fresh yellow chilies, seeded
    1 medium white onion, finely chopped
    4 garlic cloves, chopped
    1 tablespoon chopped cilantro (coriander)
    1 tablespoon chopped parsley
    ½ cup (45 g) chopped huacatay leaves (see Note)
    Salt
    7 oz (200 g) queso fresco or other firm, fresh cheese,
        finely chopped
    5 oz (150 g) roasted peanuts, chopped

MAKE THE VEAL AND POTATO STEW

Place the potatoes in a medium pot and add water to cover. Bring to a boil over medium heat and cook until soft, about 12 minutes. Drain and set aside.

Season the veal with salt and pepper. In a medium pot, heat the olive oil over medium heat. Add the veal and cook until browned, about 4 minutes. Reduce the heat to low and add the garlic, tomatoes, ají panca paste, cumin, vinegar, and 2 quarts (2 liters) water and cook until the meat is soft and tender, about 2 hours. Season to taste with salt and pepper. Add the potatoes and cook for 10 minutes.

MAKE THE UCHUCUTA SAUCE

In a medium frying pan, heat 1 tablespoon of the olive oil over high heat. Add the chilies, onion, and garlic and sauté until lightly browned, about 5 minutes. Remove the pan from the heat and stir in the cilantro (coriander), parsley, and huacatay and season to taste with salt. Transfer to a blender and blend until loosely combined. Transer to a medium bowl and fold in the queso fresco and peanuts. Set aside.

TO SERVE

Ladle the stew into bowls and top with 1 tablespoon of the uchucuta sauce.

Note: If you don't have huacatay leaves, subsitute with mint.

Virgilio Martínez

BREAD PUDDING WITH STEWED FRUIT

Serves 8

BREAD PUDDING

1 lb 2 oz (500 g) stale bread, cut into 1½-inch
   (4 cm) chunks
4 cups (960 ml) milk, warmed
3 eggs
1¼ cups (240 g) granulated sugar
4 tablespoons (60 g) butter, melted
5½ tablespoons all-purpose (plain) flour
1 teaspoon ground cinnamon
Pinch of salt
1½ cups (260 g) raisins

STEWED FRUIT

1 lb 2 oz (500 g) plums, diced
9 oz (250 g) strawberries, diced
1⅓ cups (250 g) granulated sugar

MAKE THE BREAD PUDDING

Preheat the oven to 350°F (180°C/Gas Mark 4). Butter
a 10-inch (25 cm) round baking dish.
   In a blender, combine the bread and milk and process
until smooth. Add the eggs, sugar, melted butter, flour,
cinnamon, and salt and blend. Transfer to a large bowl and
mix in the raisins. Transfer to the prepared mold and bake
until a wooden pick inserted in the center comes out clean,
about 25 minutes. Let cool.

MAKE THE STEWED FRUIT

In a medium bowl, stir together the plums, strawberries,
and sugar. Set aside for 5 minutes. Transfer to a medium pot,
bring to a simmer over low heat, and cook until reduced and
syrupy, about 10 minutes.

TO SERVE

Place a slice of the bread pudding on each plate and drizzle
with 1 tablespoon of the stewed fruit.

Note: You can use any fruits you have on hand for the
stewed fruit.

RECIPE NOTES:

Jeremy Charles &
John Winter Russell

Jeremy Charles and John Winter Russell, two young and ambitious Canadian chefs, joined us at the Refettorio to share their vision of working with salvaged food. Growing up on the island of Newfoundland, Jeremy had spent the majority of his summer vacations selling cod tongues to the locals and tourists in Old Perlican, a quaint fishing village on Trinity Bay. This is where Jeremy's passion for working with wild and local ingredients comes from. At his restaurant Raymonds in St. John's, partridge, seal flippers, and moose chops are featured on the menu. John, of Candide in Montréal, works obsessively with seasonal ingredients, foraging many himself, and he choses to rely on a restricted number of ingredients in order to reduce the chance of food waste in the kitchen.

It was obvious that these two chefs were friends by the way they worked together. I walked in halfway through the preparations and was surprised to find that they were making a lot of Italian-inspired food. I think I must have said something like, "I didn't know Canadians knew how to cook Italian," and they both turned red. John admitted that he was nervous about making ice cream in a machine he had never used before and Jeremy was worried about serving polenta to Italians. "We don't want to mess up such cultural staples as polenta and gelato!" they both said laughing.

Every time I have ever cooked in Canada, I have succumbed to the desire to cook Canadian-inspired dishes, adding native ingredients like maple syrup to a classic recipe. Whenever you leave your kitchen and change your perspective, your kitchen changes and evolves. This is a good thing, and one of my favorite aspects of working with so many different chefs at the Refettorio. A chef's identity—cultural and personal—really comes through in the dishes, no matter the ingredients or the circumstance.

Jeremy wanted to make sure that his meal felt earthy and simple, but with substance—something to get people through their day. This attention to the guests touched me. In normal circumstances, chefs often get lost in their imaginations and think more about the way a dish looks, the technique, or the concept rather than how it will be received on the other end. The Refettorio guests helped remind us all that we were cooking for people who needed nourishment and food that was above all welcoming.

Jeremy began the meal with a refreshing starter of grapefruit and fennel with an anchovy aioli. The raw and cooked fennel had different textures and sweetness, which contrasted nicely with the savory anchovy and the tart grapefruit. He followed with a hearty plate of polenta and ragù, which was very traditional and very Italian.

John was taking care of the dessert. He overcame his initial hesitation about making ice cream and made a wonderful brown butter ice cream that he served with roasted plums. John cleaned three cases of plums without finding one that was overripe or bruised. "One or two had tiny small black dots, but they were easily removed with a paring knife. So much of what gets thrown out is because of aesthetics," he said while shaking his head in disbelief.

He pitted the plums and infused the pits in the milk for the ice cream. This gave the ice cream a slightly almond-y flavor. Then he macerated and roasted the plums. He topped everything with a bread crumble made with day-old bread.

Later, John told me he was shocked that the fridge was so well stocked. He had the sense that it didn't look much different than any other restaurant fridge. I told John that many chefs had this very same reaction. John reflected on this for a moment and said, "You know, Massimo, when I walked in and saw the neon sign 'No more excuses,' it all made sense." I can't say how much I appreciated this comment and maybe only then did I realize that now was the time to act, not only for chefs but for everyone.

Jeremy Charles & John Winter Russel

October 8

Serves 6

3 large fennel bulbs, 2 trimmed and 1 whole
2½ cups (600 ml) grapefruit juice
1 bay leaf
2 grapefruits, segmented and cut into small pieces
3 tablespoons extra-virgin olive oil
Salt
⅔ cup (150 ml) Anchovy Sauce (recipe follows)

Halve the two trimmed fennel bulbs through the core. Place them in a medium pot and add the grapefruit juice and bay leaf. Cover and cook over medium heat until soft, about 20 minutes. Remove from the heat and let cool in the grapefruit juice. Cut into 6 wedges and set aside.

Very thinly slice the remaining fennel bulb on a mandoline and place in a medium bowl. Add the grapefruit pieces and olive oil. Season to taste with salt, toss, and set aside

To serve, place 2 tablespoons of the anchovy sauce on each plate and top with a spoonful of the fennel and grapefruit salad and a braised fennel quarter.

ANCHOVY SAUCE

Makes 1⅔ cups (400 ml)

1 can (5 oz/140 g) tuna packed in olive oil, drained
5 anchovies filets
2 tablespoons capers
3 tablespoons fresh lemon juice
½ cup (125 ml) extra-virgin olive oil
½ cup (110 g) mayonnaise
½ tablespoon salt
½ teaspoon freshly ground black pepper

In a blender, combine the tuna, anchovies, capers, lemon juice, olive oil, mayonnaise, salt, and pepper and process until smooth and creamy. Cover and refrigerate for up to 2 days.

RECIPE NOTES: _____
_____
_____
_____
_____
_____
_____
_____
_____
_____
_____
_____
_____
_____
_____
_____

Serves 8

BEEF AND PORK RAGÙ

4 tablespoons extra-virgin olive oil
2¼ lb (1 kg) ground (minced) pork
9 oz (250 g) ground (minced) beef
3 oz (80 g) carrots, cut into medium dice
1 medium white onion, cut into medium dice
3 oz (80 g) celery, cut into medium dice
3 garlic cloves, sliced
1 teaspoon fennel seeds
½ teaspoon crushed chili flakes
1 bay leaf
1 cup (9 oz/255 g) tomato paste (puree)
1¼ cups (300 ml) dry white wine
4¼ cups (500 ml) milk
Salt and freshly ground black pepper

POLENTA

8 cups (2 liters) heavy (whipping) cream
Leaves from 2 sprigs thyme, chopped
Leaves from 2 sprigs rosemary, chopped
1 bay leaf
2 garlic cloves, minced
1 tablespoon black peppercorns
3½ cups (500 g) polenta
Salt

FOR SERVING

3½ oz (100 g) Parmigiano-Reggiano cheese, grated
1 cup (50 g) freshly made breadcrumbs

MAKE THE BEEF AND PORK RAGÙ

In a large pot, heat the olive oil over medium heat. Add the meat and brown. Add the carrot, onion, celery, and garlic and cook until soft, 20 minutes. Add the fennel seeds, chili flakes, and bay leaf and cook for 4 minutes. Add the tomato paste (puree) and cook for 5 minutes. Add the wine and reduce by half, 10 minutes. Add the milk and cook over medium-low heat until creamy, 15 minutes. Season to taste with salt and pepper. Discard the bay leaf.

MAKE THE POLENTA

In a medium pot, bring the cream, thyme, rosemary, bay leaf, garlic, and peppercorns to a simmer over low heat and infuse for 45 minutes. Strain through a sieve. Return to the pot and simmer over low heat. Whisk in the polenta and cook until creamy, 30 to 40 minutes. Season to taste with salt.

TO SERVE

Place some polenta into each bowl and top with the beef and pork ragù. Sprinkle with Parmigiano and breadcrumbs.

 P. 353

Jeremy Charles & John Winter Russel

ROASTED PLUMS WITH BROWN BUTTER ICE CREAM AND BREADCRUMB CAKE

Serves 6

BREADCRUMB CAKE
3¼ oz (90 g) stale bread, finely crumbled (1⅔ cups)
2 eggs
¾ cup (150 g) granulated sugar
1 stick plus 3 tablespoons (150 g) butter, melted
1 cup plus 2 tablespoons (145 g) all-purpose (plain) flour
½ teaspoon baking powder

ROASTED PLUMS
10 plums, quartered (see Note)
½ cup (100 g) granulated sugar

FOR SERVING
Brown Butter Ice Cream (recipe follows)

MAKE THE BREADCRUMB CAKE

Preheat the oven to 300°F (150°C/Gas Mark 2). Line a baking sheet with parchment paper.

Arrange the breadcrumbs on the lined baking sheet and toast until golden and completely dry, about 15 minutes. Set aside.

Leave the oven on but increase the temperature to 325°F (160°C/Gas Mark 3). Line a 12 x 16 inch (30 x 40 cm) rimmed baking sheet with parchment paper.

In a medium bowl, whisk together the eggs and sugar until pale yellow and thickened. Slowly add the melted butter, stirring constantly. Add the flour and baking powder and gently fold to combine (the batter should be thick like a pancake batter; if it is too thin, add more flour). Stir in the toasted breadcrumbs. Transfer to the prepared baking sheet and spread in a thin layer. Bake until golden brown, about 15 minutes. Reduce the heat to 275°F (135°C/Gas Mark 1) and cook until crunchy, about 15 minutes.

MAKE THE ROASTED PLUMS

Preheat the oven to 325°F (160°C/Gas Mark 3). Line a baking sheet with parchment paper.

Arrange the plums on the lined baking sheet and sprinkle with the sugar. Bake until tender, about 7 minutes.

TO SERVE

Place 2 or 3 of the roasted plum pieces in each bowl and top with a few pieces of the breadcrumb cake and a scoop of the brown butter ice cream.

>>

BROWN BUTTER ICE CREAM

Makes 3 quarts (3 liters)

5¾ cups (1.36 liters) milk
10 plum pits (see Note)
1⅔ cups (400 ml) heavy (whipping) cream
5 egg yolks (see Note)
1⅔ cups (340 g) granulated sugar
Pinch of salt
1½ oz (40 g) blanched almonds (about ¼ cup)
3 sticks (350 g) salted butter

In a medium pot, bring 1½ cups (370 ml) of the milk, plum pits, and the cream to 180°F (82°C) over medium heat, stirring constantly. Remove from the heat and let cool to 140°F (60°C). Discard the plum pits.

In a medium bowl, whisk together the egg yolks and ½ cup plus 3 tablespoons (140 g) of the sugar until creamy. Slowly add one-fourth of the hot milk mixture, stirring constantly. Return the warmed eggs to the pot and cook at 160°F (70°C) for 20 minutes, stirring constantly. Stir in the salt. Strain through a fine-mesh sieve into a bowl and set the bowl in a large bowl of ice and water to quick-chill. Cover and refrigerate the ice-cream base until cold, at least 3 hours.

Meanwhile, preheat the oven to 350°F (180°C/Gas Mark 4). Line a baking sheet with parchment paper.

Arrange the almonds on the lined baking sheet and toast for 5 minutes. Remove and let cool at room temperature. Roughly chop and set aside.

In a small pot, heat the butter over medium heat and cook until golden brown, about 6 minutes. Remove from the heat and set aside.

Transfer the ice-cream base to a blender. Add the remaining 4¼ cups (990 ml) milk and 1 cup (200 g) sugar and process. Add the brown butter and process. Transfer to an ice-cream machine and process according to the manufacturer's instructions. (If you don't have an ice-cream machine, freeze the mixture until hard enough to scoop.) Stir in the chopped almonds and freeze.

Note: Save the plum pits for the ice cream. Save the egg whites to make Meringues (pages 32 or 387).

📷 P. 355

RECIPE NOTES: _____
_____
_____
_____
_____
_____
_____
_____
_____
_____
_____
_____
_____

Mario Batali

Mario Batali and I have known each other for almost twenty years. He was the one who encouraged me to bottle my family's small-batch balsamic vinegar and put it on the market. I did exactly what he said and for many years the Villa Manodori business was what kept Osteria Francescana afloat financially. So I wouldn't be here if it weren't for Mario.

For those who know Mario, he is even more multiple than writer Bill Buford's nickname for him: "Multiple Mario." He is one of the most recognized and respected chefs in the United State, a savvy businessman—with many restaurants in New York, Los Angeles, Las Vegas, and abroad—and a philanthropist. And what many people do not know is that he single-handedly put Italian cuisine back on the table. He created curiosity among public to seek out good Italian food, cook authentic recipes, and travel to Italy.

A couple of years ago, Mario told me a story about growing up Italian-American in Seattle. He described walking up to his house on a cold night and the joy that overcame him when he saw that the kitchen windows had fogged up; he knew that meant pasta boiling on the stovetop. I love this image. It is exactly the feeling that we wanted to create for our guests at the Refettorio: A place where there was something to look forward to at the end of a long day. I had no doubt when I invited Mario that he could prepare a meal that would be tasty and, even more important, welcoming.

Mario describes growing up in the Batali household as a No Waste Zone. "Some of my best memories were the summer afternoons that my brother, sister, and I handpicked thousands of blackberries from the bushes that filled a cul-de-sac near our home in Seattle. After spending five hours gathering more berries than we could count, we headed home to make fifty-two pies and forty pints (eighteen kilograms) of jam with our mom. All of the pies were stored in the two giant freezers we had in our garage, and every Sunday we pulled one out to enjoy after dinner."

Today this attitude has become even more important for Mario at home and in his restaurants. He speaks often and adamantly about the problem of food waste, "Waste is our single largest problem and has to be managed like a business."

Mario offers solutions to the daily waste that goes on in our home kitchens. "If I'm at home cooking with carrots, I'm not throwing away the greens. I'll transform them into a delicious pesto or chimichurri. All of my restaurants and Eataly marketplaces have a huge focus on sustainability, thanks to our food safety and sustainability director, who is always finding new and improved ways to reduce waste."

Mario had the menu down in minutes. He knew that there had to be pasta or the Southern Italians would complain. He knew that everyone ate chicken and turkey, as opposed to pork or beef. And he wanted to make lots of vegetables, like baked fennel and sweet and sour onions, to create that kind of unforgettable Thanksgiving-style feast. There weren't any turkeys to stuff, but there was ground turkey for meatballs and he made them really big and juicy, the next best thing. And if he cut up the five chickens he had found on the truck that morning into small pieces, maybe no one would notice how few there were.

When I asked him about the menu, he said, "Cristina told me that there are fifteen people who don't eat pork. So I'm making vegetable pasta, basically a tomato sauce with potatoes. It's going to be a *zuppa di patate* and tomato sauce hybrid." I thought it sounded like a pretty crazy plate of pasta, but I love hybrid recipes. Zuppa di patate, adding potatoes to rice or pasta, is one of the best ways to give body to pasta or soups when the pantry is bare.

It was a big menu and a satisfying one. Mario had multiplied things before our eyes: two panettone became bread pudding for an army; five chickens ended up feeding over one hundred people, and there was pasta for second and third helpings.

Everyone was feeling good that night and no one wanted to leave. One of our guests had brought a guitar. A couple of weeks earlier he had mentioned that he was a musician and I told him to play for us sometime. The volunteers took off their aprons, the kitchen team sat down, and the musician began playing the blues. With the first chord the dining room transformed back into a theater. He was singing in Senegalese with a deep and resonating voice. His music filled up the room. I was touched by the poignancy of this moment. We were all sharing a meal with people we hadn't met before. When the music was over Mario said, "Food brings people together. Sharing your failures and your successes with someone leaves you connected to the world. So if we can provide that here, that's a dream."

October 12

PENNE WITH RAW TOMATO SAUCE

Serves 8

1 lb (450 g) penne pasta or other short pasta
1 lb (450 g) potatoes, cubed
1 lb 2 oz (500 g) tomatoes, cut into ½ -inch (1.25 cm) dice
Pinch of granulated sugar
Salt
⅓ cup (90 ml) extra-virgin olive oil
Freshly grated Parmigiano-Reggiano cheese, for serving

In a large pot, bring 3 quarts (3 liters) lightly water to a boil. Add the pasta and cook until just al dente. Reserving about ½ cup (240 ml) of the pasta water, drain the pasta.

Meanwhile, in another large pot, bring 6 quarts (5.6 liters) lightly water to a boil. Add the potatoes and cook until just tender, about 7 minutes. Drain.

In a large pot, combine the tomatoes and 4 tablespoons of the reserved pasta water and bring to a simmer over medium-high heat. Add the sugar and salt to taste. Add the drained pasta and potatoes and stir over medium heat until well coated (add a splash or two more of the reserved pasta water if necessary to loosen the sauce). Add the olive oil and stir.

Serve immediately with grated Parmigiano on the side.

COQ AU VIN
WITH TURKEY MEATBALLS AND BAKED FENNEL

Serves 8

COQ AU VIN
1 whole chicken (about 4½ lb/2 kg), cut into 8 pieces (save the wings and back for making stock)
Salt and freshly ground black pepper
All-purpose (plain) flour, for coating
4 tablespoons extra-virgin olive oil
6 oz (170 g) pancetta, cut into ½ -inch (1.25 cm) dice
2 carrots, chopped
2 celery stalks, finely diced
5 cipollini onions, thinly sliced
3 garlic cloves, thinly sliced
9 oz (250 g) button mushrooms, halved
3 tablespoons tomato paste (puree)
2 cups (475 ml) red wine, preferably Cabernet or Merlot
1 cup (240 ml) chicken stock
1 bouquet garni (6 sprigs each thyme and parsley)

TURKEY MEATBALLS
10 thin slices stale bread, cut into 1-inch (2.5 cm) squares
2 lb (910 g) ground (minced) turkey
¼ lb (115 g) unsliced prosciutto di Parma, cut into ⅛-inch (3 mm) dice
½ lb (225 g) sweet Italian sausage or other mild sausage, casings removed
3 eggs, lightly beaten
3 oz (80 g) parsley, finely chopped
¼ teaspoon freshly grated nutmeg

1¼ cups (115 g) freshly grated Pecorino Romano cheese, plus more for serving
½ cup (50 g) freshly grated Parmigiano-Reggiano cheese, plus more for serving
½ cup (100 ml) extra-virgin olive oil
Salt and freshly ground black pepper
1¼ cups (295 ml) canned tomato sauce (seasoned passata)
½ cup (120 ml) cup dry white wine

BAKED FENNEL
3 fennel bulbs, cut into 1-inch (2.5 cm) chunks
Salt and freshly ground black pepper
3 tablespoons extra-virgin olive oil
1 garlic clove, peeled and minced
4 tablespoons dry vermouth
4 tablespoons (60 g) butter, diced
3½ oz (100 g) stale bread, finely crumbled (1¾ cups)

SWEET AND SOUR ONIONS
20 small red or white onions, root and stem trimmed
3 tablespoons extra-virgin olive oil
2 bay leaves
2 tablespoons red wine vinegar
1 tablespoon granulated sugar, or more to taste
Salt and freshly ground black pepper

MAKE THE COQ AU VIN

Season the chicken with salt and pepper and sprinkle with the flour to lightly coat.

In a large Dutch oven (casserole), heat the olive oil over medium heat. Add the pancetta and cook until browned, about 5 minutes. Remove and set aside. Working in batches, add the chicken and brown, starting skin side down. Remove and set aside. Add the carrots, celery, onions, garlic, and mushrooms and sauté until slightly softened, about 5 minutes. Season to taste with salt and pepper. Add the tomato paste (puree) and cook, stirring, until a dark rust in color. Add 1 to 2 tablespoons of flour to coat the vegetables and stir. Add the wine and reduce for 1 minute. Add the chicken stock and bouquet garni. Return the chicken and pancetta to the pan and bring to a boil. Reduce the heat to medium, cover, and simmer until the chicken is tender and falling apart, about 2 hours.

MAKE THE TURKEY MEATBALLS

In a medium bowl, soak the bread in water for 5 minutes. Remove and squeeze out the excess water.

>>

In a large bowl, combine the turkey, prosciutto, sausage, moistened bread, eggs, half the parsley, nutmeg, grated Pecorino and Parmigiano, and 5 tablespoons of the olive oil and gently mix with your hands. Season with salt and pepper. Form into 3-inch (7.5 cm) balls and place on a baking sheet lined with parchment paper. Cover with plastic wrap (cling-film) and refrigerate for 1 hour to allow the flavors to blend.

In a large heavy-bottomed sauté pan, heat the remaining 2 tablespoons olive oil over high heat until almost smoking. Add the meatballs and brown on all sides. Transfer to paper towels to absorb any excess oil. Drain off the excess oil from the pan. Add the tomato sauce and wine to the pan and bring to a boil. Add the meatballs to the sauce, reduce the heat to medium-low, and simmer until the meatballs are cooked through, about 20 minutes. Transfer to a platter, sprinkle with the remaining parsley, and serve with the Pecorino and Parmigiano.

BAKE THE FENNEL

Preheat the oven to 325°F (160°C/Gas Mark 3). Butter an 8 inch (20 cm) round baking dish.

Set up a large bowl of ice and water. Bring a medium pot of water to a boil. Add the fennel and blanch until soft, about 6 minutes. Immediately transfer to the ice bath to cool. Drain and season with salt and pepper.

In a medium sauté pan, heat the olive oil over medium heat. Add the garlic and sauté until soft.

Arrange the fennel in the prepared baking dish. Top with the sautéed garlic, vermouth, butter, and salt and pepper to taste. Sprinkle with the breadcrumbs and bake until golden brown, about 20 minutes. Let cool for 10 minutes before serving.

MAKE THE SWEET AND SOUR ONIONS

In a large pot, bring 3 quarts (3 liters) water to a boil. Add the onions, reduce to a simmer, and cook until tender, 5 to 7 minutes. Drain and peel the outer layer.

Meanwhile, in a saucepan, warm the olive oil with the bay leaves over medium heat.

Add the blanched onions and cook until just browned, about 5 minutes. Add the vinegar and sugar, increase the heat slightly, and cook, stirring frequently, until the mixture begins to caramelize, about 2 minutes. Discard the bay leaves. Gently stir the onions to coat with the syrupy mixture. Season to taste with salt and pepper and let cool. Serve at room temperature.

TO SERVE

Serve the coq au vin with the turkey meatballs, baked fennel, and sweet and sour onions.

 P. 360

ALMOND JOY BREAD PUDDING
ALLA MILANO WITH VANILLA ICE CREAM

Serves 8

ALMOND JOY BREAD PUDDING

17 oz (500 g) stale panettone, cut into 2-inch (5 cm) cubes
3 eggs
¾ cup (150 g) granulated sugar
2 teaspoons salt
2 cups (500 ml) milk
generous 1 cup (250 ml) heavy (whipping) cream
2¾ cups (300 g) sliced slivered almonds
12 oz (300 g) chocolate, chopped, or chocolate chips

VANILLA ICE CREAM

3⅓ cups (790 ml) heavy (whipping) cream
generous ¾ cup (200 ml) milk
1 vanilla bean, split lengthwise
3 eggs
5 generous tablespoons sugar

MAKE THE ALMOND JOY BREAD PUDDING

Preheat the oven to 350°F (180°C/Gas Mark 4). Line a baking sheet with parchment paper. Grease a 9-inch (23 cm) square baking pan with butter.

Place the panettone on the lined baking sheet and toast in the oven until golden brown, about 10 minutes. Let the bread-crumbs cool, then transfer to the prepared baking pan.

In a large bowl, whisk together the eggs, sugar, and salt. Whisk in the milk and cream. Pour over the toasted bread and let soak for 1 hour, turning occasionally to absorb, until rehydrated. Sprinkle with the almonds and bake for 45 minutes, or until golden brown. Remove and let cool.

Meanwhile, in a heatproof bowl set over a pan of simmering water, melt the chocolate, stirring frequently. Set aside.

MAKE THE VANILLA ICE CREAM

In a medium pot, combine the cream and milk. Scrape in the vanilla seeds and add the pod. Heat over medium heat.

Meanwhile, in a medium bowl, whisk the eggs with the sugar until creamy.

Slowly add one-fourth of the hot milk mixture to the eggs, stirring constantly. Transfer the warmed eggs to the pot and bring to 176°F (80°C) over low heat. Cook for 10 minutes. Cover and refrigerate until cold. Transfer to an ice-cream machine and process according the manufacturer's instructions. (If you don't have an ice-cream machine, freeze the mixture until hard enough to scoop.)

TO SERVE

Place a slice of the bread pudding in the center of each bowl. Top with a scoop of the vanilla ice cream and drizzle with the melted chocolate.

P. 363

Mario Batali

Ana Roš

This was a girls' trip to Italy. Ana Roš and her friend Tatjana Humar had driven 370 miles (600 kilometers) over the Slovenian border to be with us in Milan. Hiša Franko, the restaurant and guest house she and her husband, Valter, own in Slovenia's Soša Valley was closed for the winter season. She had hoped to escape the Slovenian rain but only found a more determined version of it in Milan.

Much like me, Ana did not go to culinary school but learned her trade on the job and by learning her skills from local chefs, who had a deep understanding of the culinary heritage of the area. Hiša Franko is located in Slovenia, just over the border from Italy, in a large house with a lively past dating back to 1860. The house was a roadside inn, then an agricultural estate, then a hospital during World War II. Ana is not only a very accomplished chef but also an ambassador for Slovenia and more specifically the Soča Valley. I had the opportunity to meet her at San Patrignano, an agricultural property and winery above the hills of Rimini that rehabilitates ex drug addicts through gastronomy.

Ana arrived in Milan the night before at 10 p.m., just in time for a pizza with chef Mario Batali, who had prepared dinner at the Refettorio. We ate an infinite quantity of pizza, but there were leftovers. We brainstormed ideas for a recipe that could resolve once and for all the problem of leftover pizza. Finally, the winning solution was pizza soup. We left lighthearted, after saying goodbye to Mario and his team. Ana, Tatjana, and Cristina headed to the apartment near the Refettorio. On the way, they saw several men in makeshift beds on the street. Ana knew that pizza would not make it to tomorrow's lunch. Instead, she gave it to them. When I walked in the next day, I was looking forward to trying pizza soup. I was terribly disappointed to hear we would be eating something else. But then Ana said, "Imagine the day you sleep on the street and don't have anything to eat. It could happen to me. We have the power to change the world a little bit for the better."

Without the pizza, Ana had to start from scratch. She arrived in the morning with the delivery truck. There were crates of ugly apples, dried porcini mushrooms, potatoes, and lots of stale bread. She said, "It's a cold rainy day so I wanted to make something to warm people up. But I can't make pasta because I'm not Italian, so I based the starter on legumes. There is a bit of cheese and different kinds of beans—red beans and lentils—potatoes and mushrooms, some vinegar, and a bit of cinnamon. I toasted the stale bread to add crunch."

She decided to check the freezer to see what had been stocked there. She found all kinds of fish and seafood: big, small, freshwater, Mediterranean, and more exotic ones. She asked Cristina, "Where did all the fish come from?" Cristina told her that fish and seafood would come in every once in a while but it was never enough to serve fifty or one hundred guests, so she always put it in the freezer. Ana decided to make a *brodetto*—a kind of fish stew—using all the fish from the refrigerator and freezer. While she ran the fish under water to help it thaw quickly she said, "Where I come from, if fish is a little tired, we cook it this way into a stew."

She embraced the spirit and the challenge of turning these random ingredients into Slovenian comfort food for a rainy day. There was a lot of bread around and she found a way to use it all. There were breadcrumbs in the legume and cinnamon soup, bread used for savory bread pudding served with the stew, and fried bread with the apple and zabaione for dessert.

The preparations for dessert were intense. Cristina was taking care of all the small bruised and worm-eaten apples. She peeled hundreds of apples for hours. Ana baked them with sugar, butter, and honey and then marinated them with red currants. She sliced the bread, soaked it in an egg-and-milk mixture, and fried it in lots of butter à la French toast. She served it with a creamy zabaione.

Everything was prepared with care. "Sharing is very important," she said. "It's like cooking for my children. I do

it with all my heart. So I'm trying to make food that is helpful and great." At the end of the night I had forgiven her for giving away the pizza. The meal was imbued with her flavors. She had left home to be here with us, but it felt like she had brought her home across the border with her. And that is when I realized that the Refettorio kitchen has a magical way of bringing out the best in everyone.

October 13

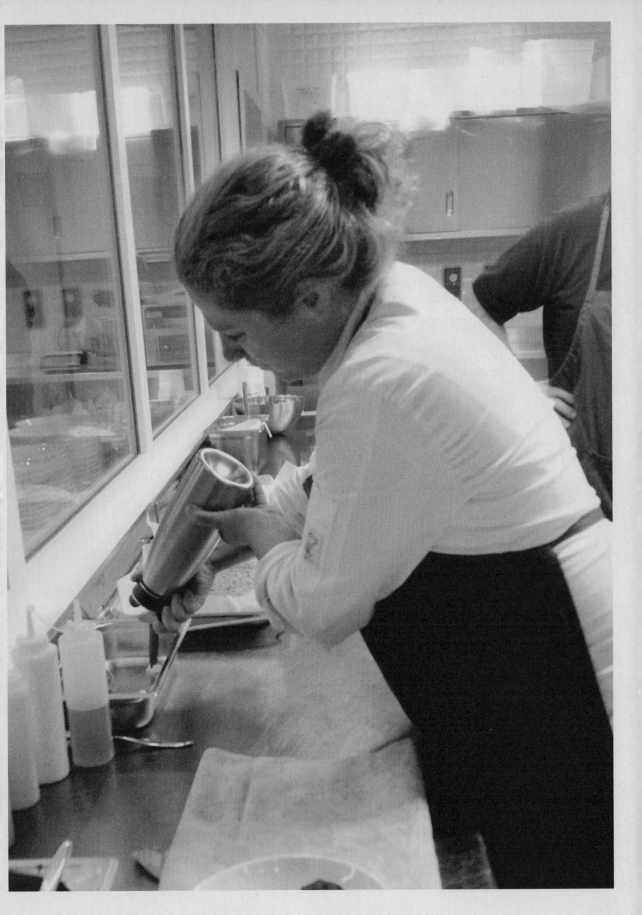

Ana Roš

October 13

FISH STEW
WITH SHRIMP MEATBALLS AND BREAD PUDDING

Serves 8

FISH STEW

1 lb 2 oz (500 g) mixed fish and shellfish (head-on
    shrimp, mullet, whitefish)
1 tablespoon extra-virgin olive oil
1 shallot, chopped
4 garlic cloves, peeled but whole
12 chives, chopped
2 teaspoons all-purpose (plain) flour
generous 2 cups (500 ml) white wine
2 quarts (2 liters) canned tomato sauce (seasoned passata)
2 tablespoons balsamic vinegar
1 teaspoon granulated sugar
1 teaspoon crushed chili flakes
2 bay leaves
Salt and freshly ground black pepper

SHRIMP MEATBALLS

10 oz (300 g) shrimp, peeled, deveined, and minced
1 teaspoon grated lemon zest
1 teaspoon salt
1 egg white, lightly beaten
1 cup (130 g) all-purpose (plain) flour
3 eggs, whisked
10 oz (300 g) stale bread, finely crumbled (5 cups)
2 cups canola (rapeseed) oil

BREAD PUDDING

1 cup (250 ml) heavy (whipping) cream
5 oz (150 g) stale bread, torn into small pieces
1 shallot, chopped
1½ slices bacon (streaky), chopped
2 sprigs rosemary
2 sprigs sage
2 sprigs thyme
3 tablespoons milk
4 chives, chopped
3 sprigs tarragon, chopped
2 lovage leaves, chopped
2 eggs
1 egg white, lightly beaten

PARMIGIANO CREAM

9 oz (250 g) grated Parmigiano-Reggiano cheese
generous 2 cups (500 ml) heavy (whipping) cream
Salt and freshly ground black pepper

FOR SERVING

Extra-virgin olive oil, for drizzling

MAKE THE FISH STEW

Preheat the oven to 200°F (100°C) or as low as your oven can go.

>>

Clean the fish; reserve any skin and bones. Cut the fish
into 2 x ¾-inch (5 x 2 cm) pieces, cover, and refrigerate.

Arrange the fish bones with meat on a baking sheet and
bake until the meat is easy to remove, 10 minutes. Remove
the meat, reserving the bones. Cover and refrigerate.

Peel the shrimp; reserve the shells and heads. Cover
and refrigerate.

In a large pot, combine 2 quarts (2 liters) water and the
reserved fish skin, bones, and shrimp shells. Bring to a boil.
Reduce the heat to medium-low and simmer for 30 minutes;
then strain.

In a large stockpot, heat the oil over medium heat. Add
the shallot, garlic, chives, and shrimp heads and sauté for
3 minutes. Stir in the flour. Add the white wine and reduce
for 5 minutes. Add 4¼ cups (1 liter) of the seafood stock, the
tomato sauce, vinegar, sugar, chili flakes, and bay leaves.
Simmer for 2 hours. Discard the shrimp heads and the bay
leaves and season to taste with salt and pepper. Add the
shrimp and pieces of fish and simmer for 5 minutes. Remove
from the heat and let rest for 20 minutes before serving.

MAKE THE SHRIMP MEATBALLS

In a bowl, combine the shrimp, zest, salt, and egg white.
Cover and refrigerate for 10 minutes.

Set up 3 shallow bowls: for the flour, the eggs, and the
breadcrumbs. Form the shrimp mixture into small balls.
Roll each ball in the flour, eggs, then in the breadcrumbs.

In a pan, heat the oil over high heat. Fry the meatballs
until golden brown, 4 minutes. Drain on paper towels.

MAKE THE BREAD PUDDING

In a medium pot, heat the cream over medium heat to 158°F
(70°C). Add the bread and mix well. Transfer to a large bowl.

In a medium pot, combine the shallots, bacon, rosemary,
sage, thyme, and milk. Bring to a boil and cook over low heat
for 5 minutes. Pour the milk over the bread mixture. Let sit
for 1 hour or until most of the milk is absorbed.

Preheat the oven to 350°F (180°C/Gas Mark 4). Line a
9 x 13-inch (23 x 33 cm) deep baking dish with parchment
paper and grease with butter.

Remove the herb sprigs from the bread mixture. Add the
chives, tarragon, and lovage, then add the eggs one by one,
mixing by hand. Gently fold in the whisked egg white.

Transfer the mixture to the baking dish. Cover with foil
and bake until a wooden pick inserted in the center comes
out dry, 45 minutes. Remove the foil and cut into squares.

MAKE THE PARMIGIANO CREAM

In a pot, simmer the Parmigiano and cream for 10 minutes
over medium-low heat. Season to taste with salt and pepper.

TO SERVE

Ladle the stew into bowls and top with 2 meatballs. Serve with
a square of bread pudding. Finish with the Parmigiano cream
and a drizzle of olive oil.

Ana Roš

P. 369

LEGUME SOUP
WITH CINNAMON, FRIED BREAD, AND GREEN OIL

Serves 8

LEGUME SOUP
4 tablespoons extra-virgin olive oil
½ garlic bulb, separated into cloves and peeled
2 whole cloves
2 shallots, finely chopped
2 carrots, chopped
1 lb (500 kg) potatoes, peeled and diced
2 bay leaves
Salt
1¾ oz (50 g) dried poricini mushrooms, soaked in water
    (change water twice)
2 quarts (2 liters) vegetable stock
2 cups (375 g) canned legumes (such as chickpeas, lentils,
    or soybeans), drained and liquid reserved
1 tablespoon soy sauce
½ teaspoon balsamic vinegar
¼ teaspoon ground cinnamon
¼ teaspoon crushed chili flakes

BREADCRUMBS
2 cups (500 ml) canola (rapeseed) oil
14 oz (400 g) stale bread, cut into medium cubes
¼ teaspoon ground cinnamon
1 whole clove
2 whole star anise

GREEN OIL
2 bouquet garnis (each with 2 sprigs parsley, 3 basil leaves,
    and 2 lovage leaves or other mixture of herbs) (see Note)
generous ¾ cup (200 ml) extra-virgin olive oil

MAKE THE LEGUME SOUP

In a medium frying pan, warm 2 tablespoons of the olive oil
over medium heat. Add the garlic and whole cloves and sauté
until golden brown. Remove the garlic and cloves and discard.
Add the shallots and carrots and sauté until golden brown,
about 5 minutes. Remove the pan from the heat and set aside.

In a medium pot, add the potatoes and bay leaves, cover
with water, and season with 1 teaspoon salt. Bring the water
to a boil over medium heat and cook until tender, about 15
minutes. Drain and discard the bay leaves. Mash half of the
potatoes using a masher or ricer. Set the mashed potatoes
aside.

In a medium frying pan, warm the remaining olive oil over
medium heat. Add the reserved diced potatoes, the sautéed
shallot/carrot mixture, and the mushrooms and cook until
golden brown, about 10 minutes.

>>

In a large pot, combine the vegetable stock, legumes,
3 tablespoons of the reserved liquid from the can, the mashed
potatoes, and the potato/vegetable/porcini mixture and
simmer over low heat. Add the soy sauce, vinegar, cinnamon,
and chili flakes and cook for 10 minutes. Season to taste with
salt. Keep the soup warm.

MAKE THE BREADCRUMBS

Preheat the oven to 275°F (140°C/Gas Mark 1). Line a baking
sheet with parchment paper.

In a medium pot, heat the oil to 356°F (180°C) over
medium heat. Working in batches, add the bread and fry until
golden brown, about 5 minutes. Transfer to the prepared
baking sheet and bake until crispy, about 40 minutes. Let
the bread cool, then transfer to a food processor, add the
cinnamon, clove, and star anise and pulse until finely ground.
Transfer to a tray and set aside set aside in a warm, dry place
to keep crispy and dry.

MAKE THE GREEN OIL

Set up a large bowl of ice and water. Bring a medium pot
of water to a boil over medium-high heat. Add 1 of the herb
bouquets and blanch for 10 seconds. Remove and transfer
to the ice bath. Remove and pat dry with a tea towel.

In a medium pot, heat the olive oil to 158°F (70°C) over
medium heat. Add the blanched bouquet and the unblanched
bouquet and warm for 5 minutes. Remove from the heat and
let cool. Strain the oil through a fine-mesh sieve into a bowl.
Store in the refrigerator.

TO SERVE

Ladle the soup into bowls. Sprinkle with the breadcrumbs
and a drizzle of the green oil.

Note: You can make green oil ahead of time, or anytime your
fresh herbs are not looking so fresh. Store in the refrigerator.

RECIPE NOTES: _____
_____
_____
_____
_____
_____
_____
_____
_____
_____
_____
_____
_____
_____
_____
_____

Ana Roš

FRIED BREAD, ZABAIONE, AND BAKED APPLES

Serves 8

ZABAIONE
    4 egg yolks (see Note)
    scant ½ cup (90 g) superfine (caster) sugar
    4 tablespoons Marsala wine

APPLES AND RED CURRANTS
    scant ½ cup (100 ml) white wine
    2 tablespoons honey
    6 red apples, halved
    1 cup (200 g) granulated sugar
    4 tablespoons (60 g) butter, melted
    Ground cinnamon, for sprinkling
    10 oz (300 g) red currants

FRIED BREAD
    4 tablespoons (60 g) butter
    4¼ cups (1 liter) milk
    1 vanilla bean, split lengthwise
    8 slices stale bread (½-inch/1.5 cm thick)
    5 eggs, lightly beaten
    2½ (300 g) powdered (icing) sugar

MAKE THE ZABAIONE

Bring a medium pot of water to a boil. In a heatproof medium bowl, combine the egg yolks and sugar. Place the bowl over the pot and whisk until foamy. Slowly whisk in the Marsala, whisking constantly. Continue whisking until the sauce thickens to a custard consistency, about 10 minutes.

MAKE THE APPLES AND RED CURRANTS

Preheat the oven to 350°F (180°C/Gas Mark 4). Line a baking dish with parchment paper.

In a small pot, bring the white wine and honey to a simmer over medium heat and cook until syrupy, about 8 minutes. Set aside to cool.

Arrange the apples cut side up in the prepared baking dish. Cover each apple half with 1 tablespoon sugar, 1 teaspoon melted butter, 1 teaspoon wine/honey syrup, and a sprinkle of cinnamon. Cover the baking dish with foil and bake until soft, about 40 minutes. When cool enough to handle, cut into medium dice.

In a medium pot, combine the currants and remaining 4 tablespoons sugar, bring to a boil over medium heat, and cook for 5 minutes. Remove from the heat, add the diced apples, and let sit for 30 minutes to marinate. Serve at room temperature or chill.

>>

MAKE THE FRIED BREAD

In a heavy pot, melt the butter over low heat. Skim off the froth from the surface, then carefully pour the clarified butter into a bowl, leaving the milky residue in the pot (discard the milky residue).

Pour the milk into a big bowl and scrape in the vanilla seeds. Add the bread and soak until most of the milk is absorbed. In a medium bowl, whisk the eggs, then dip the soaked bread into the whisked eggs.

In a deep frying pan, heat the clarified butter over medium-high heat. Working in 2 batches, fry the pieces of soaked bread until a golden brown crust forms on both sides, about 7 minutes. Remove and drain on paper towels. Sprinkle on both sides with powdered sugar.

TO SERVE

Place 1 slice of bread in the center of each bowl and garnish with a spoonful of zabaione on one side and a spoonful of the apple and red currant mixture on the other.

Note: Save the egg whites to make Meringues (pages 32 or 387).

RECIPE NOTES: _____
_____
_____
_____
_____
_____
_____
_____
_____
_____
_____
_____
_____
_____
_____
_____
_____
_____
_____
_____
_____
_____
_____
_____
_____
_____
_____
_____
_____
_____
_____

Moreno Cedroni

Moreno Cedroni's story and mine began in a similar way. When we both started out people thought we were crazy. Moreno deliberately provoked the cuisine of the Riviera Romagnola, along the Adriatic coast of Italy—famous for its spaghetti and clams and breaded grilled fish—with a radical concept he called "susci." Moreno had studied in Japan and was fascinated with the culture of raw fish, particularly Japanese sushi, which at the time had not invaded the Italian peninsula. Moreno literally changed the spelling to accommodate the Italian phonetic pronunciation, while on the plate he substituted Mediterranean flavors for Japanese ones. His restaurant Madonnina del Pescatore, located in Senigallia on the shores of the Adriatic Sea, has always had access to fresh fish. Today, it is a Michelin-starred destination restaurant, but this does not mean Moreno has lost his sense of humor nor his desire to provoke. You still never know what to expect and will undoubtedly always leave with a smile.

I couldn't believe the luck he had that morning when a truck full of fresh—not frozen—*orata* (sea bream) arrived at the Refettorio. The availability and quantity of fish was never something we could count on. Ground meat, yes, vegetables in various states, always, tropical fruit, almost a certainty, and fresh cheeses were never lacking, but fish was a rarity. And fish is tricky. It takes a trained eye to know how fresh it is and what to do with it if it isn't at its best. This is why it was essential to have chefs with experience, skills, and technique in this kitchen. They were able to teach and pass on their knowledge to the kitchen staff, and literally show them how to transform reclaimed ingredients into healthy and delicious meals. Moreno patiently demonstrated how to clean and debone the fish. The bones were used to make fish stock for the main course of *guazzetto*, a kind of fish stew that took several hours to cook.

While the guazzetto was simmering, Moreno decided to make a kind of homemade pasta called *passatelli*. I grew up with the Emilian version of *passatelli*, which is a common dish in the Emilia-Romagna region and one of the best ways to recycle day-old bread. The dough is simple enough to be made by a six-year-old child and actually comes out better when it is mixed by hand. There are three main ingredients: breadcrumbs, eggs, and grated Parmigiano cheese. The dough is formed into a ball pressed through the small holes of a ricer. It comes out the other end in long threads, like Play-Doh, and is traditionally simmered in a capon broth and served piping hot.

Moreno's *passatelli* followed the classic recipe to a point, but instead of pressing the pasta through a ricer, he rolled it out by hand into long threads and cut it into bite-size pieces. He was convinced that this process was faster and easier; nonetheless it was a production. There must have been five of us in the kitchen that morning working to have enough pasta ready by noon. After lunch, there was still more pasta making in preparation for dinner. It reminded me of Mauro Colagreco's ravioli workshop. There is just no way around it: Making homemade pasta is nothing other than an act of love.

Moreno's *passatelli* were cooked in boiling water for a few minutes, then added to a meat-based ragù and accompanied with a Parmigiano cream sauce made by infusing Parmigiano rinds into heavy cream. Every part of this recipe took into consideration the importance of using everything available. This dish was a far cry from his carefully crafted "susci" creations, but was made with the same focused attention.

When it came to the dessert, Moreno really showed his stripes. That day there was a truck full of Kinder Pinguì, a snack bar of layered chocolate cake and cream, complete with a penguin cartoon on the silver packaging. It's the kind of treat that moms would buy to reward their kids for good behavior, good marks in school, and homework completed on time. He could have served them as they were in their shiny packages, but Moreno had a devious plan in mind. Soon enough he and Cristina were opening one Kinder Pinguì after another, trying to resist the temptation to eat one. They crushed them and rolled them into hundreds of balls to accompany a milk-based flan. Once again Moreno returned to being his rebellious self, ready to provoke, this time with no other intention than to remind us of the joy of being a kid again.

Moreno Cedroni

October 16

Moreno Cedroni

PASSATELLI WITH RAGÙ

Serves 6

RAGÙ

2 tablespoons extra-virgin olive oil
9 oz (250 g) ground (minced) beef and chicken
3 medium carrots, chopped
7 oz (200 g) celery, chopped
1 medium white onion, chopped
1⅔ cups (400 g) canned peeled whole tomatoes
2 sprigs rosemary
1 tablespoon salt
½ teaspoon ground white pepper

PARMIGIANO SAUCE

3½ oz (100 g) Parmigiano-Reggiano rinds, chopped
generous ¾ cup (200 ml) milk
½ cup (120 ml) heavy (whipping) cream
4 oz (120 g) Parmigiano-Reggiano cheese, grated

BASIL AND SPINASH PUREE

7 oz (200 g) spinach
4 cups (100 g) basil leaves
Salt

PASSATELLI

10 oz (300 g) dried breadcrumbs
¾ cup plus 2 tablespoons (80 g) freshly grated
     Parmigiano-Reggiano cheese
⅔ cup (80 g) all-purpose (plain) flour
5 eggs
¼ teaspoon salt
½ teaspoon ground white pepper

MAKE THE RAGÙ

In a medium pan, heat 1 tablespoon of the olive oil. Add the beef and chicken and cook until lightly browned, about 7 minutes. Remove from the heat and set aside.

In a medium pot, heat 1 tablespoon of the olive oil over medium-high heat. Add the carrots, celery, and onion and cook for 5 minutes. Add the cooked beef and chicken, tomatoes, and rosemary and gently simmer for 1 hour. Add the salt and white pepper.

MAKE THE PARMIGIANO SAUCE

In a medium pot, simmer the Parmigiano rinds, milk, and cream over medium heat for 20 minutes. Remove from the heat and let sit for 1 hour. Return to the heat and simmer over low heat for 15 minutes. Remove from the heat and add the grated Parmigiano. Using a hand blender, blend until smooth. Strain through a fine-mesh sieve and set aside.

>>

MAKE THE SPINACH AND BASIL PUREE

Set up a large bowl of ice and water. In a medium pot of boiling water, blanch the spinach for 30 seconds. Remove the spinach and transfer to the ice bath to cool. Drain after 1 minute and set aside. Repeat the same process for the basil, reserving some of the water. In a blender, combine the spinach and basil and process until smooth (loosen with the reserved water if the mixture is too thick). Season to taste with salt. Set aside.

MAKE THE PASSATELLI

In a medium bowl, mix together the breadcrumbs, Parmigiano, and flour. Mix in the eggs, salt, and pepper. Gather into a ball, cover with plastic wrap (clingfilm), and set aside for 20 minutes.

Bring a large pot of lightly salted water to a boil over medium heat. Push the dough through a ricer or colander and directly into the boiling water. Cook until al dente, about 12 minutes. Drain and transfer to the pan with the ragù and gently toss to coat.

TO SERVE

Divide the *passatelli* among the bowls and drizzle with the Parmigiano sauce and the basil and spinach puree.

P. 377

RECIPE NOTES: _____
_____
_____
_____
_____
_____
_____
_____
_____
_____
_____
_____
_____
_____
_____
_____
_____
_____
_____
_____
_____
_____
_____
_____

Moreno Cedroni

FISH STEW WITH VEGETABLE CAPONATA
AND MASHED POTATOES

Serves 6

VEGETABLE CAPONATA
    3 zucchini (courgettes), cut into ⅓-inch (1 cm) dice
    2 medium eggplants (aubergines), cut into ⅓-inch
        (1 cm) dice
    4 Roma (plum) tomatoes, diced
    ⅔ cup (100 g) diced onion
    scant ½ cup (100 ml) extra-virgin olive oil
    Salt

MASHED POTATOES
    4 medium potatoes
    generous 2 cups (500 ml) milk
    1 stick plus 6 tablespoons (200 g) butter
    ¾ cup (100 g) all-purpose (plain) flour
    ½ teaspoon freshly grated nutmeg
    Salt

FISH STEW
    generous ¾ cup (200 ml) extra-virgin olive oil
    ⅔ cup (100 g) chopped white onion
    3 tablespoons plus 1 teaspoon white wine vinegar
    10 oz (300 g) Roma (plum) tomatoes, diced
    1 teaspoon dried oregano
    Salt
    6 sea bream, sea bass or other white fish, cut into 1-inch
        (3 cm) chunks

MAKE THE CAPONATA

Preheat the oven to 350°F (180°C/Gas Mark 4). Line a baking sheet with parchment paper.
    In a medium bowl, mix together the zucchini (courgettes), eggplant (aubergines), tomatoes, onion, and olive oil. Season with salt. Transfer to the prepared baking sheet and bake, stirring every so often, until soft but firm, about 25 minutes. Set aside to cool at room temperature.

MAKE THE POTATOES

Preheat the oven to 325°F (160°C/Gas Mark 3). Line a baking sheet with parchment paper.
    Add the potatoes to a medium pot and add water to cover. Bring to a boil over medium heat and cook until soft but firm, about 15 minutes. Drain and when cool enough to handle, peel and mash. Add the milk, butter, and flour and mix until smooth. Add the nutmeg and season to taste with salt. Transfer to a pastry (piping) bag and form ¾-inch (2 cm) mounds on the prepared baking sheet. Bake until golden brown, about 20 minutes.

>>

MAKE THE FISH STEW

In a medium pot, heat the olive oil over medium heat. Add the onion and cook until translucent, about 5 minutes. Add the vinegar, cover, and cook over low heat for 5 minutes. Add the tomatoes and gently simmer for 40 minutes. Add the oregano and season to taste with salt. Add the fish and sprinkle with salt. Cover and simmer for 6 minutes.

TO SERVE

Place 4 mashed potato mounds on each plate and top with the fish stew. Garnish with the vegetable caponata.

RECIPE NOTES: _____
_____
_____
_____
_____
_____
_____
_____
_____
_____
_____
_____
_____
_____
_____
_____
_____
_____
_____
_____
_____
_____
_____
_____
_____
_____
_____
_____
_____
_____
_____
_____
_____
_____
_____

Moreno Cedroni

VANILLA FLAN WITH VANILLA CRÈME ANGLAISE AND CHOCOLATE PINGUÌ BALLS

Serves 6

VANILLA FLAN

1⅔ cups (400 ml) heavy (whipping) cream
scant 1 cup (220 ml) milk
¼ teaspoon salt
½ vanilla bean, split lengthwise
1 cup (200 g) plus 7 tablespoons granulated sugar
3 eggs
2 egg yolks (see Note)

VANILLA CRÈME ANGLAISE

2 eggs
1⅔ cups (400 ml) milk
½ cup (100 g) granulated sugar
2 tablespoons cornstarch (cornflour)
1 vanilla bean, split lengthwise

CHOCOLATE PINGUÌ BALLS

6 packages (30 g each) Kinder Pinguì bars (or substitute with brownies)

MAKE THE VANILLA FLAN

Position a rack in the center of the oven and preheat to 350°F (180°C/Gas Mark 4).

In a medium pot, combine the cream, milk, and salt. Scrape in the vanilla seeds and add to the pot. Bring to a simmer over medium heat. Remove from the heat and let steep for 30 minutes.

Meanwhile, in another medium pot, combine 1 cup (200 g) of the sugar and 5 tablespoons water and cook, stirring, over low heat until the sugar dissolves, about 5 minutes. Increase the heat to high and cook, without stirring, until deep amber, brushing down the sides of the pan with a wet pastry brush and swirling the pan occasionally, about 10 minutes. Quickly transfer to an 11-inch (28 cm) round baking dish. Using oven mitts, immediately tilt the mold to coat the sides. Set the mold into a 9 x 13-inch (23 x 33 cm) baking dish.

In a medium bowl, whisk together the whole eggs, egg yolks, and remaining 7 tablespoons sugar until just blended. Gradually add the cream mixture, whisking constantly, without creating a lot of foam. Pass through a fine-mesh sieve directly into the caramel-lined mold. Pour enough hot water into the baking dish to come halfway up the sides of the mold. Bake until the center of the flan is just set, about 40 minutes. Transfer to a wire rack to cool, then refrigerate for 2 hours.

>>

MAKE THE VANILLA CRÈME ANGLAISE

In a small bowl, whisk together the eggs.

In a medium pot, combine the milk, sugar, and cornstarch (cornflour) over medium heat and heat until tiny bubbles form around the edges of the pan, whisking occasionally to prevent clumping, about 5 minutes. Remove from the heat. Slowly add 2 tablespoons of the hot milk mixture to the eggs, whisking constantly. Return the warmed eggs to the pot in a steady stream, whisking constantly. Return the pot to the heat and cook, whisking constantly, until the thickened, 2 to 3 minutes (do not boil). Remove from the heat, scrape in the vanilla seeds and add the pod and let infuse for 10 minutes. Remove the vanilla pod and discard. Cover the surface directly with plastic wrap (clingfilm) and refrigerate to chill.

MAKE THE CHOCOLATE PINGUÌ BALLS

In a medium bowl, smash together the Pinguì bars with your hand to form a dough. Shape into ¾-inch (2 cm) balls.

TO SERVE

Place 3 tablespoons of the crème anglaise into each bowl and top with a scoop of flan. Garnish with 3 Pinguì balls.

Note: Save the egg whites to make Meringues (pages 32 or 387).

RECIPE NOTES: _____
_____
_____
_____
_____
_____
_____
_____
_____
_____
_____
_____
_____
_____
_____
_____
_____
_____
_____
_____
_____
_____
_____
_____
_____
_____
_____

Mauro Uliassi

Cristina was on the phone all morning trying to get in touch with Mauro Uliassi to make sure he was coming to cook that day. Mauro wasn't picking up. When I arrived and saw the situation, I explained to her that when you live and work in a place as beautiful as the beach, sometimes it is just too hard to leave. I imagined the quiet beach after the summer season and the mild breeze that comes off the sea onto the porch of Mauro's restaurant. For years, the team at Osteria Francescana migrated to his Michelin-starred beach shack to inaugurate our annual August holidays. It was a ritual that we looked forward to year after year. Mauro enjoyed it much less than we did because we crashed the restaurant during the busiest time of the year. But he knew exactly how to keep us happy, with drinks and fried calamari.

Mauro and his sister Catia founded Ristorante Uliassi in 1990 along the shores of the Adriatic Riviera in Le Marche, just below the rolling hills of Senigallia. Mauro's exceptional cooking and Catia's hospitality are guaranteed to appeal to everyone. If you bring your grandmother there, she will love it. If you bring a group of gourmet travelers on a food tour, they will love it. If you bring your children, they will never want to leave.

It was 3 p.m. and I was starting to think Mauro wasn't going to show. I was pacing the kitchen and imagining what to make for dinner when I heard a car pull into the square. Mauro was wearing a funky pair of retro sunglasses and he burst into the kitchen with boxes of fresh squid, the smell of the sea filling the room. Mauro explained that he was late because he had been at the fish market in Senigallia that morning trying to get all the unsold fish from the fishmongers. When he saw them reloading fish back onto their trucks, he explained that he would be cooking at the Refettorio, and the squid were happily donated.

That evening Mauro served conchiglioni pasta in an intense squid ink broth made with simmered squid, peas, tomatoes, and potatoes. He topped it with a raw condiment of fresh tomatoes, peppers, arugula (rocket), basil, scallions (spring onions), and garlic marinated in red wine vinegar and olive oil. The dish was strikingly beautiful—dark and bright, warm and cold.

The second course took a complete detour from Mediterranean flavors. I heard Mauro shout from behind the walk-in refrigerator, "What are these?" And three seconds later he came out with a devious smile carrying thirty or more packages of chicken wings. "Let's have some fun!" he shouted. The wings came prepacked, and as Mauro began tearing off the plastic he described the sweet and sour Asian-inspired sauce he wanted to lacquer them with in the oven. Once baked, he topped the wings with a mixture of chopped scallion, parsley, and fried quinoa. I was taken aback because I didn't expect Mauro, the same guy who had arrived with a trunk full of fresh squid, to prepare a dish like this, I was pleasantly surprised, and our guests were licking their fingers and asking for more.

Mauro concluded the evening with a parfait of coffee granita, amaretti, meringue crumble, and tiramisu cream on top. It was the perfect antidote to the spicy wings. The slight touch of star anise in the granita reminded me of a *caffè corretto*, an espresso that's literally "corrected" with a drop of alcohol, often sambuca. Caffè corretto heralds back to my father's generation and I've always considered it a kind of Band-aid (plaster) for a bad day, a small escape from reality. I don't know if that's what Mauro intended, but nonetheless his dessert cast its magic, leaving everyone ready for a good night's sleep and the prospect of a new day to come.

Mauro Uliassi

October 19

PASTA WITH SQUID, TOMATO, AND BASIL

Serves 6

SQUID

2¼ lb (1 kg) squid, bodies cut into strips
Salt and freshly ground black pepper
1 tablespoon extra-virgin olive oil
1 onion, chopped
2 tablespoons squid ink
scant ½ cup (100 ml) white wine
3¾ cups (500 g) fresh or frozen green peas
5 oz (150 g) tomatoes, peeled
1 cup plus 2 tablespons (10½ oz/300 g) tomato
    paste (puree)
1 quart (1 liter) fish stock

FRESH TOMATO CONDIMENT

7 oz (200 g) tomatoes, peeled and diced
¾ cup (100 g) diced yellow, green, and red bell
    peppers, diced
4 garlic cloves, minced
20 basil leaves, torn
2 tablespoons chopped parsley
3½ oz (100 g) red onion, sliced
1½ cups (30 g) arugula (rocket)
2 teaspoons red wine vinegar
5 tablespoons extra-virgin olive oil
Salt

PASTA

Salt
6 oz (180 g) conchiglioni or other shell-shaped pasta
1 tablespoon extra-virgin olive oil
5 slices bread, toasted

COOK THE SQUID

Season the squid with salt and pepper. In a medium pot, heat the olive oil over medium heat. Add the onion and sauté until soft and lightly browned, about 6 minutes. Add the squid and stir. Add the squid ink and white wine. Add the peas, tomatoes, and tomato paste (puree) and stir. Add the fish stock, cover, and cook over low heat until the squid is tender, 30 minutes. Season to taste with salt and pepper. Set aside.

PREPARE THE TOMATO CONDIMENT

In a medium bowl, combine the tomatoes, bell peppers, garlic, basil, parlsey, onion, arugula (rocket), vinegar, and olive oil and toss to combine. Season to taste with salt.

>>

PREPARE THE PASTA

Bring a medium pot of lightly salted water to a boil over medium heat. Add the pasta and cook until al dente. Drain and toss with the olive oil.

To serve, ladle the squid broth and squid into each bowl and top with the pasta. Garnish with the fresh tomato condiment and top with a slice of the toasted bread.

📷   P. 385

RECIPE NOTES: _____

_____
_____
_____
_____
_____
_____
_____
_____
_____
_____
_____
_____
_____
_____
_____
_____
_____
_____
_____
_____
_____
_____
_____
_____
_____
_____
_____
_____
_____
_____
_____
_____
_____
_____
_____
_____

Mauro Uliassi

SPICY CHICKEN WINGS
WITH FRIED QUINOA AND ROASTED POTATOES

Serves 6

SPICY CHICKEN WINGS
24 chicken wings
All-purpose (plain) flour, for dredging
2 tablespoons extra-virgin olive oil
2 tablespoons grated fresh ginger
3 tablespoons soy sauce
4 tablespoons packed light brown sugar
3 tablespoons plus 1 teaspoon white wine vinegar
4 garlic cloves, finely chopped
4 tablespoons red Sriracha sauce
Salt

FRIED QUINOA
scant 1 cup (180 g) quinoa
1 cup (250 ml) canola (rapeseed) oil

SWEET AND SOUR SAUCE
generous ½ cup (130 ml) rice vinegar
7 tablespoons packed light brown sugar
1 fresh red chili, finely chopped
5 tablespoons tomato paste (puree)
4 garlic cloves, finely chopped

ROASTED POTATOES
2¼ lb (1.5 kg) baking potatoes, cut into wedges
4 sprigs rosemary
2 garlic cloves, thinly sliced
6 teaspoons extra-virgin olive oil
1 teaspoon salt

FOR SERVING
5 tablespoons finely chopped parsley
5 tablespoons finely chopped chives

MAKE THE SPICY CHICKEN WINGS

Dredge the chicken wings in flour. In a medium frying pan, heat 1 tablespoon of the olive oil over medium heat. Add half the chicken wings and brown, about 12 minutes. Transfer to paper towels to drain. Heat the remaining 1 tablespoon of olive oil and cook the remaining chicken wings.

In a medium saucepan, combine the ginger, soy sauce, brown sugar, vinegar, garlic, and Sriracha sauce and cook over medium heat until thick and velvety, about 6 minutes. Season to taste with salt. Remove from the heat, add the wings, and stir to coat.

>>

MAKE THE FRIED QUINOA

Preheat the oven to 200°F (100°C) or as low as your oven can go. Line a baking sheet with parchment paper.

In a medium pot, combine the quinoa and 1⅔ cups (400 ml) water. Bring to a boil and cook for 20 minutes. Drain and rinse under cold water to cool. Transfer to the prepared baking sheet and spread evenly. Bake for 3 hours.

In a medium pot, heat the canola (rapeseed) oil to 356°F (180°C). Add the quinoa and fry until it pops. Remove and transfer to paper towels to drain.

MAKE THE SWEET AND SOUR SAUCE

In a medium pot, combine the vinegar, 5 tablespoons water, the brown sugar, and chili and cook over low heat for 10 minutes, stirring often. Add the tomato paste (puree) and cook for another 10 minutes, stirring often. Remove from the heat and let sit for 2 minutes. Stir in the garlic and let infuse.

MAKE THE ROASTED POTATOES

Preheat the oven to 350°F (180°C/Gas Mark 4).

Bring a large pot of water to a boil. Add the potatoes and cook until soft but firm, about 10 minutes. Drain and transfer to a baking dish. Add the rosemary, garlic, olive oil, and salt and toss to combine. Bake until well browned, about 20 minutes.

TO SERVE

Divide the chicken wings among 6 plates and drizzle with the sweet and sour sauce. Sprinkle with the fried quinoa, parsley, and chives. Serve with the roasted potatoes.

RECIPE NOTES: _____
_____
_____
_____
_____
_____
_____
_____
_____
_____
_____
_____
_____
_____
_____
_____
_____
_____
_____
_____
_____
_____

Mauro Uliassi

COFFEE GRANITA WITH TIRAMISU CREAM, AMARETTI COOKIES, AND MERINGUE

Serves 6

CARAMELIZED ALMONDS AND HAZELNUTS

4 oz (125 g) hazelnuts
4 oz (125 g) almonds
generous ¾ cup (100 g) powdered (icing) sugar
1 tablespoon butter, diced

COFFEE GRANITA

¾ cup (40 g) instant coffee
½ cup (100 g) granulated sugar
2 whole star anise, crushed
1 cup (250 ml) hot water

TIRAMISU CREAM

6 oz (175 g) mascarpone
¾ cup (175 ml) heavy (whipping) cream
½ cup plus 1 tablespoon (70 g) powdered (icing) sugar
2 egg yolks (see Note)
1 tablespoon rum

FOR SERVING

3 Amaretti Cookies (recipe follows), crumbled
3 Meringues (recipe follows), crumbled

MAKE THE CARAMELIZED ALMONDS AND HAZELNUTS

Line a baking sheet with parchment paper.

In a medium saucepan, combine the hazelnuts, almonds, powdered (icing) sugar, and 2 tablespoons water and heat over medium heat until the sugar is melted and has a caramel color. Add the diced butter, stir until melted, and simmer for 2 minutes. Remove and transfer to the lined baking sheet. Spread evenly and let cool. Once cool, break into medium-size pieces.

MAKE THE COFFEE GRANITA

In a 10 x 12-inch (25 x 30 cm) rectangular container, combine the instant coffee, sugar, star anise, and the hot water. Stir to dissolve. Cover with plastic wrap (clingfilm) and let infuse for 30 minutes. Add the 4¼ cups (1 liter) water and stir to combine. Strain through a fine-mesh sieve. Cover and freeze for 4 hours, or until frozen. Scrape the mixture with a fork.

MAKE THE TIRAMISU CREAM

In a medium bowl, combine the mascarpone, 6 tablespoons of the cream, and the powdered (icing) sugar. Using a hand blender, blend until smooth. Add the remaining 6 tablespoons cream and the egg yolks and mix with a spatula. Add the rum and mix well. Cover and refrigerate to chill.

\>>

TO SERVE

Place a spoonful of coffee granita in each bowl and top with crumbled amaretti cookies and crumbled meringues. Garnish with the tiramisu cream and sprinkle with the caramelized almonds and hazelnuts.

AMARETTI COOKIES

Makes about 40 cookies

10 oz (300 g) sweet almonds
1 oz (25 g) bitter almonds
1½ cups (300 g) granulated sugar
3 egg whites (see Note)
generous ¾ cup (100 g) powdered (icing) sugar

Preheat the oven to 265°F (130°C/Gas Mark ½ to 1). Line a baking sheet with parchment paper.

In a food processor, grind the almonds to the consistency of flour. Transfer to a medium bowl, add 1 cup (200 g) of the sugar, and mix. Cover with a wet cloth and let rest for 24 hours.

Mix in the remaining ½ cup (100 g) sugar and the egg whites. Transfer to a pastry (piping) bag and form ¾ inch (2 cm) mounds on the prepared baking sheet. Dust with the powdered (icing) sugar and bake until an even golden brown crust, about 20 minutes. Let cool down at room temperature. Store in an airtight container.

MERINGUES

Makes 40 meringues

Powdered (icing) sugar, for dusting
3 egg whites (see Note)
4 tablespoons granulated sugar

Preheat the oven to 200°F (100°C) or as low as your oven can go. Line a baking sheet with parchment paper and dust with powdered (icing) sugar.

In a medium bowl, whisk the egg whites with the sugar until stiff peaks form. Transfer to a pastry (piping) bag and pipe 2¾-inch (7 cm) long strands onto the prepared baking sheet. Bake for 4 hours, or until completely dried. Transfer to an airtight container.

Note: Save the egg whites to make the meringues and save the egg yolks to make the tiramisu cream.

RECIPE NOTES: _____
_____
_____
_____
_____
_____
_____
_____
_____
_____

Gennaro Esposito

Before Gennaro Esposito became a chef he was a swimmer. This only comes as a surprise if you have met him in person because he doesn't fit the stereotype of a tytpical athlete. But when he tells you that he grew up on the Sorrento coast with his front yard facing the Gulf of Naples and his backyard leading to his grandfather's tomato garden, the real Gennaro, the chef and swimmer, comes into focus. Today he swims in open water with a fishing harpoon looking for his next recipe.

Gennaro opened Torre del Saracino twenty-five years ago in the small fishing village of Vico Equense. Actually, he put Vico on the map not only through the fame of his Michelin two-star restaurant but also from an annual summer festival held in early June called Festa a Vico. What had begun as an informal gathering of friends became a gathering of friends of friends, and so on and so forth. At the very beginning, Gennaro's idea was to invite a few friends who in turn would introduce a friend, chef, artisan, or winemaker to the group. This is how I was brought into the fold. And once you are in, you are there for life. Year after year the numbers multiplied and soon enough the whole town got involved. Today, Festa a Vico is open to anyone who wants to buy a ticket. Young chefs are invited to cook in impromptu kitchens that line the narrow streets and alleys of Vico. The festival is going into its fifteenth year and funds raised from the three-day event are given to selected charities.

Gennaro was the perfect chef for a project like the Refettorio because he has an instinctive ability to bring out flavor in anything. He brought with him Marco Merola, a teacher from the culinary school I Cook You in Caserta. Marco is passionate about bringing value to the area and has dedicated his career to teaching. There seemed to be an intuitive understanding between the two chefs about how to push the ingredients in the right direction with the singular goal of above all creating flavor.

They prepared pasta and potato soup that was deceptively humble. The broth (made with Parmigiano rinds), potatoes, onions, and a piece of pancetta they found in the back of the refrigerator was creamy and rich. The pasta was precooked and added at the last minute before serving to keep it al dente. When you look at this pasta bowl, it isn't pretty or neat. It is abundant, savory, solid, and soupy all at once.

To follow, they prepared a Neapolitan ragù that followed the path of least resistance. The rule goes: If the tomatoes are overripe, you go for sweetness in the ragù, trusting that you will find something savory to add in contrast. The ragù was paired with a cheese sauce and served with meatballs (that day packages of ground veal arrived in excess). This classic Italian dish should be served with a piece of hearty bread because when the meatballs are gone, the sauce remains. *Scarpetta* is an expression that means to wipe the bowl with a piece of bread the size of a little shoe (*scarpetta*) to clean the plate. When the sauce is good, this is the rule.

Up until that moment, the meal prepared that day was quite humble if you think about the ingredients, and it demonstrated to me just how much flavor can come from common pantry items. And then something magical happened. The meal concluded with a mouthwatering panettone cream served with grapefruit sorbet. Panettone is a classic Italian Christmas bread prepared with a fluffy yellow dough and candied fruit. Its flavor is infused into Italian culture from north to south and signifies the onset of the holidays. October is neither panettone nor grapefruit season and how these ingredients ended up in the pantry was a mystery to all of us. Nonetheless, this out-of-season dessert brought a magical sense of Christmas come early that illuminated the room.

October 19

Gennaro Esposito

Serves 6

2 tablespoons extra-virgin olive oil
1 onion, finely diced
1 celery stalk, finely diced
1 carrot, finely diced
3½ oz (100 g) pancetta, finely diced
5 oz (150 g) cherry tomatoes, quartered
1 lb 5 oz (600 g) potatoes, peeled and cut ¾-inch
    (2 cm) cubes
10 oz (300 g) mixed pasta shapes
1 quart (1 liter) boiling water
Salt and freshly ground black pepper
10 oz (300 g) Parmigiano-Reggiano cheese rinds, grated

In a medium saucepan, heat the olive oil over medium heat. Add the onion, celery, carrot, and pancetta and sauté until lightly browned, about 5 minutes. Add the tomatoes and simmer for 10 minutes. Add the potatoes and the pasta, then add the boiling water little by little until the liquid is almost absorbed, the soup is creamy, the potatoes are soft, and the pasta is al dente, about 12 minutes. Season to taste with salt and pepper. Add the grated Parmigiano rinds.

To serve, ladle into bowls and serve.

RECIPE NOTES:

Gennaro Esposito

VEAL MEATBALLS IN TOMATO SAUCE WITH CHEESE SAUCE

Serves 6

VEAL MEATBALLS IN TOMATO SAUCE

4 ¾ -inch (2 cm) thick slices stale bread, crusts removed
⅔ cup (150 ml) milk
14 oz (400 g) ground (minced) veal
2 eggs
⅔ cup (60 g) freshly grated Parmigiano-Reggiano cheese
2 sprigs parsley, finely chopped
Salt
½ teaspoon freshly ground black pepper
7 oz (200 g) stale bread, finely crumbled (3½ cups)
1 cup (240 ml) sunflower oil
1 tablespoon extra-virgin olive oil
1 onion, chopped
2 cup (475 ml) canned tomato sauce (seasoned passata)

CHEESE SAUCE

5 teaspoons (20 g) butter
4 teaspoons all-purpose (plain) flour
1¼ cups (300 ml) heavy (whipping) cream
7 oz (200 g) provolone cheese, finely diced
generous 1 cup (100 g) freshly grated Parmigiano-
    Reggiano cheese

MAKE THE MEATBALLS

In a medium bowl, combine the bread slices and milk and soak until the bread is soft, about 10 minutes. Drain, squeeze out the excess liquid, and transfer to a medium bowl. Add the veal, eggs, Parmigiano, parsley, 1 tablespoon salt, and the pepper and gently mix until soft. Form 1½ -inch (4 cm) meatballs and roll in the breadcrumbs.

In a medium frying pan, heat the oil over medium-low heat. Add the meatballs and fry until golden brown, about 10 minutes. Remove and transfer to paper towels to drain.

In a medium saucepan, heat the olive oil over medium heat. Add the onion and sauté until golden brown, about 6 minutes. Add the tomato sauce and simmer for 15 minutes over low heat. Season to taste with salt. Add the meatballs and cook, covered, for 10 minutes. Set aside.

MAKE THE CHEESE SAUCE

In a medium saucepan, melt the butter over low heat. Add the flour and cook until golden brown, about 6 minutes. Slowly add the cream, stirring constantly, until there are no lumps, about 6 minutes. Remove from the heat, add the cheeses, and stir until melted.

TO SERVE

Place the meatballs on each plate and spoon some of the tomato sauce over them. Top with cheese sauce.

P. 394

RECIPE NOTES:

PANETTONE CREAM WITH GRAPEFRUIT SORBET

Serves 6

GRAPEFRUIT SORBET
    1½ cups (300 g) granulated sugar
    generous 2 cups (500 ml) grapefruit juice

PANETTONE CREAM
    1¼ cups (300 ml) heavy (whipping) cream
    4 eggs yolks (see Note)
    ¾ cup plus 2 tablespoons (175 g) granulated sugar
    2½ teaspoons cornstarch (cornflour)
    14 oz (400 g) stale panettone, torn up

FOR SERVING
    Toasted almonds
    Toasted hazelnuts

MAKE THE SORBET

In a medium pot, combine the sugar and 1¼ cup (300 ml) water and cook over medium heat until a light syrup, about 10 minutes. Let cool, then cover and refrigerate to chill.

In a bowl, combine the chilled syrup, grapefruit juice, and a generous ¾ cup (200 ml) water. Transfer to an ice-cream machine and process according to the manufacturer's instructions. (If you don't have an ice-cream machine, freeze the mixture until hard enough to scoop.)

MAKE THE PANETTONE CREAM

In a medium pot, heat the cream to 180°F (82°C) over medium heat.

In a medium bowl, whisk together the egg yolks, sugar, and cornstarch (cornflour) until creamy. Slowly add one-fourth of the hot cream, stirring constantly. Transfer the warmed egg mixture to the pot and cook over low heat, stirring constantly, for 10 minutes. Let cool.

Transfer the egg/cream mixture to a blender, add the panettone, and process until smooth. Pass through a fine-mesh sieve, cover, and refrigerate to chill.

TO SERVE

Place 3 tablespoons of the panettone cream in each bowl and top with a scoop of the grapefruit sorbet. Garnish with almonds and hazelnuts.

Note: Save the egg whites to make Meringues (pages 32 or 387).

RECIPE NOTES: _____

Carles Mampel, Antonio Bachour &
Oriol Balaguer

Italian-Brazilian journalist Luciana
Bianchi and I met more than ten years
ago, so long ago in fact that I can't
remember exactly where or when. What
I do know is that as soon as she came
into our lives, we were enriched by her
observations and listening skills. She
became much more than a journalist,
she became a trusted friend. After that
first encounter, we kept running into
each other at gastronomic conferences
from Lo Mejor de la Gastronomía and
Madrid Fusion to Flemish Primitives
and Identità Golose. She finally visited
Modena in 2009, and to our embarrass-
ment we did not have a table available.
She ate standing in the kitchen, and that
is when I knew we were really friends.

Luciana was trained as a chef and
worked in many restaurant kitchens
before turning to travel writing and
journalism. She is one of those people
who lives in different time zones and
thinks nothing of being constantly on
the road researching, organizing, and,
most of all, connecting people. It was
exactly in this way that she brought together three internationally acclaimed
pastry chefs to Milan. Luciana had
flown in to lend a hand during our first
charity dinner back in early August.
She was swept up by the enthusiasm
of the night, and about a week later
she called me, so excited I could barely
process what she was saying. "I was
talking about the Refettorio with Carles
Mampel, Antonio Bachour, and Oriol
Balaguer," she told me, "and they said,
'What about a bunch of crazy pastry
chefs cooking together?'"

I had never met them in person but
their fame preceded them all. I thought
it would be an interesting experience
to have some of the top pastry chefs in
the world cooking in a soup kitchen.
Fortunately, these three friends had the
good sense to bring their own chocolate
with them, because it would have been a
tragic day in the pastry world if they had
had to rely on what was in our pantry.

That day, the fridge was almost empty,
but they took on the challenge with
smiles. They were cooking for almost

two hundred guests: a group of children at lunch and our regular guests
at dinner. The kitchen looked like a
chocolate factory, and in no time it
smelled heavenly. You could even smell
chocolate from the street outside. There
was a Willy Wonka buzz, and I couldn't
tell if all the energy in the air was from
the sugar or the pure happiness they
were producing.

Carles is a Catalonian chef with a
passion for cakes and pastries. His
Barcelona shop Bubó is not a typical
pastry shop and you can see this from
the shape, color, and design of the
cakes, which look more like modern art
than sugar confections. I was surprised,
and even a little disappointed, that he
decided not to make a cake that day,
and instead dedicated himself to the
savory part of the meal. He and Luciana
prepared paella with everything that
they could find in the refrigerator:
carrots, chicken, peppers, soy sauce,
and even rice noodles. It was a fusion
between Asia—with the noodles and
the soy dressing—and Spain. It was
the perfect dish to prepare, appealing
to both kids and adults, and surely
a discovery for every guest that day.

Antonio is one of the most passionate
people I have ever met. He was raised
in his family's bakery in Puerto Rico. He
is obsessed with the quality of ingredients. When he came to Milan he hadn't
yet opened Bachour Bakery + Bistro
in Miami—which since has become a
magnet for young pastry chefs from all
over the world—but he was telling me
about his new book on chocolate, which
happened to include an introduction
by Carles and Oriol. At the Refettorio he
prepared many different treats, but the
most delicious was an olive oil cake with
white chocolate.

We all watched mesmerized as Antonio
tempered the white chocolate to create
perfect white chocolate shards with
gloss and shine. Tempering creates the
snap and crispness that we associate
with real chocolate desserts, and for
Antonio it was absolutely essential to re-
create to the best of his ability his pastry
shop, because he only wanted to share
the best, nothing less.

Oriol was literally born into the profes-
sion, apprenticing with his father in
the family pastry shop. After working
with Ferran Adrià, he was named best
pastry chef in Spain at the age of twen-
ty-three. His pastry and chocolate shops
in Barcelona and Madrid are not only
places for continual innovation and
cutting-edge chocolate design but are
also home to classics like his world-re-
nowned butter croissant.

Oriol made a composition of chocolate,
hazelnuts, and oranges served in a bowl.
It was rich and creamy and laborious
to make. He also made lollipops with
grapes and chocolate. He set the grapes
on skewers and swirled chocolate
over them. This dessert is the perfect
solution for covering up imperfect fruit
like this day's grapes, and it makes you
happy just looking at it. The lollipops
reminded us of how easy it is to create
so much joy with so little because no
mater where you come from, sweets
connect you to your childhood.

The night was memorable. The dining
room smelled like a pastry shop and we
were all high on sugar. We had never
served three desserts during a meal, nor
generated so much joy in such a small
window of time. As I watched our guests
leave the Refettorio with lollipops in
their hands, I remembered Gene Wilder
singing to Charlie in the *Willy Wonka
& the Chocolate Factory*: "Come with
me and you'll be in a world of pure
imagination . . . . Anything you want to,
do it. Want to change the world? There
is nothing to it."

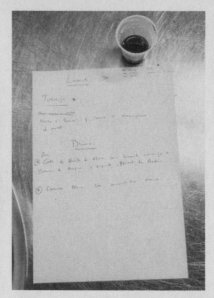

PAELLA WITH CRISPY NOODLES

Serves 6

CRISPY NOODLES
generous ¾ cup (200 ml) canola (rapeseed) oil
5 oz (150 g) rice noodles

BROTH
2 tablespoons extra-virgin olive oil
2 carrots, finely chopped
2 leeks, trimmed and finely chopped
scant ½ cup (100 ml) soy sauce
1¼ oz (35 g) dried porcini mushrooms
1 bay leaf

PAELLA
3 tablespoons extra-virgin olive oil
10 shallots, finely chopped
1 red bell pepper, finely chopped
1 green bell pepper, finely chopped
1 yellow bell pepper, finely chopped
2 garlic cloves, finely chopped
1 tablespoon tomato paste (puree)
Salt
7 oz (200 g) boneless, skinless chicken breast
    or thigh, diced
3½ oz (100 g) veal (any cut), diced
1 eggplant (aubergine), diced
1½ cups (300 g) rice

MAKE THE CRISPY NOODLES

In a medium pot, heat the canola (rapeseed) oil to 356°F (180°C). Add the rice noodles and fry until puffed, 4 to 5 seconds. Transfer to paper towels to drain. Set aside.

MAKE THE BROTH

In a medium pot, heat the olive oil over medium heat. Add the carrots and leeks and sauté until golden brown, about 6 minutes. Add 2 quarts (2 liters) water, the soy sauce, dried porcini, and bay leaf and bring to a boil. Cook for 30 minutes. Strain through a fine-mesh sieve, reserving the porcini, carrots, and leeks. Set aside.

>>

MAKE THE PAELLA

In a large shallow ovenproof pan, heat the olive oil over low heat. Add the shallots and sauté for 3 minutes. Add the bell peppers and sauté until soft, about 8 minutes. Add the garlic and tomato paste (puree), season with salt, and cook for 5 minutes. Add the chicken, veal, and eggplant and cook over medium heat for 10 minutes.

Preheat the oven to 350°F (180°C/Gas Mark 4).

Add 1¼ cups (300 ml) of the broth and sprinkle the rice evenly over the pan. Cook for 5 minutes over high heat, then reduce to low and cook for 5 minutes more. Add ⅔ cup (150 ml) more broth and the reserved porcini, carrots, and leeks. Transfer to the oven and cook until the rice is soft, about 8 minutes.

TO SERVE

Serve the paella garnished with the crispy noodles.

RECIPE NOTES:

Carles Mampel, Antonio Bachour & Oriol Balaguer

OLIVE OIL CAKE, CITRUS JAM, WHITE CHOCOLATE, AND OLIVE OIL JELLY

Serves 6

OLIVE OIL CAKE
½ cup (115 g) granulated sugar
½ cup (70 g) all-purpose (plain) flour
1 teaspoon baking powder
1 egg
4 tablespoons extra-virgin olive oil
3 tablespoons orange juice

CRUNCHY STREUSEL
1 cup (30 g) cornflakes
1½ oz (40 g) white chocolate, melted
5 teaspoons (20 g) butter, melted

WHITE CHOCOLATE MOUSSE
3 gelatin sheets
⅔ cup (150 ml) heavy (whipping) cream
scant ½ cup (100 ml) goat milk
5¾ oz (160 g) white chocolate, melted

CITRUS JAM
1 tablespoon granulated sugar
1 teaspoon pectin powder
1 orange, peeled, segmented (membranes reserved), and chopped
1 lemon, peeled, segmented (membranes reserved), and chopped
1 grapefruit, peeled, segmented (membranes reserved), and chopped
1½ teaspoons honey

OLIVE OIL JELLY
2½ gelatin sheets
¼ teaspoon invert sugar
2 generous tablespoons granulated sugar
0.8 oz (25 g) isomalt
3 tablespoons plus 2 teaspoons extra-virgin olive oil

WHITE CHOCOLATE SHAVINGS
7 oz (200 g) white chocolate

MAKE THE OLIVE OIL CAKE

Preheat the oven to 325°F (160°C/Gas Mark 3). Line a 8½ x 12- inch (22 x 30 cm) rimmed baking sheet with parchment paper.

In a medium bowl, whisk together the sugar, flour, and baking powder. In another medium bowl, whisk together the egg, olive oil, and orange juice. Add the dry ingredients and whisk until combined into a smooth batter. Pour into the prepared baking sheet and bake until golden brown, 12 to 18 minutes. Let cool on the pan, then cut into ¾ -inch (2 cm) pieces and set aside.

MAKE THE CRUNCHY STREUSEL

Line a baking sheet with parchment paper. In a medium bowl, combine the cornflakes, melted chocolate, and melted butter. Transfer to the lined baking sheet, spread into a thin layer, and refrigerate until firm.

MAKE THE WHITE CHOCOLATE MOUSSE

In a small bowl, soak the gelatin in cold water until soft, about 10 minutes. Drain and set aside.

In a large bowl, whip the cream until soft peaks form. Set aside.

In a medium pot, heat the goat milk over medium heat and bring to a boil. Stir in the gelatin until dissolved.

Place the white chocolate in a medium bowl. Slowly pour in the hot goat milk, whisking until smooth. Let cool to 86°F (30°C), then carefully fold in the whipped cream. When the mixture is firm but smooth, transfer to a pastry (piping) bag and set aside at room temperature.

MAKE THE CITRUS JAM

In a small bowl, stir together the sugar and pectin. Set aside.

Squeeze the juice from the reserved citrus membranes into a small pot. Add the honey and gently warm over medium heat for 10 minutes. Add the sugar and pectin mixture and bring to a boil over medium heat. Remove and pour over the chopped citrus. Let cool and set aside.

MAKE THE OLIVE OIL JELLY

In a small bowl, soak the gelatin in cold water until soft, about 10 minutes. Drain and set aside.

In a medium pot, heat 3 tablespoons water, the sugars, and isomalt to 194°F (90°C), stirring constantly until dissolved. Stir in the gelatin to melt. Using a hand blender, add the olive oil in slow stream. Let cool. Pour into a 9 x 13-inch (23 x 33 cm) baking pan and refrigerate until solid, about 1 hour. Cut into ¾ -inch (2 cm) cubes.

MAKE THE WHITE CHOCOLATE SHAVINGS

In a heatproof bowl set over a pan of simmering water, melt the chocolate, stirring frequently so that it does not burn. Spread the chocolate on a baking sheet lined with parchment paper. Refrigerate until solid, about 30 minutes. Break into irregular pieces.

TO SERVE

Place a spoonful of the citrus jam in the center of each plate. Top with 3 pieces of the olive oil cake and pipe the white chocolate mousse over the cake. Place a few cubes of the olive oil jelly around the cake and garnish with the white chocolate shavings and the streusel.

>>

CHOCOLATE AND GRAPE LOLLIPOPS

Makes 20 lollipops

  10 oz (300 g) dark chocolate (65% cacao), finely chopped
  10 seedless green grapes, halved

In a heatproof bowl set over a pan of simmering water, melt two-thirds of the chocolate, stirring frequently with a rubber spatula until melted. Place a candy thermometer or digital thermometer in the chocolate and do not let the temperature exceed 120°F (49°C). Remove the bowl from the pan and wipe the bottom of the bowl to get rid of any condensation. Add the remaining chocolate little by little, constantly stirring and letting it melt before adding more. Let cool to 82°F (28°F). Return to the pot of simmering water and reheat to 88° to 91°F (31° to 32°C), then remove from the heat. Spread a small spoonful of chocolate on a piece of wax paper. If it dries quickly with a glossy finish, the chocolate is ready to use; if it looks dull or streaky, repeat this process. Transfer to a pastry (piping) bag.

Line a baking sheet with parchment paper. Arrange the grapes cut side down 2½ inches (6 cm) apart on the lined baking sheet. Place one end of a 4-inch (10 cm) skewer underneath each grape. Pipe chocolate over and around each grape in a spiral pattern, making sure to go over the skewer. Refrigerate for at least 15 minutes before serving.

📷   P. 403

RECIPE NOTES:

Carles Mampel, Antonio Bachour & Oriol Balaguer

Pino Cuttaia

By the time Pino Cuttaia came to the Refettorio, Expo was coming to an end and every day fewer and fewer ingredients arrived. Thankfully, Pino is a master illusionist. The illusion I am referring to is the age-old tradition of *cucina povera*, the humble cooking from rural areas where finer ingredients were rarely available and were substituted by more realistic alternatives. *Cucina povera* belongs to every Italian grandmother who learned how to master the art of recovering anything edible to feed their families while still making it taste good. It is an approach to cooking that transforms stale bread into gold, becoming anything imaginable: soup, meatloaf, or even dessert. That day, Pino took the concept to the extreme by turning eggs into "fake fish" for a seafood-inspired pasta dish.

Pino is from the eternally beautiful southwestern coast of the island of Sicily. His culinary training brought him to the Alps, in Piedmont, which required the ability to adapt to altitude and climate, as well as lifestyle. Imagine a Sicilian guy accustomed to waking up in front of the sea, who only sees fog for months on end. Pino eventually returned to his hometown of Licata with a rich toolbox of techniques and knowledge—and his Piedmontese wife, Loredana, with whom he opened La Madia.

Back at the Refettorio there was not even the shadow of a mollusk or seaweed in the kitchen. Pino grabbed anything he could use to evoke his familiar flavors from home: tomatoes, garlic, and parsley became a poor man's rich spaghetti sauce. He scrambled eggs in the boiling pasta water to make "fake fish" resembling the shape and texture of pulled crab and folded them into the pasta with a dusting of toasted almonds on top. It didn't actually look like fish at all, but the flavors were distinctly Sicilian and there was no doubt that this dish was testimony to *cucina povera*, a recipe invented out of necessity.

Pino kept the illusions going with the second course called *falsomagro*, which literally means "fake-thin." Falsomagro is a traditional Southern Italian meatloaf, or more appropriately, a stuffed meat roll that can be filled with everything and anything like vegetables, cold cuts, eggs, and cheese. There are very few rules when it comes to falsomagro, and as with so many Italian traditions, every family has its own secret recipe. Pino's falsomagro looked deceptively simple from the outside, but when he sliced it, a decorative pattern of mortadella and sliced boiled eggs revealed itself.

As Pino cooked, he told me a story from his childhood. "When I was a kid, my mom used to reheat leftovers from the day before and cover up the flavor with pizzaiola seasoning. Whenever we smelled the scent of pizzaiola coming from her kitchen, we knew we were being tricked!"

Pino continued to play with real and imagined. When I heard he had named his dessert Profiteroles with "Almost" Chocolate Sauce, I couldn't help but laugh. The filling was a classic custard with eggs, milk, and sugar, but the chocolate sauce was made with only cocoa powder, sugar, and water (we didn't have any chocolate bars), which he drizzled over the profiteroles. No one noticed the difference.

After every service, whether lunch or dinner, there was a meal for the volunteers. Most of the time, the chefs would serve the same meal that they had prepared for the guests. The person who appreciated the staff meal more than anyone was Francesco, a young electrician who had recently lost his wife. He signed up to volunteer as a way of getting out of his house. He didn't know how to cook and was very shy, so he decided to wash the dishes three nights a week. Every time I saw him, he was cheerful and upbeat, making the least glamorous job look fun. And night after night at the staff meal, he would talk and laugh with the other volunteers. The volunteers became the family Francesco needed.

While we were eating the pasta that night, someone asked about the sauce. Pino kept the joke going as long as he could and said it was a simple fish ragù.

Everyone continued eating except for Francesco who looked closer at his plate. After a brief moment, he said, "There isn't any fish in this pasta, is there? *Chef, ci ha fregato*! You tricked us!"

Pino Cuttaia

October 27

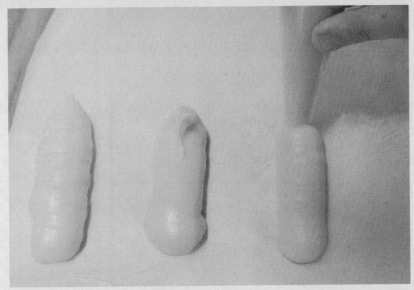

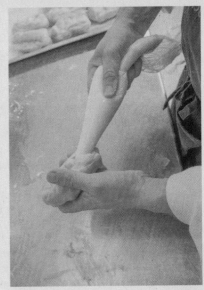

Serves 6

    2 tablespoons extra-virgin olive oil
    2 garlic cloves, sliced
    1 lb 2 oz (500 g) tomatoes, peeled and mashed
    3½ oz (100 g) parsley, chopped
    10 oz (300 g) spaghetti, broken in half
    2 eggs, whisked
    3½ oz (100 g) roasted blanched almonds, sliced

In a medium saucepan, heat the olive oil over medium heat. Add the garlic and cook until lightly browned, about 5 minutes. Add the tomatoes and parsley, reduce the heat to medium-low and cook for 15 minutes. Add 1 quart (1 liter) water, increase the heat to medium, and boil for 10 minutes. Add the spaghetti and reduce the heat to low. Add the eggs, stirring to form strings to mimic pulled crab or fish and cook until the pasta is al dente, about 5 minutes. Stir in the almonds.

P. 409

RECIPE NOTES:

Pino Cuttaia

Serves 6 to 8

FALSOMAGRO
6 eggs
5 oz (150 g) sliced mortadella or cooked ham
generous 1⅔ cups (130 g) freshly grated
    Parmigiano-Reggiano cheese
¾ cup (50 g) chopped parsley
1½ lb (700 g) ground (minced) meat
4½ oz (130 g) stale bread, finely crumbled (2⅓ cups)
1 small onion, chopped
Pinch of salt
1 teaspoon freshly ground black pepper
scan ½ cup (100 ml) extra-virgin olive oil

ASPARAGUS WITH HOLLANDAISE
24 asparagus spears, trimmed
3 egg yolks, at room temperature (see Note)
1 stick plus 6 tablespoons (200 g) butter, cut into cubes,
    at room temperature
2 tablespoons fresh lemon juice
Salt and ground white pepper

MAKE THE FALSOMAGRO

Bring a medium pot of water to a boil. Add 3 eggs and boil for 9 minutes. Remove and let cool in cold running water. Peel and transfer to a food processor. Add the mortadella, Parmigiano, and parsley and process until smoth. Set aside.

Preheat the oven to 325°F (160°C/Gas Mark 3). Line a baking sheet with parchment paper.

In a medium bowl, whisk together the remaining 3 eggs. Add the ground (minced) meat, breadcrumbs, onion, salt, and pepper and mix to combine. Transfer to the prepared baking sheet and press into an even ¾-inch (2 cm) layer. Cover with the egg mixture. Roll into a cylinder and slice into 2½-inch (6 cm) slices. In a large pan, heat the olive oil over medium heat. Add the falsomagro without crowding the pan and brown, 4 minutes on each side. Cover with foil and bake until the internal temperature reaches 176°F (80°C), 10 minutes.

MAKE THE ASPARAGUS AND HOLLANDAISE

Set up a large bowl of ice and water. Bring a medium pot of water to a boil. Add the asparagus and blanch for 3 minutes. Transfer to the ice bath to cool. Drain and set aside.

In a heatproof bowl set over a pan of simmering water, combine the egg yolks and 2 tablespoons water. Whisk constantly until thick and doubled in volume, about 3 minutes. Slowly add the butter, whisking constantly until the consistency of a thick cream. Whisk in the lemon juice. Season to taste with salt and white pepper.

TO SERVE

Place a slice of the falsomagro on each plate and top with the asparagus. Drizzle with the hollandaise.

Makes 8

CHOUX PASTRIES
5 tablespoons plus 1 teaspoon (75 g) butter
Pinch of salt
1 cup minus 1 tablespoon (125 g) all-purpose (plain) flour
4 eggs

CUSTARD
1 cup (250 ml) milk
⅓ cup (75 g) granulated sugar
Grated zest of 1 lemon
2 egg yolks (see Note)
2½ tablespoons cornstarch (cornflour)

CHOCOLATE SAUCE
generous ¾ cup (160 g) granulated sugar
⅔ cup (160 g) unsweetened cocoa powder
2½ tablespoons cornstarch (cornflour)

MAKE THE CHOUX PASTRIES

Preheat the oven to 400°F (200°C/Gas Mark 6). Line a baking sheet with parchment paper.

In a medium pot, combine a generous ½ cup (125 ml) water, the butter, and salt and bring to a boil over medium heat. Slowly add the flour, whisking constantly until a dough forms. Reduce the heat to low and add the eggs one at a time, beating well after each addition. Transfer to a pastry (piping) bag and pipe sixteen 2⅜-inch (6 cm) mounds onto the lined baking sheet. Bake until golden brown, 15 minutes. Let cool.

MAKE THE CUSTARD

In a medium pot, bring a generous ¾ cup (200 ml) of the milk, the sugar, and lemon zest to a boil over medium heat.

In a medium bowl, whisk together the egg yolks, cornstarch (cornflour), and the remaining 3 tablespoons plus 1 teaspoon milk. Slowly whisk the egg mixture into the milk mixture until thick. Let cool, then cover the surface with plastic wrap (clingfilm), and refrigerate until cold.

MAKE THE CHOCOLATE SAUCE

In a medium saucepan, whisk together the sugar, cocoa, and cornstarch (cornflour). Add a generous 2 cups (500 ml) water. Boil, constantly stirring, until thickened. Set aside.

TO SERVE

Fill a pastry (piping) bag with the custard and pipe into the centers of the choux pastries. Place 2 profiteroles on each plate and drizzle with the chocolate sauce.

Note: Save the egg whites to make Meringues (pages 32 or 387).

 P. 411

Alice Delcourt

The story of Alice Delcourt and her restaurant Erba Brusca is a fairy tale about a nomadic princess who found her home in a hidden garden surrounded by a big metropolitan city. It is also a modern-day love story about a boy and a girl, both working in the restaurant business, who met, started a business together, and then fell in love. It is also the story about being resourceful with ingredients, the land, and the lessons passed down from generation to generation.

Alice is a perfect example of a global melting-pot generation. She was born in France to a French father and an English mother. She was raised in the United States and later chose Italy as her home. She fell in love with Italy for the first time twenty years ago and later returned as an undergraduate, but she did not settle permanently until twelve years ago. It was while living and working in New York—by day in a legal office and at night in a restaurant—that she discovered her passion for the kitchen. She moved to London to work at the River Café and then to Italy to work at several Italian restaurants, among them Alice Restaurant in Milan where she worked with chef Viviana Varese.

Alice briefly met her future husband, Danilo, at a sommelier certification class in 2007, but they barely exchanged a word. Then in 2010 they became friends through work. It wasn't until right when they opened Erba Brusca in 2011 that they started dating.

Erba Brusca is located on the outskirts of Milan, but it only takes a bicycle to reach it along the Naviglio Pavese. If you follow the canal until the city fades and transforms into a rural landscape, soon enough you'll find yourself in Alice's kitchen garden.

I asked Alice how she found the restaurant and she laughed out loud, "It found me!" She added, "Danilo randomly found this site and asked if I was interested in creating a restaurant in a very different context from your average city restaurant—on the outskirts, with a garden—and the journey was kick-started."

The philosophy behind Erba Brusca is simplicity, fresh and seasonal products, and above all, respect. For Alice, salvaging food is part of her everyday life. She is clearly devoted to keeping waste to a minimum. She explained that, "Working with food in a professional kitchen, we have the chance to invent ways to use the best and the most of every product. In this sense, salvaged food becomes a matter of respect: respect for the product, respect for the environment, respect for the world."

Alice's outlook was reflected in the menu she served at Refettorio that night, beginning with classic vegetable minestrone where all kinds of vegetables and herbs shared the same bowl. Basically, she cleaned out the refrigerator and used all of those odd vegetables that would have never been enough individually to feed all our guests. Together they simmered in a broth of Parmigiano rinds to make a welcoming and hearty meal.

Alice continued on her "empty the fridge mission" with couscous and meatballs for the main course. She used many different spices, such as cumin and toasted fennel seeds, as well as chopped dried prunes and lemon zest, and added a dollop of sour cream on the side. She added toasted almonds, sesame, and sunflower seeds to give the couscous extra texture. For dessert, Alice made an apple-cinnamon cake with diced apples and raisins, and olive oil instead of butter. It was absolutely delicious.

I was impressed to see such a young chef so determined and clearheaded. She wasn't at all daunted by the challenge and seemed perfectly at ease. Cooking came naturally to her as she improvised at an upbeat pace. "The real challenge for us chefs," she said, "is to present leftovers and scraps in a way that people can enjoy."

The way she cooked was exactly how my mother taught me to work in the kitchen, with humility and intention. "Since I don't use much technology in my kitchen," she said, "the techniques stay the same as those of my grandparents: using stale bread for cakes, panzanella, and soup; animal and fish carcasses for broths; citrus peels for candies; and leaves for pesto." Her cooking is from the heart. And wasn't that the reason we had all come here to cook anyway?

Alice Delcourt

October 29

Alice Delcourt

RADICCHIO AND FENNEL SALAD

Serves 6

2 tablespoons red wine vinegar
4 teaspoons balsamic vinegar
1 teaspoon soy sauce
Juice of 1 lemon
1 tablespoon Dijon mustard
scant ½ cup (100 ml) extra-virgin olive oil
1 tablespoon honey
Salt
2 fennel bulbs, trimmed and julienned
2 medium heads radicchio, sliced into thin ribbons

In a medium bowl, whisk together the vinegars, soy sauce, lemon juice, and mustard. Slowly whisk in the olive oil, whisking constantly until combined. Whisk in the honey and season to taste with salt.

Set up a large bowl of ice and water. Bring a medium pot of water to a boil over high heat. Add the fennel and blanch for 2 minutes. Remove and transfer to the ice bath to cool. Drain.

Add the radicchio and fennel to the vinaigrette and toss. Season with salt and serve.

RECIPE NOTES: _____
_____
_____
_____
_____
_____
_____
_____
_____
_____
_____
_____
_____
_____
_____
_____
_____
_____
_____
_____
_____
_____
_____
_____

MINESTRONE

Serves 6

1½ lb (700 g) Parmigiano-Reggiano cheese rinds
2 sprigs thyme
1 sprig rosemary
3 sage leaves
2 tablespoons extra-virgin olive oil
4 carrots, diced
1 fennel bulb, trimmed and diced
4 potatoes, peeled and diced
2 garlic cloves, finely chopped
Salt
7 oz (200 g) conchiglioni or other small shell pasta
7 oz (200 g) stale bread, diced
½ teaspoon freshly ground black pepper
10 basil leaves, finely slivered

In a medium pot, combine 2 quarts (2 liters) water, the Parmigiano rinds, thyme, rosemary, and sage and bring to a boil over medium heat. Immediately reduce the heat and gently simmer for 1 hour. Remove the Parmigiano rinds and strain the broth through a colander. Set aside at room temperature.

Preheat the oven to 350°F (180°C/Gas Mark 4). Line a baking sheet with parchment paper.

In a medium saucepan, heat 1 tablespoon of the olive oil over medium heat. Add the carrots, fennel, and potatoes and sauté for 3 minutes. Add the garlic and sauté for 5 seconds. Season with salt. Add the Parmigiano broth and boil for 6 minutes. Add the pasta and cook until al dente, about 8 minutes.

Place the bread on the baking sheet and lightly toss with the remaining 1 tablespoon of olive oil and pepper. Bake until golden brown, about 15 minutes. Toss with the basil.

To serve, ladle the soup into soup bowls, garnish with the toasted bread, and sprinkle with salt.

P. 417

RECIPE NOTES: _____
_____
_____
_____
_____
_____
_____
_____
_____
_____
_____
_____
_____
_____
_____
_____
_____
_____
_____

Alice Delcourt

COUSCOUS WITH MEATBALLS AND SOUR CREAM

Serves 6 to 8

SOURED CREAM
1 cup (250 ml) heavy (whipping) cream
1½ tablespoons fresh lemon juice

MEATBALLS
7 oz (200 g) stale bread
1¼ cups (300 ml) milk
2¼ lb (1 kg) ground (minced) beef, pork, or other ground meat
3 garlic cloves, chopped
1 tablespoon extra-virgin olive oil
2 eggs
5 oz (150 g) dried prunes, pitted and finely diced
2 teaspoons fennel seeds, crushed
½ teaspoon ground cumin
1 lemon zested
2 teaspoons salt
¼ teaspoon freshly ground black pepper

COUSCOUS
1⅔ cups (500 ml) chicken stock
2½ cups (450 g) couscous
2 tablespoons (30 g) butter, melted
1 teaspoon grated fresh turmeric
1 teaspoon salt

TOASTED NUTS AND SEEDS
½ teaspoon white sesame seeds
2 tablespoons chopped almonds
1 tablespoon flaxseeds (linseeds)
2 tablespoons sunflower seeds

MAKE THE SOURED CREAM

In a medium bowl, whisk together the cream and lemon juice, whisking constantly until combined. Cover with plastic wrap (clingfilm) and refrigerate until cold and firm, at least 1 hour.

MAKE THE MEATBALLS

Preheat the oven to 400°F (200°C/Gas Mark 6). Line a baking sheet with parchment paper.
In a medium bowl, soak the bread in the milk until absorbed, about 10 minutes. Remove and squeeze out the excess milk.
In a medium bowl, combine the ground meat, garlic, olive oil, eggs, prunes, soaked bread, fennel seeds, cumin, lemon zest, salt, and pepper and mix by hand. Form into ping-pong–size balls and transfer to the prepared baking sheet. Bake until golden brown, about 20 minutes.
Set aside and cover loosely to keep warm.

>>

MAKE THE COUSCOUS

In a medium pot, bring the stock to a boil over medium heat.
Meanwhile, in a heatproof large bowl, combine the couscous, melted butter, turmeric, and salt and toss to combine.
Pour the hot stock over the couscous, cover with a tea towel, and let stand until all the liquid is absorbed, about 20 minutes. Fluff with a fork and set aside.

MAKE THE TOASTED NUTS AND SEEDS

In a large dry frying pan, toast the sesame seeds, almonds, flaxseeds, and sunflower seeds over low heat until golden brown, about 5 minutes.

TO SERVE

Place a generous spoonful of couscous at the bottom of each dish. Top with 3 meatballs and garnish with the toasted seeds and soured cream.

RECIPE NOTES: _____

Alice Delcourt

APPLE, CINNAMON,
AND OLIVE OIL CAKE WITH RICOTTA CREAM

Makes 6

APPLE, CINNAMON, AND OLIVE OIL CAKE
½ cup (80 g) raisins
2 cups plus 2 tablespoons (280 g) all-purpose (plain) flour
1 teaspoon ground cinammon
½ teaspoon salt
½ teaspoon active dry yeast
1 teaspoon baking soda (bicarbonate of soda)
¾ cup plus 2 teaspoons (160 g) granulated sugar
½ cup (120 ml) extra-virgin olive oil
½ vanilla bean (split lengthwise)
2 eggs
3 apples, peeled and cut into ⅓-inch (1 cm) dice (see Note)
Grated zest of 1 lemon
2 egg whites (see Note)

RICOTTA CREAM
10 oz (300 g) ricotta cheese
scant ½ cup (100 ml) heavy (whipping) cream
2½ tablespoons powdered (icing) sugar

MAKE THE APPLE, CINNAMON, AND OLIVE OIL CAKE

Preheat the oven to 325°F (160°C/Gas Mark 3). Grease a
4 x 8-inch (10 x 20 cm) loaf pan with olive oil and line with
parchment paper.
 Bring a small pot of water to a boil over high heat. Add the
raisins and cook until soft, about 5 minutes. Drain and set
aside to cool.
 In a medium bowl, sift together the flour, cinnamon, salt,
yeast, and baking soda (bicarbonate of soda).
 In a stand mixer fitted with the paddle attachment, beat
together the sugar and olive oil. Scrape in the vanilla seeds.
Add the eggs one at time, beating well after each addition.
Add the apples, raisins, and lemon zest and mix. Add the flour
mixture and combine until smooth.
 In a separate bowl, whisk the eggs whites until stiff peaks
form. By hand, fold the whites into the batter and combine
well. Pour the batter into the prepared loaf pan and bake until
a wooden pick inserted in the center come out clean and dry,
about 1 hour. Let cool in the pan.

MAKE THE RICOTTA CREAM

In a medium bowl, combine the ricotta, cream, and powdered
(icing) sugar with a spatula until soft. Cover and refrigerate.

TO SERVE

Serve a square of the cake with a spoonful of the ricotta cream.

Note: Save the egg yolks to make Zabaione (page 371) or ice
cream. Save the apple peels and toast them in the oven
at 300°F (150°C/Gas Mark 2) until golden and crisp, about
30 minutes, for a snack.

The Refettorio Ambrosiano was made possible with the collaborative effort of many people.

Thank you to Cardinal Angelo Scola and Monsignor Luca Bressan for your encouragement and enthusiasm.

Thank you Davide Rampello and Tania di Bernardo; Don Giuliano Savina, the parish priest of San Martino in Greco, Milano; and Luciano Gualzetti, director of Caritas Ambrosiana, Milano, for your engagement in the development of the project.

Thank you to Cristina Reni, the project manager, along with the Caritas staff, in particular, Fabrizia, Marzia, Alessandro, and Ghislain, for facilitating the day-to-day operations.

Thank you to the Caritas kitchen staff, including Davide, Ilenia, and Julien, in addition to other chefs who participated in the project, including Emilio Barbieri, Matteo Baronetto, Giorgio Damini, Giovanni Cuocci, Rino Duca, Todd Gray, Mario Ferrara, Roberto Petza, Nicola Portinari, Luciano Tona, Davide Scabin, and Digby Stirdiron for making extraordinary meals out of ordinary ingredients.

Thank you to the artists, architects, and designers who demonstrated the power of beauty through contributing artwork, ideas, and creations.

Artists: Carlo Benvenuto, Enzo Cucchi, Maurizio Nannucci, Mimmo Palladino, and Gaetano Pesce.

Architects and Designers: Anna Barbara, Mario Bellini, Aldo Cibic, Pierluigi Cerri, Antonio Citterio, Terry Dawn, Michele de Lucchi, Giulio Iacchetti, Piero Lissoni, Alessandro Mendini, Franco and Matteo Origoni, Fabio Novembre and Patricia Urquiola, Italo Rota, Matteo Thun, Origoni Steiner Architetti Associati, and the Politecnico di Milano.

Thank you to our partners: Alessi, Artemide, Riva 1920, Bormioli Rocco, BPER, Carpigiani, Consorzio del Formaggio Parmigiano-Reggiano, Eataly, Enel Cuore Onlus, Etruria Design, Farina Petra, Giblor's, Ideal Standard, Kartell, KME, l'Alberghiera Medagliani, Lavazza, Pastificio dei Campi, Pastificio Felicetti, Pentole Agnelli, Poliform, Presto, Richard Ginori, and San Pellegrino.

Thank you to all of the people who documented the events, making *Bread Is Gold* and "Theater of Life" possible.

Bread Is Gold: Emanuele Colombo for the photographs; Lara Gilmore and Francesca Mastrovito for the narratives; Karime Lopez Moreno Tagle for the recipe testing and development; and Laura Loesch-Quintin for her supervision and incredible patience.

"Theater of Life": Josette Gauthier, Peter Svatek, and their production staff.

Thank you to the team at Osteria Francescana for your sustained support throughout the project.

Thank you to the Refettorio Ambrosiano for teaching me that nothing is impossible.

— Massimo Bottura

Phaidon Press Limited
Regent's Wharf
All Saints Street
London N1 9PA

Phaidon Press Inc.
65 Bleecker Street
New York, NY 10012

phaidon.com

First published 2017
© 2017 Phaidon Press Limited

ISBN 978 0 7148 7536 1

A CIP catalogue record for this book is available from
the British Library and the Library of Congress.

Commissioning Editor: Emilia Terragni
Project Editor: Laura Loesch-Quintin
Production Controller: Adela Cory
Design: Julia Hasting
Typesetter: Ana Rita Teodoro
Documentary Photography: Emanuele Colombo
Recipe Photography: Food Editore/Piermichele Borraccia

Printed in Italy

The publisher would like to thank Kate Slate and
Cecilia Molinari for their contributions to the book.

RECIPE NOTES

Milk is always whole.

Eggs are always large (US)/medium (UK).

Herbs, unless indicated otherwise, are always fresh, and
parsley is always flat-leaf.

Butter is always unsalted.

Kosher salt is Diamond Crystal. (UK, please use coarse salt
in its place.)

Cooking and preparation times are for guidance only,
as individual ovens vary. If using a fan (convection)
oven, follow the manufacturer's instructions concerning
oven temperatures.

To test whether your deep-frying oil is hot enough, add
a cube of stale bread. If it browns in 30 seconds, the temperature is 350–375°F (180–190°C), about right for most frying.
Exercise a high level of caution when following recipes
involving any potentially hazardous activity, including the
use of high temperature and open flames. In particular,
when deep-frying, add the food carefully to avoid splashing,
wear long sleeves, and never leave the pan unattended.

Some recipes include raw or very lightly cooked eggs. These
should be avoided by the elderly, infants, pregnant women,
convalescents, and anyone with an impaired immune system.

Both metric and imperial measures are used in this book.
Follow one set of measurements throughout, not a mixture,
as they are not interchangeable.

All spoon measurements are level.

When no quantity is specified, for example of oils, salts,
and herbs used for finishing dishes, quantities are
discretionary and flexible.

Exercise caution when making fermented products, ensuring
all equipment is spotlessly clean, and seek expert advice if
in any doubt.

All herbs, shoots, flowers, and leaves should be picked fresh
from a clean source. Exercise caution when foraging for
ingredients; any foraged ingredients should only be eaten
if an expert has deemed them safe to eat. Mushrooms
should be wiped clean.